THE COMPLETE LAPTOP COMPUTER GUIDE

THE COMPLETE LAPTOP COMPUTER GUIDE

How to Choose and Get the Most Out of Your Portable PC or Mac

David H. Rothman

St. Martin's Press
NEW YORK

The author has tried as hard as he can to check such information as shipping charges, addresses, telephone numbers, and availability of updated products. However, such information is subject to change. Readers should verify costs and product descriptions with sources before ordering (costs normally do not include shipping charges). The author cannot absolutely promise that products will function as described on all computers. Nor can he guarantee that modems, hookup kits, and other communications-related products will work well on all telephone systems. If in doubt, consult with equipment manufacturers and telephone companies about issues of compatibility and legality.

Warning: Because of the vagaries of laws, lawyers, and electricity, neither St. Martin's Press nor the author can promise complete freedom of worry when you connect computer equipment directly to phone lines. If need be, check with an attorney or with the hotel or the telephone company serving it.

Design by Levavi & Levavi, Inc.

Library of Congress Cataloging-in-Publication Data

Rothman, David H.
      The complete laptop computer guide : how to choose and get the most out of your portable PC or Mac / David H. Rothman ; foreword by William F. Buckley, Jr.
          p. cm.
     ISBN 0-312-05062-3
     1. Laptop computers. I. Title.
QA76.5.R635 1990
004.16—dc20   90-36890
                                                      CIP

First Edition: November 1990
10 9 8 7 6 5 4 3 2 1

To Herman Holtz, mentor extraordinaire, even if he shuns Brand X.

Special thanks to John Deakin, Ed Stackler, Michael Sagalyn, Marie Finamore, Harry Welsh, Bonita Nelson, James Fallows, and William F. Buckley, Jr.

CONTENTS

ACKNOWLEDGMENTS

Captain John Deakin's name *must* come first. He is a born technical editor, disguised as a Japan Airlines pilot, whose eyes surely are sharp in both roles. John has been a hacker going back to the days of the ancient CP/M operating system, and perhaps beyond. For years, via CompuServe, he's been sharing his wisdom with peripatetic laptop people, not for pay from a plush office in Silicon Valley but for free from On The Road, where he is up against balky hotel switchboards, quirky AC power, boorish customs agents, and other joys of laptop use in the real world. John cut a mean bargain. He wouldn't keep helping me unless I mentioned the CP/M Forum on CompuServe. Done, John. This is Mention #1! (Remember, readers—just type **GO CPMFORUM.**)

I'll also single out:

Ed Stackler of St. Martin's Press, who helped juggle around the inserts needed to keep this book up to date. His boss, my editor Michael Sagalyn (himself no slouch!), would approve of Ed's being so high on the list.

Michael Sagalyn, for his zeal.

Marie Finamore, the production editor, another ally in the battle of the deadline.

Harry Welsh, a newsroom systems man at the *Washington Post*, without whom I could never have written my Electronic Baedeker chapter in its present form. Thanks, too, to David Vise of the business section and Curt Suplee of the Outlook section.

Bonita Nelson, my agent, whose faith in this book never faltered. Thanks, Bonita! You helped the manuscript reach just the right publisher and editor.

James Fallows of *The Atlantic*, who, like John Deakin, shared the insights of a well-traveled laptop user and slogged through the manuscript looking for glitches. (Don't blame anyone other than me if I didn't manage to find them all.)

William F. Buckley, Jr., author of the foreword. Although not a hacker, he is a veteran laptop and e-mail user in the United States, Europe, and other countries, and on the waters between.

In somewhat stream-of-consciousness fashion (no time for precise ranking), I also would like to thank:

Sandra K. Dhols, my hard-working copy editor, to whom the raw manuscript surely must have seemed Typo City; Peter O'Connor of Laptop Expositions (where would the sales section be without you, Peter?); and David Ryan of Intel, all of whom reviewed the proofs for technical accuracy; Robin Raskin, senior editor, *PC Magazine*; Dr. David Page, his wife, Dr. Socorrito Baez-Page, and her father, Luis Baez; James David Besser; John Dvorak of *PC Magazine* and just about every other computer publication in the cosmos; Paul Chernoff; Storer H. (Bob) Rowley of the *Chicago Tribune*; Mary Williams Walsh of the *Los Angeles Times*; Steve Frankel, president of Scandinavian PC Systems; Steve Goldberg of Media General; Matthew Schmidt; Jeff Ayres, Oz Communications; Ronald Gans; Tony Revis, president of Psion; Mike Fappiano and Rowan Prior of Psion; Gail Jamentz, Tina Valdez, and Danielle Morris of Bob Thomas and Associates; David Ryan, Jim Jarrett, Jean Davia, David Ramey, Saul Zales, and Markus Levy of Intel; Robert Jurik, vice president of sales at Modatach Systems; Sam Telzer, a CPA with Coopers & Lybrand; Trevor Stewart, a Deloitte & Touche partner who heads the company's software development group in Princeton, New Jersey; Jeff Knepper of the D&T Washington office; Alex Kask of Ernst & Young.

Ken Skier of SkiSoft Publishing; Floyd Beavers of Congoleum; Peter Mueller of Pfizer; Bruce Johnson, formerly with Deloitte & Touche; John Rule, president of Spectrum Cellular who helped review the cellular-related material; Kitty Thomas, Tisha Gray, Jim Ryan, and Susan Wylie of CompuServe; Alan Garratt and David Bland of MCI Mail, Jim Kelly, my local MCI Mail agent, and Gary Oppenheimer, an MCI agent in New York; Michael Cavanagh, executive director of the Electronic Mail Association; Bill Lempesis, Bart Ladd, Phil Devin, and Sohail Malik of Dataquest; Tim Bajarin of Creative Strategies Research International; Paul Zagaeski of The Yankee Group; Eric Arnum, of *Electronic Mail & Microsystems*; Margaret Moe of Amdek; Bruno Corrada of Milan, Italy (count on more overseas people being quoted in the next edition, especially now that CompuServe has European-oriented forums); Nobuyuki Makita of Japan Airlines; Don Kimberlin; William Degnan; Army Captain Bill Badger; Jerome Glenn; Jerry Oppenheimer; John McAfee of the Computer Virus Industry Association and his assistant, Aryeh Goretsky; Larry Krough of MagicSoft; Toni Nevitt of Ziff Communications; Al Louis Ripskis; Marcia Peoples Halio of the University of Delaware; Eric Meyer of the University of Oklahoma; Edward L. Wright of UCLA; Ray Hoffer of Reflection Technology; Terry George of *Irish Voice*; Mike Espindle of Home Office Computing; Terri Slater, Caroline Mei, and Melinda Hayes of Hill and Knowlton; and Ann-Marie Downing, formerly of H&K.

Gil Gordon of Gil Gordon Associates; Richard Dent of COMCO; Frank Cannata; the press office of Barbara Bush; Hugh Faulkner and Keith Comer of Toshiba; Gérry Lynn Baker of Les Goldberg Public Relations; Bill De Nicolo and Eric Andersen of Tellular Inc., Pete Packer of Runzheimer International; Marv Katz; Herman Holtz; Victor Pope; Margaret Engel; Mel Weiss of YUASA; Paul Lazar of Generation Five; Stuart Hanley of On-Trak Data; Rich Schinell and Doug Hummer of the Capital PC User Group; Kevin R. Grantham; David Labell; Priscilla Tate-Austin of the Microcomputer Managers Association; Dan White, Chuck Runquist, Philip Johnson, and Anatoly Tickin of Vertisoft; Barbara Sturken; Laura Koss, associate editor of *Business Travel News*; Marci Maule of Traveling Software; Michael Bernard of Touchbase Systems; Hayes Microcomputer; Gene Brezovsky; Frederic Hirzel and John Bloom of Vocal Technologies; Harry Newton; Sidney Nolte; Al Delio and others at Sundog Software; George Daniels of the Farm Employers Labor Service; Paul Nadler, author of ScriptWright; William Orabone of Ovonics; DEMI; Klaus Brand of Moli Energy (1990); Richard Cohen and Ellen Rony of Penamax; Rip Pett of Axonix; Larry Fitzpatrick and Karen Ruckman of Kodak; Stephen Banker; Robin Carlson of US Sprint; Frank Dobisky; Al Hodges, manager, avionics branch, FAA; Dick Stafford, FAA; Susan Lucek, FinalSoft; Rick Van Winkle; Sheila Hershow.

The public relations staff at Lotus; Bill Gross, Magellan developer for Lotus; Barbara Newman; Martha Griffin, Brian Ek, Steve Hein, and Sirajul Islam of Prodigy Services; Len Abbazia and Lisa Daniele of Dorf and Stanton Communications; Helen Kendrick, Software Publishing Corporation; Herb Tyson of Mount Vernon Economics; Chris Torem; Tracy Smith; Bill Gladstone; and Myles Thompson of the American Management Association.

If I've accidentally left off any deserving person's name, contact me c/o St. Martin's Press, 175 Fifth Avenue, New York, New York 10010, and I'll include him or her in the next edition.

FOREWORD

I have never met the author of this book, though I feel I know him
well, and know well his modi operandi. He has written evangelistic
pieces for my journal and other publications (subject: U.S. backing for
PCs spread about the world, to facilitate communications and western
technological aid); and he undertook over the telephone, during one
summer that must in retrospect seem infinitely long to him, to coach
me in a word processing update (not the XyWrite he refers to in the
text of this book). I walked away from my apprenticeship dizzy with
admiration at David Rothman's stylistic approach to problems having
to do with computers and having to do, I now suspect, with life itself.

His is a combination of utter—protracted—infinite patience com-
bined with resolution. You have a problem? *"Please push the Escape
Key. Yes, the Escape Key. Push it several times. . . ."* Before you
know it, your problem goes away. Your problem, I should add in
reflecting on this large book, whatever it is . . .

Whatever it is that has to do with the laptop computer. I know one
or two sedentary types who nevertheless use only a laptop. One of my
friends travels occasionally, but probably she hasn't taken her laptop
away from her desk more than once or twice in a year: she just likes
the size of it, doesn't need anything larger, so why get anything larger?
David Rothman is writing primarily for those who feel the peripatetic
imperative, but also for those who simply want the laptop as their
permanent primary machine. And then when we do travel, most often
on business, it becomes necessary to use our laptops to do whatever it

is we are in the field to do, whether to make sales, for instance, or to file stories or columns.

I have a continuing problem. Twenty-five percent of the hostelries I check in at defy my attempts to establish a conventional connection between my laptop's modem and the telephone. I have to admit that I became very nearly hysterical with laughter when I hit the long sections in this book on how to crack the inhospitable hotel that doesn't have a convenient jack for your modem. The only remedy David leaves out is kidnapping the innkeeper's wife and offering to release her only after the hotel provides you with a convenient outlet for your RJ-11. But he tells you everything else you could possibly need to know, including the number and kind of screwdrivers you should carry. Oh my, but this book is full of extraordinary information. I didn't know until I read it why the Diconix printer on my chartered sailboat didn't work, even though that dismal experience is ten months old.

But I am carried away. David Rothman cannot bear for you not to be aware of *everything* he knows about laptop computers, the uses to which they can be put, the things you need to watch out for when you have them, the vicissitudes of travel, and the horrors you need to be prepared to face when time comes to fetch up MCI Mail because you want to send a computer message or a fax. Reading along, you sometimes get the impression of the maître d' who begins at eight o'clock to tell you what you can have for dessert, and is still telling you at nine o'clock. Have you lost your hunger?

Yes, if it happens that along about 8:15 he hit exactly the dessert you crave, making the balance of the list supernumerary. This will happen to every reader of this book here and there. But the beauty of it is that it won't happen at the same point in the same chapter or section. My interest ceases when I run into exactly the information I was looking for. So will yours. But neither of us knows at what point we will come across that which we achingly wished to know. Conceivably, it is the very last item. All you can absolutely count upon is that if the information exists, it will be in this book.

Come to think of it, that isn't absolutely fair. If the words David Rothman wrote this afternoon were published tomorrow, his book would be in one sense anachronized, because things will change. Indeed, many of these changes, like prevailing baud rates, or bps rates, he anticipates. But that is a problem inherent in a dynamic technology, and there was never a technology more dynamic than that which seeks to enlist the chip, and electricity, for the purpose of storing memory, finding it, classifying it, and communicating it.

A learned friend (he is a literary editor) once told me that at the beginning, he read *everything* to do with computers because he wished to master one function absolutely, namely to write on his word processor his book reviews, correct them, and dispatch them to the newspaper that employs him. Having done all of that, he found that he had closed his mind to computer talk, that he didn't even bother to read the weekly computer column in his own newspaper.

I can understand that. I have zero curiosity about what goes into making my CD player work: I know now how to turn it on and off, how to increase the volume, and tune up or down the treble or the bass. I would look with amazement at anyone who presented me with a book on the technology of CDs.

But here, I think, is where computers edge out that common presumption, that I-am-entirely-happy-with what I already know. They do this because you generally suspect that you are missing out on something. What was that about 9600 bps? About a fax modem? What does *it* do? What kind of batteries? Prolong your laptop battery life by *what* percent, did you say?

For this reason I suspect that more readers are going to end up reading more of David Rothman's book than ever they thought they would. That is for the sheer pleasure of running into just so much information of a kind that is contingently useful, and rather fun just to flirt with. But another reason the book will prove valuable is that having experienced it, we will know that the answer to questions we don't yet need to ask, but some day may need to do so, is sitting here between the covers of this book. So add, to the screwdrivers and Swiss knife you will want to take along, a copy of this book, whose index will be well thumbed in a matter of months, I warrant. That will please David. He is determined to please those he serves, who include his grateful servant,

WILLIAM F. BUCKLEY, JR.

Chapter 1

AN OWNER'S GUIDE— TO THIS BOOK

Jimmy Breslin, the New York columnist and novelist, once starred in a Smith Corona ad where he heartily recommended typewriters for "people who don't like their words processed." Flash ahead four years. *Home Office Computing* is telling the planet about VIP authors gone electronic, and just above a confessional caption ("My working style was electrified out of existence"), we see a photograph taken in the Horn & Hardart Automat. It shows a certain Pulitzer Prize winner with two writing aids—a large coffee mug and a powerful laptop computer.[1]

Breslin isn't alone in lapdom. Alan Alda, the *M*A*S*H* star, uses a Toshiba portable to write scripts while jetting between coasts, and Walter Cronkite taps away on a tiny Compaq. Similarly, a GriD laptop makes sense for an author, traveler, housewife, and novice computer user named Barbara Bush. "I don't know all its talents," she says, "but am fast learning. And I am loving it!"

Laptops are no longer just exotic extravagances for Silicon Valley and the rest of the techno-elite. Now college students take three-hundred-dollar laptops back home to work on term papers over the holidays. Costlier models are standard sights on the East Coast air shuttles—the new Smith Coronas for newspaper reporters and network correspondents, turbocharged calculators for traveling auditors, time-savers and more for sales reps, executives, independent consultants, even rock stars, who use them to juggle appointments and compose music on the road.

---

[1] The Breslin example is from Terry George's article on page 45 of the March 1989 *Home Office Computing*.

WHAT'S A LAPTOP?

For this book, I'll define a *laptop* as a computer that weighs less than fifteen pounds, either has a handle or is small enough to be carried like a notebook, and most likely runs on batteries. Exceptions abound. Some AC-only portables with gas plasma screens are so small that I'll include them.

This book will also mention *lunchboxes*, since machines in this category might also be useful to some laptop owners. They're not true laptops, though.

Nor will I include the Sharp Wizard and similar gadgets used to keep lists of names, appointments, and addresses. They are computers in many ways, and in fact I'll mention them in chapter 2. But for the moment such machines lack the versatility and power of genuine laptops as defined for the purpose of this book. Most can't run the MS-DOS programs found on IBM-style machines.

Although I'll say *laptops* most of the time when discussing the appropriate machines, I'll also use *portables*. In the context of this book they are synonymous.

Thanks to brawny new portables, CPAs can do complex tax calculations while visiting out-of-town clients. Such work once might have required several trips back and forth. But not now. With the right chips added, even some four-pound machines may be able to run monster programs like the Lotus 1-2-3/G spreadsheet by the time you're reading this. 1-2-3/G typically demands five megabytes of memory. That's eight times the capacity of the typical desktop computer, but the Lilliputians by now should be up to the job or close to it.

Insurance companies, meanwhile, have outfitted thousands of agents with laptops and portable printers. Now the agents can wow clients with slick, animated sales presentations, even Snoopy cartoons, and grind out sales contracts in the field. Insurance adjusters can settle claims on the scene; they can even print out checks.

Laptops clearly have come a long way from the puny machines of the past, some of which at best were executive toys. Worldwide sales of battery-operated computers totalled just 114,000 in 1983. Dataquest, a leading research organization, says that in 1993 laptop sales will exceed 3.5 million. Once skeptics could puckishly suggest that business travelers avoid laptops and just carry floppy disks to use on colleagues' machines. No more. With a laptop and cellular phone, you can whiz spreadsheets to your boss from a desert or bayou. Laptops also should spur telecommuting. They'll help millions of Americans work at home full- or part-time and stay in touch with the office via telephones and computers. Many people will use the same machines at home and in the office; a laptop is a desk with a handle.

The possibilities are endless. But even the more seasoned users are like Mrs. Bush: they don't quite know all the talents of their machines. This book will help. It won't just tell how to *choose* a laptop, it will explain how to *use* it.

I myself have written with laptops on and off for the past several years. I've done some of my best work not at my desk but along the banks of the Potomac River or some other previously unlikely location.

One of the biggest uses of laptops is for communications, and as a writer or editor, I've swapped files with scores, perhaps hundreds, of other computer users. During the creation of the film *2010* I helped set up a trans-Pacific computer link between novelist Arthur C. Clarke and a scriptwriter at MGM/UA.

To produce the present book, however, I didn't just rely on my recollections. I turned to other experts. A leading designer of laptop software explained how to choose programs for the more affordable machines. Sales automation whizzes told how reps could use laptops to win new business and better serve old accounts; computer experts at Big Six accounting firms shared their own secrets. The *Washington Post*, meanwhile, electronically sent out a questionnaire to veteran foreign correspondents.[2] They replied with thousands of words on such topics as how to get your laptop repaired overseas, or what to do about Third World customs officials who, rubbed the wrong way, might just turn your machine into a Frisbee.

"But," you're wondering, "isn't it presumptuous to tout any guide as 'complete'?"

Yes! To write about laptops is really to write about all of computers—to cover topics from shopping tips to telecommunications

---

[2]The *Post* earlier had considered a similar survey for its own purposes, and the payoff was fast—easier coverage of the Malta summit conference. Knowing what to expect abroad, laptop users could better cope with foreign power and telephone lines. Harry Welsh, a newsroom computer expert, says the *Post* people set up "a nice news center" while some rival papers were "dead in the water."

advice. I do not claim to mention *every* product, *every* solution to everyone's problems. Rather, I've emphasized either (1) the practical or (2) the interesting. Often the two categories overlap.

Here's a quick overview of what follows:

CHAPTER 2

A Laptop Primer

This chapter offers tips not just to novices but to experienced computer users who are looking for their first laptop or their next one.

I'll explain how two major companies—Pfizer pharmaceuticals and Congoleum, the floor-covering people—are keeping up with new laptop technology. How do you prevent your corporation from being stuck with a fleet of obsolete machines?

You'll learn, too, about the classes of laptops and about machines that stand out from the crowd. Want to know which machine weighs only a pound, is smaller than a videocassette, and costs no more than a color television? Or which laptop floats? Whether you should buy an IBM-style laptop or one from Apple? How to evaluate keyboards and screens? Or whether you need a hard disk or can make do with the cheaper floppy drives? This chapter tells. It also explains the subtleties of choosing a printer to accompany your laptop on your travels. Here, too, you'll learn of a solar cell distributor with a $130 product that works with some single-floppy laptops.

In this chapter and elsewhere you'll often see prices of laptops and other equipment and programs. These are constantly changing (usually downward). Just the same, I'm including them at times, such as when I'm discussing a unique item or when I'm comparing a few items within a category. Don't just mail off a check. Call the manufacturer, dealer, whatever, for the latest pricing information.

CHAPTER 3

Software To Go

If only we all could buy deluxe laptops! The economy models offer screens that may cause eyestrain when viewed for long periods. Moreover, the screens can't reproduce the colors on which some programs depend. In chapter 3, you'll learn the criteria for choosing software to overcome the limitations of affordable laptop technology.

Expect more "laptop software" in the future. Meanwhile, there are many programs of interest to laptop owners even if they're not specifically designed for small portables.

Double Disk, for instance, can actually double the effective capacity of your hard disk when you're using it with certain programs. And a new program called Translate can magically translate English into Spanish—just the ticket for that sales rep stranded in Mexico without an interpreter handy. Translate isn't precise, but is still a breakthrough program. You'll also learn about FileExpress—a terrific database for laptops—as well as other software worth considering.

CHAPTER 4

Laptops on the Job: Software for Writers, Accountants, and Sales Reps

Writers, sales reps, and accountants are among the more common users of laptops, and this chapter discusses software of interest to them. Other readers, though, should at least skim the relevant parts of the chapter. Lawyers and consultants probably will be just as interested as writers in the selection of word processors; in fact, I've titled the first section "Writers and Other Processors of Words."

Not surprisingly, word processing leads the list of laptop applications. And in this chapter you'll learn of two programs that blow up letters and numbers so you can see them more clearly on laptop screens:

■ Eye Relief. It should suffice for business use in many situations and as an auxiliary word processor in virtually all cases.

■ Kidword, which isn't as fancy but costs just ten dollars and is dandy for children.

The author of yet another piece of software—VDE, a zippy little WordStar clone that runs wonderfully on laptops—expects nothing more than a modest donation. It can be any size you want.

Mind you, those are just a few of the programs in chapter 4. I'll also discuss XyWrite, the Maserati of word processors, a favorite of many a journalist at *The New York Times* and other leading newspapers.[3] That's what I booted up to write this guide. But my needs may not be your needs. Want to use your laptop for screenplays or teleplays rather than books? Then turn to the appendix on page 335, where I discuss a $49.49 program for scriptwriters.

Just as good software can make writers more competitive—let me know if my advice lands you a $500,000 script deal—it can do the same for sales reps. In chapter 4, you'll learn how entrepreneurs and individual reps can automate their sales operations through a program called ACT! Use it to do everything from keeping lists of prospects to writing those canned letters. This section also tells how a company, large or small, can automate an entire sales force through the appropriate use of software and electronic mail. And it will explain, too, how sales reps can use graphics to jazz up their presentations to customers. Although mainly about software, the section will briefly discuss data panels and other technology of special interest to reps.

The next section is on accounting software. Perhaps you've already chosen your spreadsheet. But what other programs are of interest? I'll offer tips from an expert on small-business accounting systems and from staffers of major accounting firms. With increasing efficiency, the firms are using laptops to audit, do tax planning, and perform other vital tasks. This section also contains a list of add-ons for Lotus 1-2-3, the most popular electronic spreadsheet. Although many of these programs are too demanding for small laptops, they should be of interest to users of portables with hard disks, the quasi desktops.

CHAPTER 5

The Murphy's Law Chapter

You know Murphy's Law: If anything can go wrong, it will. Thieves steal laptops, viruses infect them, hard disks fail, floppies go the way of all plastic, rechargeable batteries run out ahead of time, keyboards jam up, screens lose their brightness, maintenance people turn selfish and surly, and laptop users in the field somehow find themselves un-

---

[3]Writers interested in the *Times*'s use of XyWrite may want to read my book *XyWrite Made Easier* (Tab Books: Blue Ridge Summit, Pennsylvania, 1988).

prepared for the tasks at hand. Not all portables float or can be dropped on concrete the way the ruggedized models can. Most laptops demand respect. If machines are as sentient as I suspect, they certainly must have egos. I'll tell you how to pay proper tribute to these little electronic juggernauts so they'll kindly let you do your work uninterrupted.

Among other things, I'll explain how to protect against all but the most determined thieves, pass along a few antivirus tips, and tell you how to care for disks, keyboards, and other components. I'll also discuss additional countermeasures against Murphy's Law, one of which you already practiced when you bought this book: education.

CHAPTER 6

A Communications Primer: How Your Laptop Can Talk to the World

Yawn. Yawn. What could be more soporific than a discussion of modems and a jumble of technical terms like "bits per second"? If you know the basics, however, you can shop more smartly for the hardware and software to communicate with distant computers over the phone lines.

Nowadays you can even buy a modem that slips into your laptop so you don't have to haul it around. Other marvels may intrigue you. Modems with error control can help you log onto computer nets from the boonies where the telephone service is lacking. What's more, some modems even let you fax messages from your laptop. You don't have to type something on your computer, print it, then scurry to find a facsimile machine; a fax modem can eliminate the printing and speed your message directly to the fax machine at Headquarters. You needn't use a computer network to convert the message.

Cellular modems are yet another way you can get the most from your laptop; they work with cellular phones—no small help if you're gridlocked on Route 95. You can just pull off to the side and send a report to the deadline-ridden client you were rushing to see. And if you're a field engineer or traveler, you can use cellular phones and modems to bypass the switchboards that hate computers. Turn to appendix 3 for cellular modem tips.

What about software for zipping bits and bytes over the phone? Even Arthur C. Clarke, the father of the communication satellite, isn't perfect in this regard. He ended up with a program that couldn't talk to most other modem software—a woe that bedeviled him during the script-writing of *2010*, when he was in Sri Lanka trying to swap files with California. Chapter 6 will tell how to shop for more flexible software.

CHAPTER 7

How To Hook Up (and Handle Other Hassles) From Almost Anywhere

This chapter contains hookup tips from telecommunications consultants, businesspeople, James Fallows of *The Atlantic*, and other writers who have successfully used laptops overseas.

It's full of grubby specifics. What equipment should you take to ensure dependable communications, whether you're a sales rep or a reporter, whether you're in Peoria or Pretoria? How about foreign phone lines? When should you try to slide those earmufflike acoustic couplers over the headsets? And when should you actually wire into the phone system? What colors in the phone cables should you look for? How about the Murphy's Law potential in all this? Tim Bajarin, a prominent computer consultant in California, tells of a Radio Shack employee whose company had to shell out several thousand dollars to replace a circuit board in a hotel switching system. I'll help you avoid such calamities.

Among other things, this book contains a list of the common modem commands to help you hook up when no other source of information is easily available.

The next two chapters are for travelers overseas, who, more than those in the United States, may have problems using their modems. That's why those chapters appear directly after the one on connections. If, however, you care not a whit about foreign travel, then you'll want to skip ahead to chapter 10.

CHAPTER 8

The Electronic Traveler Abroad

Caryl Conner, one of the first women to become a White House speech-writer, died of a heart attack in Mexico after an ugly confrontation with bureaucracy there—precipitated by her laptop. This chapter offers general advice on dealing with customs inspectors and other officials; the bomb threat question; whether radio waves from laptops can cause jets to crash; how to hook up from abroad through the MCI Mail or CompuServe networks; and what to do if your laptop breaks down while you're overseas. Some readers may want to avail themselves of a service from a company called COMCO, which simplifies hookups overseas.

To be sure, this book is full of warnings about traveling abroad with a laptop. But there's a bright side, too. By better coping with the difficulties, you'll have an advantage over your less-prepared competition.

CHAPTER 9

An Electronic Baedeker

Here's a country-by-country account of what you *might* encounter. I'm not kidding when I talk about customs inspectors capable of turning laptops into Frisbees. An American journalist tells of one hapless journalist who saw his notebook computer held eight feet in the air and dropped to the floor. Such incidents are the exception, of course, just like Caryl Conner's fate, but a little prudence will help, even when you're visiting garden-variety destinations.

CHAPTER 10

A Quick Tour of Some On-Line Services

Some of the most exotic cities you can tour are no farther away than your computer screen. I refer to metropolises of the electronic variety. New York and Tokyo exist in the corporeal universe—places where so many things are the biggest and the best—and they have their equivalents on-line. Through such world-class services as CompuServe, you can dial up thousands of newspaper and magazine articles, academic papers, financial reports, travel listings, even clothing catalogues. Services offer forums where consultants, programmers, newspaper people, writers, lawyers, pilots can swap messages. You name it, the services might have it.

Through my electronic wanderings, I found Captain John Deakin, a veteran hacker, electronics buff, and airline pilot. He gave me the last word on whether laptops could confuse navigation gear. Without computer networks, I would have spent many more hours on research and still not have found someone with his range of experience.

CHAPTER 11

Some Basics of Electronic Mail (Including How to Send E-mail, Faxes, Telexes, and Paper Letters Via CompuServe and MCI Mail)

When will the Postal Service wise up? As I write this, I hear talk of a thirty-cent stamp. Now think about the expense of an envelope, then add on the cost in time going to the post office to mail a letter. You'll find that electronic mail, AKA e-mail, isn't such a luxury after all. Via the MCI Mail network, a short computer message costs just forty-five cents, and your words reach the other person's machine faster than it takes to lick a stamp. For long transmissions, CompuServe is the better bargain. You can send ten thousand words anywhere in the United States for less than one fifth the cost of an overnight letter.

Thanks to e-mail, John Deakin could critique this book whether he was at home in Tokyo or resting up in a hotel room in San Francisco or New York. E-mail, too, is how he used his laptop to help settle a bitter labor dispute.

E-mail is also a boon to sales reps. Now they can dial up the computers at headquarters to pass on orders from customers and find out about inventory. No more garbled messages. No more telephone tag. You can even use e-mail nets to hook up with fax machines and telexes. With a laptop and an already-compiled electronic mailing list on MCI Mail, a traveling CEO in Melbourne can fax dozens of branch offices at once—from Calcutta to Caracas.

*   *   *

Whether we travel corporeally or electronically, laptops offer a new chance for *personal* computers to live up to their name—for good or bad.

Status seekers can brandish ten-thousand-dollar laptops to inflate the perceived value of their time. Philosophers can compose treatises of cosmic brilliance on laptops bought at K-mart. Laptops, moreover, are like cellular phones: they can make you feel more free or more oppressed, depending on how you or your company uses them. A laptop at home can turn a borderline workaholic into a terminal case, with a boss perhaps abetting the machine, and portables also can help abusive employers inflict impossible quotas on traveling sales reps. On the other hand, laptops can better the lives of reps by reducing paperwork and allowing easier scheduling of visits to customers. And they can wring more than a little drudgery out of accountants' days.

Chosen unwisely, though, a laptop won't wring away anything but your money. How to avoid common mistakes? Read on.

A LAPTOP PRIMER

Congoleum gave the world Linoleum, the no-frills covering for kitchen floors.[1] When Floyd Beavers evaluated laptops for his company, he himself wasn't after glitz, just a good machine for sales reps that could pay for itself within a year or so. Beavers didn't care much whether that particular model would keep up with the latest technology. Over at Pfizer pharmaceuticals, however, another computer professional, Pete Mueller, traveled a different road and chose GriD laptops capable of being upgraded

---

[1]To be precise, one of Congoleum's founders invented Linoleum in 1888. Tougher, more attractive floor coverings have superseded the original product.

to the powerful 80386 processors and color screens. Who was right, Beavers or Mueller?

Both, it turns out. Within the area of sales alone, the needs of laptop users will vary greatly.

That isn't even to mention the differences between occupations. An accountant, for example, will want a machine with a numeric pad, while many writers couldn't care less and in fact might resent the extra space it would take up.

In this chapter I'll help you find the right laptop for you or your company, whether you're a free-lance writer or an information systems expert with a blue-chip firm. Today's buyers can choose anything from a notebook-size machine to lunchbox portables, which really aren't laptops but do merit discussion as alternatives. Here I'll discuss:

■ The classes of laptops available. I'll give you a quick overview, then some more detailed descriptions based on performance and relative price. When I use dollar figures, I'll do so only to give you an idea of how much some equipment might cost compared to other choices. Most laptop prices are declining fast.

■ General physical characteristics that you should consider in picking a machine.

■ Keyboards. The feel of the keyboard is just one criterion; what about others, such as whether it's at the right level for comfortable typing? Many portables, such as the Compaq LTE series, have keyboards that are too high for my own taste.

■ Screens. Should you buy a laptop with a watchlike liquid crystal display, a gas plasma screen, or what?

■ Random-access memory. The old 640K barriers are fading. Many laptops now come with a megabyte of RAM. For novices, 640K means approximately 640,000 bytes; each letter, number, or other character takes up 1 byte. A megabyte, or "meg" in computer slang, is about 1,000K.

■ Mass storage such as floppies or hard drives. Monster programs are overwhelming even hard disks. And in the storage department, it's hard for laptops to keep up; they don't have as much room inside for hard disks. But hard disks themselves may eventually lose some popularity. Intel, the famous chip maker, is promoting a new technology, flash memory; someday a tiny, affordable chip might be able to store thousands of pages of information. And yet this memory would be entirely solid state, with no moving parts to act up. Unlike normal chips, it wouldn't lose information after you shut off the power.

■ Kinds of batteries. Ni-cad (nickel-cadmium) batteries have reigned supreme in the laptop world; on page 151 I'll discuss them and a major alternative, lead acid. But as the decade wears on, you may have some newer, better choices, the advantages of which this chapter will explain.

■ Portable printers. How do they differ from their desktop counterparts?

■ Two alternatives to laptops: portable word processors and organizers. They aren't as powerful and flexible as the usual laptops, but they may work out for people with either very simple needs or a very well developed fear of computers.

Whatever your needs, keep in mind that laptop technology is far different from that of automobiles or television sets; it's moving infinitely faster. I remember one of the first laptops that I ever beheld, a little HX-20 from Epson. My friend Stephen Banker, a writer and trade show organizer, owned the Epson and fantasized about being able to do real work on it. I was horribly jealous. Dating back to the mid-1980s, the Epson was no longer, no wider, than a child's slate—a miracle of miniaturization—but it could display only five lines at once on the screen. Not long ago Stephen offered to give me his machine. I turned him down. Even free, this little box didn't seem worth the cubic foot or two that it would have taken up in my file cabinet.

In deciding how much you'll spend on a laptop or a fleet of the machines, and whether you'll buy or rent, you should think strategically. Don't just consider your immediate problems. Consult with the appropriate people in your company about the tax situation, for example, and the general feeling about how soon equipment should pay for itself. Normally you should avoid rental. Laptops quickly lose resale value, and leasing firms set their rates accordingly.

Both Congoleum and Pfizer *bought* their machines, though the two companies' procurement policies differed then and still do.

Floyd Beavers says Congoleum favors return-on-investment equipment payoffs within about a year. So it made sense for Congoleum to buy Toshiba 1200HD machines for the first reps the company equipped with portables. The 1200s were among the least costly hard disk laptops that Beavers could purchase then from a name vendor. And he didn't insist on the latest technology, since in his opinion the laptops would quickly be technological has-beens anyway. Laptop makers often promise expandability, then sock customers with surprise extras when they try to keep their computers up to date. Beavers figured he could always buy more modern machines later, when the return on investment justified them.

For the moment the 1200s could handle the sample spreadsheets, databases, and other programs that Congoleum's reps needed. He wasn't expecting them to run fancy graphics software, as might companies in other industries—especially financial services, where the right software often could mean the difference between a sale and no sale. Congoleum's reps wouldn't require fast machines to boot up demonstration programs in a hurry while new prospects looked on. They didn't need to worry about "dead time." After all, the reps would use the laptops not for sales presentations but for housekeeping chores, such as sales analyses.

By contrast, Peter Mueller at Pfizer was looking for speedy computers that sales reps might employ someday for demonstrations in front of doctors and others. So the GriDs were ideal. Although many manufacturers exaggerate the upgrade potential of their laptops, GriD systems did not in this case. It actually showed Mueller how it could make the machines more powerful when his needs changed.

Mueller could start out with laptops containing an 80286 processor,[2] then arrange for GriD to swap out the 286s for the even speedier 80386 processors, which could speed up computerized graphics. Moreover, in several years Pfizer could swap the orange-only screens for multicolor displays. Pfizer was further along in computerization than Congoleum (only a fraction of the Congoleum reps had computerized at the time) and therefore had more clearly defined its goals.

---

[2]*Processor* is short for *central processing unit*, or CPU (a computer's main brains). The original IBM PC's CPU was an 8088 chip from Intel and ran at 4.77 megahertz, much slower than mid-range portables today. CPU speed normally counts more for numbers crunching than for word processing.

Finally, Pfizer's sales environment differed from Congoleum's. The floor covering company's reps were not really selling directly, but were offering sales analysis, promotional support, and many other services to distributors. Pfizer's reps, on the other hand, were out there persuading customers to buy. And since Pfizer paid its reps more on the average and more money was involved, the company sensibly bought more expensive laptops than those at Congoleum.

Sales, as I've noted, is not the only field where laptop needs can differ. You can't stereotype. For example:

■ Tax accountants as a group need fast, powerful machines, especially for putting together big, complicated spreadsheets. *Typical* auditors, however, may get along fine with slower, cheaper laptops. You don't go by the size of an accounting firm; function counts more. Hence a tax expert at a smaller firm actually may need a more expensive laptop than an auditor working for Coopers & Lybrand.

■ Writers of short articles don't need the same amount of hard disk space that writers of books do. Those working in the field might even want to avoid hard disk machines if they feel they're sacrificing too much battery life. They also may value compactness over power and gravitate toward the little notebook machines. And they may not be as picky about screens. *Book* writers, on the other hand, may insist on either a good screen or the ability to plug in a decent external monitor.

■ Some high-level executives may insist on the newest, latest equipment—but may need only a modest laptop for purposes such as electronic mail. This will vary. Other executives actually may benefit from fancier machines that can use sophisticated graphics to display complex information or simplify the operation of programs.

■ Not all computer consultants, the very group expected to require the most powerful laptops, will need them. Certain consultants may be able to do their work entirely on their clients' machines, saving their laptops for light-duty tasks, such as electronic mail.

■ Some lawyers may favor small, compact laptops for taking notes during investigations, while others prefer big, hefty hard disk portables that they can fill with evidence and take with them. Of course, many attorneys will choose to buy both varieties.

■ English lit majors are not going to need as powerful a laptop as will students of engineering. On the other hand, if they're writing for long stretches, they may be more finicky about keyboards.

WHAT PEOPLE USE LAPTOPS FOR

Wonder what other laptop users are up to? Creative Strategies interviewed one thousand laptop users in 1989 and found that:

■ At least 80 percent of the one thousand users were using laptops
as a second computer—something to augment their desktops.

■ Ninety percent used their laptops for word processing.

■ Sixty percent ran spreadsheets, although often for simple purposes
such as expense accounts.

■ Fifty-five percent ran databases, everything from simple filers to
the complex dBASE program.

■ Forty-five percent used laptops for electronic mail and other forms
of communication.

CLASSES OF MACHINES

Here's a quick, simple hierarchy of laptops. My list excludes trans-
portables. By my standards they might as well be desktops; some can
weigh as much as forty pounds. Now, the laptop hierarchy:

1. Volkswagen-priced notebook computers, the slowest, least expensive portables, which often lack the IBM-style operating system.
Virtually all of the least expensive laptops, plus those in the PC and
XT class that I'll describe next, use LCDs similar to those in watches.
"But what," you ask, "is a *notebook*?" By my definition it's a computer
that weighs less than seven pounds and measures eight and a half by
eleven by two inches at the most.[3] I'm kind. In future years the weight
limit will probably decline to a pound or so.

2. VWs that run MS-DOS–style software but physically and electronically place you at a disadvantage. Keyboards and small screens
may get in the way of running your favorite programs.

3. Chevrolets for the IBM set—PC- and XT-class laptops—which
include floppies and hard disks. They use improved, lower-power ver-

---

[3]The seven-pound limit was in popular use—in both ads and computer publications—
while I was writing this book.

sions of the original 8088 microprocessor, the heart of the original PC.[4]
Usually their LCDs have backlighting, which lets you use them in dim
locations. The PC/XT-class machines can be either in notebook form
or larger. Typically they use clamshell construction, so the screen folds
on top of the keyboard. Machines in this class weigh from seven to
fifteen pounds.

4. Small, upscale sports cars like the Poqet that run IBM-style software but weigh as little as a pound because they don't include hard
disks or floppies.

5. Buicks, the AT class. These mid-priced laptops are faster than
the XT class and offer better displays, some of which may be gas plasma,
which offers an orange or yellowish glow and is more readable than
many LCD screens. The downside is that some of the early AT-class
machines needed AC power and weighed around fifteen pounds. Still,
AT-level laptops are common sights at many accounting firms requiring
more power than the PC/XT class can offer. The typical microprocessor
in use on AT machines is an 80286 or equivalent as of this writing—
but this is changing. Almost all Buick-priced laptops will start using
80386-level chips in the early 1990s.

6. Cadillacs and Rolls-Royces, the machines that magazines call
"powerhouse laptops." Count on their using equivalents of the 80386
or perhaps even the 80486 processor. Speeds can range from 16 megahertz to several times higher. Displays often are either gas plasma or
sharper LCDs than those on PC/XT laptops. For obvious reasons, fewer
of the more powerful machines run on batteries than do the 80286-level
models and below.

Not belonging in the above categories but still worthy of mention are:

■ Lunchbox-style portables, which can include the XT and AT
classes as well as 80386 machines and above. The lunchbox machines
are not really laptops; they're more like a tackle box than a lunchbox
in bulk. Still, as you'll discover, in applications requiring plenty of
power and flexibility, lunchboxes can be an alternative to laptops.

■ Offbeat machines, such as the portable version of the Macintosh,

---

[4]In this case, by lower-powered I mean a chip that drains the battery less.

a bad buy for the typical laptop user but just the ticket for some rich companies and people who prefer Mac software.

■ Hand-held laptops, such as the GridPad, an MS-DOS laptop that weighs just four and a half pounds and reads handwritten print. It's for businesses in which employees constantly fill in forms.

Below are more detailed explanations of the classes of machines.

VW-Priced Notebooks Without True IBM Compatibility

When Hemingway was scraping by on the Left Bank—eking out a living as a free-lance journalist—he might have cut back on his liquor to buy a Radio Shack Model 100 if it had existed back then. The Model 100 is no longer made. Still, it and other machines are interesting even now because of their availability on the used equipment market, and because they continue to be staples at many large American newspapers. They can sell for as little as $125 or so. If you own a deluxe laptop and are reasonably sophisticated technically, you might consider buying a used Model 100 or 102 for note taking and other simple work in places where there is danger of theft or breakage.

Otherwise you may want to shun the machines with genuine VW prices. They can't run the usual IBM-style software. And the built-in programs for word processing, spreadsheets, telecommunications, and other purposes are puny compared to the ones for more sophisticated laptops. I say this with a caveat. If you're certain you need just a very inexpensive, simple laptop, you needn't feel ashamed. Quite the reverse. I congratulate you on your frugality! Moreover, you can buy additional programs and memory for the Model 100 and some other VW-priced machines from a supplier such as Traveling Software, at 18702 North Creek Parkway, Bothell, Washington 98011, 800-343-8080 or (206) 483-8088.

Lacking built-in disk drives—and relying just on memory chips— some of the cheapie notebook machines can store as few as fifteen to twenty pages of information. Auxiliary drives usually won't work with IBM-style floppies of any size. So typically you'll use cables to transfer information to your desktop machine or turn to a modem, which allows a computer to talk to others over the phone lines.

As expected, the screens are small and not very visible in dim light. You may be able to see only eight lines at a time. Using a Model 100, believe me, Hemingway might have kept his sentences even shorter. Blessedly, however, the keyboards on Radio Shack laptops have satisfied many a nitpicking writer. The word *writer* is no coincidence. Although Radio Shack meant the machines for businesspeople—for executives and sales reps—the Model 100s and the like have never really enjoyed as much success there as they have among journalists, consultants, and techies.

Whether buying new or used, make sure you won't outgrow your economy machine too quickly. I myself own a WP-2, a Tandy word processor that is a lighter, slimmer Model 100 with a screen showing more text, and I find it dandy for in-person interviews and research sessions at the library. But I would never want a WP-2 for more than note taking or dashing off short articles.[5]

More positively, batteries for the WP-2, the Model 100, and other bargain-priced notebooks can last weeks and even months if not in constant use. While many business executives dismiss such machines, the cheapest laptops may appeal even to some well-off writers who wander miles from the nearest AC outlet and need an electronic notebook. If "Papa" had actually owned a Model 100—and if his enemies hadn't broken it in a bar fight—he might well have taken it along on a trek up Mount Kilimanjaro.

Portfolio-Class Machines: MS-DOS-style VWs

"Aaah, isn't it cute?" cooed my friend Dr. Socorito Baez-Page, M.D., gazing down at the one-pound Portfolio from Atari, which is just 7.8 by 4.1 by 1.2 inches, sells for $399.95, and is ballyhooed as IBM compatible. Her husband, David, also a doctor, nodded. Both are computer-smart—Soc knows more than she lets on—and like many other professionals, they could use a good little machine to take notes on the run. I wanted several reviewers since the Portfolio was such a talked-about product; perhaps the first MS-DOS laptop listing for less than $500. As a bonus, Soc's father, a naval engineer, was visiting the Pages and could join our test.

All of us reached the same cranky conclusion: *$400 is too much even*

---

[5]The WP-2's commands are more awkward than the ones I've encountered in most MS-DOS programs. Also, the communications software is primitive, and an early version had bugs. Still, for light-duty use the WP-2 does the job.

ATARi

for the world's best telephone dialer. It's cruel to evaluate Portfolio as a real computer.

Below are three problems with the Atari and *perhaps* with the clones that surely will be coming along:

1. "IBM compatibility" is in eyes of the beholder. The Atari's LCD screen is just forty characters wide and eight lines deep. Even with the ability to scroll horizontally—move sideways—the screen won't be the easiest way to view the usual MS-DOS–style software. RAM is only 128K. Expansion is possible up to 640K, via a memory pack, but it's expensive. And that is yet another obstacle to running normal IBM programs. Not surprisingly, Tim Bajarin, the Silicon Valley consultant mentioned in chapter 1, refers to Portfolio-class computers as "wounded-DOS machines."

Besides the first-class dialer, the Portfolio comes with a word processor, an appointment diary, and a spreadsheet, but they are not replacements for grownup IBM-style software. The operating system is a workalike of MS-DOS 2.11. That's an antediluvian version of DOS, which is now past version 4.0 and may even be at version 5.0 by the time you're reading this. Most programs will work with 2.11, but not all will.

As expected, the Portfolio won't be a speed demon in the IBM world, no matter what software you use. The 80C88 chip runs at just 4.9 megahertz.

2. The keyboard is as abysmal as I had feared; the keys are too small, too close together, for serious work. I could type no faster than thirty words per minute, a fraction of my normal speed. Even with days of practice, I doubt I could have surpassed sixty.

To Atari's credit, you hear a click when you hit the keys, one way to increase the accuracy of your typing. But the Portfolio is still slow going. For touch typists needing a cheap machine with which to take notes, the WP-2 word processor and similar Tandy notebooks would be far wiser choices even if they can't run any IBM software.

3. The prices of the odds and ends can add up. You could be well on the way to buying a second Portfolio if you want a port to plug in your modem; cards for storing data; a card reader for your desktop computer, or a cable between the laptop and the desktop; expanded memory; and the rest of the options that somehow turn themselves into

essentials. You may as well have bought a $350 WP-2 at Radio Shack or have sent off your $550 check for a mail-order Toshiba T1000. In size the Toshiba dwarfs the Portfolio. But it also dwarfs the Atari machine in performance. The Toshiba can run many more DOS programs (even though the DOS is just 2.11) and it stores files to a 720K floppy.

On the positive side, the standard AA cells inside the Portfolio are said to last for weeks with normal usage, whereas the T1000's rechargeable battery fades away long before the end of the business day.

The Portfolio's on-screen software tutorials seem *excellent*. Before your very eyes, without your touching the keyboard, the word processor zaps characters and shows off other tricks. I can see this machine moving briskly off the shelves of discount stores and making millions as a mail-order item. It'll be an easy sell to the novelty minded.

Also, I can envision Portfolios for specialized applications where people need to punch up information from small databases or fill in simple forms. Portfolios might computerize a warehouse operation or gather information from parking meter attendants. At the end of the day the employees could upload the information to a desktop. You wouldn't have to buy separate cables and other trimmings for each person.

Portfolio-type machines could appeal, too, to those sales reps who are poor typists, don't need to punch in vast amounts of information, and insist on a small machine. They might love features like the automatic dialer. You hold the Portfolio's tiny loudspeaker up to your touch-tone phone so the computer can dial the number stored inside its memory. It's a snap to include more than one number per listing. With such features, Atari might be winning thousands of customers from products such as the Sharp's Wizard organizer; those must be the people who, according to Atari's public relations firm, have complained that the Portfolio's keyboard is too *big*. Still, if that's what they want, they might like the Wizard even more.

Regardless of the Portfolio's shortcomings, Atari deserves great credit for its try at a DOS laptop for the masses. Keep at it, people! My hunch is that sooner or later Atari will come out with something like a ''Portfolio Plus,'' boasting a better keyboard, improved screen and built-in serial and parallel ports. It's almost in the stars. If Atari doesn't turn the Portfolio into more of a real computer, a rival company will prevail in the MS-DOS-VW market.

PC- and XT-Class Laptops: Chevrolets for the IBM Set (The Floppy Disk Variety)

Congoleum chose this class of machine when it wanted a bargain-priced laptop fit for business use.

SHOULD YOU BUY A USED LAPTOP?

You can buy used computers from individuals or from companies, such as laptop rental outfits. Should you? Perhaps. But be wary. Here are some rules:

1. Use as a bargaining wedge the fact that laptop technology is constantly improving. In fact, the seller probably is disposing of the machine because he or she considers it obsolete. Read computer magazines to find out what is and is not a has-been.

2. Take advantage of the fact that laptop prices keep dropping. Not long ago I called up someone advertising a used Toshiba T1000 in the *Washington Post* for maybe $500. At the time, *now* T1000s were selling for $550 in New York. When the advertiser wouldn't lower her price, I nixed the deal. A machine several years old may command as little as one-half of its original street price.

3. If possible, try to buy from a trustworthy friend so that you'll have some idea of the laptop's history. Has it been banged around a lot? You can't always tell by the looks of the case. Hmm. I'm in the Washington, D.C., area and I can just imagine the FBI asking friends of candidates for cabinet-level jobs: "Would you buy a laptop from this man?"

4. Also think about having a technically accomplished friend or other expert look over the machine. Or do the equivalent of taking a used car you're about to buy to a mechanic for an inspection. Go to a computer dealer or repair shop with a good reputation among local groups of computer users.

5. Unless you get a fantastic price, do not buy a used hard disk laptop. Sooner or later disks die. When they do, you may find that the best thing to do is just to throw the laptop away.

6. Consider buying through a broker, such as the Boston Computer Exchange. The telephone number is (617) 542-4414; on CompuServe you can reach the Exchange by typing **GO BCE**. Nothing's surefire, of course. But at least the BCE rules offer *some* protection.

PC- and XT-level laptops use refinements of the 8088 microprocessor in the original IBM PCs and XTs. The 8088 ran at just 4.77 megahertz. Don't worry about megahertz. Just realize that it's a measurement of how fast certain programs will run. The 4.77 is fast enough for simple word processing and spreadsheets; that's the speed of many popular machines used by frugal writers. Many PC/XT-class machines have shunned the 8088 in favor of the 8-megahertz NEC V-20 chips, but these still are snailish in the eyes of many accountants and other speed fans.

Within the PC/XT class, a number of laptops come with either (1) twin floppy drives or (2) a single drive and a chip that holds information even after you switch off the power. The twin-floppy arrangement can make it easier to copy data from one disk to another. On the other hand, the extra floppy increases the size of the machine. A few PC/XT machines dispense with floppies entirely; notable examples are the original four-pound version of the NEC UltraLite and the one-pound Poqet, which offer floppy drives only as accessories. A bit redeemingly, however, the Poqet and certain other PC/XT laptops have MS-DOS built into their chips. That increases the amount of space available for programs and data in addition to reducing the time it takes for you to turn on your laptop and start computing.

Some single-floppy laptops in the PC/XT class offer hard disks, but they're slow compared to those on more expensive laptops. A hard disk is a memory device built into the machine that can store thousands of pages of information—many times more than the typical floppy can stash away. Because the floppy drives are slow, you'll take longer to retrieve a "file," which is computerese for a document of any kind— a letter, a report, and so on. You'll also require more time to save the information on your disk. For short documents, the hard disks on the XT type laptops should suffice nicely. If, however, you're dealing with massive databases, you may end up with more than your share of coffee breaks.

Another negative of most PC/XT-class laptops is that they don't make IBM-style slots available for accessories, such as modems. Granted, you can plug in modems and other options that come on printed circuit cards (commonly they slide into the back of the machine). But these cards aren't of the more popular variety that fit some IBM-style desktops. Rather, the card design is proprietary, intended just for machines made by a certain manufacturer, so you don't have as many choices of cards.[6]

Screens as of this writing are no match for those of more expensive machines. Normally they're LCDs. People using the PC/XT laptops for extended periods may want to invest in external monitors, perhaps including color ones.

Despite their various shortcomings, PC/XT laptops can be excellent investments for budget-minded buyers who require neither the expandability nor power and speed found in more expensive laptops. Moreover, mobile executives, many lawyers, writers, and students may cherish the compactness of the PC/XT. Accountants should consider PC/XT machines only for use as electronic notebooks, not for spreadsheeting, unless convinced that their needs are very modest.

Smaller PC- and XT-Class Laptops: Sports Cars for the IBM Set—With Memory Cards, Not Regular Drives

Like the Atari Portfolio, the $1,995 Poqet has blazed a trail for a whole new class of machine. It weighs about a pound and is even more amazing than the Portfolio.

By the end of 1992 the Poqet's flash-memory cards might be able to store 32 megabytes each in a space the size of a credit card. And from the start you can get an 80-by-25-line screen, *true* IBM compatibility, as many as 100 hours of battery life, and the ability to slip the Poqet into a large trench coat; here's one machine that even the better computer stores may want to bolt down.

Without doubt, the Poqet is a nifty little computer for calling up price lists, entering accident claims, or fetching electronic mail. But you might not want to take the Poqet to Bangladesh as your sole machine. Why not? The screen and keyboard are better than the Atari's but still not good enough to use hour after hour. The screen requires the light and angle of vision to be *just so*. Maybe that is a blessing for the privacy-loving users who are worried about passengers in the next seat snooping on their spreadsheets, but I myself am not thrilled. At best the LCD's contrast is mediocre.

---

[6]Of course, you may be able to buy an attachment to be able to use XT- or AT-style cards. See page 62 about such products as the Won Under.

The keyboard is worse than the screen. The seventy-seven keys are where you expect them, but as with the Portfolio, I could reach just a fraction of my usual typing speed. My friend David Page did not fare any better. And mind you, he heeded Poqet's warning to me and spent many hours of learning time to give the tiny keyboard a chance. An electronic key click wasn't audible after David turned it on to help confirm when his keystrokes had registered. "The keyboard offers an uncertain tactile feedback," he said. "The problem is much reduced but not absent on a firm surface. The keyboard is quite cramped. Also, I noticed a definite lag between keyboarding a character and having it show up on the screen."

Encouragingly, Poqet says the present model is as small as the machine will get; a big brother with an adult-size keyboard could be on the way. The first Poqet is just 8.75 by 4.3 by .9 inches. It's as if a mad scientist created a tiny genius to whom you had trouble speaking because you had to bend down so far.

Flaws notwithstanding, the original machine is a classic. It offers many little wrinkles never seen before. How many other computers can run for as long as one hundred hours on just two AA batteries? The 7-megahertz, 80C88 chip—frugal with power—is just part of the explanation. The screen isn't backlit, one way to save juice. But that's just a start. You see, the Poqet falls asleep if a certain amount of time has gone by without a keystroke; you hit a certain key to rouse the computer. Meanwhile, your data survives.

Of course you can send your information back to your desktop computer, if you want—either via cable or an external 1.44-inch disk drive. If used 20 percent of the time, the drive will operate up to twenty-five hours.

The drive, however, is hardly notable compared to the Poqet's plug-in memory cards. My test unit's RAM card could store 512K, just a fraction of the 16 megabytes that the little cards may eventually hold. Alas, you must be careful that the tiny batteries inside the cards don't lose their power if you store them away from the Poqet. Otherwise, wave good-bye to your report or spreadsheet. But Poqet says a solution is on the way—flash memory cards. Such memory cards don't need tiny batteries inside to keep them from losing information. In spring 1990 a Poqet spokesman claimed that the new-style memory cards would probably fit existing machines. He expected seventy-five thousand to one hundred thousand Poqets to move by the year's end, and said the company couldn't afford to disappoint early buyers.

By the end of 1991, if the flash-memory cards live up to Intel's expectations, the roomier cards might store 16 megabytes or more. And a year later the number might reach an amazing 32 megabytes, enough room for the equivalent of sixteen thousand pages of double-spaced typing; many small companies could squirrel away all their records in less space than a woman's handbag. That doesn't mean that the companies would, since the Poqet is such a one-person machine. But the potential exists.

The creators of the Poqet, meanwhile, have been canny in other ways; they've encouraged software makers to supply their programs on ROM cards.[7]

You see, the Poqet will be able to use software directly from the ROM cards. The cards need just a little slice of the 512K RAM with which the Poqet comes; you could run programs several megabytes in size, if they're on the ROM cards. Among the software houses planning or offering cards are:

- Lotus
- WordPerfect
- XyQuest, developer of the XyWrite word processor for writers and editors
- Contact Software, whose ACT! program is a standard among sales reps

Via ROM cards, reps can also benefit from AlphaWorks, a very good mix of word processor, spelling checker, thesaurus, spreadsheet, database, graphics program, and communications program. Imagine running AlphaWorks database when the 32 megabyte flash-memory cards finally arrive. *PSION*

Although the Poqet is a classic—it brings together a number of features, everything from flash memory to its size—it won't be the first commercially available laptop to use flash memory. The prize goes to Psion. A British employee of Psion, Inc. (the parent company, Psion,

---

[7] *ROM* means read-only memory. Your computer can read information from it but cannot store information in it.

PLC, is in England) could justifiably indulge himself in a little national
pride here. "Usually," he said of those making technological breakthroughs, "it's you guys or the Japanese."

For $1,299, Psion sells a non–MS-DOS machine using flash memory.
But the model to watch is the MC 600, a 4.3 pound IBM compatible. It
offers 768K of RAM, a 640-by-200 LCD screen, and a $2,999 price tag.

That's $1,000 more than the Poqet's anticipated price. But the Poqet
people do not seem too open to discounting, while their counterparts
at Psion do, so street prices may be within $200 of each other. The
Psion machines use RAM or flash memory cartridges thicker than the
Poqet's cards. You plug the cartridges into one of four slots ballyhooed
as "solid state drives." The Psion employs the same flash technology
inside the machine; this 256K of memory stores limited amounts of data
even without your plugging in cartridges.

Keep in mind that the battle of memory lane is not over. In the next
few years, magnetic hard disks will be much cheaper and more rugged,
and they may consume much less power than before. Still, flash memory
might elbow out the rival technology—from many laptops, anyway—
if its boosters are right. Turn to page 52 for yet more details on the
flash memory's strengths and weaknesses.

AT-Class Laptops: Buicks

Many large accounting firms insist on laptops of at least AT-class power
for spreadsheeting, databases, and other major uses. Significantly, Release 3.0 of Lotus 1-2-3 can't even run on PC/XT-class machines.[8]
Release 3.0 allows the display of more than one spreadsheet on the
screen at once and expanded graphics capabilities, causing accounting
firms to push aside the older laptops with their limited memories.

Some sales organizations, too, may value AT-class laptops because
of the speed at which they can run graphics programs in demonstrations
for clients. Computer consultants may welcome the existence of a slot
or two into which they can plug cards that normally would work just
on desktops. AT-class laptops often aren't limited to proprietary cards
for modems and the like.

These mid-range laptops feature low-powered versions of the 80286
processor found in the original IBM AT. The first AT ran at 6 megahertz;

[8]Even Release 3.0 isn't as great a memory hog as 1-2-3/G.

most of the mid-range laptops cruise along at 12 megahertz or beyond. In time, the 80286-style machines will fade away, to be replaced by those using the 80386, its equivalents, or the 80386SX. Count on this. Already the trade magazines are full of rumors about Intel working on a 386-class chip that could revolutionize laptops. These little marvels will be extra thrifty with battery power. And by themselves they'll handle tasks now farmed out to different chips or different parts of the computer. The same chip serving as a CPU, for example, might also help your laptop "talk" with the screen to tell it what to display. Result? Smaller, more powerful laptops. So don't get sentimental about 286-class machines. "Buick" will be a more apt description than "AT class" as the 286s die off.

On many laptops in this mid-price range, hard disks run at a comfortable 28 milliseconds or faster. Again, you needn't worry about the details other than to realize that zippy hard disks will be helpful if you're working with big databases or very long word processing files.

The early AT-class laptops all required AC power. This changed as chip makers churned out lower-powered versions of the 80286. If you don't need battery operation, you may be able to find some real bargains among the used AT-level laptops that you must tether to the wall. I wrote much of this book on a borrowed Toshiba 3100e—an AT laptop blessed by an extraordinary keyboard that was better than the one for my desktop machine.

Screen choices range from relatively sharp LCDs to gas plasmas. Some less picky writers may find these screens adequate for long stretches of writing, but many will want to consider external monitors. Ultimately the gas plasma screen was why I decided not to buy the machine I'd borrowed.

Powerhouse Laptops: Cadillacs and Rolls-Royces

Many AT-style laptops can run the new OS/2 operating system, a successor to MS-DOS that allows easier multitasking; you can use the computer for several things at once, such as working with one spreadsheet while transmitting another to your Los Angeles office.[9] I myself

[9]OS/2 is also an improvement in that it requires different programs to have common user interfaces. That is, OS/2 encourages (but does not require) the standardization of the way commands look on screen. Once you learn a word processor for OS/2, you can apply some of the same principles to mastering a spreadsheet.

hadn't the slightest need for OS/2 while writing this book. In fact, I almost resented the new operating system as a form of planned obsolescence. Little software existed.

But in the 1990s there will be an abundance of word processors, spreadsheets, databases, and other software taking advantage of OS/2. And many will be bigger than 640K, the maximum size of programs in MS-DOS. So if you're really looking ahead, you may want to consider powerhouse laptops—more muscular than the AT class—to run this new operating system.

Powerhouse machines are also good for users of Windows. Created by Microsoft and able to run under MS-DOS, this software also facilitates multitasking. You can see views of certain programs running simultaneously in different "windows." Alas, Windows requires at least an 80286-style microprocessor for even moderately decent speed. And then you'll want special Window-specific programs if you plan to run them on the screen at the same time. Windows needs at least a 80386SX-style microprocessor to multitask regular DOS software (this may change). It also requires additional RAM.

By the time some accountants add up their megabyte requirements for Windows or OS/2, they might find themselves needing several megabytes or more of RAM if they're doing heavy-duty spreadsheeting. Plus they'll want their system to work at a brisk speed. So even if they don't work for a large accounting firm they may seriously consider a 386-based machine, or at the very least a 286.

If you do buy a program using Windows or otherwise displaying plenty of details on-screen, you should take special care to pick out a good, sharp monitor that can do justice to the software.

In the clock-speed department the powerhouses easily surpass the low- and mid-range 286s. Expect speeds of 25 or 30 megahertz, maybe even 40 or 45 megahertz, by the time you're reading this book. Of course, everything is relative. The Buick-priced machines may well be up to 20 or 25 megahertz by then.

Chips—that is, their speeds and capabilities—set the direction of laptops and the rest of the computer industry and lead to new definitions of the word *powerhouse*. People in Silicon Valley talk of a features avalanche. The first year, you see a faster processor or other twist in a desktop, then in a lunchbox or large laptop the next year, and in a notebook machine the year after that. "Power users" will keep crying for more, so they can run OS/2, Windows, and other demanding software. And as the technology improves, Silicon Valley will work to raise the expectations of the computer world at large.

Even Technoklutzes will eventually want computers with new talents. Take all those graying executives who never want to type; they are prime candidates for notebook-size computers that can understand many words and speak back. That means 386 chips and up. Likewise, the faster microprocessors will help tablet-style computers read handwriting with much greater reliability than is possible with 286s. The computer-ignorant couldn't care less what the chip is, just so their machines can do what the humans want; they are like the buyers of high-tech cars who yawn if you talk about the latest fuel-injection systems, but who can be maniacal about gas mileage. And so the Technoklutzes, too, will keep the avalanche rolling on. With the 386 poised to become the norm in the Buick class, it will lose its cachet as a chip for the Rolls-Royce people. Already clone makers are churning out 80486 desktops. So by 1992 or 1993 you should expect—yes, the 486 notebook.

Earlier I said laptop technology moved "infinitely" faster than technology in other industries. Maybe I instead should have said "infuriatingly."

Lunchbox Machines (Not True Laptops)

Unless you're André the Giant or a similar-size wrestler, you won't want a lunchbox machine on your lap. They can weigh twenty to thirty pounds or more. Still, there are advantages. The main part of the portable houses the computer and screen. In most cases you can separate the keyboard from the main unit and increase your comfort.

Another advantage of a lunchbox-style computer is that it typically contains at least several slots into which you can plug fancy accessories. That's handy, given the relentless progress of computer technology.

Lunchbox machines can be in the PC/XT, AT, and powerhouse classes. You've heard the old cliché that you can never be too rich or too thin. The same thinking can apply to RAM and hard disk space: if you're at a major accounting firm you can never have too much of either. What's more, in certain parts of the computer world you can never have too many slots available for specialized applications, such as local area networks linking together a bunch of machines. And that's where lunchboxes come in. One network user complained to Compaq that a lunchbox with twelve slots still wasn't sufficient.

Wisely, Jeff Knepper of Deloitte & Touche's Washington office recommends lunchboxes to help link together the laptops of individual accountants when they're out at client sites. They can serve as portable servers—hub machines in local area networks.

Offbeat Machines

"Don't quote me," says a laptop guru at a large company deeply committed to MS-DOS software. He pauses. Then he goes on to praise Apple's first Macintosh portable for being "perfect, marvelous, fast, wonderful, easy to use," and for having "a quick, razor-sharp screen. And on top of everything else, it runs Macintosh software." The screen, however, isn't backlit. And the batteries, although lasting as long as eight hours, are as heavy as lead. In fact, they *are* the lead kind.

For my needs—writing, no fancy graphics—IBM-style laptops are much easier on my back and wallet. The first Mac portable weighs 15.5 pounds and appeared with a $7,000 price tag in a typical configuration with a hard disk. As of spring 1990, the price was still $5,499 for a model with a 40 megabyte drive.

I equally hate the mouse, the device with which users of desk-bound Macs move the cursor.[10] Nor am I excited by the trackball. It's the ball buried in the portable's keyboard—the mouse replacement to which Apple turned when it realized that laptop users couldn't very well employ the knee of the next passenger in a 747 as a mouse pad. Roll the trackball and the cursor will move. Big deal. I'm not one for video games either. I'm a touch typist who would rather use keys on the main part of the keyboard to control the cursor. Video game fanatics are welcome to demur. I would hope, however, that they'd join me in complaining about something else—the way Apple gouges its users.

Apple uses lawsuits and other mischief to stymie some rivals who want to make affordable clones of Apple products; that's quite a change from the company that once talked of a "computer for the rest of us."

The Apple people should be careful. The worse the gouges, the more incentive exists for rivals to try to emulate the *complete* Mac legally. In the future the makers of clones might not need to buy Macs (or parts) to repackage as laptops.

---

[10] A cursor is the blinking square or other symbol that shows where characters will appear on the screen when you type.

WHY A MAC NOTEBOOK COMPUTER MIGHT NOT BE THE "WRITE" CHOICE FOR STUDENTS

Sooner or later a Mac notebook computer will sell for less than $500, making it a prime possibility for students. If one teacher's hunch is right, however, you might actually *hurt* your child by choosing a Mac-style portable. Marcia Peoples Halio is the assistant director of the writing program in the English department at the University of Delaware. In the January 1990 issue of *Academic Computing*, she questioned whether college freshmen, "particularly those who do not show a high level of verbal ability in placement tests, should use the Mac to write."

Halio and colleagues compared (1) classes of students using desktop Macintoshes to compose essays and (2) other classes equipped with IBMs. They concluded that the English of the Mac users showed less skill than the prose of the other students. The spelling was abysmal, and, in the researchers' opinion, sentences were too short. The MacEssayists, moreover, favored froth. Asked for essays on social phenomena, the Mac students wrote on "such topics as fast food, dating, bars, television, rock music, sports, relationships, and phenomena such as the foam 'popcorn' chips that come in so many packages." The IBM-equipped students, on the other hand, delved into subjects such as nuclear war and capital punishment.

"Why blame the Macs?" you might ask. "Maybe the problem was the people who were attracted to them." Halio, however, says the students chose the creative writing classes mainly with their schedules in mind— not so much according to the machines in use.

Halio wonders if the Mac's visually oriented, mouse-style interface couldn't be the villain. The way she sees it, the students think of the Macs as toys and thus are too casual about their prose. She offers other possible explanations, too, such as the size of the screen and the feel of the keyboard. But the visual interface seems to be her biggest concern. When Apple finally does come out with affordable notebook machines, the interface issue should be of prime interest to parents as well as academics. Ideally, other researchers will explore this topic under carefully controlled conditions.

For the moment, though, the Apple people are smug about their portables and desktops alike. They are selling most of their machines for just a little less than IBM's brand-name computers with the same capabilities; the world still awaits "the laptop for the rest of us." Meanwhile, by way of Windows and OS/2, even the low-cost clones of IBM machines are growing more Maclike than ever. The clones' screens are sharpening. Soon they will be as viewable as the present Mac Portables. Good, affordable color will sweep the IBM clone world in a few years, and Apple will have to scramble to keep far enough ahead to preserve the gouges.

That said, I'll recommend the Mac laptop as one of many possibilities for:

■ Millionaires and companies who love Mac software and don't care about the price.

■ People who are fanatical about common interfaces. "If you know one word processor," says Jerry Oppenheimer, a MacLoyalist and old newspaper friend of mine, "you can work with another. If you know one database, you can work with another." There won't be as many differences in their commands (and in the way they look on the screen) as with various brands of MS-DOS software. That will change, however, as IBM continues its moves toward common interfaces. Already users can do plenty on their own. In *XyWrite Made Easier*, for instance, I tell how I "trained" XyWrite to emulate most of the basic WordStar commands.

■ Graphics designers. My friend Oppenheimer insists that Mac owners as a group are "artsier, craftsier than the suits who buy the DOS machines." He could be right concerning people in the visual arts. Many creative people who work with words, however, would prefer fast, IBM-style software designed especially for writers and editors— XyWrite, for example.

■ People in desktop publishing who insist on knowing—when they're in the field—what their newsletters or other works will look like. Actually, of course, it may be more sensible for the user of a desktop Mac to buy a cheap IBM-style laptop on which to write articles, ads, or other copy in the field. Then he or she could rely on a modem or other means to transfer prose to the Mac after returning to the office.

■ Users in specialized applications, such as musical composition, computer-aided design, or engineering, that may rely on Mac-style software.

Unhappy as I am with Apple's prices, I still agree with the laptop guru that at times IBM gear can be expensive too. Consider the hoggish RAM requirements of OS/2 and Windows-style programs. By the time you're through stuffing memory chips into your portable—assuming that it allows such expansion in the first place—you might as well have bought an Apple laptop. Ideally this will change as memory prices decline.

To return to the Mac portables, please remember that they're just one species of offbeat laptops. Some other special machines use the UNIX operating system. A creation of Bell laboratories, UNIX is especially popular for scientific applications and where many people share the same computer system. At this point, however, UNIX is hardly a major factor in the laptop world.

Hand-held Computers

How's the Kleenex supply holding out? Is Part #187-15a in stock? Have the fire exits been checked in Building B? What about the gas meter at 205 North Farragut?

Hand-held computers can enter and fetch information in all of those areas. As *Byte* magazine observed (see "The Ever-Shrinking, Ever Expanding Laptop on page 91 of the August 1989 issue), hand-held computers can be useful to "maintenance and service personnel, sales representatives, workers on the factory floor or at test sites, public safety workers, building and utilities inspectors, military personnel, and many others. Computers in the field could eliminate the paperwork associated with schedules, maps, diagnostic procedures and manuals, inventory, and telemetry, to name a few."

Among the hand-held machines, some possibilities are:

■ The GRiDPad, which is really larger than a true hand-held but sort of qualifies anyway because it's so light and lacks a keyboard. (It does include a port into which you can plug a standard XT-class keyboard.) The GRiDPad weighs only 4.5 pounds, measures 9-by-12-by-1.4 inches, runs at 10 megahertz with an 80C86 chip, and offers a fairly

high-resolution LCD. And this MS-DOS machine can read printing—
well, if it's neat enough.

Government Computer News, a privately owned newspaper that
serves the feds and ought to know, recommends the GRiDPad as an
excellent device for streamlining the entry of forms. That could be a
boon, and not only to census bureaucrats. It could also help managers
and workers in private industry—those in inventory, warehouse administration, and similar jobs. Imagine being able to use a computer
while standing up or even walking!

In the case of the GRiDPad, at least, a few catches do exist. You
must enter data with an electronic pen, attached. Also, while anyone
can map out the forms, skilled programmers must implement the design.

Price is $2,370. The maker is GRiD Systems, 47211 Lakeview
Boulevard, P.O. Box 5003, Fremont, California 94537, 800-222-4743.

By the time you're reading this, incidentally, at least several other
manufacturers should be selling laptops that let you use an electronic
pen rather than a keyboard. Toshiba is expected to offer the PenPC for
$6,000. It isn't hand-held, includes a keyboard, and weighs over twelve
pounds.

Even lighter than the GRiDPad, however, is a hand-held laptop that
may be available by now from GO Corporation, 950 Power Lane, Foster
City, California 94404-218 (415-345-7400). It's reportedly an inch thick
and should sell for between $4,000 and $6,000.

■ The Agilis hand-held workstations. The 80386 version is so muscular that it could also qualify as an ''offbeat powerhouse machine.''
It's three inches thick and weighs just eight pounds. The Agilis includes
a touch screen, which you can use with just one hand, as well as a
keyboard (definitely not designed for touch typists).

Like the Apple laptop, the Agilis 80386 model commands a premium
for its uniqueness. Price as of this writing was around $12,000 for a
configuration with such goodies as a 20-megabyte hard disk and 4
megabytes of memory.

A less-powerful Agilis with an 80C88, weighing as little as four
pounds, would set you back a mere $5,000. The Agilis people have
ruggedized their machines for harsh outdoor environments.

The Agilis Corporation is at 1101 San Antonio Road, Mountain
View, California 94043, (415) 962-9400.

■ The PC/5000, an MS-DOS–compatible hand-held that you can
drop five feet onto a concrete floor or submerge in water. It even floats.

Utilities and forest services, understandably, were among the PC/5000's first users. This is an adequately powerful machine by laptop standards, but it's hardly fit for writing and other prolonged use. The screen is just a 20-character-by-eight-line LCD, and the keyboard, like those of many hand-helds, is not the QWERTY style to which most typists are accustomed. Running at 4 megahertz, the processor is an 80C88. The PC/5000 sells for $2,395 with 256K RAM for both program use and mass storage (expandable to 704K for the program use and 2.2 megabytes for mass storage). The manufacturer is MicroPalm Computers, at 13773-500 ICOT Boulevard, Clearwater, Florida 34620, (813) 530-0128.

■ Non–MS-DOS hand-helds from Symbol Technologies (116 Wilbur Drive, Bohemia, New York 11716, [516] 563-2400) and Telxon Corporation (3330 West Market Street, Akron, Ohio 44313, [216] 867-3700). By now both companies may be offering MS-DOS hand-helds, so check with them.

Obviously, in price the more expensive hand-helds are a long way from the Atari Portfolio. As much as you may esteem your clerks and warehouse people, can you really afford to equip everyone with a laptop costing more than two thousand dollars? If they're just filling out forms, and if the software requirements aren't that impressive, do they really need such expensive machines?

You may be better off either (1) buying Portfolio-priced laptops, commissioning the writing of custom software, and letting employees hunt and peck on the keyboards, or (2) waiting for the prices of the sophisticated hand-helds to drop.

Ironically, the $400 Atari—one pound, and smaller than a videocassette—is more portable than most of the so-called hand-helds for industrial use. On the other hand, the Atari is not ruggedized for harsh environments, and you and your programmers may not enjoy the same level of support you'd get from manufacturers accustomed to industrial and commercial markets.

GENERAL PHYSICAL CHARACTERISTICS

The experts can jabber on and on about bits and bytes and megabytes, but what I look for in a laptop first is whether I enjoy using it. I refuse to buy a machine unless I've toyed around with it for at least two hours in the store.

Here are questions that you should ask, whether you're buying for yourself or a large corporation:

■ How comfortable does the laptop feel in your lap and elsewhere? Do you hate writing on desks? Would you like a machine you can curl up with in the privacy of a hotel room? I know of at least two hardworking professionals who do some of their best work in bed. Don't think only of yourself if you're making a mass purchase. Even if you're strictly a desk person, some of your company's people may be a little less conventional, at least in private.

■ Is the laptop easy enough to tote around? Weight and size aren't everything. How about the handle? Is it comfortable in your hand? Is it in the front of the machine or the back? As always, consider the other people involved. The needs of big, burly sales reps who carry their laptop for short distances may differ from those of smaller people with long hikes between taxis and airport gates. Speaking of the jet set, will the laptop fit easily on an airline tray, especially when the person in the seat ahead of you reclines? And can it fit easily into the overhead luggage rack?

■ How about the distance between the keyboard and the screen? Alas, most—though not all—laptops lack detachable keyboards. You can't separate the built-in keyboard of the typical portable from the main unit. Yes, you probably can alter the tilt of the screen, but the distance between the keyboard and the portable's own screen must remain basically constant.

Please note that the optimal distance between you and the keyboard may conflict with the best distance between you and the screen. I like to put my elbows on the table when I type, but that moves the screen farther away and makes it harder to read—not a bad argument for large, legible characters.

Comfort issues matter less for machines that people use only for short periods of time. Even so, your needs or the needs of your company may change. You may buy the machine thinking that it'll suffice for short bursts of work, then find that you're using it hour after hour in the field.

■ How easy is the laptop to use with an external monitor? Will the built-in machine fold out of the way entirely? Granted, you or your people can position an external monitor off to the side. But that invites a sore neck if you're using the laptop for a long stretch of time.

■ How ruggedly built is the machine? Don't shy away from asking the dealer and manufacturer how much abuse a portable can take. Just how many inches off a table can you drop it? I'm not suggesting that you put the unit through an actual test. Just try to establish how well it will survive life on the road.

■ To what extent is the laptop protected from dust and the elements? You'll want to carry your laptop in a well-padded case, especially if the machine includes a hard disk; don't count on it surviving a good rain. Even so, you might feel better with a machine whose disk drive holes are not exposed. Also, consider how well the manufacturer has protected the parallel port (into which you'll typically plug your printer) and serial port (for the modem). Toshiba has cleverly arranged for the handle of some units to be able to slide over the ports.

THE KEYBOARD

Why do the keyboards of so many portables deviate unnecessarily from the classic IBM Selectric layout familiar to millions of touch typists? Why do some portables have a \ between the left Shift key and the Z? That particular stupidity is a mindless imitation of the original IBM PC. Alas, there are other idiosyncrasies—for example, strange foreign characters between the *P* and the Enter key. I suspect that some portable makers started out trying to satisfy large overseas customers. Ordinary users in the United States must pay the penalty.

Here are keyboard-related questions:

■ How high is the keyboard from the table? In my opinion—feel free to disagree—the best keyboards do not require you to raise your hands much while you're typing. This reduces wrist fatigue. Certain portables have handles that do double duty as wrist rests; still, I prefer a machine with a low-slung keyboard. Of course, the comfort of the keyboard may not seem so crucial if you aren't using the laptop hour after hour.

■ What about the tilt of the keyboard? Some laptops cleverly use the handle to raise the backs of the machines so that the keys in front are a little lower than those in the back. I like this wrinkle, just so the keys don't become too elevated.

■ How hard must you tap the keys? Using a keyboard hour after hour, I like a light touch.

■ How far must you depress the keys? Many users favor "full-travel" keys—ones with typewriterlike characteristics—rather than those that register the stroke when a key is barely pressed. Can you tell when you've depressed the key? Does the keyboard make a click sound, whether natural or electronic?

If the keyboard does click, is it still quiet enough to use during meetings? Ideally you'll find out before you buy. Still, some owners of the original Model 100s have succeeded in quieting their machines by inserting rubber bands—the kind used by orthodontists—under the key caps. Check with a repair shop familiar with the machine you're considering to determine the feasibility of this.

■ How large are the keys? The little Chiclet-like keys on some notebook machines can slow down both hunt-and-peck and touch typists.

■ How far apart are the keys? Will a big-fingered sales rep—a nontypist—feel at home? Please note that preferences do vary. Some touch typists know their way around a keyboard so well that they actually favor keys that are close together, so their fingers needn't wander around as much.

■ In particular, what about the sizes, shapes, and positions of the Tab, Enter (Return), and Backspace keys? Too many portables demote the Enter key to the size of a normal key.

What about the Caps Lock, Ctrl (Control), Alt (Alternate), and function keys? I hate the new PS/2-style keyboards on desktop machines. They've switched the Caps Lock and Ctrl keys. The Caps Lock is now on the home row of the keyboard, the row where a touch typist's hand normally would rest. To be sure, that's where the Caps Lock is on a Selectric. But in this case, anyway, the Selectric's layout won't do. After all, many programs, such as WordStar, rely heavily on the Ctrl key for issuing commands. It's been compared to a gear-shift. Holding down Ctrl, you can make an ordinary key issue a command. Which command—if any—depends on the program. WordStar heavily uses Ctrl combinations. By holding the Ctrl key and hitting the S, for example, a touch typist can easily move the cursor to the left. A combination of Ctrl and E (Ctrl-E) will move the cursor up, Ctrl-X will move it down, and Ctrl-D will move the cursor to the right.

Many touch typists, and I am one of them, love this arrangement. But IBM stupidly moved the Ctrl key from the home row to a position below the main part of the keyboard. Grrr! Luckily, programs such as SWITCH.COM—provided with WordStar—can correct the problem. But sometimes such auxiliary programs won't work with other software.

As for Alt ("alternate")—another gearshift key—it too should be in a good position for you to combine with other keys to issue commands.

You'll also want conveniently located function keys. Typically these keys are numbered F1 through F10. For me, the best place for them is to the left of the main keyboard, but Nancy Breckenridge, my ace transcriptionist, has long, nimble fingers and likes the function keys above the main board. That, indeed, is the arrangement found on most laptops, since it allows for a narrower case.

■ How about the numeric pad? Does the laptop have a true numeric pad, where the numbers are in the same order as they would appear on a calculator? How about the keys for Home (the top of the screen or file); End (the bottom of the screen or the end of the file storing a document); PgUp (up a screen, or "page"); PgDn (down a screen); Ins (insert mode); and Del (delete a character)? Are their locations the same as on an IBM PC? What about the PrtSc, Minus, and Plus keys?

As a writer, I normally couldn't care less about numeric pads. In fact, I often think such pads are space hogs on laptops. But certain programs—even some for word people—depend on the keys on the traditional IBM PC's numeric pad. If your portable lacks the numbers pad, does it include a special function key that turns regular keys into those normally found on the pad? For example, the 7 key may become a 7 (no surprise there), the 8 key an 8, the 9 key a 9, the U key a 4, the I key next to it a 5, the O key a 6, and so on. To gauge whether a keyboard will work with your pet program, don't just *look* at the portable, *try it out*! If you're about to buy the software and the computer at the same time, see if you can locate any existing owners of the laptop who use the program.

■ If the laptop lacks a numeric pad, can you plug one in?

■ Does the computer let you plug in a whole keyboard, so you can use the same board as you would with a desktop? Can you use a keyboard from another company, not just the one that made the laptop?

■ How easily can touch typists use cursor keys and other ways of positioning the cursor? Are these keys close to the keyboard? And what about devices other than keys? Consider the trackball. Is it close enough to the main keyboard so that your hands don't have to wander too far? Best of all, perhaps, would be a key in the main keyboard that functioned as a pointing device. Then you wouldn't have to go very far. Tim Bajarin, whose consulting clients include Apple and Compaq, among others, says that such alternative positioning systems may become common in the 1990s. Let's hope so. I'm tired of mice and trackballs being regarded as the only alternatives to the cursor keys.

THE SCREEN

Printer ads keep harping about the need to make a "good impression." Just as important, however, is a good screen, which can be a godsend when you're editing your work, searching for typographical errors, and checking the accuracy of what you've written.

Several of the more common video standards for laptops are:

1. CGA "color graphics adapter," even if "color" doesn't apply to the normal laptop. This is a leftover from some early desktops. Screens with CGA resolution can be more than a mite fuzzy. In the beginning CGA typically offered 640 dots across and 200 dots up and down—in other words, 640 by 200. By contrast, the cheaper monitors for desktops usually sport 720 by 348 displays. Regrettably, as of this writing the 640-by-200 form of CGA is still found on the lowest-end laptops and even a few mid-range ones, such as LTE machines from Compaq.

By now, however, most mid-range models with CGA should be capable of 640 by 400 CGA, through a technique called double scan, which makes letters and numbers appear sharper. Extra dots *vertically* fill out the blanks between the old CGA dots, so a seven by seven character can become fourteen dots high while remaining seven dots wide. Toshiba's T1000SE is an example of the new generation of CGA machines. For reasons of price and compactness, CGA probably won't disappear entirely in the early 1990s.

The earlier, 640 by 200 CGA standard normally should suffice for people using laptops for short periods or for those in the field, such as service technicians or sales reps. Primitive CGA is no joy for writers, accountants, and others who stay put and stare at their screens hour after hour. What's more, some color programs behave bizarrely even on the more advanced CGA laptops; yellow and green shades may appear the same on the screen if you can't use corrective software (supplied with some makes, such as Toshiba).

2. EGA, "enhanced graphics adapter," which typically allows 640 by 350 resolution. For the most part, EGA monitors for desktops are color models. On monochrome laptops you won't see colors, but ideally you'll perceive subtle differences in shades.

3. VGA, "video graphics array." As with other standards, resolutions can vary. The first VGA laptop widely distributed in the United States was Compaq's SLT/286, an AT-class machine debuting with a 9.5-inch screen and 640 by 480 dots in as many as eight true shades of gray. VGA is the most common graphics standard today for desktops. Ideally, laptops will soon catch up.

Not only different resolutions, but different technologies exist to create the images in the first place. Among the possibilities are:

■ LCDs, nonbacklit, nonglowing ("nonemissive," in the jargon of some computer mavens). This is the least costly screen technology, the same kind found in nonglowing wristwatches. Typically an LCD display contains two plates of polarized glass. Electrodes crisscross one of the plates. The electrodes influence the orientation of tiny, crystal-like parts of a gooey chemical mix. In one direction the crystals reflect light; in the other they block it. The greater the angle of the "twist," the sharper the contrast between the background and the dots that form characters and numbers. "Supertwist" displays (up to 270 degrees) are now standard in the industry, allowing high contrast compared to earlier laptops' displays.

Unfortunately, you can't read LCDs if you're off very far to the side, at least not the cheaper screens. Heavy-duty laptop users should check out the machines with more expensive LCDs. See if they'll be large enough and offer a big enough range of viewing angles for writing, sales presentations, and similar uses. You may be disappointed even with the upscale LCDs.

On the, er, bright side, plain LCDs without backlighting are the camels of display technology when it comes to energy consumption.

Perhaps that's why Apple didn't include backlighting in its Macintosh portable that offers eight hours of battery time.

Apple also overcame another problem: the slowness of LCD screens. In typical LCDs, you may see ghosting as you move on to another screen view. You may see traces of the characters earlier displayed. But by speeding up the screen, using an active-matrix LCD, as this new kind of screen is known, Apple's engineers helped the cursor keep up with the movements of the trackball.

Each pixel, each dot on the screen, needs a transistor, so production costs are high. But that could drop as the Japanese use active-matrix technology in hand-held televisions. "Active-matrix," says Sohail Malik, a display expert with Dataquest, "is where things are going." Tim Bajarin agrees. What's more, he believes that the industry may be headed toward laptops with a mix of backlighting and active-matrix.

Even now, however, because of sharper screens available through active-matrix, you may find that you don't need backlighting.

■ Backlit LCDs, the glowing kind. The backlighting lets you use your laptop on the red-eye when the cabin is too dark to see otherwise. However, backlighting isn't entirely good news. One negative is that with age, some backlit screens diminish in brightness. And backlit LCDs eat up more power than do those without this capability; batteries in a laptop with backlighting may last only half as long as they would in an equivalent laptop without backlighting. Some backlit machines allow you to turn off the light and save power by using the reflective capabilities of the screen. However, in a dim room, without backlighting, such screens are not as visible as those of nonbacklit LCDs under similar conditions. If you're planning to use your laptop for long periods outside—or if you're constantly in well-lit rooms and value battery life—you may be better off without the backlighting. On the other hand, if you're constantly writing in dim hotel rooms, then backlighting clearly is called for.

■ Color LCDs. One of the first color laptops, the ProSpeed CSX from NEC, appeared with a price tag almost two thousand dollars higher than a more powerful black-and-white model. Some shades on the screen were washed out, and streaking and shadowing appeared in some areas. Also, power requirements were hefty enough for the CSX to require AC current. But count on color technology becoming much more sophisticated and eventually appealing widely to sales reps and other potential users of graphics. In some areas, such as financial services, sales organizations may be willing to pay a premium for truly portable color.

■ Electroluminescent, or EL. Such screens typically give off an orange or yellowish glow and offer good resolution (as much as 640 by 480 for eight-by-five-inch displays, according to Dataquest). The glow comes from electrodes acting on a zinc- or manganese-style material inside two plates. One problem is high power consumption. ELs, at least as of early 1990, are for either AC machines or those with short battery lives. Within the next few years color EL screens may surface.

■ Gas plasma. Gas glows when electricity excites it; gas plasma screens work somewhat like neon lights. Just as neons do, they can burn out with heavy usage. Until recently gas plasma screens were known as power hogs, but Toshiba now offers a battery-operated laptop with a plasma display and a claimed running time of more than three hours. Some analysts think color gas plasma is on the way.

A Few Words about the Private Eye

If you don't want other people to sneak peeps at your laptop screen, you have two choices. You can buy:

1. A laptop with an LCD so bad that only you can see the secret report it's displaying. The snoopers won't be at the right viewing angle.

2. A machine permitting use of the Private Eye, which is a little to CRTs what Dick Tracy's watch was to radios.

The Private Eye attaches to your head like a sweatband and includes a small screen suspended near your eyes. It gives you the feel that you are two feet away from a 12-inch monitor. The image is 720 by 280 pixels.

This 1.2-by-1.3-by-3.2-inch gadget could be a natural to use with small notebook computers. Also, if you combine the Private Eye with voice recognition, you could even do work on your laptop while it's tucked away inside a closed briefcase with the lid shut. That's exactly what one laptop maker has envisioned. But enough dreaming. Can you get the Private Eye to work with your present laptop? Well, sort of.

I must say "sort of" because the Eye requires a special card even though it's CGA compatible. The gadget's developer, Reflection Technology (240 Bear Hill Road, Waltham, Massachusetts 02154, telephone

[617] 890-5905), is selling the IBM-compatible card and the Eye for $795. Check with Reflection to see if this "half-size" card can plug into your computer. Remember, many of the cheaper laptops either don't allow cards or require that they be of special design. But who knows? Maybe someone in the future will make the necessary cards for the Toshiba T1000 and some of the other economy machines that right now can't use the Private Eye. As for newer laptops, some of them may end up with special connectors for the Private Eye.

If You're Doing Presentation Graphics

The makers of laptops should thank Big Bird and the other denizens of Sesame Street: TV has whetted the appetite for flashy graphics in sales, financial services, and other fields. Even without a color laptop screen, you needn't confine yourself to black and white. See pages 115 through 122 to learn what color add-ons might work with today's affordable machines.

When you give a presentation, you may want to use both the laptop screen and an external monitor at the same time. That way, your tiny portable could rest on a table or even the lectern and you could look *toward* your fans. Does this capability matter? If so, ask about it before pulling out your credit card to buy your laptop.

RANDOM-ACCESS MEMORY ("I'M OK, YOU'RE 640K")

Robin Raskin, a friend of mine, is gathering anecdotes for a collection of bizarre computer stories.[11] I love her wonderfully descriptive title: "I'm OK, You're 640K." In the computer world, power users now consider 640K computers to be passé, and at times they can be snobbish about it, now that some personal computer memories reach 16 megabytes.

The 640K, of course, refers to the number of kilobytes in the random access memory, the temporary memory containing bytes from the programs and data that you've loaded. A RAM of 640K was once like the sound barrier in the days before Chuck Yeager's bright orange jet roared

---

[11] Please write Robin Raskin, Senior Editor, *PC Magazine*, 1 Park Avenue, New York, New York 10016.

past Mach 1. Under MS-DOS you just couldn't run software needing more than 640K of RAM.

But clever computer people figured a way around the limit. They gave us:

■ Expanded memory. This special memory works with conventional memory under 640K. Your computer grabs pieces of memory above 640K and switches them in and out of conventional memory. Programs using expanded memory run more slowly. But certain software can work with more information; for example a spreadsheet may include more cells. And some computers can use expanded memory for tasks such as disk-caching, a way to jack up the effective speed of a hard disk.

■ Extended memory. That's "normal" memory above one megabyte. Many spreadsheet programs such as the more powerful versions of Lotus 1-2-3 can use this space. OS/2 and UNIX, which do not recognize expanded memory, use extended memory. Extended memory is available only on computers with the 80286 processor, or more advanced chips.

In the eyes of computer designers and software developers, expanded and extended memories differ sharply. But most laptop buyers won't care as much. Disk-caching, for example, may take place inside either expanded or extended memory, and you may find that your pet programs can store data inside either. Besides, you can set up some machines to treat parts of memory as either expanded or extended.

Check out these matters, though, before you buy. If you think your programs will be memory-hungry, ask the software house to tell you whether expanded or extended memory would be better. Also find out how much memory to purchase. See if you can add the proper memory chips to your machine in case future versions of your favorite programs need more RAM.

Of course, you may get along just fine with 640K or less. Word processing, after all, is the number-one use for laptops, and it isn't as demanding as numbers crunching. Here's a quick idea of how much RAM you may need for common applications:

■ Very basic word processing with a VW-priced laptop and short files. A total RAM of 32K or even less could do the trick in non–MS-

DOS computers like my WP-2 laptop, which has the word processor in ROM. The WP-2 needs 10K for odds and ends. That leaves me with 22K, or the equivalent of maybe eleven double-spaced pages.

■ Some more-advanced word processing, as well as the less-powerful databases, and spreadsheets. You may get away with anything from 64K to 512K. A few word processing programs require as little as 40 or 50K, excluding whatever the operating system requires. With several hundred K of RAM, you can run standard programs, such as XyWrite and WordPerfect, although you won't enjoy all their features. For instance, you may not be able to call up an electronic spelling-checker while you're in the middle of a file. Databases and spreadsheets for RAMs of this size may not enjoy all of the power and flexibility that more memory will allow.

■ Normal versions of word processors, spreadsheets, databases, and other common programs. You'll want 640K of RAM. Fortunately, with a few big exceptions such as the Toshiba T1000—limited to 512K without added memory—640K is now a standard among the Chevrolet-priced laptops. By now the Toshiba itself may be priced in the Volkswagen category! Because 640K is still a standard, Lotus offers 1-2-3 Release 2.2 for machines incapable of running 1-2-3 Release 3 (requiring 1 megabyte of RAM under MS-DOS) or 1-2-3/G (typically needing 5 megs).

■ Demanding programs, such as 1-2-3/G, sophisticated desktop publishing software,[12] and the fancier Macintosh-like interfaces, where you "point" a mouse at symbols on the screen and rely less on typed commands. "I can remember when we thought that 64K was enough," says Jeff Knepper of Deloitte & Touche. "Now you look at 640K and think that's not nearly enough. The machines around here carry 4 megs or more. In our business, if you configure a machine at the low end, the day will come when someone will take a machine somewhere and try to do something and be stuck." Of course, his firm employs less-muscular laptops for tasks such as note taking. If, however, you're going to use OS/2 for *anything*, you'll probably want at least several megabytes.

[12]Desktop publishing is a step up from mere word processing. In desktop publishing you're producing newsletters, instruction manuals, and other documents with a personal computer and high-quality printer, such as a laser. Normally laptops aren't used, because of the limitations of their monitors. But over the next several years this may well change.

Price, of course, not just the programs you're running, should count when you're deciding how much RAM you need. RAM prices go up and down, but over the long run they're falling, and even now you may find that one megabyte of RAM is only fifty dollars more than 640K. So you might as well go for the meg. In the future you just may want a program that needs more than 640K.

Some manufacturers have come up with ingenious uses for RAM chips. Toshiba, for example, offers optional RAM for the T1000 so that, for example, you can load your software entirely into RAM, then use the T1000's single drive to store data. There are other tricks. Certain machines let you turn off your laptop, then resume work with your programs and data instantly ready to go. When you flip the switch, you may think you've powered down your laptop. But you haven't entirely. A small amount of juice continues to reach the memory chips.

MASS STORAGE, SUCH AS FLOPPIES OR HARD DRIVES

My first computer, a Kaypro II the size of a small suitcase, had two 5.25-inch floppy disks that could store just 200K apiece. I was all too aware of the limits of this 1983 technology. If chapters were very long, as mine tended to be in draft, I often had to divide them up.[13] How things have changed. Today just one 3.5-inch drive can stash away 720K—or almost as many words as are in this book.

Below is a review of floppy drives, hard disks, and some other storage technologies. I'll start with the basics for novices, then work up to a brief discussion of new trends in hard disks, CD-ROM, and other areas.

■ Floppy disks. Buy a one-floppy machine for simple tasks like word processing and communications (sending information from one computer to another). Very likely you already own a desktop. Single-floppy portables are also a possibility for budget-strapped students who insist on a laptop even though a desktop probably could mean a lot more computer for the money. If nothing else, single-floppy machines offer obvious advantages in weight and size.

But they come with problems. A 720K disk won't even store the current version of WordPerfect, at least not in full. Laptop manufacturers

[13] WordStar produced backup files—electronic carbon copies of my work—which helped fill up my floppies and lessened their effective capacity.

have tried to get around this problem. Some single-disk machines, such as the Toshiba T1000 and the Tandy 1100FD, come with the MS-DOS operating system already built into the computers. So DOS doesn't take up disk space. The Tandy machine, moreover, includes a simple word processor; hence, in a crunch you can devote the entire 720K of storage space to data.

Just the same, you shouldn't buy a single-floppy laptop as your only machine unless you know that your needs will be limited. Still insist on the single-floppy route? Then see if you can't end up with a 1.44K floppy, such as the one used on the Toshiba T1000SE. And be prepared to invest in extra memory into which you can load programs, then use the floppy to store data. Even a twin-floppy laptop may prove trying at times. That's why I've devoted so much of chapter 3 to the topic of special software suited to the limitations of the economy laptops.

Mercifully, by the time you're reading this, and maybe before, IBM may have introduced its 2.88-megabyte standard for floppies. Floppies exist in sizes of 20 megabytes or greater—enough to store ten thousand pages of double-spaced typing—but so far the monsters are too expensive.

Another problem with floppies is that they are more likely than hard disks to lose data. They're thin plastic disks. Yes, the 3.5-inch floppies are enclosed in cases, but they're still far more subject to wear than the hard disks are. Likewise, floppies don't run programs as fast. Software that takes ten seconds to load from a hard disk may take forty-five seconds to a minute from a floppy.

■ Hard disks. Typically they're aluminum platters coated with magnetic material and spinning at around 3,600 revolutions per minute. "Heads" read and write magnetic patterns on the material. Most of the platters come in diameters of 2.5 or 3.5 inches. The smaller disks are more rugged and lend themselves to notebook-size laptops; the larger ones can store data more economically and show up in the larger models.

Often hard disk manufacturers and computer makers express ruggedness in terms of Gs. Compaq says the hard disks in its new notebook-size computers can survive shock equal to four hundred times the force of gravity. It often uses disks from Conner Peripherals, currently the market leader in hard disks for laptops. A Conner rival, PrairieTek, a young company in Longmont, Colorado, claims to outdo the ruggedness of Conner products (I won't offer any definitive conclusions here). PrairieTek makes a 2.5-inch hard disk that is "ramp loaded." In other words, if the disk isn't in use, it lifts its heads off the sensitive magnetic material and moves them off to the side. So the heads don't slap against the platter as they would on some disks. Two companies, GriD and Agilis, plan to include PrairieTek drives in their laptops, and I wouldn't be surprised if Toshiba and others followed.

When PrairieTek torture-tested its ramp-loaded hard drive on a Toshiba laptop, the plastic case went before the drive did. Disk drives, moreover, should become even more rugged over the next few years. Phil Devin, a drive expert at Dataquest, even expects some hard drives to be tiny enough to be mounted on printed circuit boards like the usual chips. They'll be no larger than a small matchbox.

Yet another survivability issue is mean time between failure, or MTBF. Over the next five years the typical MTBF should reach two hundred thousand hours—for all practical purposes, the life of a computer. I won't mind. On one desktop computer alone, I went through *two* hard disks. The typical laptop now has a hard disk MTBF of twenty thousand to thirty thousand hours.

Oh, but what about the fun parts, storage capacity and speed? Today most hard disks on laptops can hold at least 20 megabytes—some ten thousand double-spaced typewritten pages. That's the standard for a 2.5-inch hard disk. An increasing number of 3.5-inch drives can hold 40 megabytes or more. The best is yet to come. "In 1992," Devin says, "I expect a 2.5-inch drive to offer 80 megabytes per platter" (a drive can have more than one platter). A 3.5-inch drive may hold 160 to 200 megabytes. By 1995, if Devin is right, you'll be able to drop by your friendly discount computer shop and leave with a notebook-size computer storing 100 megabytes and costing less than five hundred dollars. Access times[14] could be well under the twenty to forty milliseconds of today's hard drives for laptops. Faster access times will make the hard disk reply more snappily to commands such as CHKDSK (this "check disk" command will reveal how many bytes your drive is storing, so the head must first wander all over the disk).

You should also consider another kind of number: disk throughput. It means how quickly you can load a file into RAM. The first drives for the IBM PC had throughputs of 625K per second; the new disks for laptops have throughputs as fast as 2 megabytes per second. Despite

[14] Access speed is how quickly the head can find the proper location of the desired information on the disk.

these advances, however, the hard disk speeds of most laptops tend to lag somewhat behind those of desktops. The faster the disk, the more power it needs. So as a rule, if you want to stretch your battery life you might be better off buying a laptop with a slower disk.

By now some of the more advanced hard disks for laptops should require only two or three watts of power when they're reading or writing data and just a tenth of a watt when in standby. Except for backlit LCDs, hard disks are the biggest power sappers in the world of the laptop.

■ CD-ROM drives. They're the silver platters that can store whole encyclopedias of information; look for some laptops to start including them in the next year or so. The disadvantage of CD-ROM is that you can only read from it; you can't write new information on it. There is a technical problem with portables because of the power requirements of the lasers used. For more on CD-ROMs, see page 367.

■ Plug-in RAM cards (powered by batteries). At the moment these are not truly mass-storage devices, even though some portables, such as the Poqet, the NEC UltraLite, and the Atari Portfolio, use them to hold data. Just a megabyte of RAM for the UltraLite can cost you hundreds of dollars. Compare that with the $2, 1.44-megabyte disk I buy through the mail. The RAM cards are rugged, but if you forget about them long enough and they lose their power, you may find that they've dumped your data.

■ Flash memory, another kind of storage for data. This technology, found in the Psion computers, is functionally like regular RAM except that the information remains even after the power is switched off.

Flash memory has its roots in EPROM technology (EPROM means erasable programmable read-only memory). The contents of traditional EPROMS can't be altered on the fly. Why, the "ROM" in "EPROM" means exactly that—"read-only memory." You can't write a spreadsheet or word processing file to a ROM. But flash memory is more accommodating. Electrons can do the work, make the changes that once required ultraviolet light. It's truly A Revolutionary Technology. Intel is betting heavily on it, even if the economics aren't the best right now.

A Psion card with 512K of flash memory as of this writing was to sell for $399.00. That's more than 80 cents per K. At that price, one megabyte of such storage would cost $800; two megabytes, $1,600. But—and this is a big but—Psion and Intel expect prices to slide down steadily. Sooner or later you might even be able to buy generic memory cards, just as you can purchase no-name floppy disks. The first Psion cards don't meet any industry standards. The Poqet cards will. If Intel has its druthers, electrical and physical standards will prevail for flash memory just as they do now for floppies. And that could help lower prices drastically.

If prices do plunge, then flash memory may supplant floppies and hard drives as a means of mass storage in many machines. So what's the trade-off? Speed. For the moment, flash memory can write no faster than floppy disks. Hard-disk addicts will notice the difference. But that could change as the technology improves. Besides, most of the time you'll be reading files from flash memory rather than writing to them. And flash memory can read at an adequate 128K per second. What's more, the power consumption of flash memory is negligible compared to hard disks or floppy drives. Remember, the drives are the biggest power hogs in a laptop computer.

Think about a statement that Tony Revis, president of Psion, Inc., made to me. He said his company would offer 2-megabyte cards with flash memory, and that the tiny Psion IBM compatible could store four cards in its slots. Meaning? Eight megs of memory and no hard drive to break down! Let's just hope that Silicon Valley can slash the cost of flash memory technology.

A few other questions persist. If flash memories are so great, why is Psion giving buyers a choice between them and RAM cards? Well, it's because RAM cards both read and write at blinding speeds. Then again, they have those pesky batteries inside them. If you remove a RAM from a Psion slot, it will die after several months unless you replace the little battery inside the card. And who will *always* remember?

I also asked Psion about risks to flash memory, such as static electricity. The word is, don't worry. For good measure, the Psion people told me you could dunk one of their computers underwater, let it dry, and put it to work again without losing a byte. Let me bail out the lawyer for St. Martin's Press: I hereby urge curious readers not to give their own Psions a bath.

Psion appears to be onto a very good thing. Compaq, GRiD, and Apple are considering flash memories.

■ Bubble memories. The per-megabyte cost of these solid-state devices is too high for most uses; you rarely encounter bubble memories in laptops for office use. They are, however, a possibility for field, outdoor, and industrial purposes because of their ruggedness.

■ Tape drives. You normally don't find tape drives in laptops, but they can be useful for backing up the contents of a portable's hard disk. Tape is cheap for storing data. The drives work like a normal tape recorder, writing and reading the magnetic patterns on the tape. Costs can run from $300 to $700 for an external tape drive with a 40-megabyte capacity, around the same as a hard drive. A tape cartridge for 40 megabytes costs just $20 or $25. The downside is that tape drives take forever to store data; you may want a drive to do the backups after hours or while you're at lunch. If your disk is big enough, you could have a perfect excuse for a long lunch.

■ Bernoulli boxes, another backup device used outside a laptop. In a Bernoulli, a floppy disk spins at high speeds with a small cushion of air separating it from the head that reads and writes data. A Bernoulli disk is more reliable than the usual floppy. It comes in a removable cartridge. The disadvantage of this technology is the expense—several times the costs of an equivalent tape drive. On the other hand, a Bernoulli box is many times faster. The technology, incidentally, comes from a company named Iomega, which named the boxes after Daniel Bernoulli, a Swiss scientist whose theories led to this invention.

Alas, in trying to squeeze programs and information into your laptop, you may come up against a Silicon Valley corollary to Parkinson's Law, the observation that work expands to fit the time available. The valley's corollary: the roomier the hard disks get, the less interested the software companies in producing tightly written programs. You cannot run OS/2, IBM's new operating system, on a typical floppy disk machine (let me allow for a few exceptions, such as the freakishly large floppies that the R&D geniuses keep messing around with).

Sophisticated spreadsheets and ancillary programs may sprawl over 5 or 10 megabytes, perhaps more, and of course, mammoth files can emerge even from the simpler databases. I pity accountants and business-people with large spreadsheets and databases that they want to squeeze into their laptops. Such people just can't think of laptops as full-powered substitutes for desktops—unless they're willing to pay dearly for the extra mass-storage space and other goodies. So instead they should try to find compact programs for their portable computing. This advice applies to writers, too. Normally writers shouldn't buy disk-hogging software just so they'll have a pretty, Macintosh-like interface on their IBM-style machines.

BATTERIES

Batteries are a subject that makes me grouchy.[15] Their run times—how long they'll last between charges—are disgraceful in many ways. One of the most notorious offenders is the Toshiba T1000SE, an otherwise wonderful laptop that runs only two hours before you must recharge. And this is just a single-floppy machine, mind you, not a model with a hard disk that eagerly sucks up every stray electron.

I'm also irked that many laptops have batteries you cannot change. So you don't have the privilege of bringing along spares when, say, you're doing fieldwork in the middle of Death Valley, miles from the nearest outlet.

Ideally the computer industry will wake up. At a major laptop company, for instance, when I posed the question of longer battery life, an employee there said in effect, "Does anyone care? Do people really want to pay for a battery that runs twenty hours?" I couldn't believe my ears. If you're using a laptop as a quasi-desktop, then battery life doesn't much matter. But think of the millions of customers and potential customers who would be thrilled to have batteries last longer than a flight from Milwaukee to Baltimore.

How about the consultant cranking out spreadsheets on deadline? Or the journalist whose competitive standing is partly a function of how much copy he can crank out on the campaign bus, away from power outlets? Or the archaeologist in the field? True, the Apple Macintosh already can last well over eight hours—twelve hours, in fact, according to a friend of mine who tested it—but there are trade-offs, such as weight.

Poqet has been pushing power management to the curent limits. But like the Macintosh portable, the first Poqet computer lacks a backlit screen. Eventually the need for power-performance trade-offs could diminish. But tell me this: have *you* seen any laptop lately with a 30-megahertz processor, a color screen, and one hundred hours between battery charges? Battery limits are a major reason why laptops as a group may never be quite the equal of desktops of the same vintage. Oh, yes, we do have powerful, AC-operated portables, such as the heftier Toshibas, but they're in a different league from the typical laptop designed to work off batteries.

---

[15]See pages 151–153 of my Murphy's Law chapter for a discussion of the kind of rechargeable batteries now complicating life for users.

Although I'm grouchy about batteries at the moment, I should be much happier in the near future. One of several promising solutions might lie in nickel-hydride cells. Already a small Michigan firm, Ovonic, makes long-lived C cells that knowledgeable users can install in the Toshiba T1000, and the firm's AA versions should be on the market now. (See page 152 for more about replacements.) But skeptics abound.

"A lot of companies are talking about nickel hydride," says Bill Lempesis, a laptop specialist at Dataquest, which has major computer companies among its clients. "It's sort of like new versions of software. People will believe it when they see it."

William E. Orabone, Ovonic's manager of technical marketing, claims that the problem isn't technical, it's commercial. Battery plants are costly, and Orabone says just half a dozen companies are equipped to make the rechargeable cells that Ovonic lacks the capital to produce in large numbers. Nickel-cadmium is the prevalent technology. "If you're a ni-cad manufacturer and your business is growing 25 to 30 percent a year," Orabone says, "do you really want to retool immediately?" I won't take sides here. At least one large Japanese company, Matsushita Battery Industrial Company, has announced plans to make nickel-hydride batteries, and it predicts that prices will be about the same as for ni-cads.

A second solution could come from Dreisbach ElectroMotive Incorporated (DEMI), which has been perfecting "Aerobic Power."[16] Why *Aerobic*? Because these batteries need to "breathe" air when they're working. They even have air doors. Yes, doors. The laptop must shut these doors—perhaps through electrical or mechanical links to the on-off switch—when the batteries aren't running. So production models of existing portables can't go Aerobic, at least not without tinkering.

Just the same, DEMI has won attention from laptop makers. At the November 1989 COMDEX, Toshiba and DEMI quietly showed off their Aerobic batteries to corporate buyers. NEC also is investigating this technology.

As with Ovonic batteries, the rewards of new technology could be impressive. DEMI literature says that when used experimentally on a Toshiba 1600 hard disk laptop, Aerobic Power offered a run time of

---

[16]DEMI's address is 212 Anacapa Street, Santa Barbara, California 93101, (805) 965-0829.

six to eight hours. That's maybe twice the normal time. Given enough of a charge, the batteries could even last twelve or fourteen hours. Total battery life—as distinguished from run time—could be 150 to 200 hours; it isn't as long as the life of nickel-cadmium, but Aerobic batteries may soon sell for a fraction of the costs of ni-cads, making the newer technology a better deal for laptop owners.

A third solution might be lithium batteries, which, in fact, the NEC UltraLite laptop has already used. Boosters of lithium cells say their batteries in an AA size can offer 1.44 watt hours per charge compared to .84 for a ni-cad of the same size and 1.2 for nickel-hydride technology. Like all other battery figures, these are subject to interpretation. At Ovonic, for example, Orabone says his company's AA cells offer just as many watt hours as the lithium batteries do. Still, lithium batteries are prized for their light weight and may hold great promise. But there's a big if: the safety question. In Japan, a cellular radio with a lithium battery caught fire, forcing a massive recall of batteries from NEC's supplier, Moli Energy, then headquartered in Vancouver, British Columbia. Moli folded. But new backers revived the company under the name Moli Energy (1990), Ltd.

Klaus Brand, Moli's vice-president for research and development, says the radio fire was caused by a correctable manufacturing defect.[17] None other than Matsushita, the very same company flirting with nickel-hydride technology, is said to be ramping up for mass production of lithium cells. So clearly, lithium seems far from dead.

A fourth solution could be a refinement of lead acid batteries, which the Macintosh and some other laptops use, and which I discuss in chapter 5. I wouldn't bet heavily on lead acid, however. Too many problems exist with bulk and weight. It's hard to make a good lead acid battery for a slim laptop, a big negative when notebook computers are among the fastest-growing categories within the laptop world. So expect one of the other three technologies to fare better in the battery wars.

But what to do *right now* if you must do fieldwork in the middle of Death Valley? Two possibilities are:

1. A device that lets you run your laptop off your automobile battery. If you're using a battery-powered laptop, then you might need a gadget

---

[17]The address of Moli Energy (1990) is 20000 Stewart Crescent, Maple Ridge, British Columbia. The telephone number is (604) 465-7911.

to regulate precisely the electricity from automobile, boat, or whatever. Check with your manufacturer. If your laptop is AC-only, there's still hope. Computer Products Plus (16321 Gothard Street, Huntington Beach, California 92647, 800-274-4277) sells a DC-to-AC adapter for autos and boats. It even works with machines as powerful as the Toshiba T3100. The big question is whether the auto or boat battery can bear the added load.

2. An oft-overlooked solution—one especially apropos for Death Valley: solar power. For $130 you can buy a one-pound, twelve-by-twenty-five-inch, six-watt panel from a dealer or a distributor like Solar Electric Engineering, 175 Cascade Court, Rohnert Park, California, (707) 586-1987 (inquiries), or 800-832-1986 (orders). Solar says the panel typically can power a small floppy drive laptop (for instance, the Toshiba T1000) for six to eight hours a day if you go easy on printing. Other computers may require a larger model of panel which, however, at $199 is hardly a budget-buster. It's one-by-four feet, weighs five pounds, and is rated at twenty watts. Solar tries to work closely with Toshiba and is eager to cooperate with other laptop makers. Presumably some other people offering solar cells are ready to do the same.

PRINTERS

Portable printers can be a must for writers who want to work off their notes without having to split their screens between the research material and their electronic manuscripts. My friend Barbara Newman, a TV producer, discovered the hard way that she needed a printer. She carried a laptop to Europe, but not a printer, so she suffered many hours of rewriting her book on her return to the States, because she couldn't make sense of the manuscript without being able to flip through the pages.

Printers in the field can be even more useful for sales reps. On the spot a rep can print out a contract for his or her customer; then, back at the hotel, the rep can dash off a thank-you note—perhaps summoning a canned letter, which will appear customized even though the rep just filled in a few blanks.

If you have sympathetic clients with compatible printers or your branch offices are well equipped and obliging, then you might get by without a printer. Even then, however, you may still want to go ahead with the purchase. Why depend on favors from others? Get that printer if you need it and your or your company's budget allows it.

The next question is whether the printer should be a "portable printer" or a regular one. I'd go for the portable if the laptop is to be moved around more than once a week or so. If you do need superb print quality, travel by car, and can easily lug equipment around, then you might investigate one of the DeskJet printers from Hewlett-Packard, a leader in inkjet technology. They're quite unwieldy to carry, but quiet, and the print is laserlike.

But what if you want a true portable printer? Consider:

■ The basic technology. The main choices today are inkjet, dot matrix, and thermal transfer. In inkjet printers, little nozzles spray out dots that form characters on the paper. Traditional dot matrixes use little hammers to create the dots. Thermal transfer uses heat to transfer the ink from the ribbon to the paper.

■ How much noise the printer makes—an important consideration when you're printing in a client's office. Inkjets are quieter by far. Quite understandably, Kodak ballyhoos its Diconix series of printers by showing them in advertisements next to a sleeping cat.

■ How fast the printer goes in the draft mode. The Diconix is rated at some 180 characters per second, not bad for a printer that sells for as little as $300 through the mail. Be warned that printer ratings often are no less optimistic than some of the mileage ratings we've seen for automobiles. The ratings often reflect extra-favorable conditions—described with euphemisms such as "burst speed."

■ The quality mode. The Diconix, alas, can do less than thirty characters per second in this mode. Some dot matrixes can go faster than inkjets. In the case of either technology, print quality is in the eye of the beholder; the output still is dotty enough to be distracting.

■ How many characters or pages the ink cartridges or ribbons can print, how much each costs, and how widely available they are.

■ How rugged the printer is. As with laptops in general, ruggedness is important if a unit won't be assigned to just one user.

■ How reliable. Manufacturers can provide statistics, but that's no substitute for trying to talk to some actual users, even if the printer has been on the market just a short time.

■ Whether the printer uses the parallel port of your computer. The term *port* means a plug or socket into which wires go from a modem, printer, or other accessory. It also includes the related circuitry. *Parallel* refers not to the position of the port, but rather to how the bits flow back and forth—in parallel streams of 8 bits rather than just 1 bit at a time. Another term for a parallel port is *Centronics port*, named after a printer manufacturer whose products worked with a parallel port.

The parallel port is generally the best port for a printer. The typical laptop has only one *serial port* (the kind where, yes, the bits flow 1 bit at a time). And you might want to save the serial port for your modem or another gadget. An external modem—one outside the laptop rather than inside on a card or chip—most often uses the serial port.

By the way, in the computer world, the jargon for a serial port is *RS-232 port*. To be more precise, the term is *RS-232C port*. The letters *RS* mean "Recommended Standard" of the Electronic Industries Association. The numerals *232C* identify the current versions of the standard.

TWO ALTERNATIVES TO LAPTOPS: PORTABLE WORD PROCESSORS AND ORGANIZERS

In those prehistoric times before the dawn of personal computers, two machines were the rage in American offices: word processors and electronic calculators. They survive even today, and now there are some new twists:

■ "Personal" word processors: machines sold with a screen, a keyboard, and a printer, usually of letter quality. Most personal word processors are the size of luggable computers. Others are laptops. All are smaller than the old Wang-size behemoths. Boosters of personal word processors say they're simpler to use than the normal PC. True, a tricycle is easier to master than a racing bicycle or a Harley; still, how many of us can get by with commuting on a tricycle?

■ Organizers, most notably the Sharp Wizard, Casio B.O.S.S., and Psion Organiser, which are about the size of calculators but offer many capabilities besides mathematical ones. *Organizer*, in fact, normally refers to features such as electronic address books, phone directories, and calendars.

In the sense of having a central processing unit (CPU) and related trimmings, both personal word processors and organizers are indeed computers. They're just specialized—designed for specific tasks—although in some cases you can plug in cards to expand their capabilities.

For most readers of this book these quasi-computers won't work out as "only" machines—at least not now. But perhaps they can augment laptops and desktops. Anyway, differences are getting fuzzy between product categories. I own a Tandy WP-2 "portable word processor," yet think of it as a grown-up computer and have mentioned it with the bigger, more powerful machines earlier in this chapter. The WP-2 has a full-size keyboard, for example, and includes communications software and other features of interest to PC users. It lacks a printer. But it can easily send files via an RS-232–style cable to my AT clone. So in my mind, logically or not, the WP-2 is a true laptop *computer*.

Likewise, the blurriest of divisions exists between computers and organizers. Some students of the organizer market would toss the tiny Atari Portfolio into this category even though it can run some MS-DOS programs.

Quite understandably, then, Peter O'Connor, the owner of Laptop Expositions, called his trade show "LAP&PALMTOP '90."[18] O'Connor says many of the objections first raised against laptops—such as the skepticism that something so small could be so powerful—also are being used against organizers. Organizers, of course, have a ways to go; their keyboards are tiny and memories are still minuscule by the usual standards for personal computers. Still, under the laws of electronic evolution, the small-fry inherit the earth. Even now, for specialized functions, such as calculation of interest on loans, organizers could be a viable alternative.

Personal Word Processors

For fifteen years Mary R. Patton, a forty-nine-year-old editor, has lived in the same apartment. She still has a rotary phone. Patton is an intelligent, articulate woman, but at the time we talked, she had yet to master

---

[18]O'Connor holds his shows in the spring and/or the fall. His address is: Laptop Expositions, 104 East Fortieth Street, Suite 808, New York, New York 10016, (212) 682-7968.

the complexities of MS-DOS. Many would say she's the perfect candidate for a word processor. After all, most are simpler to run than a computer.

In the long run, however, the future of personal word processors is just as bleak as the prospects for the old Wangs and CPTs, a dying breed.

TIPS ON USING EXPANSION CARDS WITH YOUR LAPTOP

Expansion cards are printer circuit boards that add new capabilities to your computer—for instance, modem boards to let your laptop talk to other machines over the telephone.

Most IBM-style laptops can physically accommodate only the plug-in cards built for them. They can't use standard cards designed, say, for XT- or AT-class desktops. Sometimes, though, you can get around this limitation—by way of gadgets like the Won Under.

The Won Under (Or Similar Attachments)

Contrary to rumor, the Won Under isn't the name of a Chinese or Australian restaurant. It's a device that attaches to the bottom of a laptop and provides a slot into which you can plug cards, such as:

■ A modem card. You may want one that transmits information faster than the add-on modems designed especially for your computer. In this case, as in others, consider how much the extra circuitry will shorten battery life. Also, consider whether the card is XT-size or AT-size. A product designed for an AT-class computer may not work with your card adapter.

■ A fax card, which lets your computer send and receive faxes.

■ A video card, otherwise known as a graphics card. Check with the Won Under people and your laptop manufacturer. You may find, for instance, that a computer with a built-in EGA adapter won't accept a VGA card. On the other hand, according to the Won Under people, there may be a way to tweak your laptop to eliminate conflicts between the built-in adapter and the external card.

■ Hard disk cards, the jargon for plug-in printed circuit boards with hard disks mounted right on them. I won't mention these as the most likely option. That's because of (1) the size of such cards and (2) their effect on battery life, and (3) the possible risk of damaging your laptop's power supply.

■ A MIDI interface. A what? *MIDI* means "musical instrument digital interface." The Won Under people know of at least one musician who flies between coasts and stores his music inside his portable's hard disk. Via the MIDI interface he can hook up the laptop to the synthesizer that generates the music.

For more information on the Won Under, contact Connect Computer, 9855 West Seventy-eighth Street, Eden Prairie, Minnesota 55344, (612) 944-0181.

Please note that Won Unders are not available for all laptops. Check with the Won Under people.

By the way, the Won Under people pass on a shopping tip that reflects their selfish interests but is valid just the same. When you buy a laptop, see how many third-party products work with it. Toshiba in particular has been nurturing toward makers and sellers of third-party products to increase the usefulness of laptops.

Expansion Boxes (Also Known as Expansion Chassis)

Connect Computer sells an AC-powered expansion box into which you slide five full-size cards. Some laptop makers may sell their own boxes.

Docking Stations

Docking stations plug directly into the laptop. They fit alongside the machine. Or the laptop might go atop the station.

*   *   *

All of the above gadgets hook into a laptop's bus—the network through which bits flow between the CPU and other devices, such as the keyboard and the optional plug-in cards. You might, in fact, hear an expansion box called an "expansion bus."

Like the full-size models, the new personal word processors are nothing more than computers with limited capabilities—the electronic equivalents of overbred dogs. Consider Smith-Corona's PWP 7000LT, a laptop-size machine. However sleek the 7000LT may look in ads, its 3.5-inch disks cost $3.50 each and can store only 100K—a mere fifty or sixty double-spaced pages. That's less than one-seventh the capacity of the 720K disks now standard in the laptop world. The printer crawls along at just fifteen characters per second. Furthermore, although the 7000LT offers an optimal spreadsheet program, it lacks the full versatility of a personal computer. Even at $899 list price, the PWP 7000LT isn't the best of buys, given its limited powers.

By now Smith-Corona may be offering an improved replacement for the 7000LT, but the problem will remain the same—pygmy-size power compared to the usual personal computers. An acquaintance of mine, a former ambassador now doing consulting, gave up in disgust on another make of word processor. With long reports to grind out, he bought a Zenith laptop.

As an associate editor–analyst with Datapro's Office Products Evaluation Service,[19] Patton would understand why the man went the laptop route. "If you limit yourself to small typewriters or small personal word processors," she says, "you'll be doing small jobs for small money." She sees the personal word processor as a machine mainly for high school students and others with less-sophisticated needs—or for people who are jittery around computers.

You may not fall into those categories, but a few friends of yours may. If they insist on a personal word processor and really need a lot of hand-holding, they might consider buying from an office equipment dealer rather than a discount chain. They should look for many of the same features that you would want in a laptop, especially a good screen and keyboard. Software should include at least basics like the ability to move and delete blocks of text. Advise your friends, also, to compare spell checkers, thesauruses, and punctuation checkers. The 7000LT, for example, can tell you how many times you've used a certain phrase. "That," says Patton, "is why these things are good for the student market."

[19]Datapro Research, a McGraw-Hill company, is at 600 Delran Parkway, Delran, New Jersey 08075, 800-328-2776. Many public libraries carry Datapro publications rating electronic products. The address of Marketing Research Consultants is 124 Hebron Avenue, P.O. Box 776, Glastonbury, Connecticut 06033, (203) 633-7988.

Ideally, however, students won't have to do any fancy footnoting. Patton couldn't recall any personal word processor with automatic footnoting—a must, I think, for students writing longer papers.

With more and more schools teaching computers, the student market for personal word processors should wane in time. Even now (in my opinion, not necessarily Patton's) a used IBM-style machine would be a better gift for a sixth-grader.

In any event, don't expect the personal word processor in its present form to make sense to many people in future years. Smith-Corona, Brother, and the other manufacturers understand. Frank Cannata, president of Marketing Research Consultants in Connecticut,[20] says that floppy disks eventually should catch up with the 720K and 1.44-meg standards of today's laptops and share the same formats. Also, presumably, personal word processors will run MS-DOS programs sooner or later. Why, the manufacturers then might even start calling them "computers."

Organizers

Long ago, calculators weighed fifty pounds and cost thousands. Something happened. Size dwindled. Powers increased. Calculators, in fact, fueled the development of the miracle chips that made the first personal computers possible. Today *Time* and *Newsweek* give away tiny calculators during subscription campaigns. Very likely that is the future of organizers—the hand-held gadgets that can store names, addresses, and phone numbers and much, much more.

Organizers, by the way, have other ancestors, too. For years companies have been buying tiny computers for extremely specialized purposes, such as calculating interest rates or insurance premiums. But today's organizers are infinitely more flexible than the calculators and hand-held computers of yore.

They don't just include the usual built-in address books, telephone directories, and calendars. Take the Sharp Wizard series. For $329 list—the price may be lower by the time you're reading this book—you can buy a model with 64K internal memory. The model OZ-7200 stores up to 1,540 names, addresses, and phone and fax numbers. But

[20]The telephone number of Marketing Research Consultants is (203) 633-7988 or (203) 659-1165.

that's just the beginning. This Wizard also lets you expand the memory or plug in a variety of cards for special purposes, including:

■ A card for BASIC programming, algebraic, power, root, exponential, logarithmic, and trigonometric calculations, math conversions, and correlation and regression analysis.

■ A spreadsheet compatible with Lotus 1-2-3, permitting storage of as many as 999 rows and 26 columns.

■ An electronic money planner for calculating loans and savings, translating annual rates into effective annual interest rates, and investment analysis. For personal equations, 8K of memory is available.

■ A city guide with hundreds of phone numbers for hotels, restaurants, stores, and other businesses in cities across North America.

■ A time-expense manager for such purposes as "do lists" and the recording of expenses.

■ A thesaurus and dictionary. The thesaurus contains forty-five thousand entry words, their meanings, and more than half a million synonyms. The card also can correct the spelling of more than eighty-seven thousand words.

■ A translator containing the most common phrases and words in English, French, Spanish, German, Italian, Chinese, and Japanese. The translator includes thirteen categories, ranging from "at airport/on plane" to "doctor and emergency."

The cards, typically listing for around $100 or $120, are among the big strengths of the Wizard series. In its earlier models the keyboard was the downside. It was alphabetical rather than designed in the QWERTY configuration that touch typists favor. Reacting to criticism, Sharp brought out some QWERTY Wizards.

A model from another manufacturer, the $260 B.O.S.S. ("Business Organizer Scheduling System") SF-8000 from Casio, debuted with a "tactile" keyboard whose feel was more typewriterlike. The screen was better, too—six lines by 32 characters, compared to the Wizard's eight-line-by-sixteen-character screen. Unlike the Wizard OZ-7200, the SF 8000 doesn't accept plug-in cards. But you may decide that the SF-8000 (or succeeding models) will suffice anyway. By choosing one of seven yellow buttons, you can call up phone numbers, "business cards," the equivalent of a memo pad, a scheduler, a calendar, "home time," or "world time." Plus you can enjoy the usual calculator functions. Internal memory is 64K.

Despite the Casio's keyboard, some people feel that the best bet for word processing could be the $279 Laser Computer pc3. As with the WP-2, this product straddles two categories: laptops and organizers. The pc3 includes the usual calculator, telephone directory, alarm clock, and so forth. But it's laptop-size. At 10-by-7.6-by-1.3-inches, the 30-ounce pc3 dwarfs the Wizard OZ-7200 (6.4-by-3.7-by-0.8 inches, 8.6 ounces), the Casio SF-8000 (6.4-by-3.2-by-0.9 inches, 10.6 ounces), and the Psion Organiser II LZ (6-by-3.8-by-1.2 inches, 9 ounces). It would put a noticeable sag in your trench coat pocket, assuming it could fit there in the first place.

As a reward, however, you get a full-size keyboard whose layout in many ways is like a PC's. With 32K of usable memory, you can squeeze in perhaps nine pages of single-spaced text. Notice the word *single*. Double spacing would waste half the screen, a mere two lines deep. And each line is just twenty characters wide. As a word processor, then, the pc3 is a best bet only if judged by the standards of organizers rather than laptops. It's not the machine on which to write a sequel to *Moby Dick*.

The Psion Organiser II LZ has a reputation for being harder to use than some rivals; on the other hand, hackers will appreciate its programming language, known as OPL. Large companies or consultants might tweak the Psion for special applications. Among its features are a diary, a calculator, a memo pad, and a calendar. The memory is 32K, though I suspect that a successor with a larger capacity will be in the stores in due time.

Into the Psion you can plug "Datapaks" for language translation, word processing, and finance, among other applications. Accessories range from a printer to a bar code reader and even a modem. You can also hook the Organiser into a personal computer to swap data. (That's true of most organizers.)

Ideally, of course, organizers soon will be able to not just communicate with PCs but come closer to them in power. It could happen. Perhaps in the next decade or two Wizard-class machines will be able to recognize voices—mitigating the frustrations arising from the Lilliputian-size keyboards. And voice synthesis could reduce the frustrations arising from organizers' tiny LCD screens.

Breakthroughs may also occur in the screen departments, though. Consider the gadget mentioned on page 45; the Private Eye, the LCD screen that you wear like eyeglasses. The price may drop to $100 or less. And when it does, organizers can sport 25 line, 80 character screens.

Who knows, maybe there will even be folding keyboards to make the organizers easier to carry without being such a burden to type on. That's one marketer's prediction. Combine such wrinkles with voice recognition, voice synthesis, more memory, and faster, more powerful chips, and it's clear that organizers someday could comfortably run the same MS-DOS and OS/2 programs that are now limited to desktops and laptops. (See page 333 for predictions further into the future.)

I return you now to the world of laptops—genuine, grown-up laptops—circa 1990. It's clear: nirvana is still far away. Unless you pay a steep price, portability can mean trade-offs in memory capacity, screen quality, sometimes keyboard quality, even print quality. Just the same, there is much that you can do to compensate, through selection of good software, discussed ahead.

Chapter 3

SOFTWARE TO GO

- Ideal software for laptops. Page 70.
- Interesting software for the road—of appeal to many professions. Page 73.

Laptop makers often brag that their machines are powerful desktops with handles; in many cases, no pun intended, that's true. But scads of the more affordable laptops are weaklings, the computer versions of the scrawny kid into whose eyes the muscular bully kicked sand on the beach.[1]

Take desktop technology and go back a few years or more and you have an idea of where the economy laptops stand. One of the more popular models, deservedly, has been the pokey Toshiba T1000. With its 4.77-megahertz clock speed, 512K of factory-supplied RAM, and single floppy drive, it may as well be a museum exhibit from the mid-1980s. Most of the newer laptops are far fleeter than old PCs in processing information. Their screens, however, aren't as viewable as the monitors of those bulky antiques. Besides, many laptops cannot do justice to software that requires frequent taps on oddball keys such as Home and End; you wonder how many laptop designers have ever beheld a touch typist at work.

Clearly, then, users of those somewhat-hobbled computers can benefit from special software. Exactly which programs can help?

---

[1] Thanks to Ken Skier for the beach metaphor.

And what about software for common users of laptops, such as sales reps, accountants, and writers? In this chapter I'll discuss:

■ The traits of ideal software for small, inexpensive laptops. The words *ideal* and *small*, and maybe *inexpensive*, too, are important. Mainstream software may justify the complications of using it on a cheapie laptop, even if the program isn't ideal. Moreover, some software for small laptops with limited disk space may waste the power of larger portables.

■ Interesting software for the road—of appeal to many professions. I won't just discuss cursor control programs and other software of special interest to owners of the smaller or more affordable machines. I'll also introduce you to the Double Disk program. This marvel greatly increases the amount of space for programs and data on a hard disk. Owners of the more powerful computers can save hundreds of dollars that might otherwise go toward upgrading their hard disks or buying auxiliary disk drives or tape backups. You'll also learn about Translate, which turns English into Spanish.

IDEAL LAPTOP SOFTWARE

Ken Skier of SkiSoft Publishing is one of the best-known writers of laptop software. Headquartered in Lexington, Massachusetts, his company markets the No-Squint cursor program, which thousands of laptop owners have bought to remedy a design flaw of their machines. Alas, the laptop companies were maniacally intent on making shrunken IBM PCs. So they imitated one of the worst features of the PC, the thin, swiftly blinking line that served as a cursor. They did this as if oblivious to the differences between the ubiquitous LCDs and the cathode ray tubes that the conventional PC monitors used. A square or rectangle would have been far more noticeable than that little line.

The cursor, of course, is just part of the problem on laptops. The LCDs of the more affordable laptops don't display *anything* as sharply as the usual CRT—hence the possible need for a second program that Skier wrote for laptop owners, Eye Relief. This word processor can adjust the size of characters and the spacing between lines.

Ahead are Skier's rules for ideal laptop software. Again, keep in mind that trade-offs may be necessary; if your laptop is powerful enough, for instance, you may not care so much whether software gobbles up RAM and disk space. Now, the rules:

1. The software should run on almost any laptop PC you can pick up. "That's quite a demanding requirement because you can buy a laptop with one drive, no hard disk, a speed of 4.77 megahertz, and only 512K of RAM," Skier says. "We haven't seen this class of machine on a desktop for at least five years. But this is exactly the type of machine that's continuing to emerge as lightweight, notebook, and pocket computers. The most exciting portable computers today are very small, very light, and very underpowered." Ideally your software will run well on those machines.

2. The program will stretch battery life. Even a floppy disk adds considerably to battery strain because of the need to power a motor. So a program can prolong battery life by reducing the number of times you need to use your disk. Ideally the program will require disk access only when you're loading the program in the first place or want to save data.

3. The software maker should realize that laptops don't have full keyboards. "All the keyboard makers will claim that their keyboard emulates an 84- or 101-key keyboard," Skier says. On many laptops, however, you must hit an FN key—a special kind of function key, not to be confused with F1 through F10—if you want to use Home or End or PgUp or PgDn. What's more, rather than offering a separate numeric pad, laptop makers often embed it in the regular keyboard, and you need to press the FN key to use the pad.

"Some software products require you to hit the missing keys a lot," Skier says. For instance, some outline programs make use of the gray + key on the numeric pad on IBM-style desktops. And WordPerfect —at least the regular desktop version—relies heavily on the Home key. On the other hand, with Skier's word processor Eye Relief, you can press F5 instead of the Home key, F6 instead of the End key, F7 instead of PgUp, and F8 instead of PgDn.

4. Good laptop software doesn't require the use of a mouse—obviously impractical if you're far from flat, desklike surfaces. In Apple's overpriced portable version of the Mac, the company built a trackball, a mouse substitute, into its keyboard. Few of the truly affordable laptops boast trackballs.

5. The software shouldn't include color combination that will display

poorly on a monochrome LCD screen. "Often," Skier says, "a program will use screen colors that are absolutely unreadable on an LCD display. If you can't change the colors that such a program uses, then you can't run that program on your laptop. That's bad design." To give one example, a spreadsheet might hold out real possibilities on color machines and laptops with EGA and VGA. But it might not look so good on laptops with the older CGA display—it could depend too much on color.

6. Ideally the software will let you change the sizes of letters and the spaces between lines. For centuries typographers have noticed that wider spacing will contribute to readability—a point that virtually all other programmers seem to have missed. Of course, future laptops will boast sharper screens. Just the same, I suspect that many laptop displays will always be less readable than those on the larger computers, simply because the little portables' screens must be smaller. Yes, I know. Maybe some technological breakthrough will throw me a curve ball, or we'll all be viewing text through special eyeglasses that we wear while computing, but I wouldn't count on it to happen in a big way *soon*.

7. The software also will provide a font in a variety of sizes, each designed for maximum readability on a laptop. For the moment you'll just have to satisfy yourself with Eye Relief if you value that trait above all in a word processor for laptops.

The above rules come from Skier, not me, but I do agree with them, even if he modestly demoted the screen-related features to the end of the list. I would add, however, two more rules for ideal software for laptops:

8. Laptop software should be able to read and write to a variety of formats for word processors and other programs, not just to ASCII. (I'll explain ASCII further on page 166.) It's somewhat of an Esperanto for microcomputer software, allowing different programs in some cases to swap information. Unfortunately, Skier's own word processor, along with virtually all rivals, can't replicate a WordPerfect format, a WordStar format, and so on.

9. The more highly customized the package, the less training time you or your employees should require—a good rule for any software, not just the laptop variety. This rule is especially true at a large corporation. If similar applications exist throughout the company, it may

pay either to tailor an off-the-shelf package to the firm's needs or to develop the software from scratch. Think strategically. Avoid counting just the up-front costs. Also ponder training costs; ease of use, not just ease of learning; and productivity gains. Too many companies are blind to the ease of use criterion. Don't buy or commission the writing of "dumbed-down" software that prevents employees from reaching their full potential.

INTERESTING PROGRAMS FOR THE ROAD

Here are some programs of special interest to laptop people. Please pay attention to my word *interesting* in the heading above. *Interesting* is a favorite cop-out of software reviewers when they're discussing novel products; *interesting* differs from the words *good* or *excellent*. Like laptops themselves, all of these programs have trade-offs. Still, they're all of interest to at least some laptop users. The programs discussed are:

■ No-Squint, Ken Skier's little cursor program, which can save time and prevent eyestrain when you're searching for the cursor.

■ CTYPE, a free, public domain alternative to No-Squint.

■ XWORD, a conversion program that can turn WordPerfect into ASCII, XyWrite into WordPerfect, and so on.

■ FileExpress, a good database that you can trim to function as a filing program for laptops.

■ Magellan and other programs that help you find information on your disk. Attention, owners of hard disk laptops!

■ Double Disk, which, though the name is a little too optimistic, does indeed raise the number of megabytes of data that you can squeeze onto your hard disk.

■ Translate, the English-to-Spanish program.

■ Integrated programs, which can, for instance, combine word processing, spreadsheeting, and communications.

Please note that in chapter 5 I'll briefly discuss other software of interest to many laptop owners—for instance, programs to help you back up your data onto floppies and help stretch your battery's time between charges. Appendix 4 explains communications programs and those that transfer files between portables and desktop machines.

No-Squint

Straining to see a cursor on a laptop isn't just a question of the characters being smaller than on a desktop machine. LCDs aren't as quick-witted as cathode ray tubes, so they can't keep up as well with the rapid blinking of the classical, IBM-style cursor. Besides, compared to desktops, laptop screens tend to be of poorer resolution.

Using No-Squint on his laptop, however, a California computer consultant says he can work several hours longer at one stretch than he could in the past. No-Squint lets him see more than a faint, blinking sliver. It turns into a big, viewable rectangle.

What's more, you can adjust the blink on a one-through-nine scale, from very slow to very fast. To activate the program just type **LCD 1** (or as high as 9 for a faster blink) and press Return. You can even modify AUTOEXEC.BAT—a file used to tell MS-DOS how to set up your computer—so that your machine automatically loads No-Squint. The program needs just 1K of RAM.

Needless to say, No-Squint has its fans. Skier says one user even "called while on a break from jury duty to tell me that 'You're better than a doctor. A doctor just sees you—but you solve the problem.' " I myself get along nicely without No-Squint, since XyWrite gives me my favorite kind of cursor, a nonblinking rectangle. But for people whose favorite software lacks this option, this program may well be a must. No-Squint also could be good for some owners of gas plasma machines whose cursors sometimes disappear when running certain software in the EGA mode; that's how Toshiba owner Rich Schinnell, a vice president of the Capital PC User Group, benefits from No-Squint.

To be sure, No-Squint is not without problems. One fan of the program, for instance, found that it worked fine with WordPerfect but clashed with an auxiliary pop-up menu from another software house. Also, No-Squint may have trouble with certain communications software, specifically the Mirror program, a clone of CrossTalk. A cure is easy if your problems aren't with the program you mostly use. Just go to DOS, type **LCD OFF**, and press Return, thereby deactivating No-Squint. If need be, you can set up a batch file—in this case, a file consolidating MS-DOS commands—so that you automatically turn off No-Squint just before loading the program that doesn't get along with it.

Although not officially a function of No-Squint, the capability exists to give you a nonblinking cursor. SkiSoft won't support this function, since it won't necessarily work properly with all machines and all programs. But try it if you want. Use the command **LCD ALWAYS ON** and press Return.

No-Squint costs $39.95, plus shipping, from SkiSoft Publishing Corporation, 1644 Massachusetts Avenue, Suite 79, Lexington, Massachusetts 02173, (617) 863-1876.

Let me emphasize that among commercial products, No-Squint isn't necessarily the last word in cursor control. I've just learned of a program called Redline that, judging from a photo in *PC Magazine*, makes the cursor even more visible than it is with No-Squint. For more information about Redline call DynaCorp in Houston at 800-777-8320 or (713) 664-1492.

CTYPE (Another Cursor Enlargement Program)

Before buying any commercial cursor control product, you might try CTYPE. It not only can enlarge the cursor, it also can change its height. Unlike No-Squint, CTYPE won't adjust the blink rate. Also, as with No-Squint, CTYPE may not influence the cursor within every program. But considering CTYPE's price—zilch—it's well worth trying.

CTYPE is a public domain utility available on some bulletin board services (BBS's) or through *PC Magazine*'s MagNet section of CompuServe.[2] At least in the form I received it, CTYPE was "zipped," compressed through the ZIP utility, which you also can find on BBS's. You can stick the line CTYPE into your AUTOEXEC.BAT file. Then the CTYPE will take effect whenever you fire up your machine. You can even tell CTYPE from the beginning to give you the cursor size and location that you favor. You might start out with **CTYPE /AA** and press Return.

To answer the inevitable question, no, I couldn't use a combination of No-Squint and CTYPE to both stop the blink and reposition the cursor.

XWORD

Ideally you'll be able to use the same word processor on your laptop as you use on your desktop. Suppose, however, that that isn't possible.

[2]A listing for CTYPE first appeared in the November 10, 1987, issue of *PC Magazine*.

And what if the formats differ? Then you might buy XWORD, a file conversion program that has a devoted following among writers and editors who must deal with different formats. I've been using it happily for two years.

XWORD can translate among:

1. ASCII, with carriage returns at the end of all lines.
2. XyWrite.
3. MultiMate.
4. Classic WordStar. In this case and others, check with XWORD's makers about translation to and from newer versions.
5. WordStar 2000.
6. WordPerfect.

XWORD can also translate from various word processors into dBASE III comma-delineated format. Eventually it may be able to handle Microsoft Word, MacWrite, Wang, and IBM's DCA standard.

For $40 plus $5 shipping you can buy XWORD directly from the author, Ronald Gans, 350 West Fifty-fifth Street, Apartment 2E, New York, New York 10019, (212) 957-8361. Before you send any money, however, please contact Gans. By now, he may be marketing his product commercially, under a different name. Also, be certain that his product covers the versions of the word processing formats with which you'll work.

FileExpress

This database packs enough power for inventory use—it can deal with as many as 16 million records—but you easily can trim it to laptop size, and it's a snap to master compared to dBASE.

"I was first attracted to it because it is so easy to use," says Jo Allan, who owns a Zenith laptop and runs Tech-Comm Services, a technical writing firm in Richardson, Texas. "Anyone who can follow instructions on the screen can be entering data in a few minutes. It's also very small and can be made even smaller by deleting the report, label, or sort modules if you don't need them." If you're just taking short notes, the FileExpress people say the program needs only 195K of disk space and 235K of RAM (the extra RAM is needed for data).

"Probably the best way to describe my use of FileExpress is that it turns my laptop into an automated note taker," Allan says. "If I'm in a meeting, bidding a job on-site, or in some similar situation, I can set up a suitable form in a minute or two. It is actually quite speedy and much more efficient to enter notes directly into a form, rather than scribbling on a note pad.

"When I get back to the office I export to dBASE to organize my notes, create an outline, etc. I often use my laptop in this manner, even at the office. I keep it set up next to the AT and use it for note recording." That's easy, since FileExpress exports to the ubiquitous ASCII format, readable by dBASE.

FileExpress costs $69.95 for a registered version or $15 for evaluation disks without technical support available. The $15 includes a coupon for $10 off the $69.95. You can also download the software directly from Expressware's BBS; telephone (206) 788-4008. Expressware's address is P.O. Box 230, Redmond, Washington 98073; voice telephone is 800-753-FILE or (206) 788-0932. The package requires 639K of disk space and 320K of RAM if you're using all modules.

Among FileExpress's customers are General Dynamics, IBM, Ford, DuPont, the U.S. Department of Justice, and the U.S. customs authorities.

Magellan and Other Programs to Help Find—Or Help Organize —Information on Your Disk

Every now and then, you *know* some information is on your hard disk but just plain can't recall the name of the file. No, you're not growing senile. Rather, you're like many people—a candidate for a program like Magellan II. Just key in the word or phrase that you want, and Magellan will locate it. Other programs of this kind exist, but at the moment, Magellan ($139 from Lotus Development Corporation) is commanding the most attention. Magellan lets you search for words from files created in a number of programs—anything from spreadsheets to word processors. Both programs help you find patterns of information that may otherwise escape you.

Among the many questions to ask here are:

■ How fast will the search take? On the faster hard disk laptops using the 80286 processor or an equivalent, Magellan can take just a few seconds to find all files with the word or phrase you're seeking.

■ Will the product do Boolean searches using the words *AND* or *OR* to determine the scope of your search? **Susan and George** would bring up all files where the two names appear. **Susan or George** would include all files containing "Susan" or "George." Unfortunately, Magellan can't do Boolean searches.

■ Does the software allow searches by keywords—words that sum up the document but aren't necessarily a part of the original material? The word *friends* may be the keyword for a file containing "Susan" and "George." You'd have had to enter the keyword ahead of time.

■ Can you easily use wildcards—for instance, **Su*** to pick up not only **Susan** but **Sue** and **Suzy**?

■ Can it easily cut across the subdirectories of your disk, the areas where you'd store programs and data?

■ If the electronic product creates an electronic index to sum up the contents of your disk and speed searching, what's the ratio between the size of the index and the indexed material? To index 20 megabytes of material, Magellan needs just 1 megabyte of space.

■ Can you easily open up files and view them in the formats in which they were created? On the left of the screen Magellan offers you a list of files. Moving the cursor through the list, you'll see a window showing the files' contents in sixteen programs. A letter created in WordStar will look as it would in WordStar, complete with formatting.

Besides Magellan, you also might check out ViewLink—from Traveling Software—which lacks some of the latter's search power but can be made memory resident so that it pops up when you need it.

Another possibility is GOfer, which sells for $79.95 from Microlytics, Two Obey Village Office Park, Pittsford, New York 14534, 716-248-9150. GOfer can take up as much as 120K of RAM. But it needs as little as 8K of the memory below 640K, if you can shift the bulk of the program to your hard disk or to expanded or extended memory. GOfer isn't as fast as, say, Magellan. But you can speed up your searches by confining them to one area of your hard disk. Like many search programs, GOfer not only can find words, it also can help you move material from one file to another even if file formats are different. GOfer does Boolean searches.

It's slower than Magellan and much less ambitious, but it sells for about a third of the cost, and it, too, can pop up.

Yet another possibility is PC-Browse, from Quicksoft (219 First Avenue North, Seattle, Washington 98109, 800-888-8088). PC-Browse permits you to search for information without your word processor or spreadsheet and lets you paste the outside information directly where your cursor is. In fact, it even allows you to search for the word on which the cursor rests. The command structure is clumsy, though, requiring too many repetitive keystrokes. Also, unlike Magellan, PC-Browse can't display underlining and other formatting in the native formats of the files that it's reading.

Double Disk

Back in the old days, your 20-megabyte hard disk seemed the electronic equivalent of the Wild West in the 1800s—a capacious frontier impossible to fill. But what can you do now that you've settled the Great Plains?

To the rescue comes Double Disk. Its name is from the claim that it enables a hard disk to store twice as much data. That's a bit sweeping. The statement is easily true if you're working with database files, or if you have a number of short files; in those cases there will be plenty of slack on your hard disk. But what if you're dealing with a long file from a word processor? Then the compression might drop to 30 to 40 percent. Why? Because word processor files in their original forms will use the hard disk more efficiently. The same idea applies to program files, the ones ending with extensions such as .COM or .EXE; don't expect Double Disk to live up to its name in such cases. Still, even if your average compression is only around 40 percent, Double Disk seems well worth its $100 list price. I suspect that the street prices will eventually sink to $50 or $60.

Other than giving up 40K or 50K of RAM for the program, I appeared to be making no sacrifices except for the increased need to be vigilant about making backups on floppies.[3] I simply ran Double Disk's automatic installation program, then enjoyed use of a disk called Drive E. The disk wasn't a new hard drive or floppy. Rather it was a logical

---

[3]Philip Johnson, vice-president of engineering with Vertisoft, says there will be slowdowns in rare instances when you're using databases and when you're doing sorts, or in some other disk-intensive applications. Normally, however, you should not notice any difference in execution speeds, especially if a program runs mainly in RAM. If a slowdown does occur, you can probably get around it. Just try running your database software, et cetera, in a normal section of your hard disk while storing your data in a compressed area.

disk, a part of my original hard drive that now existed as a separate disk. I could have created as many as ten drives by way of Double Disk. Each would have stored much more material than normal.

Significantly, Double Disk provides for an easy backup procedure, a must when you're trying to squeeze more information onto your hard disk. It also should work with backup tape drives; find out about compatibility with your model.

I asked the Double Disk people about their data compression technique. The word I got is that Double Disk doesn't "crunch or rearrange" data. Instead Double Disk removes the fat—blank spaces that DOS wastes on a hard disk. Philip Johnson, vice-president of engineering for Vertisoft Systems, Double Disk's developers, says the program "compresses 4 bytes of information into the space normally taken up by 2 bytes." Double Disk does this by functioning as a "device driver," a program that tells DOS how to do its job in a new way.

Johnson says Double Disk isn't like ARC, ZIP, or other compression programs that simply crunch individual files and require you to uncompress. You needn't do this in Double Disk. It's automatic.

Material stored through the program appears as one monster file *to DOS*. The Double Disk device driver knows where a file (or what you perceive as a file) is located within the monster file. The monster file is a "hidden file" not visible on your file directory.

Although Double Disk ran safely on my system, I'd still urge you to exercise care. If you use SpinRite II or another disk optimizer to rearrange your hard disk so it stores files most efficiently, you must first remove Double Disk (see the DD manual). That shouldn't be a problem normally. Just back up your data regularly; if you don't, you shouldn't try a product like Double Disk. Most laptop users, however, should seriously think about Double Disk and other new software that could radically boost the power of their machines. Don't limit your repertoire to, say, dBASE, 1-2-3, or other applications programs.

Double Disk is available for $99.95 from Vertisoft Systems, Inc., 100 California Street, San Francisco, California 94111, (415) 956-6303, or 150 Highway 9, Freehold, New Jersey 07728, (800) 548-8115.

Also think about Squish Plus, another good compression program, which sells for the same as Double Disk. Like Double Disk, Squish Plus makes just modest demands on RAM, gets along fine with most applications programs, and allows password protection.

Sundog Software (264 Court Street, Brooklyn, New York, 11231,

718-855-9141) claims that Squish Plus doubles the average effective disk space. As with Double Disk, I learned that the "double" isn't universally true. Squish's compression, in fact, is a little lower on the average than Double Disk's is. But in another way Squish beats Double Disk. It can work with both hard disks and floppies, and the Squish people say their product can also jack up the effective capacity of silicon disks (RAM chips or other devices used to imitate physical disks). Do you own a diskless machine like the Psion, Poqet, or one of the early NEC UltraLites? Then consider Squish Plus.

Translate (Translation Software)

Language barriers are bad enough for big companies; think of the small fry without a pile of money for translation. High-tech firms face special problems. There are masses of technical documentation to be written, not just the usual contracts, product information, and letters to local dealers. How to reduce translation costs and speed up the process, especially if you're a lone rep traveling abroad with a laptop? One solution, if time and money permit, may be to check with your e-mail vendor to see if there are any translation services on-line.

But there's another approach, too—translation software, which also could be useful in communicating bilingually in the heavily Hispanic areas of this country.

Such programs, of course, will not translate your golden prose into the other language perfectly; you must beware of serious inaccuracies that could cause technical or legal problems. Just the same, translation software can be a real lifesaver in deadline situations when no human help is available.

One of the more interesting programs in this category is Translate (from FinalSoft, 3900 Seventy-ninth Avenue N.W., Suite 215, Miami, Florida 33166-9791, 800-232-8228 or [305] 477-2703), which lists for $495. Translate goes from English into Spanish. You can type in your English—and get Spanish output—or you can feed Translate an English file in the ASCII format. Translate's usefulness can be improved by writing short, simple sentences, of which Hemingway would approve. And, helpfully, you can tailor Translate to your needs via a "Dictionary Update and Maintenance Editor."

As described by the newsletter of the Farm Employers Labor Service in Sacramento, California, translation is 60 to 80 percent complete.

Typical users should handle the output the same way they would treat output from a scanner that keys the contents of a book into a computer. For most purposes the output should be considered just a start. It will need polishing. Here is original English, then Spanish as Translate produced it.

> *The company may require any applicant or employee at any time to submit to testing for alcohol or other drugs. The company will require the test when, in the company's opinion, the physical or mental impairment of the applicant or employee in performing a job duty, such as operating machinery, would pose a threat to the safety of any person or to company property or to its interests.*

And now the Spanish:

> *La compañía puede requerir cualquier solicitante o empleado en cualquier momento para presentar a probar para alcohol u otras drogas. La compañía requerirá a la prueba cuando, en la opinión de la compañía, el deterioro físico o mental del solicitante o empleado al ejecutar un deber de trabajo, como operando maquinaria, es una amenaza a la seguridad de cualquier persona o para propiedad de las compañía o sus intereses.*

That's not sales brochure or technical documentation, of course. But you get the idea. If you write simply—the rule for a good brochure or documentation—you might enjoy even better results from Translate.

Beyond the normal question of accuracy, do be aware of gender problems. My friends David Page and his wife, Socorrito Baez-Page, who is a native speaker of Spanish, found many gender mistakes. Ideally a new version of Translate will improve in that regard.

I hope, too, that Translate will run faster. Even on the Pages' 80386 desktop, Translate needed about forty-five seconds to process just one paragraph of English.

Luckily, some relief is available in the areas of both accuracy and speed. Translate lets you customize your dictionary with new words and even phrases. The more you use the program and "train" it, the fewer mistakes it will make in terms of gender or other areas. You can teach Translate the jargon of your trade. After you've enlarged Translate's vocabulary, fewer words will befuddle the program and slow it down. FinalSoft promises good telephone support to customers doing customization.

Translate requires 512K of RAM. Alas, it takes up at least 10 mega-bytes of disk space, ruling it out for virtually all floppy-only portables or for hard disk users with cramped space (things could change when the 10-megabyte floppy becomes the norm). Double Disk to the rescue? Speller-checkers and thesauruses often employ special compression techniques to reduce demands on disk space; I wonder if FinalSoft can either refine such techniques or use them to begin with. Regardless, many grateful users may regard Translate as just as much a breakthrough product.

To answer the inevitable question, yes, FinalSoft told me it's working on a Spanish-to-English program.

Integrated Programs

Integrated programs mix several functions. Among the common ones are word processing, spreadsheeting, graphics, and communications.

SLIMMING DOWN REGULAR SOFTWARE FOR YOUR LAPTOP

Don't give up if the manual for your regular software says it can't run on a laptop. *Sometimes* you can succeed anyway. In a word processor, for instance, you may be able to jettison:

- Printer files (if you're not planning to print on the road).
- Files for using the word processor to generate mailing lists.
- "Help" files that you won't need. Perhaps you can condense information about your software—or hardware—for use on the road.

I'll mention integrated programs with less than full enthusiasm, since the software typically isn't as powerful as one-purpose programs. Still, if your disk space is limited or if your needs are modest, you may want to check out this possibility. Here are some criteria worth considering:

1. The extent to which different parts of the software use the same command structure. Granted, a word processor doesn't do the same thing as a spreadsheet, and so on, but do the software's modules share

as many commands as possible? For instance, will Ctrl–Left Arrow in both cases move the cursor to the left end of the line you're on?

2. How smoothly can you switch from program to program. Is the master menu helpful? Are its commands efficient?

3. How easily you can move information from one part of the program to the next. Will graphics files easily merge with the word processor? Also, what about compatibility with your normal word processor?

4. To what extent you save disk space. That's an issue with all laptop software, of course, at least if your space is limited; but the question might be asked especially of integrated software. Since integration involves trade-offs, you may as well enjoy benefits in return, such as conservation of valuable disk space.

5. The criteria for choosing executive word processors and laptop software in general. If nothing else, most integrated programs include word processors.

Among the major integrated products are:

■ WordPerfect Executive, $249 from the Orders Department, WordPerfect Corporation, 1555 North Technology Way, Orem, Utah 84057, (801) 225-5000. Executive's word processor is a slimmed-down version of 5.0, without all of the formatting features and minus the thesaurus and speller.

Are you a WordPerfect devotee? Consider WordPerfect Executive if your laptop doesn't have lots of memory above 640K and works with just one 720K floppy. Or get a regular version of WordPerfect that is older than 5.0. Single-drive machines, such as the Toshiba T1000 and the Tandy 1100FD, simply cannot run the newer, fatter versions of WordPerfect—at least not without giving up the speller and the thesaurus.

Beyond the word processor in WordPerfect Executive, you'll also get an appointment calendar, a calculator, note cards, a phone directory, and a streamlined spreadsheet compatible with PlanPerfect. Even though I have reservations about the main WordPerfect program in its present incarnations, I'll mention Executive first on this list—because of its file compatibility with the best-selling brand.

■ Microsoft Works, $149 from Microsoft Corporation, Box 97107, Redmond, Washington 98073, (206) 882-8080. Works offers word processing, mail merge, and graphics and is highly recommended as a good program for novices.

■ Symphony, $695 from Lotus Development Corporation, 55 Cambridge Parkway, Cambridge, Massachusetts 02142, (617) 577-8500. Symphony is regarded as harder to master than Works. It offers a word processor, outliner, database, and communications module. Symphony's database permits up to 8,000 records with as many as 256 fields per record. A record is a listing for a person, a product, and so forth, and a field is an item within a record, such as a name.

■ PFS:First Choice, $169 from Software Publishing Corporation, 1927 Landings Drive, Mountain View, California 94043, (415) 962-8910. First Choice includes a word processor, a database, mail merge, and presentation graphics, whose capabilities may be handy for sales reps. "We decided to use it for the sales-force automation product," says Peter Hutchinson, a technical analyst at Ciba-Geigy Pharmaceuticals in Summit, New Jersey, who was impressed with both the price and functionality.[4]

■ Framework III, $695 from Ashton-Tate, 20101 Hamilton Avenue, Torrance, California, 90509-1319, (213) 329-8000. Word processor, mail merge, spreadsheet, database, graphics, communications, outlining, electronic mail, and programming language.

■ Alpha Works, $195 from Alpha Software Corporation, 1 North Avenue, Burlington, Massachusetts, 01803, (617) 229-2924. Word processor, spelling checker, thesaurus, spreadsheet, database, graphics, and communications. It can work with dBASE and Lotus 1-2-3 formats and has enjoyed many favorable reviews.

■ SideKick. $84.95 in the basic version from Borland International, P.O. Box 660001, Scotts Valley, California, 95066-001 (800) 331-0877. Word processor, phone list and appointment calendar, among other things. "It makes for the portable office more than anything else," says my friend Jim Besser, a hard-working writer for Jewish-oriented newspapers, who turns out ten thousand words in a typical workday.[5] Often Besser takes Amtrak from Alexandria, Virginia, to New York,

---

[4]Peter Hutchinson's remarks are from *PC Week*.

[5]Besser is also the author of *Do They Keep Kosher on Mars?* (New York: Macmillan, 1990), in which Sol the Answer Man discourses on Jewish laws and customs, reveals how many of the Chosen People have become police chiefs, and whether a pious woman would be better off marrying a good Christian or an evil Jew.

and he loves SideKick because "you're able to bring your portable phone list with you. My whole Rolodex is on my SideKick phone dialer. It has numbers, addresses, just anything I want. Second, it has an editor that has WordStar commands. You can install as much or as little as you want. For example, you can drop the calendar." The real glory of SideKick, however, in my opinion, is that a quick keystroke can bring this program up on your screen, even if you're in the middle of another program. Unlike the other software here, SideKick is most often used as an auxiliary program rather than a main one.

*   *   *

As much improved as today's integrated programs are compared to predecessors, I'd still recommend that you see first if you can work with specialized software. It has many advantages. For instance, at least one word processor, Eye Relief, is specially designed for laptops and might be of strong interest to you even if it isn't as powerful as some competitors. Read about it and additional word processors in the pages ahead.

Chapter 4

LAPTOPS ON THE JOB: SOFTWARE FOR WRITERS, ACCOUNTANTS, AND SALES REPS

■ Software for writers and other processors of words. Page 88.
■ Software for sales reps. Page 105.
■ Accounting software. Page 122.
■ "ScreenWright: A Delightful $49.95 Program for Screenwriters and Playwrights," Appendix 1.
■ "Software Tips for Owners of the Mac Portable," Appendix 2.

God knows what word processor Mailer uses, if any. Bellow, last I read, was sticking to a typewriter. Fitzgerald truly *wrote* —in longhand. Thank goodness. Otherwise some drudge of a grad student would no doubt be slaving away, explaining the effect of word wrap[1] on the symbolism in *The Great Gatsby*. We'd all know, wouldn't we, about the green screen and Daisy's green light?

But enough Lit. You needn't be Scott Fitzgerald II to cherish a good word processor.

Although canned letters are popular among some sales reps, others may take pride in individualized notes. Even accountants can be word processing addicts. On the consulting side of major accounting firms, some staffers may use word processors almost as much as they use spreadsheets. In fact, all things considered,

---

[1]Word wrap automatically places a word on the next line if it won't fit on the original line.

word processing is by far the most popular application of laptop computers.

This chapter, then, while also addressing the software needs of sales reps and accountants in detail, begins with writers and other processors of words. Hard-core numbers crunchers are welcome to skip ahead to the discussion of accounting software.

WRITERS AND OTHER PROCESSORS OF WORDS

The programs discussed in the following pages include:

■ Eye Relief, a tightly written word processor capable of blowing characters up to newspaper headline size on your screen.

■ QEdit, another worthy product for word jugglers with limited disk space and problems seeing their cursor. It should enjoy great appeal among laptop users doing communications; after all, the files come out in pure ASCII of the kind that most e-mail networks prefer.

■ ZEdit, a dressed-up version of QEdit.

■ VDE, a slick little WordStar-compatible editor that's just dandy for portables—it needs only 90 to 140K of RAM. The main file is a mere 40K.

■ Kidword. Like Eye Relief, this word processor features large letters on the screen. At just $10, Kidword is a possibility for children; what's more, it could be a training aid for some computerphobics who are novices to laptops.

■ EDTGREEK, an editor for scientists and engineers with laptops and a need to work with large characters in both the English and Greek alphabets. It costs $9.95.

■ XyWrite, my favorite word processing program, designed especially for writers and editors.

■ A few auxiliary programs for writers. See Appendix 1 for a description of a $49.95 screenwriting program that's powerful enough for some frugal writers to use as their main word processor.

Eye Relief

If software publishers really want to woo the laptop crowd, then they'd better listen up and heed the lessons imparted by a pioneering product from SkiSoft: a word processor called Eye Relief. It can enlarge characters on the screen and greatly vary the spaces between lines, while you're in an editing mode. You don't need to be in "preview" to see jumbo letters. Outside the Windows environment—a real memory hog—most MS-DOS word processors lack this capability.

Eye Relief may benefit even those with normal vision. With bigger characters, for instance, proofreading may be easier.

Granted, some veteran laptop users might shrug off the importance of Eye Relief. After all, via a quick DOS command, they can make their screens display forty letters a line rather than the customary eighty. Check your DOS manual to see if the command works on your computer. From my C:\ prompt, I typed **MODE CO40**, then pressed Return, and I instantly saw the new mode.[2]

But when I ran XyWrite, my usual word processor, I beheld some bizarre sights. The customary ruler line near the top of the screen, for instance, split into two lines. What's more, I had to readjust my margins.[3]

Eye Relief, however, without much ado, lets you change the sizes of the letters on the screen for editing purposes. In fact, SkiSoft's Ken Skier may have been overzealous. You can't shrink the characters enough. On a portable with a CGA-style display, his "Tiny" characters are equivalent to someone else's medium size or large letters—a hindrance when you want to see a few hundred words at once while editing. You can't bring the lines closer together than maybe one and a half times the normal distance. Moreover, even the nearsighted might welcome the ability to use a *single* keystroke to switch from huge letters to much smaller ones. Skier's product lacks that ability right now.

Eye Relief disappoints in some other ways:

■ This software can't work with files more than 60K long; nor can you change the keyboard commands without an auxiliary program, such as SmartKey.

■ The word processor's first version lacks an amenity that, on second thought, is really a necessity: a working Tab key.

---

[2] Some computer systems might lack this capability; others may require the command **MODE BW 40**.

[3] Despite my problems, XyWriters might want to experiment with the **MODE CO40** command. Try it! (Thanks to my friend Herb "XySon" Tyson for the tip.)

■ Eye Relief won't give you a headline in 14-point Helvetica and body text in 10-point Times Roman. Font control just isn't available.

■ The product can't even insert underlining or italics. You'll need to bring the files back into your usual word processor to fancy them up for decent printing.

■ Eye Relief cannot be taught to imitate WordStar commands or those of other word processors. Of course, some well-regarded keyboard macroprograms, such as SmartKey, Keyworks, or ProKey, probably could do the job, but I'd rather not bother with this (although I do recommend them anyhow as a way to deal with the quirks of portables' keyboards).

■ Frustratingly, Eye Relief cannot read files unless they're in pure ASCII. Almost all word processors allow ASCII conversions, but it is still an inconvenience. (You can save time by not using your word processor's formatting features until you're working on absolutely the last draft; then you can rely on the ASCII conversion—which won't, however, preserve the formatting.)

Just the same, when you're thirty thousand feet up, the reading light is no good, and you envy the pilot because he has radar while you enjoy nothing comparable to guide you around a tiny laptop screen without good backlighting, then you'll be very thankful that Skier wrote Eye Relief. His brainchild will appeal to at least four classes of users:

1. Those who, like me, can use Eye Relief to complement an existing word processor. I won't give up XyWrite. Rather, I'll use Eye Relief at times as auxiliary software on a laptop when my eyes are tired, after which I can edit the results on my desktop running XyWrite. What's more, Eye Relief should be just the ticket when I want to transcribe parts of a taped interview and don't need to edit my output.

2. People with bad eyes—both laptop and desktop users. Considerately, Eye Relief starts out with letters the size of a newspaper headline reporting an earthquake. Even some legally blind people can use the program. Skier has even been thoughtful enough to write his instruction manual in large type.

3. Computerphobes who simply will feel more comfortable with a machine that can generate large letters.

4. Children who are just learning computers and how to type on

them. They too should enjoy the large, friendly letters that Eye Relief brings to the screen.

5. People making presentations on monitors smaller than they would like. Audiences can view Eye Relief's huge characters much more easily than they can those of most word processors.

Eye Relief runs on machines with CGA, EGA, VGA, and Hercules/ monographics displays, 512K RAM, and 3.5-inch disks or the older 5.25-inch ones. The main program itself takes up just 48K on the disk, and even with overlays and options, the disk from SkiSoft contains less than 170K of material. It's like diet food, except Skier is selling something of value, not just watered-down cheese. Installation on most machines is a snap. On a hard disk laptop, for example, I just carved out a new subdirectory on my hard disk and copied the files from the installation disk to my own via a simple DOS command. That, more or less, was it. Skier provides detailed instructions for users of floppy-only machines.

Even a novice computer user can be turning out work within hours, because of the program's easy menu structure. Eye Relief uses pull-down menus. Suppose you want smaller letters on the screen. Type F10, which takes you to the main menu, and press V for Video. Then move the cursor to "Tiny," "Jumbo," whatever, and hit Return. Bingo! Your type is as small or large as you want it—well, within the bounds I've already described. By the way, via the menu summoned by F10, you can quickly reach the commands for editing, file handling, and so on. And Skier tutors you via this main menu. After you press F10 and then F (File), for instance, you'll see that Ctrl-S will let you save a file. So next time around, you just hit Ctrl-S without having to go through the F10 routine.

What's more, Eye Relief provides some limited macro capabilities. You can trigger a series of keystrokes—as long as you want them to be, and including either text or commands—if you hit Ctrl-X, type the name of the macro, then press the return. Regrettably, Eye Relief lacks the ability to activate macros through single keystrokes (although Skier is thinking of adding this).

Faults notwithstanding, Eye Relief is a welcome departure from the me-too programs that characterize the American software industry. I'll be rooting for Skier to do the logical follow-up and create a large-character spreadsheet—before some of the big boys turn a buck on the concept he pioneered.

Eye Relief costs $295 plus $4.95 shipping for a copy directly from SkiSoft at the address mentioned earlier. It's also available at some computer stores and through Traveling Software, 18702 North Creek Parkway, Bothell, Washington 98011, (206) 483-8088.

QEdit

I wish someone could make a hybrid of Eye Relief and QEdit. The hybrid would be better for cheapie laptops than either product by itself. Like Ken Skier's program, QEdit is weak on formatting features, but it makes up in ways that are especially helpful if you're using your laptop with a modem. Here's how the two products stack up:

■ Price. No comparison. QEdit sells for $54.95, Eye Relief for $295, even with the usual discounts. If anyone deserves to make money off software, it's a gutsy, innovative programmer like Ken Skier. But at $295 list, his word processor may be shunned by people who would welcome it as auxiliary software if it were more affordable. The auxiliary market presumably was on the minds of QEdit's creators.

■ Wear on batteries. Tie. Both QEdit and Eye Relief operate almost entirely within RAM, reducing the need for power-hogging disk accesses.

■ Paragraph reforming when new words or letters are inserted. When you insert new words in a paragraph in Eye Relief, everything immediately slides into the correct place. With QEdit you must press Alt-B or an equivalent command for that to happen. And then, if you want to return to your previous place in the text, you need to tap out yet other keystrokes.

Moreover, rather disturbingly, you must insert spaces between paragraphs; otherwise you'll get one huge paragraph when you type Alt-B. An executive at SemWare, QEdit's publisher, was surprised when I reminded him that there are thousands of users who actually compose without blank lines separating paragraphs. Amazing. To his credit, he said QEdit eventually would eliminate the need for the Alt-B commands. Meanwhile I've suggested that Semware consider using tabs as a way to tell the program, ''Hey, don't blend that material with the stuff above; it's a new paragraph!''

■ Other formatting. The programs are roughly equal. Both allow the creation of page numbers and offer other basics, but not underlining, italics, and so forth, in most cases (QEdit lets me insert control characters that WordStar will recognize as underlining). I find this to be ironic considering that in his promo material Skier at times has put the name of his products in boldfaced italics. I suspect that the QEdit people themselves like to use something other than plain text. Oh, well, at least they've *priced* their product as an auxiliary program.

■ Amount of RAM consumed. QEdit wins, since the program itself takes up just 64K of memory (that doesn't include the RAM that your computer's operating system requires). Eye Relief needs several times as much. What's more, QEdit itself can require as little as 50K of disk space, or even less than Eye Relief does. QEdit, like Skier's program, would be a natural for notebook computers with limited disk space or no disk at all.

■ Visibility on laptop screens. Eye Relief wins. QEdit won't let you vary the size of the letters and the spacing between them. I may be unfair to QEdit here. It wasn't designed to fill the special niche where Skier is at home. On the other hand, I wish the special niche—software that lets you vary character size and line spacing were the main market. QEdit, at least, is easier on the eyes than many other programs; it uses boldfacing or a different color to set off the line that the cursor is on. And the cursor is big and blinks. What's more, QEdit lets you change the colors of the text and the background.

■ Ability to scoot back and forth between the main word processor and the auxiliary one. QEdit is better for me when I take a XyWrite file and farm it out to a laptop running the auxiliary software. XyWrite itself is almost pure, traditional ASCII. But in a few places XyWrite uses special characters—European quotes—such as for boldface or italics. QEdit won't print these characters but will preserve them in the raw form (for instance, «MDUL» to indicate underlining and «MDNM» to show a return to normal text).

Eye Relief, on the other hand, gives me an error message and won't let me edit those files because they aren't 100 percent ASCII.

Redeemingly, however, Eye Relief is kinder to me when I'm going in the other direction—from the auxiliary word processor to the main one. It doesn't clutter up my files with carriage return symbols at the end of each line, just at the ends of paragraphs, the way XyWrite prefers.

WordPerfect, WordStar, Microsoft Word, you name it—most word processors can more gracefully import files produced through other means if the carriage returns show up only at the paragraph ends.

■ Communications. No contest. QEdit is the victor because of the same, ubiquitous carriage returns that show up at the end of each and every line. Both QEdit and Eye Relief are pure ASCII. It's just that if you transmit a raw, unmassaged Eye Relief file on a network like MCI, you'll confuse the network because the carriage returns show up only at the end of each paragraph. To obtain the right format through Eye Relief, first you must print to a file on your disk (although it's possible to streamline this through a macro).

Of course, just as the QEdit people might object that I compared their software's viewability against that of a program designed partly for the visually impaired, Skier might protest that he didn't really have e-mail in mind when he designed Eye Relief.

By the way, QEdit's designers appear to have had something even more than e-mail in mind: the editing of programs. QEdit comes up on the screen almost instantly with the kind of ASCII that programmers love.

■ File length limits. QEdit triumphs. Eye Relief can handle files of only 60K or so in length—maybe twenty-five or thirty pages. Skier correctly points out that few business documents are that length. Just the same, as a book writer who has produced his own share of computer guides, he should realize that some authors like their chapters *long*.

■ Macros. Both programs offer some capabilities. QEdit, however, allows macros triggered by mere keystrokes; you don't have to type in a file name.

■ Command structure. QEdit's victory. The software can emulate basic WordStar commands; not only that, QEdit also offers a well-designed pull-down menu. Would that QEdit also feature those wonderful fonts and enlarged letters that Eye Relief does!

■ Printer compatibility. I haven't really tested this aspect of the program, but I suspect that QEdit would win. A QEdit-style program, ZEdit (see below), supposedly works with any microprinter as long as you have the proper cable.

See why the ideal laptop word processor may be a combination of both programs? If you can afford it, you might consider buying them both—Eye Relief for long writing stints without editing and QEdit for communications or programming.

QEdit is available for $54.95 plus $3 for shipping and handling from SemWare, 4343 Shallowford Road, Suite C-3, Marietta, Georgia 30062-5003, (404) 641-9002.

ZEdit

Also check out ZEdit, a dressed-up cousin of QEdit. Like QEdit, it lets you use WordStar-like commands. In fact, in at least one important case, ZEdit resembles WordStar more. You use Ctrl-B rather than Alt-B to realign paragraphs where you've made insertions (though you'll still need blank lines between paragraphs to avoid making everything below the cursor turn into one gargantuan paragraph).

On top of everything else, ZEdit offers a cursor line and an enlarged cursor, as QEdit does. Alas, it lacks Eye Relief's ability to enlarge fonts. Certainly, however, ZEdit provides greater flexibility of commands and more of them than Eye Relief does. The price is $59.95 from Traveling Software or directly from Telcom Library, 12 West Twenty-first Street, New York, New York 10010, (212) 691-8215, 800-999-0345, or 800-LIBRARY.

VDE

When Eric Meyer was in graduate school he used WordStar but found it "too slow for the actual writing process." To him, the old version 3.3 was especially lacking. Not everyone would agree. Regardless, Meyer was impatient with such functions as Ctrl-QF (the search function). He seldom printed. Meyer didn't need fancy formatting wrinkles in a word processor, just a nice, brisk feel.

The outgrowth of his unhappiness was VDE, short for Video Display Editor.[4]

It's exactly that: an *editor*. The version I downloaded from CompuServe doesn't include more than three printer drivers. One is generic, a second is for Epson-style printers, a third is for the Hewlett-Packard inkjet called the DeskJet. (Meyer would appreciate copies of printer drivers that users come up with.) Formatting is nothing to brag

---

[4]Thanks to John Dvorak for bringing VDE to my attention.

about. So while VDE is indeed a word processor, and a great one for laptops, it's far from the most powerful. But a fast editor it is indeed.

"Finding a string near the end of a 60K nondocument file," says Meyer, who now teaches the history of science at the University of Oklahoma, "takes WordStar 4 about twenty seconds." On the same machine, an 8-megahertz computer with an 8088 processor, VDE can do the job in half a second.

You can squeeze VDE into just 40K of space on a disk, and it will run in a mere 90 to 140K of RAM.

Not surprisingly, VDE is terrific for e-mail notes, for programming chores, or for writing on laptops with limited memory. If I ran Atari, I'd buy up the world rights to Meyer's brainchild, adapt it to the Portfolio, and bundle it with RAM cards to augment the 128K of RAM already built into the laptop.

What's more, the **MODE CO40** command—the one to enlarge letters on the screen—disrupts VDE less than it does many other programs. Admittedly some text in the upper-right-hand corner will vanish. And **MODE CO40** mutilates the menus and requires narrower margins. Still, I could live with those limitations.

VDE's biggest marvel is the cost. Meyer would like "contributions" from happy users but doesn't require a registration fee from individuals. A corporation or institution can license VDE on twenty computers for just $50. That's all of $2.50 a machine. Meyer, moreover, gives permission for a software dealer or library to sell VDE for just $5 (apparently, royalties are required if the price is higher; to be on the safe side, please contact Meyer). I can just see the ads in *The New York Times* science section: "Buy our $550 laptop and we'll throw in a $5 WordStar clone!"

Please note some caveats:

■ You'll appreciate VDE more if you're already fond of WordStar. Meyer provides both a WordStar-style interface and an alternative. I loved the former and am indifferent to the latter. A friend, who loathes WordStar, hates VDE's "menubar" mode. I'd hope that all VDE users would try the WordStar interface, even though it requires more time to learn, for if you touch type, you'll hardly ever need to take your hands off the main keyboard. VDE shares WordStar's S-E-X-D diamond. Ctrl-S moves the cursor up, Ctrl-E moves it to the left, Ctrl-X moves it to the right, and Ctrl-D moves it down.

■ VDE's file output isn't 100-percent WordStar compatible. You probably won't be able to enter *all* the formatting commands for WordStar 5.0 on up.

■ Some of the commands also deviate from WordStar's; for instance, VDE normally will ignore the dot commands.

■ As with older versions of WordStar, you must type Ctrl-B after you've inserted a word or words in a paragraph.

■ Your file size cannot exceed 80K. You can, however, edit multiple files, splitting up material too cumbersome for one file. Plus VDE can divide into usable parts a long file created elsewhere. Ideally, in the future VDE will offer the ability to process monster files without such splits—a feature already in QEdit. I doubt that I would write a book chapter too long for QEdit and a 640K machine to handle. On the other hand, I'd have the same problem with VDE. Would that Meyer have split his dissertation into fewer chapters so he could understand my plight! This chapter, for example, is more than 111K long.

■ I've read complaints on BBSs that some of VDE's features, such as the macro capabilities, do not always work smoothly. I don't know who is at fault—the users or the program. But if it's the latter, Meyer should be quick to correct the problems.

Despite the VDE's limitations, it's an amazing piece of work from one person. Meyer, hacking during off-hours, has written a program with features missing from some software developed by multimillion-dollar corporations. VDE, for instance, included a quick, accurate little word counter. It offers WordStar-ASCII conversion, automatic saves if requested, an undo command, sophisticated keyboard-macro capabilities, and windows, among other things.

What's more, Meyer seems attentive to the desires of reviewers and plain users. Within a few days, at my request, he added a feature that enabled his program to produce files editable in a format well suited to XyWrite.

Obtain a copy of VDE from a local BBS or CompuServe, or write the Public Software Library, P.O. Box 35705, Houston, Texas 77235. The disk in the PSL catalogue is now number 1933; the cost is $5 per disk plus $4 postage and handling. Prospective dealers should contact Meyer through PSL.

Kidword (A $10 Word Processor for Children—and for Adults Learning How To Use a Laptop)

Flash! As I was moseying around on a local BBS, I ran across an intriguing little program called Kidword. "Little" is right. The .EXE file, the only one you need, it just 49K long. Kidword offers a fraction of Eye Relief's power but does give you headline-size characters on the screen of IBM-style machines. Like VDE, it's "shareware." You may obtain the program over the phone from a local BBS, try it, see if you like it, then pay Kidword's author if you do. And as with most shareware, the cost is reasonable, just $10 (plus $2 shipping and handling if you buy the disk version).

Granted, I wouldn't recommend Kidword for normal business use. The program, after all, is kid-specific. If you fire up Kidword and don't hit a key, your laptop's speaker will play "Twinkle Twinkle Little Star." That's not the kind of software you'd want for a laptop in the boardroom. Furthermore, the file limit is only ten double-spaced pages, hardly enough for a long business report. And files aren't in ASCII, even though Kidword can bring in ASCII files from other word processors.[5] There's another flaw. Originally written for the early Epson printers, Kidword may not get along too well with yours.

But if one of your employees is computerphobic and needs a friendly word processor to start out with, then Kidword is well worth the ten bucks. It starts up with a screen showing choices—for instance, creating a new file or retrieving an old. That's not unusual. What is unusual is the electronic pencil that you move around to make your selection. In an apt, childish way, Kidword is visually oriented. A specialist in childhood education teamed up with Kidword's author and made certain that the big letters would be the same shapes as those commonly seen in elementary school.

If you take a child along on a business trip, or if you simply want to keep him or her entertained and educated at home while you're away, then you should give Kidword a try. For more information write the author, Sidney D. Nolte, 13858 Peyton Drive, Dallas, Texas 75240. The telephone number is (214) 233-6178, but please do not call Nolte unless you're seriously inquiring about the program or are a registered

---

[5] Kidword files, however, based on a brief test, are readable in any version of WordStar. Moreover, Kidword can read WordStar files, at least those through Version 3.3.

user. Remember to mention your preferred disk format; also check with him about the printer you use.

EDTGREEK

EDTGREEK is a simple, no-frills way to work with large characters —even Greek letters—and use subscripts and superscripts.

My friend Edward L. Wright, an astronomer at UCLA, designed EDTGREEK to run on his T1000. This compact program, however, should delight users of other low-end laptops. If it won't work right off the bat on the Atari Portfolio—I haven't checked—then it could be well worth adapting. The most grateful fans of EDTGREEK will be scientists and engineers who are tired of squinting at small screens and will relish a built-in scientific calculator.

EDTGREEK, to be sure, is no XyWrite or WordPerfect at this point. It isn't even a full-fledged word processor with editing and printing functions carefully integrated; the program is just an editor. You must use a separate program (included) to prepare files for printing. Also, EDTGREEK lacks word wrap. You must hit Return at the end of every line, just as with an electric typewriter. Also, the cut-and-paste feature works only on whole lines, and the screen flickers when you scroll. The flicker, though, isn't so bothersome on screens without backlighting; what's more, there are other compensations for the eyes—namely, the large characters. EDTGREEK shows only thirteen rows of characters at a time in a CGA mode.[6]

They're much more readable than the normal font on a T1000, the Radio Shack equivalent, or a similar machine. Plus you can *see* Greek letters, not strange coding, the moment you create them. If you type Ctrl-N A, the Greek letter alpha will appear; Ctrl-N B will give you a beta; and so on.

EDTGREEK is just 30K long and runs entirely within random-access memory; with a 640K RAM, you can work with files exceeding 400K.

Print drivers are available for:

■ The Epson FX-85.
■ Hewlett-Packard DeskJet printers.
■ The VAX computer used with LN03 printers.

---

[6]The version especially for the EGA displays 24 lines, and the VGA version displays 34 lines. All of the versions give an 80-character-wide screen except the Hercules Graphics Card version, which shows 90 characters.

If EDTGREEK catches on, Ned undoubtedly will create other print drivers. Meanwhile, if you don't need to create Greek characters, you can always confine yourself to conventional ones and use search and replace with the scientific word processor on your desktop. Except for the Greek characters, EDTGREEK's output is pure ASCII.

EDTGREEK costs $9.95 and is available from Edward L. Wright, 10541 Seabury Lane, Los Angeles, California 90077. It's shareware, so it might be found by now on bulletin boards or in an IBM-related section of CompuServe.[7] Try it out. If you like it, send the $9.95 to Ned and he'll respond with a copy of the latest upgrade.

XyWrite: Why Flaubert's Ghost Would Choose It

Thomas Wolfe would have favored an early version of PC-Write. No frills. He'd let Max Perkins clean up with something fancier. James Joyce might have insisted on a Macintosh-based word processor; somehow a mouse would be more in keeping with a stream-of-consciousness writer, and of course, since he suffered from poor vision, he would have appreciated the large characters that Mac systems could give him on the screen. Ever the conservative, John O'Hara would have favored WordStar, just as William F. Buckley, Jr., does today.

Being a fan of both XyWrite and WordStar, I once suggested via MCI Mail that Buckley try the former, but I might as well have recommended a change from English to Etruscan. Most writers simply will not switch word processors. Still, in case you're an exception and are ready for a change, I'll tell you what *I* look for in a word processor for writers, and I'll use XyWrite, my pet program, as an example. I just know Flaubert's ghost would choose XyWrite. He'd want to edit fastidiously on a keyboard with his own custom set of commands—something that XyWrite could give him.

Most of the following traits should be of interest to fiction and nonfiction authors alike.

■ Speed. The sooner I finish a book, the faster I'll get paid. Oh, sure, we can talk about time to reflect, time for cosmic thoughts; but I myself find it a lot more enjoyable to think them when I'm out for a

---

[7]Try typing **GO IBMAPP**, going to the "Libraries," and looking under a category like "Text Editors."

walk than when I'm at the computer keyboard, where I spend *enough* time. I know Flaubert's ghost would agree. With XyWrite, Flaubert the man might have been able to finish *Bouvard et Pecuchet* before his death. Just as important, he would have felt more free to experiment with his prose, since each change would have required less of an investment in time. Newspaper writers especially value speed. I'm not the least surprised that XyWrite is the standard for bureaus of *The New York Times* and the *Washington Post*.

When I say *speed*, I don't just think of how long it takes the program to store material or go from the start to the end of a fifteen thousand-word file. I also consider how many keystrokes the common commands require. With XyWrite—via its keyboard macros—I can easily consolidate keystrokes of oft-used commands. I also think about the locations of the keystrokes; I'm not so keen on WordPerfect and other processors that require constant excursions to the Home and End keys. That's not just because I use laptops at times. I'm a touch typist and hate to take my fingers off the home row. In my opinion—and I can hear the WordPerfectionists demurring—no word processor has ever surpassed the logic of WordStar's commands. I've done the inevitable and given my XyWrite a WordStar-like keyboard. (Works the other way around, too. In a forthcoming WordStar book I tell how, XyWrite fashion, you can instantly delete a paragraph without marking with blocks.)

■ Reliability. Will the word processor blithely trash a chapter on which you've toiled for the last two weeks? Yes, no matter which word processor I use, I back up my material. Still, I'm egotistical enough to be disgusted by the thought of losing even a few minutes of work—at least due to a computer mishap; let me do my own word killing.

■ Maximum length of files. Unless Ken Skier raises his limit from thirty pages, I'll never use Eye Relief as my main program. With XyWrite I never worry about fifteen-thousand-word chapters.

■ The ability to move large blocks of material easily from one file to another. What starts out in one chapter may end up in another. Moreover, newspaper and magazine writers like to move quotes from their notes into actual articles. By the way, it helps if your word processor offers many windows so that you can quickly move from note to note to peek at their contents. XyWrite allows me as many as nine windows, among which I can move by pressing Ctrl-Shift-1, Ctrl-Shift-2, and so on. The SmartWare II WordProcessor reportedly allows as many as thirty-five windows on the screen at once and can cope with as many as fifty—though I'm baffled why anyone would want *that* many. When I work with windows on a desktop or laptop, I prefer to have only one window on the screen at a time. That's because I usually want to see twenty-four lines at a time rather than dividing the screen into two eleven-line views (I'd need space for the border between windows). Because of the size of the screen on the typical laptop, you too might prefer full- rather than split-screen windows.

■ Respect for the writer's eyes. With XyWrite I can change the cursor to a solid, nonblinking square and vary the screen colors (on a gas plasma screen at least I can switch from light characters against a dark background to dark characters against a light background). And as noted earlier, the new XyWrite will allow you to change your font sizes, see the results on the screen, and edit. The larger-than-normal type should be a real godsend.

■ Ability to handle oddball formatting requirements. That's not so important to me, but it will be to others. XyWrite, WordStar, and other powerful word processors can produce snaking columns and other goodies of interest to newsletter editors. If you're writing documentary scripts, then you'll also want to consider a word processor's ability to handle multiple columns. And if you're a technical writer, by now you well know the usefulness of being able to merge graphics into text. No matter what your formatting needs are, try to make certain that the word processor will work smoothly with popular printers and produce the appropriate styles (fonts) and sizes of characters. I know. You can't tote LaserJet when you board a jet of the 747 variety. But someday you just may want to feed your copy into a client's printer and dress up your work with a Times Roman or Helvetica font.

■ The presence of other special features, such as footnotes or endnotes. I've set up XyWrite so that a simple Alt-F opens up a space where I can enter an endnote.

■ The ability to produce ASCII, either for communications to a newspaper or for a disk that you hand over to a publisher.

■ Whether the program has a built-in spelling checker, thesaurus, and index, and how good they are. XyWrite's checker beeps at me if I type a word that isn't in its electronic dictionary—a feature I can turn off. Moreover, I can add several thousand words to the speller. I can even set up the speller to correct common typos automatically, and to let me use abbreviations. Just now, I didn't type XyWrite; I typed Xy.

In evaluating spellers and thesauruses, consider the size of the voca-
bularies. How many original words are in the thesaurus? How many
synonyms? Also, what about indexing? How flexible are the indexing
formats, and how long does it take to make and compile entries?

■ The presence of a word counter, a must for newspaper and magazine writers facing deadlines and strict word limits.

XyWrite is available from XyQuest, 44 Manning Road, Billerica,
Massachusetts 01821, (508) 671-0888. Check to confirm current pricing.

A Few Auxiliary Programs for Writers

Below are add-on programs that I use or think may be of interest to
other writers:

■ Hotkey. This small program—available for free from many
BBS's—speeds up my cursor movement. Without it I'd go berserk. As
usual, many laptop makers imitated the worst features of the IBM PC
and made the cursor too pokey. By the way, Hotkey could also be
valuable to users of spreadsheets, though it offers fewer options than
does the Cruise Control product mentioned on page 128. Writers might
consider Cruise Control, too. But Hotkey is the right price for a free
lancer: free.

■ PARSE. Another public domain program available from BBS's.
It measures not only the number of words in a file, but also the number
of words with three or more syllables, the number of sentences, the
number of characters per word, the number of words per sentence, and
the minimum level of education at which the material is comprehensible.
If an editor asks about a word count, I can cite figures from both XyWrite
and PARSE.

According to PARSE, the final draft of this chapter runs eighteen
thousand words and the comprehension requirement is at the junior
college level (should I jack it up if genetic engineering arrives and future
readers can all be Ph.D.'s?). I'll add a warning: you can't *always* believe
a computer's assessment of comprehension level. PARSE, for example,
doesn't even consider the length of paragraphs—although I suppose
that even without this factor, Faulkner's prose still would seem to require
several decades of graduate school.

■ Corporate Voice. If you like readability formulas—and I've already warned you of their limitations—you'll love Corporate Voice.

Voice lets you evaluate your writing either by the formulas or by the standards that you yourself can set up. Like PARSE, it has flaws. Voice, too, doesn't allow for short or varied paragraph lengths. Newspaper people often use such techniques to make articles easier to read, yet Voice does not make allowances for this. Voice's creators are working on the problem. Their program also is unfair to computer writers who aren't churning out manuals of the "Push the Ctrl key" variety, where it's easy to break sentences down to "byte" size.

Still, Voice is far, far slicker than PARSE. The two programs aren't even in the same class. PARSE is just above a word-counter, nothing more. Voice, on the other hand, uses snazzy graphics to help you analyze your prose in countless ways. For example, Voice can measure the percentage of common words versus unusual, hard-to-understand words. It even lets you exclude trade jargon from the "complicated" category, so you're not penalized for writing for a special audience. What's more, Voice encourages you to vary your sentence lengths and hew to many other rules of good writing. Just remember: Voice goes by formulas, yours or the program's. It won't turn you into Saul Bellow or even Tom Clancy, notwithstanding its ability to compare your prose with an already charted sample of the latter's.

Flaws aside, let me urge Voice for the Internal Revenue Service and other masters of the opaque. The insurance industry is also a splendid candidate. I'd like state insurance agencies to require all automobile policies to score well as replicas of *The Hunt for Red October*. Used wisely, Voice could do much more good than harm.

Corporate Voice lists for $119.95 from Scandinavian PC Systems, 51 Monroe Street, Suite 1101, Rockville, Maryland 20850 (301-294-7450 or 800-288-SCAN). Steve Frankel, one of Scandinavian's partners, is a friend of mine and his company may help market *The Complete Laptop Computer Guide* in Europe. I don't know if he's been bold enough to try Voice on this book.

■ The Keynotes Associated Press Electronic Stylebook. A pop-up program residing in RAM, it includes business, sports, and computer terms and punctuation preferred by the country's largest wire service. Check with the vendor, Digital Learning Systems—located at 4 Century Drive, Parsippany, New Jersey 07054, (201) 538-6640—about compatibility with your laptop if it lacks the usual Home, PgUp, PgDn, and End keys. The stylebook requires a computer with at least 128K of RAM and DOS 2.0 or above. Not everyone will like Keynotes. A friend, for instance, found that he couldn't customize it; nor could it supply him with cross references. He found the hard copy stylebook to be more convenient. Still, Keynotes has garnered its share of favorable reviews. You may find it worth taking along when you've got enough space on your laptop's hard disk and you don't want to tote around the actual stylebook.

■ REMIND, whose author, Robert M. W. Tsou, correctly describes it as "a program that won't let you forget." Have an important deadline? Just enter the date—in the proper format—into a file called REMIND.DTA. Then a window will pop up on your screen as your computer is booting up; your machine will display the reminder until you press Return and either go on to another tickler or else begin your regular computing. What I like about REMIND is that I can set up XyWrite—via its customized keyboard—to get me into REMIND.DTA with just one quick keystroke. REMIND.DTA is just plain ASCII, so XyWrite works fine as an editor (the data entry program isn't as slick as I'd like it to be).

Needless to say, REMIND remembers holidays. It will even play the appropriate music on certain occasions, such as New Year's Day; and on or around Mother's Day, perhaps a little pushily, it will ask whether you've bought your mother a gift.

For REMIND to work right, your computer needs an internal clock and calendar to set the time. REMIND is available on some bulletin boards. The author requests a $10 donation. For more information, including shipping and handling charges if you order a disk, write Robert M. W. Tsou, 28441 Cedarbluff Drive, Rancho Palos Verdes, California 90274.

HOW SOFTWARE CAN GIVE SALES FORCES A COMPETITIVE EDGE

Not surprisingly, computerization of sales reps is far behind that of accountants and journalists. Stereotypically—of course there are plenty of exceptions—the sales rep is less of a detail person than are most other laptop users. Often he or she hasn't a choice. The rep hasn't time to master a complex program. His or her boss wants sales *now*.

I don't envy the people who sell laptops or software to sales reps; if they mess up, their changes wreak havoc on a client's cash flow. "Other consultants play in the World Series," says an expert in sales software. "We play in the Super Bowl. When we automate a sales force, we've got one chance to do it right." Similar pressures beset information systems people who make recommendations in-house for equipment and programs; if they value their jobs, they will tread very cautiously.

How can sales reps and managers and others switch to laptops in a cautious way that ultimately can yield big results? They can use several strategies to minimize the risks. Companies and individuals who are computerizing should retain the old ways of doing things for as long as possible while phasing in the new ones.

Large firms should not discard the old ways until the laptops—and the equipment to tie them into the mainframe—are proving themselves. They should seriously consider hiring consultants with a good track record within their field, or at least one where the sales and cash flow situations are similar. And they should make certain that, within the limits of time, sales reps receive good training.

Small companies should think twice before computerizing their sales forces extensively without good professional advice. Certainly they should feel free to experiment. But they should make certain that safeguards are in place. Individual sales reps should not discard their old-fashioned tool, the address book—which is highly unlikely anyway, considering that reps hoard the names of prospects in anticipation of a job change. Whether you run the sales force of General Motors or are your own sales rep in a one-person business, it *is* healthy to be paranoid about technology.

This section will discuss:

■ How contact management software can be useful, even for one-person companies.

■ How small firms can process orders electronically—via laptops and modems and MCI Mail or an equivalent network. Bigger companies can use similar techniques to see if they'd be amenable to larger-scale use of the machines and software by sales reps. I'll discuss communications in a general way. Other chapters offer many more specifics about communications and the best ways to use laptops and modems in various locations. The present section is more on strategy than on specifics, which you may want to turn over to your data processing people or a consultant.

■ More ambitious use of laptops for sales automation, especially by large companies using highly customized programs.

■ Presentation graphics software. With it, sales organizations of all sizes can whip up catchy shows for clients—an especially tantalizing prospect now that laptop displays have improved and high resolution screens are becoming somewhat more affordable. As color laptops grow cheaper, presentation software should become a must for sales reps.

Contact Management Software

Except for some clerical help, Peter O'Connor runs his Laptop Exposition by himself, mailing out invitations to countless exhibitors and tens of thousands of others interested in his trade shows. O'Connor used to own a computer store, and therein lies part of the reason for his success today as a one-man sales force. Thanks to sales software called ACT! (Activity Control Technology is the full name), the names of old contacts from years ago survive on the disks of his laptops.

ACT! is the best-selling contact software on laptops, including those of more than five hundred sales reps at Zenith, NEC, Toshiba, and Epson. It speeds up the process of reaching people. You can automatically dial phone numbers; whip out letters, form letters, memos, and mailing labels; and compile electronic versions of file cabinets, address books, phone directories, and yellow stick-on pads. At a glance you can tell what's on your electronic calendar and see your to-do list.

Not surprisingly, then, O'Connor wanted his sales people at his laptop store to become faithful users of ACT! Whenever a rep dealt with a customer at the laptop shop, O'Connor insisted that the name go on disk. That way he could track their performance effortlessly and get a good feeling for the number of contacts they were making. What's more, reps might come and go, but the names would stay behind. O'Connor, after all, collected names regularly from the reps' disks, adding them to his master collection ("It's like backing up your computer. It's not good to go more than a week without backing up your sales information"). Only O'Connor enjoyed access to the master list. That way, if the reps defected to his competition, the only list they would be taking along was one of their own contacts.

Imagine the potential of such software for other people in sales of

all kinds. A sales rep could benefit from a database showing
(1) customers' wishes and (2) existing and forthcoming machines.
Then, say, when an 80486 laptop materialized, the rep could order the
software to print out a report identifying prospects. He or she also could
track other useful information. If ambitious enough, the rep even could
record customers' birthdays and be reminded about sending them
cards—not such a bad idea, considering the cost of cards compared to
the thousands of dollars that one sale could bring. ACT!, moreover,
could gather some of the information automatically. For instance, via
the electronic clock inside the rep's computer, it could tell the rep when
he or she last spoke to the prospect.

Obviously, too, contact software could reveal the subjects of prior
conversions, how many times the rep had called, how often the rep had
been able to reach the customer, and so on. It could even provide the
rep with form letters to match the needs of the moment—for instance,
cover letters to go out with product information or post-sale notes of
thanks. Ideally the program could do all of this by picking up notes,
address, and so on from information already entered, because if there's
one thing sales reps despise, it's typing.

Here's what others are doing with ACT!:[8]

■ Coulter Electronics, which makes blood-cell counters, is using
this type of software on about a hundred Zenith 286 laptops. "It's one
of the best territory management tools I have ever used," says one rep.

■ Connie Gato, an award-winning sales rep for the *Chicago Tribune*'s travel and tourism section, has used contact software to compile
profiles of clients and their needs and to remind herself of important
meetings and deadlines. She's found it especially useful for reminding
seasonal resorts—ski lodges, for instance—to place off-season ads.

■ Scott Henderson, a systems consultant with Entre Computer Center in North Dallas, has found contact management software to be a
lifesaver when dealing with large corporations that favor sales reps who
are familiar with their corporate jargon and culture. With this software,
Henderson effortlessly compiles customer profiles to look at during
phone conversations, or at meetings.

[8]Contact Software provided the case histories of ACT! in use.

ACT! sells for $395 from Contact Software, 9208 West Royal Lane, Irving, Texas 75063, (214) 929-4749.

Of course, ACT! isn't the only program handy for keeping track of clients, scheduling, and other tasks. You might also look at Agenda—also $395—from Lotus Development (55 Cambridge Parkway, Cambridge, Massachusetts 02142, [617] 577-8500). Agenda isn't as structured as ACT!, at least not as it comes off the shelf, so it may not be as fit for the typical sales rep. As its name implies, however, Agenda is wonderful for scheduling. For example, if you type October 13, Agenda will recognize "Oct. 13" or "two weeks after October 1." For technical-minded sales reps with plenty of hard disk space, another possibility would be IZE, which wasn't designed as a scheduler but could be good for tracking large numbers of clients and their needs. IZE—and let me acquaint you with a vested interest in the product, my book *IZE Examined* (Homewood, Illinois: Dow Jones Irwin, 1989)—sells for $445 from Persoft in Madison, Wisconsin ([608] 273-6000). Also consider AskSam, an unstructured database from AskSam Systems that, like IZE, lets you set up templates to simplify the entry of data. AskSam Systems's address is P.O. Box 1428, Perry, Florida 32347; the telephone number is 800-327-5726.

All of the products I've mentioned so far either require a hard disk or run more smoothly on one, at least if you're dealing with large quantities of information.

Sales reps with floppy-only laptops might also take a look at Primetime Personal, $99.99 from Primetime Software in Santa Ana, California (800-777-8860). The core program is less than 300K. You can even run it in a memory-resident mode—it takes up 124K that way—so it can pop up instantly when you want it. Primetime does have its limits. At least as of Primetime Version 1.23, if you are entering to-do items, the explanatory notes can contain no more than five lines. Rival products don't crimp you like that. Still, Primetime's thrifty use of disk space may make it worth the trade-offs.

How Small Firms Can Process Orders Electronically

You're the sales manager at a small manufacturing company. Your people travel all over the country. Unfortunately, wherever they go, they're drowning in paperwork. They sell a complicated product, and their customers don't like to have their orders mangled; nor do the customers want the goods to arrive late. Sales fluctuate widely. You hate it when the cash flow suffers, because during peaks the people in the home office can't keep up with the sudden rush of orders.

Ideally, to automate the entry of information from the reps, such as order forms and expense reports, here's what will happen next:

1. You talk the owner into hiring a software expert familiar with dBASE or another program whose format is fit for MCI Mail or an equivalent service. In MCI parlance, the electronic forms are "scripts." Jernay Freeman, the script coordinator for MCI Mail, says that consultants typically charge less than $500 for simple scripts. You can find such a consultant by calling MCI Mail at 800-825-6887 and requesting the script coordinator (MCI also can refer to you to local agents). Freeman, in turn, will pass on names. Please regard this as just a starting point; check out the consultant's references and see if he or she is capable of understanding your business and sales automation software.

Above all, the consultant should be able to grasp your business's mission—your company's five-year plan. Is your main goal to increase market share, sales, profits, or visibility in the marketplace, or is it to trim costs of sales? If your business is too complex, you may want to start in the other direction and see if a database expert in your industry is familiar with MCI Mail and communications in general. Or you might seek out a sales automation expert from the start. Your company, for instance, may be growing rapidly, and you may feel you'll soon need a mainframe or a minibased order entry system—or a connection with one.

2. Simultaneously, you sell the reps on the idea of automation. It means less paperwork for everyone and more time for befriending customers and getting to know their needs. This kind of automation won't dehumanize your employees, if you implement it right; it will make them less robotic. Make it clear to your employees that you'll think in the long term in monitoring their sales activities and will factor in things like illnesses and family emergencies.

"Sales people want to know if the new system will make them money," says an expert. "If you can confidently say yes, they'll accept the system better. Describe the benefits in detail. Not just more money but more sleep. They won't have to stay up all night messing with paperwork. And they'll get home to their families sooner."

If you feel comfortable doing so, you might want to consult with your employees in setting up the specifications for the system. What features do *they* want to make the system easy?

3. MCI Mail or a local MCI agent arranges for the appropriate MCI accounts, a procedure that can happen within a week and a half or so. The costs are low, too. An MCI Mail account costs just $25 a year. The script service is $25 a month beyond that (this allows up to ten scripts; additional ones are $2.50 each per month). Once you create a script, MCI Mail will charge you twenty-five cents a minute for your revising it on-line. MCI won't bill your company when your sales reps respond to script (it doesn't matter whether one employee or ten thousand employees log on during the month), but there is a $1 cost if a rep cancels an entry.

4. The consultant uses Lotus Express or a similar communications package that automates the log-on procedure for MCI Mail. You're not a computer whiz. And you're not trying to turn your sales reps into experts, either. With just a keystroke or two your people will be able to log on with their laptops. The consultant, moreover, can prepare a brief letter that sales reps can show the hotels they stay at regularly. The letter describes the rep's modest technical needs; they simply require a traditional RJ-11-style jack into which they can plug the modems with which the computers can communicate through the phone lines. Of course, the consultant also writes step-by-step instructions for the reps.

5. With the automated entry system in place, the sales rep logs on MCI Mail and fills out the appropriate form; it can be for an order or for an expense report. MCI leads the reps through a series of prompts requesting specific information. The rep responds. The script can ask for part numbers, number of units, and so on. The consultant can set up the script to reduce the occurrence of mistakes. When the rep is entering parts numbers, for instance, the system can require a minimum number of digits.

6. Your headquarters office can work with the information directly. Or, if the system is elaborate enough, it can have the facts electronically screened by a computer to make sure that all of the ordered items are in stock. Via human or computer, the home office can trigger a message back to the rep's account that the order has been processed.

Again, let me emphasize the need for companies—especially small firms—*not* to automate sales forces without making certain that the appropriate backups are in place. And for the nth time, keep remembering that your goal is to boost sales, not turn reps into software geniuses or clerks. You'll enjoy a far better chance of success if you grasp the differences between sales reps and more sophisticated computer users.

Sales Force Automation at Larger Firms

Bigger companies might experiment with a modest system for order entries, such as the one above. After they successfully try it on a limited number of sales reps, then they can call in a sales automation expert to install powerful, highly customized software. Ideally such an expert will have an MBA; if nothing else, he or she should be able to grasp your company's mission. Among other things, the automation may include these features:

■ The ability to dial up the home office's computer directly for an update of the latest information on product price and availability. The dial-ups can happen from the hotel at night, when phone rates are low. While a rep is asleep, the home office computer can update the contents of the hard disk of his or her laptop.

■ The automatic transfer of orders that the sales rep keyed into the computer earlier that day—while he or she was face to face with a customer. Since the hard disk is updated nightly, the rep can verify almost instantly that an item is in stock. The software also may issue a warning if the customer is ordering the wrong deal, promo, or quantity (you wouldn't want to promise the customer thirty-six units if an item only comes in boxes of forty-eight). All this can happen in front of the customer. Imagine the psychological boosts to both the rep and the customer. The customer knows that almost surely the goods are on the way.

If inventory has declined to the point where the delivery could be late, the sales rep can warn the customer on the spot. (Or first thing the next morning, after the laptop has received the latest facts on inventory availability and pricing.)

Please note that before a rep is absolutely confident with a laptop, he or she can make entries before and after sales calls rather than appearing nervous in front of customers. On-the-spot entries may not occur for four to six months, but in the meantime, the computerization is well worth it.

■ The tracking of already ordered goods by invoice number or otherwise. Customers can find out instantly if and when your company has shipped the order, the identity of the carrier, and (perhaps) the identification number that the carrier has assigned the shipment.

■ Monitoring of the customer's inventory. Your own sales reps can be responsible for helping to replenish it. Bar code readers can be used to check the quantities of goods in the store; the readers can be hooked up directly to laptops to produce these replenishment orders. Imagine the reduction of pencil and paperwork by sales reps, their companies, and their customers.

■ Instant recall of credit histories and other information that the reps use to assure almost-instant confirmation of orders. If there is some problem with a customer, the sales rep can help work out a solution on the spot.

■ Three- to five-year historical trend analysis—for instance, the sales that your company has made to an account over the years, or what your firm's market share is in a product area, even using SKU numbers if you want.[9] "What this does," says an expert in sales software, "is increase the reps' credibility with customers. This is the ultimate in customer service. You could show how your products have moved compared to your rivals'—using data from Nielsen, SAMI, Polk, and similar data sources."

■ The ability to monitor step by step the progress of individual reps and help spot patterns—such as whether they are strong or weak in certain product areas.

■ Other forms of analysis, or forecasting, both for management and for individual reps.

■ A word processor and software for sending conventional electronic mail, as opposed to forms.

■ Connectivity. Ideally, the hardware and software will adapt to future corporate hardware and software, meaning that the information systems people should make the sales automation experts aware of their own five-year plans.

---

[9] SKU numbers are stock control (yes, with a K) units. They're equivalent to the publishing industry's ISBN numbers.

■ The ability for reps to insert oft-used names and other common entries into forms just by making choices with single letters or numbers or by using cursor arrows and pressing Return. Or your company might eventually experiment with the new laptops from GriD and other models that rely on handwriting rather than typing.

Think of the manifold advantages. Of course, the benefits from the system can vary greatly according to your industry; for instance, rather than worrying about counting hundreds of cans of soup on a grocery shelf, a pharmaceutical sales rep can be compiling a call report containing a list of the topics discussed with a doctor. The pharmaceutical firm Upjohn, by the way, uses its sales automation system to help coordinate sales calls to doctors and other customers. What better way to mitigate the age-old problem of repetitive calls from different reps?

If you shop carefully, you probably can outfit the typical rep for less than five thousand dollars. That will include hardware and software. Minimum hard disk size is 40 megabytes, and you may want a 286 machine to speed up the running of the software. Very likely you'll work with a consultant with close ties to GRiD or another major laptop company. That way the consultant can better integrate the hardware and software. The only other cost, beyond hardware and software, will be phone charges of two minutes per rep each night.

There is more than one way of automating. Rather than owning the equipment, you can rent it—or rent computer time to have sales orders processed or information dispersed to your reps. Then you may enjoy some tax advantages and reduce the chance of the equipment becoming obsolete. Of course, an old high-tech adage applies: as long as equipment works and is doing the job you expect of it, then it isn't truly obsolete. In the majority of cases, probably the most cost-effective way is to buy the laptops yourself and hire an appropriate consultant or other software expert.

With the right computer advice, you may enjoy a return on investment in as little as a few months. More commonly the payback will require one or two years, according to Bob Jurik, vice president of sales for Modatek, a company specializing in sales software for consumer package goods, apparel, and publishing. Among users of the MS-DOS–based systems from Modatek are Kayser Roth Hosiery, Londontown, and Jantzen USA. Modatek is at 50 Charles Lindberg Boulevard, Suite 400, Uniondale, New York 11553 ([516] 229-2336).

Three other major companies in customized sales software are Dynatec Systems (1113 South Milwaukee Avenue, Libertyville, Illinois 60048, [312] 816-5000), a generalist serving many industries; Sales Technologies (3399 Peachtree Road, Atlanta, Georgia 30326, [404] 841-4000), a specialist in large sales forces, especially in consumer goods, oil, petrochemicals, and pharmaceuticals; and Dendrite International (7 Powder Horn Drive, Warren, New Jersey 07060, [201] 271-8383), whose sales software is for reps in pharmaceuticals and related areas, consumer products, and beauty and health aids.

Presentation Graphics

You and your rivals are vying for the goodwill and money of a mass buyer with a Pentagon-size budget. Companies X, Y, and Z bring the usual boring flip charts, but you've got a surprise to set your firm apart—presentation graphics. Now the buyer can see multicolored charts showing your product's glories.

She enjoys the show. You do too. In fact, you win the $10-million contract. It's worth, of course, far more than the laptop and the graphics equipment. All along you knew that computer graphics weren't just for IBM or nerds with glasses held together with Scotch tape.

Granted, if you want to run graphics on a laptop, it may be a hard row. Your usual LCD screens may not be sharp enough or big enough, or the viewing angle might not suffice even for an audience of two. What's more, you'd hate to use the gaudy glow of a gas plasma screen—so reminiscent of a neon sign—to show off your upscale product. No, you won't settle for anything less than full color—or at least a large black-and-white screen.

And yet you know that:

■ Most affordable laptops with LCD screens are monochrome.

■ To enjoy EGA- or VGA-quality color, in many cases you'll have to hook up an EGA or VGA video card—assuming that one will work with your laptop in the first place. Chances are that you'll also need an external monitor for color.

■ Large-screen monitors are expensive. At the same time, you don't want your buyers to squint or jam uncomfortably around the display.

What can you do within these parameters? Here are six possible solutions.

Solution 1. Buy a film recorder, with which you shoot color slides off the high-resolution screen of a desktop computer. This isn't a laptop solution, but honor requires that I mention it. You can load the slides in a carousel and easily change the order in which you show them; what's more, very likely you can use the client's projector. A film recorder can be pricey; you may have to pay several thousand dollars. But the image quality will excel. A film recorder has a tiny CRT screen built into it. In the newer, better, digital film recorders, the information reaches this CRT, pixel by pixel, and is digitized on the screen. Then a "camera" photographs it through filters: red, green, and blue.

The Polaroid Palette Plus, the cheapest film recorder as of this writing, sells for $2,999—most of the cost of a color laptop! It's based on older analog technology and doesn't offer as high a resolution as its pricier cousins. Polaroid is at 549 Technology Square, Cambridge, Massachusetts 02139, telephone 800-225-1618 or 617-577-2000.

Of course, you and your colleagues can share the Palette or a bigger, more expensive model. For information on deluxe recorders, contact the Matrix Corporation (One Ramland Road, Orangeburg, New York 10962, telephone 914-365-0190). Matrix offers the widest selection of recorders.

Solution 2. Use a program like Freelance Plus on your laptop, then hire a service bureau to prepare slides (more on software in a moment). My friend Robin Raskin, a top graphics expert in New York City and a senior editor for *PC Magazine*,[10] says that the image quality can be good to excellent. The cost is often $10 or more a slide, but at least you don't have to invest in a film recorder.

Service bureaus offer overnight, and sometimes even same-day, turn-around, but often you can save money by allowing a bureau several days to do the job. "Locating service bureaus is a bit of an art," Raskin says. "If you look up *Service Bureau* in the yellow pages you'll come to a dead end. The best thing to do is to call your software vendor and ask which service bureaus it supports. The vendor will at least know the national bureaus, but if it's been doing its homework, it should also know about mom-and-pop shops."

---

[10] I'm grateful to Robin Raskin, who spent many, many hours giving me insights for this section via MCI Mail. In some cases, outside of the quotes I have attributed to her, I've changed her language only slightly.

The national bureaus are typically linked to the graphics product. For example, Freelance Plus—from Lotus Development Corporation —works well with both MagiCorp service (800-FORMAGI or [914] 592-1244) and the Autographix service (800-548-8558 or [617] 890-8558).[11] When you sign up for a national service bureau, it provides a special software driver and also the software you need to send your images via modem or disk to the bureau.

Good bureaus can be astoundingly nimble with Freelance and similar programs; what you get out will actually be better than what you sent in. Autographix, for instance, can replace the usual on-screen Freelance fonts with its own super-high-resolution fonts. Moreover, Autographix can let you drop in an exciting special effects background. MagicCorp offers special tricks too.

A mom-and-pop bureau may not be so closely aligned with the vendor or have the resources to develop neat special effects. Still, perhaps there is one just a few miles from your office. If so, you may be very lucky.

Mom and Pop and the rest might fuss over you—in a nice way— much more than some out-of-town services would. While Barbara expertly critiques your presentations, Peter helps you line up a good artist to give your work more polish. Juan bends a little when you're in a crunch and need your work done yesterday. What's more, you find that Barbara, Peter, and Juan go to the same photography production house that you've already hired for other purposes.

Solution 3. Use overhead transparencies from plotters or printers. It's easy to arrange the slides in the order you want them. And you probably can use the client's own overhead projector if you don't want to buy your own. For $600 you can buy a Ricoh MP30, billed as the world's tiniest overhead projector (it folds to nine inches wide by ten inches deep by 1.9 inches tall). Ricoh is at 1555 Passaic Avenue, Fairfield, New Jersey 07006, telephone 201-882-2000.

The downside of overheads is that rather than employing a plotter, you may want laser printing to assure good image quality, and laser printing for most people means just black and white. There are, of

---

[11] MagiCorp also has a relationship with Ashton-Tate, among others (check out Ashton-Tate's Applause II graphics package, a possible alternative to Harvard and Freelance Plus). Autographix has a relationship with the publishers of Harvard Graphics and additional companies.

course, other methods. Whether it's a laser printer, plotter, or inkjet, Hewlett-Packard is associated with good quality and reliability. Every graphics package drives the Hewlett-Packard devices. A good bet for nice overhead slides is a new Hewlett-Packard PaintJet XL. It's an inkjet color printer that has a special mode for creating transparencies without either the smears or light colorings that inkjets used to cause.

Solution 4. Get an LCD panel and use it with an overhead projector. Such panels may list from around $800 to $5,000, and even with the more expensive models the image quality is only fair. Raskin says that most reasonably priced panels are monochrome, so "you won't enjoy the vividness of good color images." LCDs have been rugged, durable, and easy to cart around; they're top-notch for software demos. You could buy only monochrome LCDs at first, but the latest crop of LCDs is offering glorious color. The Kodak DataShow is one of the most reliable monochrome LCDs. Prices of monochrome models have been dropping dramatically; in two months, for instance, the discounted price on the entry-level DataShow went from $899 to $499.

Kodak's address is: Kodak Company, Sayett Technology Division, 100 Kings Highway, Rochester, New York 14617; the telephone number, (716) 342-0700.

For a color LCD panel you might consider the 480C PC Viewer or its possible successors; the vendor is Focus Systems (7649 Mohawk Street, Tualatin, Oregon 97062, 800-327-7231 or [503] 692-4968). The 480C works with CGA, EGA, or VGA boards. As of this writing it offers what *PC Magazine* has called "the only true color LCD panel on the market." The eight colors, moreover, are "stunning," and "a clear image provides great contrast."

Solution 5. Set up a data projector. Data projectors hook into the back of your computer and use three beams of light—red, green, and blue—to project the image from the computer onto a large screen. They can be used in very large rooms and they have vivid color. The big names here are Barco and Electrohome, which is Canadian. Barco is at 1500 Wilson Way, Smyrna, Georgia 30082, telephone 404-432-2346. Electrohome can be found at 809 Wellington Street North, Kitchener, Ontario, Canada N2G 4J6; their telephone is 800-265-2171.

Typically a data projector costs more than $10,000. And you must install it in one place, unless your company enjoys the wherewithal to hire a technician to make the machinery feel at home. If you move the projector, get set for trouble. You might jar the red, green, or blue beam out of alignment, causing convergence problems; electron beams for the three colors might wander from the same, precise, locations that they must hit for the view to be first rate.

However finicky, data projectors are the Rolls-Royces of presentation technology and a must for important presentations. Just give your techie a lot of time to align the projector well before the CEO walks in for the show.

"What?" you're asking. "Why mention a bulky projector in a book on laptops?"

Answer: "Who says the projector has to be moved? Why not have it available at headquarters for laptop owners to use when the occasion requires? Even the most inveterate of electronic travelers may want to impress clients in a home-office auditorium." So if someone hopes to include a $10,000 data projector in your corporate budget, don't blanch.

Solution 6. Use your own CRT monitor or your prospect's. Of course, some complications may arise. Your laptop may run just CGA.

Then again—please check with your laptop's manufacturer—you may be able to buy an EGA or VGA card and use it with a card holder such as a Won Under.

If you bring your own color monitor, you'd better also buy something else: a little truck to wheel it around in. After all, if you don't want your audience to squint or have to crowd around the screen, you'll probably need a CRT monitor with a thirty-five- to thirty-seven-inch screen.

Luckily you can rent monster monitors in advance from audio-visual rental companies, which can also supply cards. Such monitors, unlike some data projectors, shouldn't make you suffer fuzzy pictures or out-of-kilter dots representing red, green, and blue. Mitsubishi, at the top of this heap, is renowned for its thirty-seven-inch monitors, which alas, as of this writing, cost more than ten thousand dollars each. Mitsubishi is at 999 Knox Street, Torrance, California 90502, telephone 800-556-1234. Sony also makes a very popular line of sixteen- to nineteen-inch monitors. Sony Customer Information is at Sony Drive, Park Ridge, New Jersey 07656, telephone 201-930-7669.

In choosing your displays, consider the size of the audience; even a thirty-seven-inch Mitsubishi monitor is only good for up to twenty people. Overheads and LCD displays are good for rooms with no more than fifty to seventy-five people. A bigger audience requires the use of either a slide projector or a data projector that works with a full-size screen.

Whatever monitor you use, place it carefully within the audience's view. Don't scatter several monitors around the room. "This can be very disconcerting," says Raskin.

So much for the display. How about the graphics software that you'll use to create images for the screen? You have two choices:

1. Buy a small program that fits on your laptop—something for the traveler.

2. Get a "run-time" version of a larger graphics program. Then you won't need the entire six-hundred-pound gorilla with you to play back your presentation. You can boot up the run-time module on your laptop. To oversimplify grossly, it's like showing home movies of the gorilla rather than having him there. You won't have to squander your laptop's hard disk space—or your client's.

"SML Services' Present," Raskin says, "is a good example of a small, unknown program, built to travel. It's easy to use and compact, but it does the things you need to create a presentation. Present captures images from the screen and strings them together with a few transitional movements in between. Say you're using five different software packages back at your office. To create a presentation you simply put the creation you want up on your screen and use a program like Present to capture the image.

"Present is perfect for traveling and giving demos where you might have to show a spreadsheet, a bulleted list of items, and maybe even a software package's interface. It just picks up the images from the other programs. And it lets you organize them into the electronic equivalent of a slide show. You can put the images on the screen, you can color them, you can write in transitions. It's a good, quick, dirty package.

"It doesn't do presentations as fancy as other packages, but it's easy to use. You could take one screen from your Lotus 1-2-3 spreadsheet, one screen from your drawing program, and one screen from your outliner and integrate them into a presentation."

Present sells for $80 from SML Services, 6095 River Chase Circle,

Atlanta, Georgia 30328, (404) 953-0792. It needs as little as 128K of RAM, one disk drive, and a CGA video adapter—all present on most inexpensive laptops. Do check with SML, however, about Present's screen color combinations to make sure they'll be compatible if your laptop has an LCD screen instead of an auxiliary monitor. SML seems eager to help users get the system going on their machines.

Despite the many virtues of the small, SML-style programs, and they lack the flexibility and power of their bigger cousins. Among the programs in the King Kong category, Harvard Graphics stands out. In market share it *is* Kong. Also popular is the similarly talented Freelance Plus, discussed earlier (see page 117).

Harvard offers full charting capabilities, drawing tools, and output to all sorts of printers, plotters, and other output devices. It sells for $495 and is easy to use once you get the hang of it. "You can create all your images with this program and animate them and create transitional effects," Raskin says. "You can bring in data directly from a spreadsheet like 1-2-3 or from an ASCII file, and have the data transformed into a business chart in a matter of moments. Harvard and Freelance both let you do things like decide whether to display the data as a bar or pie. Or whether to explode a slice of the pie, or create a 3-D effect with the bars. Or how to adjust the axis data scaling and other controls.

"In addition to the charting component," Raskin says, "there's a drawing component. These aren't as robust as drawing tools in full-featured drawing programs like Micrografx Designer, but they provide the basic drawing features to create attractive diagrams, word charts, and even some distinctive clip art. You can draw circles, squares, polygons, and even simple curves.

"Best of all, both of the programs come with canned, ready-to-use art called clip art. This makes nonartists look good. Clip art for both of these packages is also available from third-party sources. A typical piece of clip art for a business presentation might be a man at his desk, or a map of the world."

Both Harvard and Freelance also have built-in screen shows. You can chain images together and specify the duration and the transitional effects—fades, wipes, or pans—between images.

Both packages, of course, need plenty of hard disk space. You won't want to take them on the road with you or depend on them being installed on a customer's machine.

Mercifully, however, Harvard and Freelance let you create run-time versions. An optional Screenshow module works with Harvard; such features are already in Freelance. Basically you ''write'' images to a self-booting playback disk, so the machine you show them on doesn't have to be running Harvard Graphics or Freelance.

Harvard is available from Software Publishing Corporation.

Raskin also recommends three add-on programs for laptop users trying to jazz up the display of data:

1. Graph-in-the-Box, from New England Software, Greenwich Office Park, Suite 3, Greenwich, Connecticut 06831, (203) 625-0062. ''It's useful for converting spreadsheet output or text to display as charts on the screen.''

2. QuickGraphs, $99 from Sumak Industries, 39 Dawson Street, Sudbury, Massachusetts 01776, telephone 508-443-0205. ''It's making a splash. It does quick data charting but has no screen show.''

3. PFS: First Graphics, $149 from Software Publishing. It is a scaled-down version of Harvard that does charting but not drawing.

''If you display *only* data,'' Raskin says, ''then any of these three should be suitable.''

Fans of WordPerfect might take a look at yet another program, DrawPerfect ($495). WordPerfect Corporation says DrawPerfect offers ''a full set of graphing features, including pie, bar, line,'' and others; twenty-five built-in fonts; drawing tools; slide show features; a figure library with ''500 ready-to-use clip art images''; the ability to swap graphics and text between it and WordPerfect; compatible printer and display drives; and many similar commands. Critics of WordPerfect will regard this last feature—the commands—as an ungainly burden rather than a help. Just the same, if you're a WordPerfect loyalist, DrawPerfect may make you very happy.

ACCOUNTING

From the early days of laptops on, word processing has been far ahead of spreadsheeting as an application. Random-access memories were miniscule. Floppy disks were nonexistent. Imagine running a sophisticated spreadsheet on the first Tandy 100, or using it for a database in a major audit.

Times certainly have changed. Word processing is still the main application, but laptops can handle spreadsheets much more gracefully than before.

The laptop with which I'm writing this chapter runs at 12 megahertz, compared to the 6 megahertz of IBM's original AT, the machine that some people thought would be too powerful for individual users. It can handle spreadsheet files with thousands of cells.

By far the favorite spreadsheet program among accountants is Lotus 1-2-3 (which dominates accounting much more thoroughly than WordPerfect dominates word processing). Most show little willingness to change. So in this section I won't compare one spreadsheet to another in detail. Instead I'll briefly list some other software useful to accountants, including 1-2-3 add-ons. In the second part of the accounting section you'll learn about programs that three giants of the accounting business—Deloitte & Touche, Ernst & Young, and Coopers & Lybrand—are running on portables.

If many of these programs don't seem laptop-specific, well, there's a reason. Generally, though not always, accountants insist on laptops that are just as powerful or maybe more powerful than the typical desktop.

A Software Sampler for Accountants

For much of this software sampler I turned to Doug Hummer. He is accounting chairman of the Capital PC User Group; a computer consultant in Arlington, Virginia, who specializes in accounting systems; and an alumnus of a medium-size accounting firm in Washington, D.C. Below are some favorites of Hummer and his clients, followed by a separate list of some Lotus 1-2-3 add-ons that may be of interest to accountants and auditors.

■ Lotus Agenda, the same program that I've suggested for sales reps who are more comfortable with software than most. Agenda can prove a challenge even for accountants to learn. "But," says Hummer, "it's a good way for accounting firms to manage people and projects. You can have columns for time and clients and staff. It will let you know which staffers will be working for which clients at 3 p.m. on Tuesday. And it can make cross-references automatically. If you have a phone call coming in and the client suggests a meeting at a certain time, Agenda is a quick way of making sure that your calendar is clear. It can give people a to-do list. And have-done lists.''

On the less-positive side, Agenda is a memory hog; don't count on using it as a pop-up program, which you can trigger with just a quick keystroke. Agenda requires DOS 2.0 or higher and 512K of RAM. The program costs $395 from Lotus Development Corporation, 55 Cambridge Parkway, Cambridge, Massachusetts 02142, (617) 557-8500.

■ Calendar Creator Plus. It lets you present your staffers with calendars showing their schedules—for a whole year, if you want. Your computer also can spew out a master calendar consolidating the schedules of all your staffers. Here's one more way to keep up with the birthdays of family, friends, employees, and clients. Requires 320K RAM. Cost is $59.95 from Power Up Software, P.O. Box 7600, San Mateo, California 94403, 800-851-2917.

■ TimeSlips. "It's well recognized," Hummer says, "as a leader in its field. It can be a pop-up program with a stopwatch on it. If a client calls up, you set the clock running and you can bill by the minute. It's good for a partner whose time is spread out." The partner can capture a lot of time that he or she may miss without TimeSlips. TimeSlips can work with ASCII and dBASE formats—one way to save retyping. And via an auxiliary program it can transfer accounts receivable information to off-the-shelf accounting packages, such as DAC Easy. With TimeSlips you can create a list of clients and use letters or numbers to pick the proper one to bill after the phone rings. You can even use your cursor to "point and shoot" at the appropriate target. TimeSlips requires 448K and a hard drive. It costs $299 from North Edge Software, 239 Western Avenue, Essex, Massachusetts 01929, (508) 768-6100. For $79.95 TimeSlips also sells a product called Remote, which includes a timer and ways to compile and track schedule-related information. Remote uses 80K of RAM, needs 256K of disk space, and requires DOS 2.1 or higher.

■ DAC Easy–Light. Hummer recommends it to clients with small businesses; the product covers accounts payable, accounts receivable, payroll, and general ledger and can export information to ASCII or dBASE formats. Hummer says it's powerful enough and far easier to use than DAC Easy. "I have had *much* trouble with this program and do *not* recommend it," the owner of a small importing business said in a message on CompuServe. But DAC Easy–Light is different. "If you can't get DAC Easy–Light up in two or three hours," Hummer says, "you're in the minority." He also recommends an up-and-coming product called Quicken, another small-business accounting package that, sure enough, also is finding fans among the CompuServe crowd ("The New Quicken 3 is great"). Don't completely give up on DAC Easy, though. If possible, check with a friend who owns DAC Easy 4.0 or above. DAC Easy–Light costs $70 from DAC Software, 17950 Preston Road, Suite 800, Dallas, Texas 75252, (214) 248-0205. Requirements are DOS 2.0 and 256K.

■ Quicken. Requires 320K and DOS 2.0 or higher. The price is $59.95 from Intuit, 540 University Avenue, Palo Alto, California 94301, 800-624-8742.

■ Turbo Tax. "It's the number-one tax package in my evaluation," Hummer says. "Turbo Tax can give you the complete federal tax forms as well as schedules for the bigger states." Turbo requires a hard disk. Regardless, it's a terrific laptop possibility; you can work out a preliminary version of your client's returns at your office, then bring your hard disk portable to the client's home or office and fine-tune your earlier work. Turbo Tax, by the way, works well with Quicken. The simplest version of Turbo Tax costs $75 (the most elaborate costs $395) from ChipSoft, 5045 Shoreham Place, Suite 100, San Diego, California 92122, (619) 453-8722. DOS 2.0 and 256K or 512K (depending on your version).

■ Sideways. This 1-2-3 add-on lets you print spreadsheets sideways—just the ticket for your portable printer, which can make its letters only so tiny. Why let the width of your paper limit you to just a small number of columns? Requires DOS 2.0 or above and 156K of RAM. Sideways costs $70 from Funk Software, 222 Third Street, Cambridge, Massachusetts 02142, (617) 497-6339.

To Hummer's list I'll add another—a list of Lotus 1-2-3 add-ons. Check with the publishers of these programs to make certain that the software described below will be compatible with your computer and the version of 1-2-3 that you use. Also ask about availability. Please note that the information comes from the *Lotus Products Enhancement Guide*—the 1989 rather than the 1990 edition, which appeared too late for me to quote here. The guide is a directory of add-ons, templates, and other software compatible with Lotus products. Lotus compiles the guide based on rapidly changing information from the individual software vendors. You might want to contact Lotus for your own, updated copy. Call Lotus at (617) 623-5680 and ask for the *Lotus Products Enhancement Guide*, part number 121141. The guide is now free.

■ 3-2-1 Blastoff. This spreadsheet quickens worksheet recalculations by two to ten times, according to the Lotus guide, "and provides security for proprietary formulas. Compiles worksheets into fast machine code which loads with your original worksheet into 1-2-3. Uses all 1-2-3 features—macros, graphs, data tables—even changes formulas in previously compiled cells. Standard edition gives 2–3 times speedup on all systems. Premium edition optionally uses math co-processor for 5–10 times speedup and takes advantage of 386 if present." 3-2-1 Blastoff needs 48K of RAM and will work with DOS 2.0 and above. The standard edition costs $99.95 and the premium one sells for $149.95 from Frontline Systems, 140 University Avenue, Suite 100, Palo Alto, California 94301, (415) 327-7297.

■ ABC Audit. Automated workpaper software. The guide describes it as good for "audits, reviews and preparation of corporate and partnership tax returns; account summaries and trial balances for tax returns; bank credit ratio monitoring; consolidation (up to 25 entries)." Cost is $495 from Hemming Moore, CPAs, 160 Bovet Road, San Mateo, California 94402, (415) 574-1908.

■ ABC Quick Statement. "An innovative client write-up package that can be used by accountants, bookkeepers, or anyone to summarize a client's 'shoebox' of cash receipts and disbursements, prepare financial statements monthly, quarterly, or yearly, maintain small business accounting records. Worksheets are fully integrated and menu-driven." 1-2-3 template needs 512K of RAM and DOS 2.0 or later. Cost is $195 from Hemming Moore (see item above).

■ Accelerate! This program speeds up cursor movement. "Increase the relative speed for the keyboard about three times," says the Lotus guide. Needs 11K of RAM and DOS 2.0 or later. Price: $19.95 from Spreadsheet Solutions, 111 Beach Road, Kings Point, New York 11024, 800-634-8509 or (516) 487-1424. See also the listing for Cruise Control on page 128.

You might also want to consider BBS-distributed programs such as Hotkey, described on page 103, or KBFIX2. I've just learned of the latter program. A KBFIX2 fan tells me it takes up just "2,560 bytes of RAM. The user can set the cursor speed, keyboard repeat tripoff delay, repeat rate, straighten out the abominable IBM CapsLock mess, and more. Haven't found a program or MS-DOS machine that it won't work with."

■ Accounts Payable. The Lotus guide says it can "efficiently" handle three thousand vendors "with complete vendor history. Handles purchases on accounts, check payments, and credit memos. Retains history of invoices, payments and adjustments. Provides the necessary information for preparing most 1099s. Includes on-line help, look-up windows for easy data entry edit, and tutorial." Files are compatible with 1-2-3. Needs 512K of RAM, DOS 3.1 or later, and the Report Maker Plus program. Cost is $795 from Great Plains Software, 1701 Thirty-eighth Street S.W., Fargo, North Dakota 58103, (701) 281-0550. In the past, Accounts Payable and similarly sophisticated programs would have worked only on desktop machines. Now, however, an accountant might encourage his or her clients to buy a hard disk laptop—backed up with a tape drive, ideally—that clients or their employees could take home at night to keep the books up to date. Think of the benefit to sophisticated people who prefer to spend evenings with their families, even if the work follows them.

■ APS Fixed Assets. "Complete fixed asset accounting system with schedules for property additions, asset values, depreciation, and a property plant and equipment summary. Includes all significant conventional and tax depreciation methods including TRA '86 modified ACRS. Computes and tracks depreciation for book, federal/state tax, and Alternative Minimum Tax purposes. Handles luxury car limitations and Section 179 deductions. Provides supporting schedules for IRS forms 4562, 4255, and 4797. Totally integrated and menu-driven with a user's manual and on-line help." 1-2-3 template needs 640K of RAM and DOS later than 2.0. Price: $195 from Professional Services Microsystems, 360 Seventeenth Street, Suite 1350, Denver, Colorado 80202, (303) 825-0461.

■ Check Writing Manager. "Easy to use, fully menu-driven program prints checks, reconciles accounts, tracks income and expenses. Can print checks from user-defined list of payees. Creates paychecks and employees' payroll records. Handles checks, deposits, bank service charges, and expenses. Can print checks from a user-defined list of payees. Creates paychecks and employees' payroll records, handles checks, deposits, bank service charges and cash disbursements. Provides reports and totals by category. Expense category list is defined by the user. Check printing can be bypassed when desired. Provides facility to customize printout formula to fit exact layout of check form. Prints checks individually or in batch mode. Option to transfer entries to separate 1-2-3 file for individual analysis. Template for 1-2-3 requires 512K of RAM and DOS 2.0 or above.'' Cost is $49 from RD Software, 18 Briarcliff Avenue, Poughkeepsie, New York 12603, (914) 462-1879.

■ CPA Tickler. "A Due Date Monitoring System for any office, not just CPAs. Designed to track upcoming events such as tax returns, extensions, meetings, project deadlines, estimated tax payments, note payments, report filing dates, contract expirations, etc. Organize by user-definable categories such as person, office, location, department, client, etc." Four different reports, index and Rolodex cards. Print or view using any criteria. Sort in any order. Menu-driven. Template for 1-2-3 requires 256K of RAM and DOS 2.0 or later. Price: $89 from Front Row Systems, 3158 Maple Drive, Suite 44, Atlanta, Georgia 30305, (404) 231-0349.

■ Cruise Control. This is a more sophisticated cursor control program than Accelerate. "The anti-skid braking," says the Lotus guide, "allows you to stop the cursor on a dime. The Cruise Control feature allows you to repeat any key, hands free." Check out the possibility of using Cruise Control with your word processor. Needs 3K of RAM and DOS 2.0 or later. Price: $59.95 from Revolution Software, 4 Century Drive, Parsippany, New Jersey 07054, (201) 455-0995.

■ General Ledger. "Retains financial detail for a full fiscal year. Prints comparative financial statements at any time. Handles 2,000 accounts, 36 locations, and 999 departments efficiently. Provides a flexible year-end close and up to 13 accounting periods. Handles recurring batch transactions. Includes a sample Chart of Accounts. Provides on-line help, look-up windows for easy data entry/edit, and tutorial. File compatible for 1-2-3. Requires 512K of RAM, DOS 3.1 or later, and the program Report Maker Plus." Cost is $795 from Great Plains Software, 1701 Thirty-eighth Street S.W., Fargo, North Dakota 58103, (701) 281-0550.

■ Inventory. "Accommodates 6,000 inventory items efficiently, with part numbers of up to 15 characters. Offers 'component maintenance' for tracking light production/assembly work. Handles 36 locations per inventory item with individual 'bin locations.' " File compatible for 1-2-3. Needs 512K of RAM, DOS 3.1 or above, and the Report Maker Plus program. Cost is $795 from Great Plains.

■ Payroll. "Handles 'after-the-fact' payroll. Allows a breakdown of payroll expenses by department, with customer defined departments and job descriptions. Efficiently handles 250 employees, with an unlimited number of deductions and pay types per employee." Cost is $795 from Great Plains.

■ Payroll Administration. "Contains all salaries from both exempt and non-exempt employees. Allows accounting to analyze the effects of changing the percentage between steps within a grade, the percentage between grades, or the maximums for one or more grades." Template for 1-2-3 needs 256K of RAM and DOS 2.0 or after. Cost is $150 from Conhigh, 1429 Colonial Boulevard, Suite 103, Fort Myers, Florida 33907, (813) 939-7690.

■ Purchase Order. "Provides four different types of purchase orders: regular, drop ship, recurring, and blanker. Allows non-inventoried items to be ordered. Formats can be customized, and partial shipments or shipments to be received with an invoice can be entered. Prints Back Order Status, Back Ordered Items Received, Purchase Order Analysis, and projected flow reports." File compatible for 1-2-3. Needs 512K of RAM and DOS 3.1 or later. Cost is $795 from Great Plains.

■ Ready-to-Run Accounting. "Transforms 1-2-3 into a powerful, flexible, and professional accounting system. Includes six modules that can integrate or stand alone. Modules include General Ledger, Accounts Payable, Accounts Receivable, Payroll, Inventory/Order-Entry, and Financial Analyst. Each module is full-featured and prints a full range of financial reports. Instant graphic analysis built into each module. Audit trails are maintained on all transactions for an entire year." Template for 1-2-3 needs 384K of RAM and DOS 2.0 or after. Complete system costs $199.95 and the executive version with financial analysis sells for $299.95 from Manusoft, 1050 East Walnut Street, Pasadena, California 91106, (818) 304-2762.

Software of the Giants: Accounting and Auditing Programs at Major CPA Firms

Quick! What kind of software do laptop users with major accounting firms run most of the time? Lotus 1-2-3, right? Only partly. First off, although Lotus 1-2-3 is enough of an industry standard for me to justify my section on 1-2-3 add-ons, SuperCalc is alive and well among some top CPAs. Second, word processors and other programs at times rival spreadsheets in the extent of use, at least in the consulting sections of the large accounting firms. Accountants do not live by numbers alone. Nor are they all resistant to innovation.

Oh, computerphobia lingers in some quarters, but in many respects the big accounting firms are blazing the way for other businesses. Deloitte & Touche, for example, has developed an audit system that is comprehensive and integrated, blending everything from spreadsheeting to workpapers (complete with electronic versions of tickmarks to indicate the completion of various stages of a job).

Coopers & Lybrand uses scanners and sophisticated optical character recognition software to read clients' documents.

Ernst & Young packs some forty programs onto the hard disks of portable computers and uses software for three-dimensional graphics and flow chart creation—hardly amazing in the computer world, but light years ahead of the typical American company.

Billing clients as much as several hundred dollars an hour, the big accounting firms leap at the chance to try out new programs, even if the productivity gains are minor. Because of the importance of familiarizing employees with software, some managers at the big firms are encouraging employees to take laptops home at night and bone up on programs while airborne.

Software and hardware budgets, not surprisingly, can dwarf those of many smaller firms and independents, even on a machine-by-machine basis. And there are differences in the way the big-leaguers use the laptops. Smaller firms may employ portables for visits to client sites, where firm members sort through clients' paper records and enter data. Big firms, however, are more likely to review records electronically and pick up already-entered information.

At Deloitte & Touche—and perhaps many other major accounting firms—you'll encounter three kinds of laptop users:

■ Accountants who audit; they engage in word processing, spreadsheeting, and the electronic perusal of client files.

■ Those doing tax work. With hefty spreadsheets, the tax people can expect more of machines and software than the auditors do.

■ Management consultants, whose application can vary from simple word processing to computer-aided systems evaluation (done mainly on desktops now but expected to become more common on laptops).

"I found the auditors to be easier in their demands on computers than the others were," says Bruce Johnson, a computer consultant to accounting firms and a former laptop expert at Deloitte who is now a staffer at the New York law firm of Sullivan and Cromwell. "That's partly because they are more dependent on the client doing a lot of the data entry."

At Deloitte, auditors can avail themselves of a proprietary package called AuditTape/PC. With it they can confirm accounts receivable balances, select inventory items, check inventory balances, and so on. As you'd expect from the name, a portable running AuditTape/PC can hook up to a tape reader; then the auditor can feed the information in directly. The software can be adjusted to the client's tape formats. Deloitte's auditors also use proprietary programs, such as ControlPlan, to assess internal controls, such as the separation of duties involving the signing of checks and the authorization of invoices. Among some clients—at smaller firms, for instance—certain conflicts may be unavoidable, but Deloitte's software at least helps bring such situations to light. The company's analytical review software, meanwhile, can compare warranty claims and similar items to see if patterns are in line with the client's industry.

Such marvels are possible through the Statistical Techniques for Analytic Review program, or STAR (check with your local Deloitte office about possible availability and price). It's a multiple regression analysis package.

"Let's say you want to audit sales over a twelve-month period," explains Trevor Stewart, a Deloitte partner who heads the company's software development group in Princeton, New Jersey. "Then you might obtain thirty-six months of information on goods shipped, price index information, seasonal variables such as daylight savings time, and other variables that could affect sales.

"You might end up with six columns of variables and a seventh with sales data. The multiple regression program could develop the relationship between sales and the six other variables. It could develop mathematical models and extrapolate the data over the months you were auditing." Then you could learn whether the sales performance was in line with your expectations. What's more, through STAR you could make sophisticated comparisons based not only on time but on performance of various branches or regions.

Think about the potential for monitoring corporate performance of clients. Star could give the players a level field. Among other things, in analyzing trends and identifying significant fluctuations in financial results, STAR takes into account the auditor's judgment of materiality as well as the statistical reliability level he seeks to achieve from the analytic test. To simplify, materiality is the maximum amount of total monetary error that could exist without "materially" distorting the financial statement.

As impressive as STAR seems, the auditors at Deloitte might consider another package to be a crowning accomplishment. This program, developed for internal use, is a comprehensive and integrated audit support system. "It will integrate all the tools that we use," says Stewart. "It will computerize the whole workpaper preparation task. What we have is a combination of text processing, spreadsheet processing, and a whole bunch of specialized things peculiar to how auditors work, including tickmarks, review notes, and cross references."

The package also includes communications software (which can tie in with a global e-mail system, no small advantage considering that Deloitte is an international firm, with more than sixty thousand professionals worldwide) as well as extensive on-line documentation.

Like all good integrated software, the program offers modules with common interfaces, an act of mercy toward new users. The modules, moreover, will effortlessly pluck data from the same files, saving disk space. Even so, the program still requires a 40-megabyte hard disk and an 80286 processor. But in today's world of AT-class laptops—easily affordable to big accounting firms—that's no big deal.

In the tax area, Deloitte's people use customized packages as well as the firm's own 1-2-3 add-ons for real estate returns, partnership papers, and other applications. "The tax people probably are among the heaviest users of PCs within Deloitte," says Johnson. He says that laptops aren't used as heavily in tax work at Deloitte as in auditing, where fieldwork obviously is more common. Still, the hard disk portables can be a blessing, too, for tax-oriented people elsewhere. At Peat Marwick Main & Company's office in Costa Mesa, California, a tax partner uses a hard disk laptop for sophisticated tax forecasts and other services for his four hundred individual clients. Some tax accountants report serious addictions even to underpowered, single-disk machines —good enough for some "what if" work when conferring with clients about tax strategy.

What about Deloitte's consultants? As you might expect, they're big word processing users and demand sophisticated packages with thesauruses and spelling checkers. Among the common programs are MultiMate (because the firm used to be heavily Wang-based and MultiMate boasts a Wang-like interface) and Microsoft Word (because of the formatting features useful in developing quality reports).

At Coopers & Lybrand a CPA named Sam Telzer, a general practice audit manager, favors MultiMate (because some clients prefer that format) and WordStar (to which he personally is partial) in addition to a word processor called Mass 11 (in common use at the firm, which has a site license). He spends more than a third of his computer time doing word processing of one kind or another—for instance, churning out reports.

Telzer also uses proprietary analytical-based packages and databases to evaluate the pricing of securities. Too, he relies on 1-2-3 from Lotus. "My office uses 1-2-3 for time management as well as for analysis. And for reporting expenses. In a typical engagement we might have fifty people keying their time into worksheets which we can then combine." Hard copy can go to C&L clients and the firm's own accounting department.

At C&L, meanwhile, some people have become old hands at using scanners to pick up data from clients' files or from the firm's previous audit reports. Telzer himself relies on a Hewlett-Packard flatbed scanner and optical character recognition software, the True Scan program and a related interface card from Calera Recognition Systems (2500 Augustine Drive, Santa Clara, California 95054, [408] 986-8006); hardware and software cost about five thousand dollars, although by now the price should be considerably less.

"The scanner reads the document the way a human does," Telzer says. "It asks you questions such as, 'Is it facing the right way? Is it text or graphics? What format? A memo or a spreadsheet?' If it's putting something into word processing format, then it tries to put in the proper command for things like underlining and italics. It can even work with columns or proportionally spaced fonts. It can read an 8½-by-11-inch typed page in about thirty seconds. You just have to tell it before you feed it whether you're working with dot matrix or typed print.''

If the scanner can't read material, True Scan uses asterisks or other symbols to indicate the problem characters. Telzer, however, says: "We found that out of every one hundred characters, ninety-eight were correct. This assumes that the document is of good quality. Humans have trouble reading fourth-generation Xeroxes, and so do scanners." Usually, however, clean-up time is minimal. So a scanning system should easily pay for itself in labor costs within about a year.

In the above case, at least, Telzer is using canned software. What about the complexities of commissioning the creation of the proprietary kind? How do you avoid breakdowns in communication between the accountants and the programmer?

Telzer offers a solution, a good, obvious one that too many companies don't always try: accountants should sit down with programmers and try to show screen by screen what they want the program to look like and what they want it to do. They shouldn't just spew forth specs. Rather, accountants should describe the program exactly as they'd like to see it in action.

At another major accounting firm, Ernst & Young, Alex Kask, a senior manager in the computers audit division, repeats other accountants' opinion that word processing matters far more to the profession than laypeople might expect. In fact, he says it's just as important as spreadsheeting.

"When you write an audit document detailing procedures," he says, "that can be fifty to seventy-five pages of word processing. And a lot of the work papers are narrative memorandums of what you find."

Among the traits Kask values most in a word processor are the ability to merge in spreadsheets and graphics; the ability to format effortlessly; ease of learning, partly through on-line help; support for a wide variety of printers; and a decent upgrade policy.

To the aforementioned he adds a criterion important to major firms and corporate America at large—economical site licensing. That way, Ernst & Young can make as many copies as it wants for its own use and not worry about employees furtively making unauthorized copies. A site license partly explains why Ernst & Young is still a SuperCalc stronghold in a Lotus era. "I don't have Lotus on my machine," Kask says. "With SuperCalc you usually have one keystroke less for everything. You don't need the @ mark in front of formulas. I also like

SuperCalc's graphics. They're easy to use and very powerful. SuperCalc can produce three-dimensional graphics, 3-D bar and line charts, and exploding pie charts. Font selections are very wide, in just about any use. And you can do some very nice word graphics for text slides.''
Kask is also a fan of:

■ FAST! (Field Audit System Technology), a workpaper system with support schedules for expenses, trial balances, financial statements, internal review reports, income tax workpapers, and tax returns. The main product costs $495 and includes the audit features; tax modules are extra. FAST! is from Prentice-Hall Professional Software, 2400 Lake Park Drive, P.O. Box 723597, Atlanta, Georgia 30339 (800) 241-3306.

■ EZ Flow—software that allows the creation of flow charts for systems and procedures. ''I use it myself for program documentation,'' says Kask. ''It's fairly easy to use the graphics. You can have standardized shapes and rectangles automatically linking the steps, and draw the lines on the paper.'' EZ Flow is from HavenTree Limited, P.O. Box 2260, Kingston, Ontario K7L 5J9, Canada, (613) 544-6035 ($144.95, U.S.; $180, Canada)

■ Silverado, $149 from Computer Associates, 1240 McKay Drive, San Jose, California 95131, (408) 432-1727. ''Silverado lets you use a database on the disk rather than having the entire database in memory.''

In Kask's office at Ernst & Young, programs remain on hard disks until the computer is returned and an update of the usual forty programs occurs. But the data itself disappears. He tries not to depend on laptop security software with passwords. Not everyone would agree with this approach, but it is one way to rule out the possibility of people being able to steal the firm's secrets by filching one of the laptops. Instead employees preserve the information on floppies.

*   *   *

Regardless of your field, you probably can empathize with other laptop users when it comes to that great leveler, Murphy's Law. Let me tell you how you can at least improve your odds of a fair trial.

Chapter 5

THE MURPHY'S LAW
CHAPTER

A New York executive once warned me about "MIAs," a new form of slang among laptop users in the corporate world. The military term *MIA* means missing in action. Nowadays it also refers to lost or stolen laptops, some of which, because of their high value per ounce, seem to be almost in the same category as jewelry—well, the fake kind, anyhow.

Some weeks later, a thief educated the executive about MIAs by carrying off a three-thousand-dollar borrowed portable computer.

In the end, though, the victim must have been at least somewhat grateful. For one thing, the MIA was the insurance nightmare of the executive's employer, not his own personal one. For another, nobody was depending on the machine yet to store crucial files. Think, however, of the lesson learned: if a thief can steal a laptop from a seemingly secure office, what are the risks in a strange hotel room?

The executive was a victim not only of a crime, but also of Murphy's Law: anything that can go wrong, will. Murphy's Law is bad enough in the world of desktop computers; it's even worse among laptops. A thirty-pound bargain-basement AT clone won't fit inside a thief's briefcase or tumble off a desk as easily as a tiny, pricey GriD will. That doesn't mean you should shun laptops, of course; their blessings easily outweigh the aggravation. Just be careful. This chapter will help you by addressing the following problems:

■ Theft and loss. I'll elaborate on this topic first for the sake of continuity.

■ Protecting secrets from thieves or others, including office snoops who might boot up your laptop when you're not around.

■ Accidental or deliberate loss or corruption of programs or information. Plain, simple, prosaic mishaps are actually the biggest risks to laptops and the data in them.

■ Hungry, temperamental batteries that run out of juice before you expect them to. (Naturally, this will happen within the first half hour of a ten-hour airplane trip.)

■ Temperamental keyboards.

■ Screens. A backlit LCD may gradually lose its brightness if you don't take special precautions.

■ The business of maintenance. Where should you get your laptop repaired? And should you buy a maintenance contract?

■ Training. Not all laptop users have benefited from desktop experience. Training can especially help sales reps, who must never appear ignorant in front of customers.

THEFT AND LOSS

Anyone spotted a Toshiba 1200HB laptop in the area of West Fiftieth Street in New York City? The "borrower," unfortunately, is still MIA.

Theft isn't the major threat to laptop owners (don't expect any FBI statistics here; I've already tried the bureau), but it should grow in importance as laptops replace desktops in American offices and more people take them on the road. Already, for instance, the *Washington Post* counts on a half dozen or so laptops vanishing each year. The tiny Radio Shack notebook computers are at special risk. One sportswriter has lost at least two of them from press boxes at ball games.

"A whole new issue of security arises with laptops," a PC manager at a Fortune 500 company has observed. "When you can fit a $7,000 computer into a briefcase and then let your people carry them to and from work in Manhattan, you're going to see a lot of the computers stolen."[1]

Remember, global travel won't immunize you against muggers and thieves in the vicinity of your own headquarters. In fact, many destinations, such as Japan, are safer than the United States.

Here are ways to fight theft, either as a corporation or as an individual:

■ Make employees personally responsible for at least part of the cost of stolen or damaged laptops if they appear to be at fault.

■ Consider assigning laptops to individual employees. The price of computer equipment is coming down to the point where you needn't worry about micros being in constant use. If each employee has an individual machine—especially one with a hard disk—it should be easier for him or her to master the software. Beyond that, he or she will be more watchful.

■ Don't leave your laptop unattended, if possible. Take it to the john. That's often impossible in the case of the bigger, AC-powered units, but even in those cases there are alternative safeguards.

■ If you travel regularly, buy a Kablit cable or something similar to attach your laptop to the column of a building or another unmovable object. Cables can be snipped, of course. The idea isn't to make the computer theft-proof but to reduce the temptation to the casual thief. If you really want to decrease the risk of theft, consider an Anchor Pad, which I'll describe in a moment. As for the Kablit cable, you can order it from Secure-IT, 18 Maple Court, East Longmeadow, Massachusetts ([413] 525-7039).

■ Follow common sense and, especially if you're not using a cable,

---

[1] The PC manager's quote appeared in *PC Week*, Dec. 12, 1988.

at least hide your laptop in a hotel closet or drawer or check with the hotel about a storage place for valuables.

■ If you're staying at a hotel just briefly, put a sign on the door saying: NO SERVICE TODAY! DO NOT DISTURB! Threaten homicide— well, almost—if someone ignores your request.

■ For use back at headquarters, why not consider an Anchor Pad, a registered trademark for a metal pad that glues onto a desk. You glue little feet onto your laptop; the feet lock onto the pad. Without a key, it will be hard to remove the laptop from the pad without destroying it, especially if the desk is metal. Anchor Pad sells regularly to the military and civilian agencies of the federal government, so this product seems well worth checking out. The pad's makers, under certain circumstances, will even reimburse you for the cost of your computer if their product has failed.

To answer the obvious, yes, a thief may sic a buzz saw on your wooden desk or even use a torch or other tool on a metal one. But why do that, when there are other, less protected machines to steal? Imagine a fence walking up to you on the street and saying, "Psst! Wanna buy this hot laptop? As an extra, you even get a piece of the previous owner's mahogany." Unless the thief is more interested in the information in the laptop than in the machine itself—or unless it's easy to steal the desk—you should be well protected.

According to the Anchor Pad's makers, a heat gun can remove the pad. Supposedly this won't mar even wooden desks. The pads cost around fifty dollars each and cannot be reused with confidence, so this is no solution for someone working at a site just a few days. Still, it is a possibility for consultants who are there for weeks at a time. So are two obvious safeguards: (1) locking the laptop overnight in a heavy filing cabinet or (2) taking it home after-hours.

For more information contact Anchor Pad International, 4483 McGrath Street, Suite 103, Ventura, California 93003, 800-4-ANCHOR outside California or 800-6-ANCHOR in California.

■ Use an etching tool from your hardware store to scratch your name on the case—or at least in an out-of-sight location; also, keep a record of the serial number handy. Then you'll be in a stronger position when dealing with police and your insurance company. What's more, the thief who sees your name on the case will consider the laptop less attractive as booty.

As for loss, in many large metropolitan areas you may as well wave good-bye to your laptop if you lose track of it. But in the boonies you just may stand a chance of recovering it. Adults train children to blurt out their parents' names if they're lost; why not teach your laptop to @do the same? A *PC Magazine* editor wisely recommends that you insert lines at the end of your AUTOEXEC.BAT file on a hard disk or the floppy that you use as a program disk. Here, based on editor Bill Howard's idea, plus some wrinkles of my own, is an example of what the relevant lines might include:

CLS
@ECHO OFF
ECHO REWARD!
ECHO Year's Stock of Superb Burgundy
ECHO If You Return Me to:
ECHO Francois Mignet
ECHO Chief Wine-Taster
ECHO Vineyard Vanities, Inc.
ECHO 9480 South Washington Street
ECHO Alexandria, Virginia 22308
ECHO Telephone: 703-555-1717 (call collect)
ECHO Will pay for shipping if need be

AUTOEXEC.BAT, for the uninitiated, is the file that can perform feats like firing up a program as soon as you turn on the computer—no need to key in the program's name. That's oversimplifying matters, but you get the idea. Read your MS-DOS book to learn more about AUTOEXEC.BAT (among other things, you must use ASCII to write or edit such files).

What about insurance? You can help by accurately describing your equipment to your insurance company and being very specific about the ways in which you expect it to be used. Make sure that your policy will cover portables on the road and that its upper limit suffices for your equipment. Also, if you're constantly borrowing equipment from other people or companies, see if your insurance company still will protect you. The New York executive's employer was lucky; its insurance company reimbursed it for the MIA.

Free-lance writers or entrepreneurs may face special insurance problems. "Most insurance companies do not like to write policies for small businesses," says Jo Allan, a laptop owner in Texas, "so the best way to go is usually a rider on your homeowner's policy, and even that is not easy. My agent had to do some real searching to find one who would take my business—and I am a semi-good person who has paid out approximately one zillion more in premiums than I've ever collected or filed for.''

The agent "finally found a 'floater,' which means it covers my stuff wherever it happens to be—at my home, my office, my car, a customer's office, et cetera. I pay one hundred dollars per year for twenty thousand dollars' worth of coverage. Regular business policies cover your stuff only in your place of business.'' Allan is describing her experiences in Texas, but similar frustrations will await laptop owners in many, perhaps most, other states.

PROTECTING SECRETS

Remember, if your computer is stolen, the information inside it might be fair game. Imagine toting several thousand pages of confidential information through airport lobbies. That's what you do when you stash it away on your laptop. How to prevent the wrong people from seeing your corporate secrets?

■ Buy a laptop with either a combination lock or software that restricts access to the hard disk.

■ If your laptop lacks such protection, or if you want it to comply with military standards, consider a program such as Secret Disk II to limit access. It's available for $125 from Lattice, Inc., 2500 South Highland Avenue, Lombard, Illinois, 60148, (708) 916-1600.

■ Also consider products that offer the ability to encrypt individual files, such as the IZE textbase.

Whatever your protection, make sure it's easy to use and doesn't come with risks of its own. If you lose the electronic keys to access the encryption products, even the manufacturers might not be able to bail you out.

Of course, in the case of laptops, much of the information might end up outside the machine—either as e-mail or on a local area network (LAN)—a network through which users can share programs, data, and peripherals, such as printers. Act accordingly.

Don't worry, however, about encrypting LAN files or electronic mail unless you're handling extremely confidential financial or medical data, or unless you're a bureaucrat at the Department of Agriculture with early access to the crop statistics that the Russians or commodity brokers would kill for.

But do check with your e-mail vendor about the confidentiality of files that the services might keep to back up your messages. For how long is the information preserved? What would the vendor do if faced with a subpoena? In the past, the e-mail industry has lobbied for safeguards; check out the present situation as it applies to your vendor now.

Still, the corporate world's real vulnerability isn't from security lapses on the part of MCI Mail or CompuServe. Rather it's from companies' own mistakes. Exxon, for example, kept backups of its e-mail correspondence around longer than it had to: a big help to government lawyers investigating the company's oil spill in Alaska. I was delighted to see the government pursuing Exxon, but as a writer I felt a little schizophrenic.

On one hand, just as in the Oliver North–contra case, where prosecutors subpoenaed data backups, I was glad to see abuses of power and trust come to light. On the other, as a past user of confidential sources, I wondered if next time around some government sleuths might indulge in a wholesale tour of the computer files of a reporter or an entire newspaper. You may share my ambivalence if you're a corporate executive worried about protecting sensitive information.

While the politicians and lawyers are hashing out the legal issues, why not protect yourself by making certain that no one keeps sensitive e-mail backups or other kinds around longer than needed.

LOSS OR CORRUPTION OF PROGRAMS OR DATA

Rest assured that the most troublesome data security issues are quite mundane. Flaky floppies or sick hard disks can bedevil laptop owners and desktop owners alike. Laptop drives, of course, do not just get unhealthy on their own. Sometimes humans help, often by dropping them.

Below I'll discuss:

■ Viruses, such as the notorious Columbus Day virus of a while back.

- How to care for floppies.
- Protecting hard disks.
- Recovering information from defective hard drives. Often experts can reincarnate files, even from drives in smashed laptops. Here I'll describe this kind of service, which frequently is more cost-effective than re-creating your work.

Computer Viruses and Similar Threats

A few minutes ago I booted up my XyWrite word processor and suffered a nasty series of RAM-related problems. Had the Columbus Day virus struck a little late?

Micro managers throughout the world will long remember October 13, 1989, when a virulent bug was supposed to scramble hard disks and destroy data. Electronic bulletin boards and free software were to transmit it. The bug would pass from computer to computer and reproduce itself—hence the description of the problem as a "virus."

I'm hopelessly addicted to BBS's and free software, and the worst thoughts crossed my mind. I checked my COMMAND.COM file, a vital MS-DOS file that viruses often will infect; it was the same size in bytes as it always had been. Then I returned to XyWrite and saw that the program was flashing its "out of memory" message just after it loaded a file for the spelling corrector. I shortened the file, recalling that the spelling corrector had only so much room for new words. Breath bated, I tried XyWrite again and everything was fine. *Whew.* Still, it was a good, sound scare—even considering that *at times* the media have somewhat exaggerated the virus threat.

Here's how to reduce the risks from viruses and other human-made threats:[2]

- If you're really paranoid, don't use any programs but commercial ones. Avoid the public domain programs and the shareware—the try-before-you-pay software—that you find on bulletin boards. Similarly avoid such programs from friends, at least if you don't know the soft-

[2]For help with these tips, I'm grateful to John McAfee, who, along with Colin Haynes, is the author of *Computer Viruses, Worms, Data Diddlers, Killer Programs, and Other Threats to Your System: What They Are, How They Work, and How To Defend Your PC, Mac, or Mainframe* (New York: St. Martin's Press, 1989). McAfee writes knowledgeably as chairman of the Computer Virus Industry Association.

ware's origin. This is an extreme precaution. I myself am a big believer in freeware and shareware. Even by shunning shareware, you'll still face minor risks; for example, at least one commercial program for Macintosh computers was unknowingly distributed with viruses in it.

Just like automobile companies, some U.S. software firms are eagerly importing cut-rate work. As America relies increasingly on foreign programmers, including many in the Third World, I won't be surprised to see more viruses in commercial programs in the future. Even now, many of the worst threats are coming from abroad—from Pakistan, Israel, and other places where most hackers and other computer users mean no harm but where a small minority find joy in disrupting the rest of the planet.

■ Make frequent backups of all data and of parts of the program that you customize—for instance, the keyboard file for XyWrite or macro[3] material for WordPerfect. I've set up XyWrite so that just one keystroke issues simultaneously instructions to preserve information on both the hard drive and the floppy. I did this, appropriately, through the keyboard file. Also, make separate backups of programs and data, and keep copies of old backups in case new ones are corrupted.

No matter what programs you're using, you can usually do the same with Smart Key, Keyworks, or similar software that lets you automate keystrokes. See page 361 of this book for information on copying a number of files to a floppy at once through some ordinary MS-DOS routines.

If you isolate your text files and other data on a backup floppy, they'll be safer. Some viruses prefer to attach themselves to program files, such as those ending with .EXE or .COM. and also overlay files such as .SYS, .BIN, .OVR, and .OVL. Likewise, viruses can attach themselves to the boot sectors of both hard disks and floppies. (The boot sector contains the instruction to start up the operating system after you turn on the computer.)

Keep in mind that a backup floppy itself may be contaminated even when the data files on it are clean. Do not back up more than one program per disk. Be careful, too, that the backup disk is not in a drive when you're booting up your computer. In fact, if you have a virus

[3]Macros combine commands or keystrokes. For example, via a macro I can leave XyWrite and dial up an electronic mail network.

removed from your hard disk, you should consult with your rescuer before recopying the data from the backup floppy to the hard disk.

■ Follow my example and try to monitor the number of bytes in the programs on your disk—or at least compare them with the number on the floppies from the factory. Beware if program or overlay files mysteriously shrink or grow in size. This method isn't foolproof, but it's better than nothing.

■ Use write-protect tabs on the floppy disks that store your original copies of programs from the factory. On 3.5-inch disks—the kind most common on laptops—use the little sliding bars to tell the computer not to write to the disks, just to read from them.

Incidentally, if you're recopying valuable data from a floppy to a recently disinfected hard disk, please write-protect the floppy. The disinfection may not be as complete as you thought.

■ Consider waiting a week or two before you try out programs downloaded from bulletin boards. See if other board users have used them safely. Let the other people's computers do the electronic equivalent of food tasting. This method, mind you, still won't protect you from programs set up to spread viruses on a certain day or after a certain number of times of use.

■ Try not to pick up files from BBS's or information networks that don't keep excellent records of who uploaded the files. On nets like CompuServe or GEnie, you'll often find that it's the author himself or herself. So there's less chance of programs being tainted.

■ If you know that a virus is supposed to strike on day X or day Y—determined by your system's internal clock—reset the date with the MS-DOS date command! Let the rest of the world serve as guinea pigs before you let your electronic calendar advance to Columbus Day or the equivalent. That's what at least one computer user in the Washington, D.C., area did.

Keep in mind, of course, that the virus creator just may be perverse enough for the bug to do its deeds before the rumored date, or even when you reset the date. Still, you might consider freezing the calendar. To learn how, read the MS-DOS manual supplied with your computer; procedures may vary from machine to machine and perhaps among versions of DOS.

■ Investigate the possibility of using a virus detector or killer program on your laptop. Contact McAfee Associates/InterPath, 4423 Cheeney Street, Santa Clara, California 95054, (408) 988-3832, or locate McAfee's shareware distributed through BBS systems, including his own ([408] 988-4004).

I found the SCANV60.ZIP file, a collection of virus weapons, to be useful. Within a few minutes I was able to check an entire 40-megabyte hard disk for scores of viruses ranging from the New Jerusalem virus to the Dark Avenger, the Alabama virus, the Fu Manchu virus, and the SunDay virus, the latter of which kills files and displays on-screen the message: "Today is Sunday, why do you work so hard?"

The price may increase, but as of this writing an entire antivirus package from McAfee costs well under one hundred dollars. Also check CompuServe for antivirus software. As Columbus Day neared, many machine-specific sections of CompuServe began mentioning "vaccines."

Remember that no virus detector, killer, or vaccine will provide total protection. For security, nothing beats frequent backups. Moreover, some vaccines and other antivirus software may make your laptop less convenient to use; instead you may as well spend the extra time and money on backups. Still, if you feel more secure, why not consider such precautions? If nothing else you may want to do a quick scan of your disk with a quick, easy-to-use virus detector like McAfee's.

■ Be extra careful if you're transferring programs from your laptop to your company's LAN.[4] Consult with the appropriate computer people.

■ If, alas, a virus does infect your machine, then you can almost surely obliterate it by reformatting your hard disk. Please note that you must switch off your computer and turn it on again after reformatting the hard disk. If you don't, remnants of the virus might still lurk in RAM. When you switch off your computer, wait at least one minute before turning it back on to drain *all* power from memory. Check with your laptop manufacturer if your machine uses battery-backed RAM. If you reformat, don't use the original MS-DOS disk from the factory; use a write-protected, knowingly virus-free *copy* of that disk. The same holds true of any word processors, spreadsheets, and so on that you'll reinstall. "Many software companies," says John McAfee, the virus expert, "are not automatically replacing infected software."

[4] A separate issue is the legality of transferring software—purchased for one user—to a network. Check with your company's computer people and, if need be, with its lawyers.

With the above safeguards, you and your laptop will be much, much safer than otherwise. I've heard of a bug that can burn out monitors (at least cathode-ray tubes); plus there are rumors of one that will damage hard disks, but I have yet to hear of documented instances. Maybe they've occurred, but surely they're rare.

Viruses, of course, aren't the only risk. Beware, for instance, of Trojan Horse.[5] They don't automatically infect files. Instead, in the words of Peter Norton of Peter Norton Computing, they "must be run explicitly to cause any damage."

Norton should know. His company found an unauthorized file called NortStop in circulation on a bulletin board. "When run," he said in 1989, "it lists the directory and claims the system is virus-free. Between December 24 and December 31st, however, it will erase [certain] files in several directories."

Here, too, the main precaution is obvious: constantly back up your files and write-protect your program disks.

Floppy Tips

Let me confess up front. I haven't always observed the following rules. I have (shudder) imbibed orange juice near floppies containing an electronic version of this manuscript. Still, I'm a reasonable hypocrite. I've backed up the manuscript on not one but several floppies; moreover, I rely mainly not on floppies but on my hard drive, even if I am all too aware of its own frailties. And now the rules:

■ Don't eat or drink around floppies (the same principle applies to keyboards). I know of the wonders that Polaroid offers through a recovery service for buyers of its floppies. Still, no pastrami sandwich is worth risking irreplaceable files. If it's a good sandwich, treat it with proper respect and get up from your desk to concentrate on the food.

■ If you use off-brand, generic floppies, then you should make frequent backups. Do so even if you have good luck for a number of months. Generic floppies can come from a number of manufacturers. Of course, frequent backups are a good idea no matter who made your floppies; they're simply more important if your floppies are of uncertain

[5]McAfee likens Trojan Horses to tumors, viruses to metastasis.

pedigree. Think about the cost of developing and entering data compared to the expense of the disks themselves.

■ Keep floppies away from dust; invest in a good floppy container for your desk top and, inside your desk drawer, store the floppies in their original boxes. Don't just store them naked in the drawers. The trap door on the 3.5-inch floppies makes them less vulnerable than the older, 5.25-inch variety, but they still aren't entirely dust proof. I'll deliberately use the term *floppy*, by the way, even if the disks are now in plastic; it's as useful a way as any of reminding you of their delicacy, which remains. Some people, in fact, have said that the new-style floppies have a higher failure rate than the old.

■ Make sure the floppies don't fall off your desk. Rich Schinnell —vice president of the Capital PC User Group, a micro manager for a Washington area engineering firm, and source of much of the wisdom in this chapter—says that life on the floor can be especially dangerous for floppies. All too often people roll over them with their chairs! In fact, Schinnell says that such prosaic mishaps ruin more 3.5-inch floppies than do any other kinds of accidents.

■ Don't expose the floppies to heat. Avoid leaving them under your windshield in the middle of Arizona—or, for that matter, Massachusetts. If you're storing a large amount of confidential information on floppies, consider a heat-proof safe (check with your fire department).

■ Keep floppies at least six inches—just to be extra safe—away from old-style bell telephones that truly ring. The newer bell-less electronic telephones aren't such a threat.

■ In moldy surroundings, be careful how you store floppies. See page 271 for tips from James Fallows of the *Atlantic*, who lived in the tropics without air conditioning.

My friend James Besser, the writer for Jewish-oriented newspapers, says he no longer suffers data loss as he did before he became a staunch believer in the CHKDSK procedure.

■ Consider buying a program—such as Norton Utilities—that can help you recover files you accidentally deleted. You'll probably have to use such a program immediately to correct the mistake. But it's one more safety net.

Hard Disk Tips (Including Basic Backup Possibilities)

Knocked around enough, the heads on floppy drives can lose their alignment and be unable to read data. There's even the possibility of the heads destroying a disk. But the problems of floppy drives pale beside those of some hard disks. Consider the technology. A disk— often an aluminum disk coated with an oxide—whirls at high speeds.

As with a floppy drive, a head reads the data. It's just a fraction of an inch from the "platter," another name for the disk or disks (there may be more than one). Only a thin layer of air is between the platter and the head. If you jolt your laptop hard enough, the head will hit the platter and lose data. Dropped just a few inches onto a tabletop, some portables may develop drive problems.

Here are some hard disk tips to discourage breakage and other problems:

■ Invest in a good, thick padded case for your computer. Any old carrying case isn't enough; the cushioning must be thick. Needless to say, computers—with or without a hard disk—should never be checked as airline baggage without plenty of protection.

■ Try not to operate your hard disk after you've come in from the cold. Let the computer have maybe forty-five minutes to accustom itself to room temperatures.

■ Buy a surge protector. Hard disks can be extremely sensitive to power surges. Check with your computer's manufacturer about an appropriate protector. To be sure, many hard disks are buffered from weird electrical current because they aren't hooked directly into the wall—they're running off batteries that the wall juice is constantly recharging. But a surge protector can help.

■ Run the CHKDSK /F procedure to help get rid of odds and ends of data that hard disks can accumulate when programs don't quite work as expected. In fact, you might even want to insert the line **CHKDSK /F** into your AUTOEXEC.BAT file. Then, whenever you turn on the machine, it will automatically do the check for you. This won't be a complete test, but it will help.

■ Consider buying a disk optimizer program such as SpinRite or Norton's Speed Disk if you have even a modicum of technical ability. As a hard disk fills with data, the disk can scatter parts of the same file every which way on its platters. Disk optimizers can reunite the separated parts, often improving the effective speed of the disk and making data recovery easier in the event of catastrophe. Before installing the disk optimizer, make certain you've removed all TSR (terminate and stay resident) programs from your RAM.

Above all, consider investing either in software to help you back up your hard disk on floppies or else in a tape drive.

Check out a program like Fastback, which has a menu to guide you step by step through the back-up process; also look for a data compression capability so that you can squeeze more information onto each backup floppy. Check too about the ability to make backups only of files that you've modified since the last back-up session.

Typically, your first backup may include everything on the hard disk, followed by the aforementioned "incremental backups," which can be done in a fraction of the time that a full backup may take. If your hard disk is 20 megabytes, a full backup may take half an hour—perhaps more, perhaps less, depending on the backup product.

One way to get around this drudgery is to invest in a tape drive that works with your portable and relieves you of the need to swap floppies in and out during the procedure. Check with the manufacturer of your laptop for a list of approved drives that can plug in to your serial port or elsewhere. With a tape drive, you can lunch, sleep, consummate a million-dollar deal, do anything you want, while making your backup.

Data Recovery Services

On a snowy day, you slip on your front doorstep. Your hard disk portable turns into a sled—with you atop it. Even though it was in the case, your hard disk won't work. What to do? Fortunately, data recovery services exist to retrieve material off damaged hard disks.

"We have a 90-percent success ratio on dropped drives," says Stuart Hanley, manager of engineering at OnTrack, a data recovery service in Minnesota. Don't depend on data recovery services to recover your material, though; just realize that you at least have a fighting chance.

One of the worst scenarios involves the destruction of the file allocation table, the information on the disk that records files' size and location for the benefit of your computer. But even in those cases, OnTrack can often bring back data if it's in ASCII. "If it's readable by humans," he says, "we can see, 'Andrews, Jac,' and know that's 'Andrew, Jackson' if we see 'Jackson' in some other places." Special programs can speed up the process once the humans at OnTrack have picked up patterns.

Program files—for example, those ending in .EXE or .COM—are a far greater challenge because the guesswork involved is much more complicated. Then again, how many laptop owners are going to throw away their originals of WordStar or dBASE?

Physical damage to a hard drive is just one possibility. For instance, your controller—the device that helps the drive write to the proper part of the spinning platter—can go bad and cause the disk to write data to the wrong parts. Or yours may have a software-related calamity.

Whatever happens, I would be very wary about nontechnical people using special utilities to recover information from a failed drive. Leave it to the professionals. Otherwise you may just aggravate your problems. Needless to say, the same applies to damaged floppies. If the information is important, have a repair shop or your company's techies spring into action.

BATTERIES

Nickel-cadmium batteries are treacherous. One minute everything is fine; the next, your power's gone and you're losing data. The little critters have nasty memories. If you shorten the period between chargings, then the batteries in effect will think, "Aha! I can reduce my capacity to accept charges. Next time I'll give the human only two hours of battery life, not four." This problem isn't so bad with lead-acid batteries, which fade away more slowly and, by the way, are cheaper. Alas, the lead-acid cells are also heavier.

The ni-cad and the lead-acid factions have an Avis-versus-Hertz-type rivalry. Within the laptop industry the ni-cad side is *now* Hertz, the, er, powers that be, although this could change; the lead-acid people say that the use of their technology in Macintosh portables marks the beginning of a comeback of sorts. Having collected figures from both sides, however, I find that ni-cads as a rule do last through many more cycles of charging. And newer technologies—such as nickel-hydride and aerobic power—could prove to be better bets than either ni-cad *or* lead-acid.

There isn't much to say about lead-acid batteries, but here are ni-cad tips:

■ Use a program like Battery Watch—or your laptop's own built-in monitoring software—to monitor your battery life. But allow for fudge time. Even the well-reviewed Battery Watch can't always account for modems and other peripherals. Battery Watch is available for $39.95 from Traveling Software, 18702 North Creek Parkway, Bothell, Washington, 98011, 800-343-8080. In Washington, call (206) 483-8088.

■ Don't discharge your battery completely by hooking it up to a light bulb or by shorting it outright. You could cause it to lose track of its polarities (what's positive and what's negative). Instead, discharge your batteries by leaving your laptop on all night or by using a Battery Watch–style program. That way you'll avoid the polarity problem while preparing the battery to receive a full charge.

■ Be aware that the contents of ni-cad batteries can be highly toxic.

Whether you use ni-cad batteries or the lead-acid kind, you might:

■ If possible, stretch out the run time of your batteries by turning off your hard disk, built-in modem, or other peripherals. See your computer's instruction manual. As noted in the software chapter, your batteries will last longer between charges if your software doesn't depend on use of the disk drive.

■ Also consider setting up a RAM disk to reduce the use of a physical disk. A RAM disk can exist, electronically, inside your computer's memory chips. Please note that the usual RAM disk loses its contents as soon as you turn the power off, so if it's storing data, you'll want to copy over to your floppy or hard disk.

■ Buy spare batteries and keep them charged, assuming that your laptop lets you remove the batteries easily. Are you always running your portable off AC power? Then take the batteries out. No need to wear them down. With constant charging and recharging, by the way, the typical ni-cad should last maybe two years. Don't count on a longer life.

■ Consider replacement batteries—with longer times between charges—from third-party vendors. Check with the laptop manufacturer for a list of such companies.

One of the best bets for replacement batteries may be Ovonic Battery, maker of nickel-hydride cells. Reportedly, Ovonic batteries enables a Toshiba T-1000 to run more than 75 percent longer than it does on the batteries from the factory. Mind you, that's without a special charger. Supposedly the right charger would allow the batteries to triple the time a laptop could run without a recharge. "Ovonic batteries," the company claims in its literature, "can generally be expected to deliver from 400–500 cycles, and in some cases, over 1,000 cycles."

John Rehak, a Toshiba owner, swears by Ovonic batteries. With factory-supplied original cells, his T1000 showed a red warning light after he'd been running his laptop four hours and three minutes without accessing the floppy disk. With four replacement cells from Ovonic, the time zoomed to seven hours and ten minutes.

What's more, Rehak found that the Ovonic batteries didn't have the usual memory problem of ni-cads, which won't last as long on the next charge unless they are discharged completely. Rehak paid just $40 for the four C cells from Ovonic. (AA-size batteries cost three dollars each.)

William E. Orabone, Jr., the company's manager of technical marketing, tells me that many other Toshiba T-1000 owners have substituted Ovonic batteries. He says that his company really isn't wooing small, individual buyers and that it may farm out this task to a middleman. Meanwhile, to find out more, you can write the Ovonic Battery Company, 1826 Northwood Drive, Troy, Michigan 48084 ([313] 362-1750). Please note, however, that:

■ I don't know which other laptops the Ovonic batteries will work with.

■ If you own a Toshiba and substitute Ovonic batteries for the originals, you'll void your warranty.

■ You'll need to do some soldering.

■ You'll want to be very careful to get a feel for how long the batteries will last. If you're using Battery Watch or a similar program (see page 151), ask the software house how accurate it will be with the Ovonics.

■ Some Toshiba owners say that unused Ovonic batteries lose their charges faster than unused ni-cad cells do. "Put your ni-cad-powered T1000 on the shelf for a month," says one owner, "and you can probably fire it up, with all work retained in battery-backed RAM. With nickel-hydrides you probably wouldn't get away with a week, and the whole works would be dead." Check with Ovonic for the latest on this issue.

■ I have not personally tested Ovonic batteries.

■ Plenty of scoffers exist, though Orabone makes some good counterarguments (see page 56).

What if you need a replacement battery but don't want to try the Ovonic variety? Contact the Axonix Corporation, 2257 South 1100 East, Salt Lake City, Utah 84106 (801-466-9797). For $79 you can buy a C cell for the Toshiba T1000. An Axonix sales rep says the replacements will power the T1000 for five hours with the disk drives being accessed about ten percent of the time. That's without a modem or extra RAM. As usual, check with the maker of your laptop to see if the installation of a third-part battery will void your warranty.

Let me mention two other kinds of batteries:

1. Tiny lithium cells. Some laptops use these to power memory chips; be careful to replace them in a timely manner. Turn back to page 55 for a brief discussion of lithium technology.

2. Garden-variety alkaline cells. Especially if you use the cheap, drugstore variety in your laptop, check regularly for signs of corrosion. Ideally, of course, you'll rely only on premium brands. As much as laptop prices have fallen, I doubt that alkaline batteries will ever cost more than a portable computer.

Alkaline cells do have one big advantage: As a rule, they keep their power much longer than rival technologies do. If you're using your laptop away from the AC socket just a few times a year, alkaline might make sense. What's more, they are fine for Poqet-style laptops with low power needs.

KEYBOARDS

A smart maker of dandruff shampoos should try a different pitch on TV in the Silicon Valley area: "SQOOZE, the new, improved shampoo for laptop users!" And why not? Laptop keyboards don't cotton well to dandruff or other kinds of dust. The boards, after all, bristle with tiny switches of one kind or another, and the flakes can wreak havoc with the electrical connections and, in some cases, force you to hit the affected keys harder. Cigarette smoke isn't helpful, either.

Nor, obviously, do keyboards thrive on spilled food or drink. Columnist John Dvorak wrote of an airline stewardess who spilled a drink on one of his colleagues' laptops. The victim got a free drink but not, alas, a replacement computer.

Unfortunately, keyboards are one area where laptops are greater risks

KEEPING OTHER MACHINERY IN GOOD SHAPE: YOUR WRISTS

Murphy's Law strikes not just computers but also the wrists and hands of the humans who type on them. Muscular strain—and pain—may result. And that's not all. Sometimes surgeons must repair the damage from repetitive motion.

Carpal tunnel syndrome, as it's called, can dog professional word processors, data entry people, journalists, and others who are constantly at the keyboard. Portable computers can be among the worst offenders. The height and angle of the keyboard aren't as adjustable as those of many desktop machines.

In the early days of laptop computing, the syndrome wasn't exactly a cosmic issue; little portables normally were not people's main machines. This may change somewhat, however, as laptops replace desktops. What can you do, besides taking regular breaks from typing?

"Dr." Rothman's Rx is a cushion on which your weary hands and wrists can relax while you're typing. The cushion may slow down your typing a bit, but you still can use it from time to time. By varying your position, you'll lessen the chances of developing carpal tunnel syndrome.

If you go the cushion route, some possibilities include.

■ Homemade rests—perhaps nothing more than some sponges bought at the grocery store and cut up and taped together, I have not tried this; please don't sue me if you get carpal tunnel syndrome! My hunch, however, is that a homemade product may actually be the best solution, since you can customize it to fit your precise needs.

■ Wristrest, selling for $13 from Metaphor, the Hypermedia Group (91 North Bond Street, Hamilton, Ontario L8S 3W4, Canada, [416] 574-3272). The price is low. However, this product is an example of the one-size-fits-all variety. It's for desktops and laptops alike.

■ The KB Pillow, priced at $24.95 for laptops, $24.95 for standard desktop keyboards, and $29.95 for the longer, "extended" variety, sold by Computer Giftware (521 State Street, Glendale, California 91203, [818] 500-1718.

than desktop machines. The beast on your desk probably uses a detachable board, a replacement for which may cost as little as fifty dollars discounted. In a laptop, however, the keyboard is an integral part of the computer case.

Here are some solutions to the keyboard problem, beyond the obvious one of good personal hygiene:

■ Don't eat or drink near your computer. I know that's difficult. More than one high-tech ad has tried to humanize its offerings by showing a coffee mug near the machine. Perhaps, too, there's a second reason for the mug. Ideally you won't douse just the keyboard, you'll also flood the computer itself and give the manufacturer some repeat business.

■ Protect the keyboard and the rest of your computer in wet or dusty places by way of a garbage bag or perhaps a pair of them. Or buy a sealable, disposable bag like the kind used to store food. That's worked successfully for army captain Bill E. Badger of Springfield, Virginia, while on training exercises. You don't need Gucci's best to protect your laptop.

■ Order a plastic-membrane key cover designed for your machine. I tested a cover from Viziflex-Seels and could think of nothing but horrible condom jokes. The experience—the tactile sensation—just was totally unnatural. What's more, I had trouble closing my machine's lid because Viziflex interfered with the latching mechanism.

On the other hand, if I were in a smoky or dusty area—or on a small boat—I'd be very grateful for the existence of products like Viziflex's. There's another advantage, too. The keyboard cover greatly reduces the usual clickety-click, a blessing for writers taking notes at meetings or over the telephone.

So a keyboard cover may be worth checking out. Viziflex's address is 16 East Lafayette Street, Hackensack, New Jersey 07601-6895; the telephone number is (201) 487-8080. Price is about $30.

The Viziflex cover is just one of many possibilities. Please also ask your computer dealer about alternatives.

■ Go to Radio Shack or a similar store and buy a can of compressed air to squirt at your keyboard—after checking with the manufacturer. A Toshiba technician recommended that I do this to my borrowed T3100e. Other manufacturers may worry about the air driving the dust and other matter *into* the switches. By the way, I can think of another source of air that can be used if in a pinch: the air from the tire pump at your gas station, if you're certain that it isn't full of dust and you can struggle successfully with the valve. A tire pump did just the trick in the middle of a desert for Badger when he was on a training exercise and sand spilled into his Radio Shack Model 100. He just unscrewed the computer case and blasted away at the keyboard.

■ Use one of the minivacuum cleaners sold at discount stores and advertised on TV. Here again first check with the manufacturer.

■ Have a repair shop remove the keyboard and spray it with liquid nitrogen if the laptop manufacturer considers this appropriate.

SCREENS

LCDs just don't wear out, at least not according to the service people I talked to. Even backlit LCDs—the ones that glow—will probably outlast your laptop if you're careful. That's the good news. The bad news is that if you drop your machine, the video panel stands a good chance of shattering. And you may be out hundreds of dollars. Users of gas plasma face similar risks. On a BBS, I ran across a plaintive note from the owner of a gas plasma unit with a broken display—a hapless soul who figured it would be better to sell his machine than fork over a thousand dollars for a new screen.

Here are some screen care tips:

■ Try not to expose your LCD display to intense heat. I doubt that cold is as risky. Still, your display may need to warm up for an hour —maybe much longer—if you've just come inside after a trek through the Alaskan tundra.

■ Use a screen dimmer or blanker program if the screen is a backlit LCD or a gas plasma display. The dimmer or blanker will take effect on the screen if a certain amount of time has passed since you last used the keyboard. Check with the laptop manufacturer about a suitable program

■ Consult with your manufacturer about running your gas plasma machine for extended periods with reverse video—that is, dark letters against a glowing background. I've run across mixed opinions here.

■ Clean your screen with Windex or a similar product. Don't spray directly on the screen, just on a soft cloth with which you can wipe the screen. Another possibility would be eyeglass cleaner in small spray bottles.

THE BUSINESS OF MAINTENANCE

Brace yourself for rate shock; maintenance of a laptop isn't cheap. Keep in mind that even in cities that aren't in high-cost regions, repair rates may exceed seventy-five or even one hundred dollars an hour, perhaps because of lack of competition. What's more, a laptop is full of parts peculiar to just one manufacturer, and, aware of this, many companies will put on the squeeze.

As Rich Schinnel points out, you should realize that a maintenance contract is like a car loan. A no-money-down deal probably won't be the one with the lowest interest rate. A cut-rate service provider may squeeze into the contract all sorts of exclusion clauses, ruling out coverage for hard disk failure, screen damage, labor charges, you name it. You won't get something for nothing, not when a replacement gas plasma screen may cost more than a thousand dollars. Even if you're paying top money for service, read the contract carefully for nasty surprises.

A two-year contract on a $4,000 computer, by the way, may cost $650 and be *non*renewable. On the other hand, as a way of dealing with Murphy's Law, maintenance contracts certainly would be one solution, especially if you need a fast turnaround. Check with users groups—or via a vendors section of a network like CompuServe—to learn about the experiences of others with maintenance contracts and other support agreements.

Shopping for a maintenance contract with either a manufacturer or a third-party organization, you should consider:

■ The maximum life of the agreement. How long can the agreement be extended? It can't go on forever. Some laptop makers won't let you sign up for more than several years of protection.

■ Whether you'll have to bring the units in for repair. Of course, an on-site agreement will be more costly than the carry-in variety.

■ Possible mailing arrangements. Who pays for the freight? And will the repairpeople, the manufacturer, and so on, ship you a replacement laptop for temporary or permanent use, even before yours arrives?

■ Whether you're responsible for making backups of data before the shop works on your laptop. The maintenance people may have to reformat your hard disk, destroying all of the work stored there. What better argument for constantly backing up your data?

■ How long, at the most, the repair shop will keep the laptop. What happens if the shop can't live up to its promised turnaround time? Do you get a loaner unit?

■ Whether you'll enjoy a discount on the loaner if the repair shop won't pay for it.

■ Whether your warranty will self-destruct even if you do simple work with the innards of the laptop or your software. Will the agreement let you install a modem card, or must everything be done by the shop? And can you reformat your hard disk without voiding the agreement?

■ Whether the contract will pay not only for the usual service but also for preventive maintenance.

■ The closeness of the repair shop's relationship with the manufacturer and other sources of parts. This issue shouldn't arise, obviously, in the case of authorized dealers.

TRAINING

Training is a good way to try to defy Murphy's Law. Learn the basics of the MS-DOS operating system, for example, and you'll have much less chance of accidentally erasing your hard drive. You'll also be more certain of sending an urgent report to the home office from Belfast.

Mercifully, in many cases, you can draw on the knowledge you've amassed by way of your desktop machine. Switching to a laptop isn't a big deal for many people. It's like changing over from a Buick to a little Honda used as a second car. Sure, the Honda drives a little differently, but the steering wheel (at least in the United States) is still on the left side. The motor still starts when you turn the ignition key. The instrument panels are basically the same.

Of course, there are many issues specific to laptops, such as battery wear and selection of software that runs well on small screens. If you're like many laptop users, you'll find yourself using your modems more and worrying about connections from strange cities. But not to fret—you're reading this book, right? And very likely, too, you can buy guides to master the software you've bought.

Not everyone, however, has either the time or inclination to learn by reading or experimenting. Some writers are such technoklutzes that they need tutors or classes. The preceding is even more true of sales reps, especially the ones working under pressure for organizations. They're the least hackerish of all laptop users.

Granted, exceptions abound, especially among self-employed reps, such as my friend Al Louis Ripskis, a real estate salesman who has more or less turned computers into an avocation and who'll spend hours and hours optimizing his word processing setup. Commonly, however, sales reps are using computers for the first time. Laptops haven't been fixtures for years in sales organizations the way they have been at accounting firms.

Below are several forms of education for laptop users, beginning with the least expensive in investment up front.[6]

Approach Number One: Sink or Swim

Self-training is often the way to go for independent professional people. I've been writing about and on computers for half a dozen years, and I have yet to suffer through a single course. I say "suffer through" because I'm impatient to try hardware and software and don't want a lecture. My first reading of a laptop manual is primarily to tell me what can go wrong. Then, aware of how I could damage the hardware, I'll experiment—unafraid. If I'm learning a program, I try to keep backup disks handy. I have a stable of hacker friends I can consult if my new toys befuddle me even after a good look through the manual (especially the table of contents and index).

For writers, lawyers, accountants, and other professionals accustomed to wading their way through large masses of information, this method is often the best and cheapest. If you fly often and don't want to work with sensitive documents while jetting along, why not use your time in the air to learn more about useful programs?

---

[6]Thanks to Gene Brezovsky of Seaport, New York—a laptop expert and former systems consultant at Metropolitan Life Insurance—for helping me categorize the kinds of training and offering other advice for the training section. Brezovsky helped Metropolitan set up a laptop purchase program for thousands of sales reps.

Approach Number Two: The Self-Training Approach With Special Phone Backup

If a company's laptop users are reasonably sophisticated, then you might just hand them the usual manuals. Many actually may prefer it this way. Knowing how to get the technical information they need, and having widely varying needs, they may resent having to take time out to attend a class.

Just the same, if your company is large enough, you may want to set up a special hotline where the users can enjoy fast answers to their questions. Otherwise you may find that they're wasting time on the phone, trying to get through to technical support people. Being high tech, computer companies love to inflict obnoxiously modern phone systems on customers and would-be customers.

Once I called WordPerfect—a paragon of good technical support compared to the computer industry at large—for information about WordPerfect Executive. I wasted several dollars in long-distance charges as I wended my way through the company's automated phone system. If I punched one number as the electronic voice requested, it would lead me to a host of choices that, in turn, have options of their own.

How much better for your own company to offer a hotline to unravel common hardware and software mysteries! If nothing else, you might ask vendors for the names of third-party organizations that offer such services.

Approach Number Three: Simplifying the Instruction Manuals

"Just rewrite the manuals and limit them to the information that people need to do their jobs," suggests Gene Brezovsky, a former systems consultant at Metropolitan Life Insurance. You can augment the manuals, of course, with a hotline.

Approach Number Four: Providing Videocassettes or Tutorial Disks

More than half of all households in America own videocassette recorders. Why not record and duplicate a demo of how to use laptops and software? Your few employees without VCRs can watch on company-provided machines. Others can view the tapes at home at their own pace. Step by step you can guide your employees through the proper procedures for the laptops and software.

Alternatively—or perhaps with the tapes—you can offer tutorial disks that explain various procedures. The disks can require the employee to hit the appropriate keys to proceed.

Warning! Test the tapes or tutorial software on employees who are only average or below in technical mastery. Before duplicating the material, make sure it works on the technoklutzes. Do this even if you hire professionals to produce the training aids.

Needless to say, you'll also want to investigate what commercial aids are out there for your hardware and software; your vendor can tell you. The commercial products, of course, won't be customized for your company the way your own efforts can be.

Approach Number Five: Classes

Hold classes yourself or hire outsiders to conduct them. Ideally the instructors will know your business and be able to frame their lessons accordingly. Instead of just teaching word processing, for instance, they can show how to crank out a letter in the format that your company favors. Needless to say, overhead projectors—displaying programs in action—can speed up learning. The students can compute along, on the laptops assigned to them.

Approach Number Six: Individual Instructors

Top executives—or lower-level people who are already overworked and have scant time for normal classes—could benefit from tutoring rather than classes. That way the instruction can be tailored even more to the requirements of individuals.

You might, in fact, decide that rather than training many of your people in a routine way, you'll want a few employees to receive intensive tutoring—so that they can bring others up to speed on specific programs or machines. Presto! The multiplier effect.

*   *   *

Communications is an area where Murphy's Law often reigns. How can you prepare yourself with the right facts and equipment to escape the reach of the law? Ahead lie some suggestions.

Chapter 6

A COMMUNICATIONS PRIMER: HOW YOUR LAPTOP CAN TALK TO THE WORLD

■ The basics of computer communications. Page 165.
■ Modem shopping. Page 168.
■ Choosing the proper communications program. Page 181.
■ Fax modems (and alternatives). Page 187.
■ Some basics of electronic mail. Chapter 11.
■ Cellular modems for laptops. Appendix 3.

Your Fortune 500 company is about to merge with a large rival. This event will be fodder for *USA Today*, the *Wall Street Journal*, *The New York Times*, the *Washington Post*, the financial desk of the perestroika-era *Pravda*—and maybe some predatory traders if word leaks to them ahead of time. Jetting around the country, overseeing area offices, you've tried to stay thirty thousand feet above the paranoia. But Headquarters wants a steady stream of secret reports about the planned merger's effects, and there in rural New Mexico, you're desperate for a way to please your bosses without entrusting the corporate jewels to the local fax operator, who happens to be married to an ambitious UPI stringer. Yes, you could buy a portable facsimile machine. But you're already carrying a laptop to do spreadsheets, so why not use that? If you transmit to headquarters' computer, the people in New York can easily edit your reports after they arrive, something much harder to do with faxes. What's more, you won't have to churn out sensitive *paper*work in the field. You can keep everything inside your laptop's memory.

You're still in fine shape even if you have to send your confidential reports directly to a senior executive who's innocent of high-tech knowledge and insists on your using fax. Just dial up MCI Mail or another computer network. The network will convert your reports from a computer format to a fax format and zip them on to the fax machine that the Cro-Magnon vice president has finally befriended. The VP probably won't care that your laptop produced the faxes. In fact, most likely your computer-oriented facsimiles will look sharper compared to those created the usual way.

For all this wizardry, you'll need little more than a laptop with a modem, the device that lets the machine talk over the phone lines to another computer. You'll also require the right software and perhaps a few tools to hook up from your hotel room. That's it.

Laptops and modems, of course, aren't just for Fortune 500 executives contemplating megamergers. You'll benefit too, for instance, if you're a free-lance writer whose clients want you to squirt electronic versions of your stories directly into their computers. Some editors won't even accept paper copy anymore. What's more, through careful planning ahead of time, you can use even some Cadillac-price business databases. Who knows, if the UPI stringer breaks the news about a corporate merger, it may well be as a result of on-line detective work rather than his relationship with the local fax operator.

In this chapter you won't just learn the basics of computer communications; you'll also find out how to choose the right modem and software *before* you're thousands of miles from your favorite computer shop. Remember, travelers' needs aren't the same as those who stay at home.

The present chapter also will introduce you to modems of another kind—facsimile modems, which increasingly will be built into the normal computer modems. Fax modems let you transmit directly to your office fax machine from almost anywhere in the world. As I've said, you can send faxes via MCI Mail and other networks that translate computer messages into a format for fax machines. But fax transmissions often can survive telephone noise that would thwart computers used the normal way, including those connected to e-mail networks.

Please note that this chapter deals with basics. Chapter 7, "How to Hook Up (and Handle Other Hassles) From Almost Anywhere," discusses the details of making connections from pay phones or hotels with customer-hostile phone systems. Chapter 8, "The Electronic Traveler Abroad," tells how to deal with bureaucracies abroad—including the infamous PTTs ("Post and Telegraph"), the overseas telephone companies that torment telephone users in much of the world. Chapter 9, "An Electronic Baedeker," discusses communications, customs, and other issues in more than twenty countries. Chapter 10, "A Quick Tour of On-line Services," will help you appreciate the rich assortment of databases and other services that you can dial up. Chapter 11, "Some Basics of Electronic Mail," discusses e-mail further.

THE BASICS OF COMPUTER COMMUNICATIONS

Computer communications by telephone usually takes two forms:

■ *Instant communications.* The message that you tap out on your keyboard reaches the other computer immediately. If you're communicating with another person, it's as if you two are using an old-fashioned Teletype. If the software allows it and the printers are connected, you can even keep a paper record of the conversation. If nothing else, however, you'll see each other's keystrokes as they're appearing on the respective screens. You can also communicate instantly with a network like CompuServe—to key in your identification number or a password or to issue a command, such as the one to pick up your electronic mail.

■ *Transmission of files.* You'll recall that files are letters, reports, electronic spreadsheets, or other information that you've entrusted to your computer. Left over from the glory days of mainframes are two terms that are still popular among micro users. *Upload* means to transfer a file *to* another system. Somehow, the *up* suggests that your equipment is talking to a bigger, better machine. *Download* means to receive a file *from* another system.

Whether used in the classical Teletype fashion or to transfer files, computers think digitally—that is, in streams of 0s and 1s. Most telephone circuits, however, demand analog signals: sounds that can vary over a whole range of frequencies. And a modem converts back and forth between digital and analog.

For the benefit of the phone, the modem assigns a low frequency to a 0 bit and a higher one to a 1 bit. You'll recall that letters and numbers—bytes—are made up of bits. Modulation is the name of the process that varies the frequency according to whether the bit is a 0 or 1. The *mo* in *modem* means "modulator." The *de* means "demodulator." Remember, however, that both computers will be thinking digitally. Something is either on or off—a 0 or a 1—a fact that makes computer-related equipment more reliable than old-fashioned electronics.

The various mixes of 0s and 1s stand for letters, numbers, and other symbols meaningful to people or computers.

A capital *A* would be 100001; a capital *B* would be 1000010; a capital *C* would be 1000011; a capital *D* would be 1000100. This is part of a binary numbering system in which the positions of the places marked by 1 are all important and all numbers consist of nothing but 1s and 0s.

The binary system is wonderful for computers but clumsy for mere humans. Mercifully, however, the same series of numbers also have more conventional decimal values, based on the usual progression from 1 to 10. Capital *A*, or 100001, would possess a decimal value of 65 according to the American Standard Code for Information Interchange (ASCII), which, as the name implies, standardizes identities of letters, numbers, and common symbols. A capital *B* would be ASCII 66, and *C* would be ASCII 67.

Conventional ASCII allows up to 128 characters, and "extended" ASCII, as found in IBM-style machines, offers twice that number. Virtually all electronic mail networks in widespread use can transmit the 128 ASCII characters. Not all can transmit symbols, such as squares and brackets, that are outside conventional ASCII characters. Nor can they all send programs, which are in a raw binary format. Of course, some networks can easily transmit files in binary format rather than just as ASCII characters. CompuServe, for instance, can send binary. That capability is helpful if you want to transmit underlining, boldface, and other amenities of files from word processors.

So much for some background. Now, here are the steps of communications from one computer to another via telephone lines.

Step One: The Signals' Trip to Your Modem

Commonly, though not in every computer system, the digital signals travel through an RS-232C-style serial port to a cable and from there to a modem.[1] (Turn back to page 59 for an explanation of serial and parallel ports.) In rare cases, a parallel port connects the computer and modem. But normally the link is through the serial port, for which most modems are designed.

There's one more exception—a major one. Some modems, especially those for laptops, fit on cards that plug into the computer and don't need RS-232C or parallel ports. I'll discuss these "internal" modems shortly. Forget about them for the moment.

Step Two: Modulation

The modem turns the digital signals—the 0s and 1s—into analog ones for the telephone lines.

Step Three: Transmission

The signal travels over the phone lines. If static interrupts the flow of 0s and 1s, the data may be incomplete or garbled. Luckily, however, a sophisticated computer system can keep track of the number of 0s and 1s transmitted and ask the other machine to re-send.

Step Four: Demodulation

At the other end, the modem turns the analog signals into the usual bits, depending on the frequencies of the tone. The frequencies for the 0s and 1s aren't completely standardized around the world. That's one reason American modems don't always work overseas.

---

[1]RS-232C is a triumph of common sense in that it's impossible for you to cause damage by miswiring a RS-232C connection. The standard states that any two pins can be cross-connected. Never, never, however, hook an RS-232C port to a parallel port (also known as a Centronics port). You may damage the parallel port. The serial port won't be damaged; the voltages are in its favor.

Step Five: Processing of Received Signals

After the signals enter the destination computer—through the RS-232C or otherwise—the machine can process them and electronically record these bits and bytes on a floppy or hard disk. Communications software, such as CrossTalk or Procomm, will tell the computer how to handle the incoming signal. "Comm" programs can even tell a printer to spew out a copy of ASCII as it pours over the wires, provided that the printer is fast enough. Or the machine can print out at leisure from the files written to the disk.

QUESTIONS TO ASK WHEN SHOPPING FOR A MODEM

Reporting for the *Washington Post*, Patrick Tyler could gaze out his hotel window and see tankers aflame in the Persian Gulf, the victims of Iranian gunboats. His scanner radio crackled with the Maydays from captains pleading for American protection. The tanker attacks were front-page news. In reporting stories of this significance under deadline pressure, Tyler decided he needed more than his Radio Shack laptop, which couldn't hold more than a few articles, memos, and letters for quick reference. So he ordered a Toshiba T1000 equipped with a modem from the 1000's makers.

Unfortunately, however, a battle of a different sort raged after the Toshiba arrived—a conflict between the local phone system and the laptop's modem. Designed for use in the United States, it emitted an audio tone whose frequency warred with the phone system.

What's more, variations in the voltage on the phone line burned out three Toshiba modems. A fourth modem, which a Swedish firm had designed for Toshiba, also flopped; it couldn't coexist peacefully with Tyler's communications software. Imagine Tyler's chagrin. For him, as for countless other journalists and businesspeople, communications "is every bit as important as any other aspect of the box. Really, it is the most important after basic word processing."

This section will spare you some of the travails that Tyler suffered at the tip of the Arabian Peninsula. It will help you answer thirteen questions that you should mull over before buying a modem—although, since needs vary, you shouldn't ascribe any importance to the order in which I lay out the criteria. If you're a journalist in India who habitually dials up a mainframe in Los Angeles, for instance, you'll be keenly interested in a modem's ability to punch signals over weak or noisy telephone lines.

If, however, you're a constantly traveling sales rep who confines his international wanderings to large cities with good phone systems, then you may care more for compactness.

And if you're a businessperson who dials up a local computer, nothing more exotic, then you may get along splendidly with the very Toshiba modem that tormented Tyler. Presumably it will work well on American phone lines; plus you won't have to drag along a separate box, since the modem slips inside a Toshiba laptop.

Question One: Should the Modem Be Internal or External?

Modems come in two physical forms, internal and external

An external modem, a "stand-alone" model, is separate from your computer and plugs into the serial port, the RS-232C.

External modems will work with virtually all computers that include RS-232C ports. So your laptop and desktop computer probably can use the same modem, as long as it's small enough to be taken on trips. Indeed, some special modems for portables, such as the WorldPort modems, are the size of a pack of cigarettes.

The second form of modem is a card, a printed circuit board that plugs into a slot on your computer. As a rule—though this is changing—laptops can use only "proprietary slots" designed for particular makes of machines.

Question Two: Direct Connect or Acoustic?

Some modems plug directly into the phone lines. These "direct-connect" modems offer the clearest connections, a must when you're sending data at high speeds. Less positively, however, direct-connect modems can be nightmares to hook up to electronic phone systems. Moreover, suppose that a wire runs directly from the hotel phone to the wall and there is no jack into which you can plug the modem?

An "acoustically coupled" modem could be a solution. A tiny loudspeaker, in a rubber cone or earmuff-style cups, pipes the whine from the modem into the phone transmitter within the walls of the cone. Conversely, a microphone in another cone picks up the sounds from the receiver inside the phone handset. You can buy an acoustic coupler to work with the WorldPort modem and perhaps other brands if you can't easily make a direct connection to the wire in the wall. Alas, acoustic couplers aren't reliable for computer modems transmitting data at high speed. They're dicey at 1,200 bits per second, though I've *heard* of successes at 2,400 bits. At that speed you'd better use your acoustic coupler in a quiet room and perhaps bury it under a pillow. What's more, especially if the coupler is an earmuff-style one with a fixed distance between the microphone and loudspeaker, then you may find yourself defeated by an odd-shaped telephone handset.

For the serious traveler who needs reliable connections from many hotels, the ideal approach could well be a direct-connect modem with the ability to accept acoustic couplers. Try the couplers that Radio Shack makes for its notebook-size portables. Generally, though not always, they'll work on both American and foreign telephones. An interesting alternative, however, may be available by now. Vocal Technologies (332 Scott Boulevard, Santa Clara, California 95034, [408] 980-5181) told me that for around $40 it will sell a coupler that can work with *any* phone. Via straps, it reportedly attaches to any kind of telephone, even those with square-shaped receivers and transmitters.

Question Three: Full or Half Duplex?

The next issue is whether the modem can operate at either half duplex or full duplex. Half-duplex modems have been likened to CB radio transmitters. That is, the other person can't hear you if he or she is sending, and vice versa, so phone lines needn't be as good as they'd have to be otherwise. Normally, however, you'll need a full-duplex modem, since that's the standard among most dial-up networks as well as among individual computer users. In fact, this is really a nonissue. I mention it here just to make sure you don't get stuck with a cheapie half-duplex modem.

Question Four: How Fast?

The next big question is speed—how fast the modem will transmit information.

Years ago I worked for a newspaper and found myself awed by the Associated Press teletypes clattering away at sixty or seventy words per minute. The slowest computer modems in common use, however, whiz information over the wires at several hundred words per minute, and the business standard today is more than a thousand words per minute—although two-thousand-word-plus modems and faster ones probably will be the standard by the time you're reading this book.

I've recklessly simplified this description of modem speed, by the way. Computer professionals don't say "words per minute," they say "baud" or "bits per second" (bps). A slowpoke modem sending several hundred words per minute would run at 300 baud or 300 bps. For technical reasons that I won't bother to explain here, "bps" is preferable to "baud" and is what I'll use in this book.

A speed of 2,400 bps is the present business standard in the United States. By 1992 or 1993 the standard may well approach 9,600 bps. However, you'll still want to be able to slow to 1,200 bps or even 300 baud if the phone lines are weak or are crackling with static, which, if too bad, may prevent any computerized communications. As a rule— exceptions abound—phone lines overseas are not as good as they are in the United States.

Question Five: What About Software?

Does the modem come with its own "free" software? "Bundled" programs can be both a boon and a bane.

On the positive side, you'll save money compared to buying the software separately. And in theory, at least, the modem should get along well with a factory-supplied program. That's especially true if the bundled software is a winner, such as ProComm.

On the other hand, some manufacturers will supply their own software or tweak other people's software to hide deficiencies in the modem. I own a cheap 2,400-bps modem, for instance, that often won't stop hogging my phone line unless I actually snap the switch off. I don't have this problem if I use factory-supplied software. But I often use the popular Mirror program instead, and when I do, the modem balkily ignores the hang-up command that Mirror issues. And that's the modem's fault rather than Mirror's, since the communications program is issuing industry-standard commands to the modem. I won't complain, since the modem cost me little; still, this incompatibility is an annoyance.

To avoid such frustrations, be sure that your modem will *completely* obey the Hayes AT commands. Hayes is the IBM of modem makers, and other manufacturers love to ballyhoo their adherence to this standard.

Question Six: How About Other Ease-of-Use Issues (Including Setup)?

Do you have to flip some tiny switches—DIP switches, as they're called in the trade—before the modem will function properly? Ideally you don't. If possible, check with someone using both your brand of computer and the same software. Also, see if the explanations in the manual are clear. Many modem manuals might as well be in encrypted Japanese.

Notice, too, whether the modem boasts a speaker, so you can hear it dial and confirm that the connection is working out. Another good feature would be LEDs that tell whether the modem has detected a tone from the machine with which it's communicating. LEDs may also show the number of bps selected. Pocket modems and fax boards often make you suffer trade-offs—simply because of their compactness—so don't expect as much as you would from a full-size model. Still, it's nice to have amenities, such as the speaker, that can alert you instantly that something is amiss.

Question Seven: How Big Is the Modem?

"I've seen guys walking through airports with full-size modems the size of a phone book under their arms," says Scott Stogel, an engineer with Touchbase Systems in Northport, New York, who helps design the WorldPort series of modems.

Mind you, Stogel has a vested interest in the size issue. After all, his employer's product is a midget compared to some of the boxes of the past. Keep in mind, too, that rather than buying a cigarette-pack-size modem, you might compromise with one that's no larger than a paperback (and I'm not talking about the *Ulysses*-size variety). If, however, you're not exactly an Olympic weight lifter or if you regularly use an airport designed for Himalayan-class hikers—an O'Hare, say, or a Heathrow—you'd do well to heed his advice.

Question Eight: How Well Built and Engineered Is the Modem?

Check with existing owners about this and other issues. If the modem gets banged around—as those in the field are wont to be—will it survive? How are the printed circuit boards made? Does the manufacturer use surface-mount technology?

In surface mounting, most of the components do not have leads on them, and they don't go through the printed circuit board. "They're actually mounted directly on the board on the surface," says Glenn Checketts, an engineer with Holmes Microsystems in Salt Lake City, a maker of internal modem boards. "They're not touched by human hands, so you don't get the corrosion of body oil from production workers."

What's more, boards with surface mounting are less susceptible to broadcast signals. Lacking leads to serve as little antennas, the surface-mounted parts are more secure against this interference.

Proper electrical filtering helps, too. Three years ago a test model of a Holmes modem picked up a country music station at a frequency of about 1 megahertz. Checketts could actually hear the singers twanging away. "We were kidding around about offering the option of radio music as a background," Checketts jokes. Holmes corrected the problem. It remained, however, in the modems of three competitors.

Question Nine: How Good Is the Modem When the Phone Lines Are Bad?

Modem engineers disagree as to whether mere "end" users should try to delve into arcania such as signal-to-noise ratios. My suggestion is not to worry. Instead check with friends and colleagues about how the modem has performed in real life, not just in the lab. If you're making a mass purchase, leave the question in the hands of your management information system (MIS) guru.

According to my friend David Page, the operator of my favorite BBS, the all-time noise resister is the Telebit TrailBlazer series of modems, most of which, as of this writing, list for over $1,000.[2] Except for the $795 T1000—9,600 bps maximum—they can whiz at 19,200

[2] Telebit's address is 10440 Bubb Road, Cupertino, California 95014. Its telephone number is 1-800-TELEBIT or (408) 996-8000.

bps over good phone lines.[3] And they have been known to manage 4,800 bps over phone lines too noisy for an ordinary 300-bps modem. At least one of the TrailBlazer models, the T2500 ($1,495), doesn't come with just the Telebit error-control method (the packetized ensemble protocol, or PEP). It also includes the international V.32 modulation standard, the V.42 error-control standard, and the V.42bis compression standard discussed later in this chapter.

David's interest in this matter, by the way, is more than academic, since he's one of the pillars of Fidonet, an international communications network whose hacker members extend as far as Australia. For several years Fidonet has been fighting the good fight for reliable trans-Pacific connections at 9,600 bps.

Alas, the TrailBlazer that Fidonet uses for its Australian link is almost as big as a portable computer. But sizes have declined. Meanwhile, however, you may decide that the trade-off between bulk and error control is worth it at the higher speeds if you truly have a noise problem.

Question Ten: What About Power?

If the modem is a stand-alone unit, can you get a power supply that runs off foreign power? You may fry your U.S.-made model if you try it on the 220–240 volts widely encountered in Europe. One solution to the problem is the use of batteries, which also can be handy if you're struggling with a pay phone many feet from an outlet. You'll want to know, of course, how long the batteries will last. Ideally a single set should suffice for a two-week business trip. Just how many hours of communicating will the batteries allow? Does the modem have a shut-off feature so it doesn't draw that much power unless it's transmitting or receiving?

Better still, can the modem draw power from the phone lines? That can have a downside. Such modems are illegal in many countries, especially Germany, and there are risks of damage from unpredictable line voltages. Still, Vocal Technologies (332 Scott Boulevard, Santa Clara, California 95034, [408] 980-5181), says that its phone-line-powered, $185 Stowaway modem has worked fine overseas. By now the company should be selling a modem that allows the use of batteries when phone power is too dicey.

---

[3]The Telebit T1000, of course, is not to be confused with Toshiba's T1000 laptop.

Suppose your modem is internal—on a card that plugs inside your laptop. Then the issue is how much power it will drain from the other parts of the system. The modem should draw well under half a watt.

Question Eleven: In What Countries Can You Use the Modem?

Two issues can prove pesky at times: (1) whether the modem will talk to other modems in your host country, including those of e-mail networks, and (2) whether the local phone company there considers your modem to be legal.

You can't always depend on the compatibility of Bell-style U.S. modems outside this country, not unless you're directly dialing another American-style modem. That's the general rule. There are major exceptions, such as Canada, but not many. Here are the basic compatibility rules for different speeds:

■ **300 bps.** Europeans and the planet at large ignore Bell's 300-bps standard. Instead they adhere to the recommendation of the Consultative Committee on International Telephony and Telegraphy (CCITT)), the organization setting global communications standards. The CCITT standard for 300 bps is known as V.21.

■ **1,200 bps.** The Bell 212 modems and the CCITT V.22 modems usually get along, but not in every case. They process information in basically the same way. But their frequencies differ enough for problems to dog you if a modem is inflexibly Bell-like or CCITT-like. Even if a modem can use the CITT standard, you may have to give it a special software command to enjoy this flexibility. I'll explain the **B0** command and the related **B1** command on page 226.

■ **2,400 bps.** Virtually all 2,400-bps modems adhere to the CCITT's standards. American boosters of the metric system can find some solace here; our 2,400-bps modems and the rest of the world's are thinking alike, even if we humans in America refuse to buy our gas in liters or measure our children's height in centimeters. Several CCITT standards exist for 2,400-bps transmission, of which V.22bis is the most common.

■ **9,600 bps.** V.32 is the CCITT's standard for full-duplex modems at this speed.[4] Many U.S.-marketed 9,600-bps modems can't even talk reliably to those from other manufacturers, much less to products from

---

[4]V.29 is the CCITT's *half*-duplex standard for 9,600 bps.

other countries. But that's changing as true V.32s take over the market. You can almost always expect your V.32 modem to get along with another if you're using a CCITT-compliant model. Don't confuse *compliant* with *compatible*. The word *compliant* means that the modem meets all the V.32 standards, not just some.

Normally you should forget about a modem for overseas use unless it honors all CCITT standards precisely. Check with the manufacturer if the dealer doesn't know. Try to make your deal contingent on this compliance, and if you're buying in bulk, you might even ask about field testing under actual conditions. Also, mass buyers could join and consult with such groups as the Microcomputer Managers Association and perhaps even participate in field tests together.

Of course, often mass buyers purchase modems in bulk for internal purposes. What if a company knows that its modems won't be talking to other people's machines and that it won't use dial-up networks, just engage in direct communications? Then it may be better off saving money and not worrying about communications standards, so long as the modems comply with local regulations.

Aside from the problem of modem compatibility, there is the matter of whether a phone company will let you hook up a particular modem to its lines.[5] Voltages in some wires within phone cables can be higher than other voltages. And the companies like to keep high and low voltages apart to avoid burning out equipment. So, for this reason and others, they have construction standards for modems. For example, phone companies may require a certain physical gap between wires within the modem that carry voltages at various different levels. One modem maker flunked a Europe test because the spacing requirement was too great for a portable modem—even though the maker of the modem had tested it at a whopping 1,500 volts. Bureaucracy!

An interesting question arises: should you defy a phone company, private or government run, if you know your equipment won't hurt it? You may be breaking the law. On the other hand, your business may be urgent. The only quick way out of the dilemma may be acoustic cups, which, however, can slow transmission speeds.

Often, though not always, a slow speed of 300 bps won't make that

---

[5]At least one major modem maker, Hayes, says that overseas it sells modems that the local telecommunications officials have approved.

much difference in your business. So try to build extra time for the modeming into your travel schedule if you think direct modeming could be risky.

In the future, businesses will be sending more and more graphics-type information, increasing the attractiveness of higher speeds and direct connections. But by then maybe the more opaque of the world's telecommunications bureaucracies will have gotten the message that they could harm their countries' economic development by warring against businesspeople who rely on modems.

Question Twelve: How About Error Control?

Should your modem include an error-control scheme to cope with noise on phone lines?

Thus equipped, modem one sends data in blocks to modem two, which, in turn, confirms that it has received the same number of bytes. If not? Modem one will retransmit the block. Error control can help in such cases as when you are:

■ Communicating to or from areas with horrid phone connections.

■ Relying heavily on elaborate scripts that automate procedures for CompuServe.[6] These scripts can go far beyond automatic log-ons. They can, for example, guide you to your favorite areas of CompuServe and download new messages. If you're addicted to such capabilities, then an error-control modem may be worth the expense. Errors, after all, can befuddle the scripts.

■ Sending at extra-high speeds.

■ Handling sensitive financial, legal, or medical data where the wrong zero can bankrupt someone or even cost a life.

Error control isn't for everybody. It's overkill for most hobbyists and even for many business users, especially in locations with good telephone lines. Error control, also, can be a little unnerving on occasion. Crackling phone lines mean that blocks in files will take a long time to get through; in fact, a file-transfer may not make it at all if the racket doesn't clear up. So error control isn't always the answer. If

[6]Scripting programs, such as ATO, TAPCIS, or Navigator, are especially good for automating routines on CompuServe. Lotus Express is good on MCI Mail. You also can use other programs and home brew your scripts.

you're sending plain, noncritical text, you might be better off with garbage here and there.

What's more, if you're transmitting directly to a human at the other end of the line, you might not see your keystrokes until you've typed enough for the error-control scheme to show mercy and display the characters. Nowadays I use my modem mainly to call local BBS's and packet-switching numbers[7] in my area, so I've survived nicely without the added complications and cost of error control.

Then again, my present modem can't whiz beyond 2,400 bps. When I do make the next leap—to 9,600 bps—my new modem probably will have error control.

Granted, software-based file transfer protocols, such as XMODEM (discussed on page 184), also can reduce errors. But error control can be a real sanity saver in many situations. You may be talking in real time to a distant computer, for example, and need to give it exact commands over noisy phone lines. Even humans may have problems reading you at times if you aren't using error control at 9,600 bps. What's more, the data-compression schemes that accompany many error-control protocols can greatly cut long-distance charges. Even without compression, error control alone under certain circumstances can speed up transmissions.

When buying a modem with error control, of course, you should make certain that you can switch off the capabilities when you *don't* want them. That's not all. Also see if the control scheme is compatible with the ones at the other end. I know. You can't always pick out the humans and the computers you'll need to communicate with. Here, though, are some common possibilities:

■ V.42, the CCITT's error-control standard. Don't let the "V.42" confuse you. It refers not to speed or modulation methods but to the form of error control. Remember to insist on a "CCITT-compliant" V.42 modem rather than just a "compatible" one. Modems can use V.42 with a data-compression scheme called V.42bis, which, under

[7]Packet switching means to send information in blocks of bytes known as packets. Through technical wizardry, this method can greatly lower the cost of transmitting data over phone lines. That's why networks like Tymnet and Telenet employ packet switching. Because of it, you can use networks such as MCI Mail while calling local numbers and avoiding the usual long-distance charges.

ideal conditions, can approximately more than triple the amount of data that a computer can send in a given time. *Ideal* means a good, quiet phone line, a speedy computer, and data that lends itself to compression—for instance, a database, a spreadsheet, or a word processing file with the normal number of blank spaces.

V.42bis is based on the Link-Access Procedure for Modems (LAPM), an error-control standard that V.42 includes. Among other things, V.42 also covers classes two through four of yet another error-control scheme, the Microcom Networking Protocol. In case you're curious, V.42 and other error-control methods are available only for modems running at 2,400 bps and above. By the time error control hit the market, many users in business had already forsaken 300- and 1,200-bps modems for faster models.

■ The Microcom Networking Protocol, developed by Microcom of Norwood, Massachusetts. You'll find MNP capabilities in some 2,400-bps modems, and it's one of the standards on MCI Mail, CompuServe, GEnic, and other networks. Using the special compression in advanced classes of MNP, some 2,400-bps models at times can more than triple the amount of information sent in a given period. The top classes can talk and do error control with class four MNP, a fact of interest to class four users hoping to reach colleagues with V.42 modems.

I don't have room here to discuss all of the MNP classes in detail. Simply put, however, classes one, two, and three let the modem detect and control errors; four helps the modem cope with the vagaries of telephone lines; five compresses data; classes six through nine allow other advanced features. Higher classes, of course, include capabilities from lower classes.

For a detailed explanation of the MNP hierarchy, please see page 499 of *Dvorak's Guide to PC Telecommunications* (Berkeley, Calif.: Osborne/McGraw-Hill, 1990), by John C. Dvorak and Nick Anis—an instant classic for students of microcomputer communications.

■ The X.PC protocol, employed by Tymnet and MCI Mail.

■ X.32 (Dialup X.25). Hayes offers modems with either V.42, X.25, or both built in. X.25 is the international standard for connecting to packet-switched networks.

■ The Telebit PEP protocol mentioned on page 174—a solution for people wanting direct, transoceanic communications at high speeds under the worst conditions.

Please distinguish between (1) being able to talk to another modem and (2) being able to use error control with it. Two modems that don't share error-control techniques may be sociable in other ways.

TWO OTHER WAYS TO TURN BINARY INTO ASCII FOR E-MAIL

Lotus Express isn't the only program that can turn binary information into ASCII, then back again. Some others are:

■ Mail-It-All, a shareware program from my friends Herb Tyson and Stephen Banker. Like Lotus Express, it will preserve such goodies as boldface and underlining. It's designed for all nets, not just MCI Mail. Unlike Lotus Express, however, Mail-It-All isn't a complete communications program, just a converter used with your other software.

You can order it from Consummate Software, 5078 Fulton Street, N.W., Washington, D.C. 20016. For $25, Consummate will send you a disk (the licensing fee is $15 if you run across the program on a BBS).

■ DEBUGSC, a public domain program from *PC Magazine* (described in the November 28, 1989, issue), which also will convert binary files into ASCII for e-mail systems, then reverse the process. It works on files as large as 60K. Look for DEBUGSC on local BBS's or in the Magnet section of CompuServe.

Question Thirteen: Can the Modem Communicate Synchronously?

In synchronous transmission—a familiar form of communications in the mainframe world—the two modems electronically decide the time between each bit or character. They also decide how long to set aside for each one.

The synchronous method sends data one-fifth faster than does asynchronous communications, the kind that microcomputers normally use to talk to each other. However, synchronous modems and software, at least in the past, have been more costly than the asynchronous type. And for the most part, too, the asynchronous equipment works better with noisy phone lines and other problems, such as satellite-created delays (even radio waves don't travel twenty or twenty-five thousand miles instantaneously). So you should stick to asynchronous unless your computer will be talking to a mainframe computer or LAN that needs synchronous. If you need synchronous, you might consider buying a modem capable of both forms of transmission.

To address an important issue—if you haven't noticed already— asynchronous modems don't need timing because stop bits and start bits separate characters from one another.

SHOPPING FOR COMMUNICATIONS SOFTWARE

Arthur C. Clarke, the science fiction writer, is the father of modern satellite communications as well as the author of countless articles on technology. In 1983, when I was hoping to reach him as part of the research for my book *The Silicon Jungle*, I expected that he would enjoy the best and latest communications software, even if he did happen to be in Sri Lanka.

Consider my frustration when I learned that he was using an oddball program that worked fine with his computer but clashed with the popular communications software of that time.

We made our connection only after Clarke switched both computers and software.

This ordeal had stretched out for months, because of the logistics, and it soured me forever on oddball programs whose developers couldn't envision their customers wanting to communicate via computer with users of other products.

Today most software houses put out more versatile communications programs. But lesser troubles remain. Many programs, for instance, don't offer all means of exchanging files—all the protocols—that they should. So flexibility is one of *my* more important criteria. Over the years I've "talked" to dozens, perhaps hundreds, of different computers, either individuals' or companies'. So I want both my modem and my software not to be too picky about what's at the other end of the phone line.

Here, now, are my three big questions to ask when choosing communications software:

Question One: What's the General Ease of Installation and Use?

How easy is the software to install and learn? The program that I normally use—Mirror, which began life as an imitation of the CrossTalk program and has progressed from there—led me step by step through an installation menu.

Like CrossTalk's commands, many of Mirror's are in English or close thereto. If I want to set the speed down to 300 bps, I can tap the Esc key, type out **SP 3** (short for **Speed 300**), and press the Return key.

I also enjoy the fact that CrossTalk can be command driven. That is, I can quickly accomplish what I want without suffering a tortuous series of menus.

What's more, without ado, I can call up a screen that shows the bps rate and other important settings.

Question Two: How Flexible Is the Software?

Can you *easily* create, set, select, or choose:

■ The command or script file you use. Ideally these files will store all or many of the settings below. The slickest software packages can even record your keystrokes as you're logging on a network so that you can dial it up easily in the future. Please note, of course, that I'm describing ideal software for the serious modem user. Not all programs will have all of the command or script features listed here. What's more, if your communications needs are simple, you may need only some of these capabilities.

■ The number you're dialing. Do you have to go through countless machinations to add a new number to a directory of numbers for automatic dialing? Or is everything simple? This feature is invaluable even to casual users who regularly dial certain numbers.

■ Automatic redialing, a must feature if you want to log on a busy BBS system with a constant stream of callers. This feature ideally will be easy to invoke as well as to change if, for example, you want to shorten or lengthen the delay between tries at reaching a number.

Mind you, not everyone likes automatic dialing. I have a consultant friend, David Labell, a saint of a hacker who prides himself on avoiding it when he's trying to log on a certain BBS in Washington, D.C. Maybe David will change. For the moment, however, he'd no more use an automatic dialer than he would push ahead in a movie line or check out ten items at the express grocery counter reserved for people with nine. David, of course, could easily cheat if he wanted to. His programmer wife could log on the BBS ahead of him with her automatic redialing, and then he might beat the next caller.

I'd side with Leti Labell. Auto dialing, used on an e-mail net with only so many dial-up numbers, just might make the difference between an important report arriving on time or being late.

■ Whether you're in "originate" or "answer." Your modem can't share the same mode with the machine at the other end. When you dial the other modem you'll automatically be in originate. Sometimes, however, especially when faced with irascible hotel switchboards, you won't be able to dial—you'll have the other person call you, or the two of you will talk first (the ordinary way) before switching on the modem tones.

■ The speed—the bps. A must feature in almost all cases.

■ The number of data bits. Data bits form each character as transmitted. The standard is typically seven or eight bits.

■ The number of stop bits. Modem one uses a stop bit or bits (the normal number is 1 or 2) to tell modem two that it's finished transmitting a character. The more common setting is 1 stop bit.

■ The parity setting. Parity bits are extra bits used in error checking to make sure that no data has disappeared. Possibilities are "odd," "even," "mark," or "space." Don't worry about the meanings. Just follow the settings specified by the other person, your company, or your computer network. A common parity setting—but not a universal one—is "none."

Get the picture? If you don't know what the other person is using, try 8 data bits, 1 stop bit, and no parity, or "8, 1, and none" in popular parlance. You might also experiment with 7, 1, and even. Don't worry about another kind of bit, a start bit. It's always a digital one.

■ Whether you're full duplex or half duplex. If you're in full duplex, you'll be depending on the other computer to "echo" characters back to your screen. The other person must then be in half duplex. Otherwise he or she will see MMOORREE than one character when one is enough.

■ On-off flow control. Via flow control, during an ASCII file transfer the receiving computer can tell the transmitting one, "Hey, hold off while I write the material to my disk.'' Another, more generic term, "handshaking," encompasses flow control or any other means that computers use to verify that they're on speaking terms or to arrive at common communications settings.

■ Which character, if any, that you want to filter out when you're receiving ASCII files or the other person's typing. Suppose you're logging on your office computer network late at night and your spouse is sleeping nearby. Ideally you can tell your software to filter out Ctrl-G (ASCII 7), the control character that makes your computer beep when you're logging on many networks or BBS's. The filtering system ideally will also screen out characters that could drive your word processor crazy, such as form feeds—Ctrl-L (ASCII 12)—which cause your printer to move on to the next page prematurely.

■ Which characters you want filtered out while transmitting. You don't want to confuse the other computer either.

■ Whether you want line feeds—Ctrl-J (ASCII 11)—when you press the carriage return while typing to the other person. If your software won't let you insert line feeds, some words may be broken in two and appear on different lines.

■ The lengths of delays between characters and between lines. This feature at times can be invaluable when dealing with some mainframes that can't accept files sent the usual way.

■ Which terminal you're emulating. On occasion, must your communications software fool a mainframe into thinking you're logging on with a specific terminal made by Digital Equipment Corporation, IBM, Wang, or another company?

■ Whether you're in the "capture" mode. That's when you can record all incoming keystrokes or incoming ASCII files.

■ What protocol you'll use to transfer files. Just like the diplomatic kind, a protocol is a set of rules to which the parties involved have agreed. A popular protocol in the micro world is XMODEM. It sends files in blocks of 128 bytes, to which it adds an extra byte (or more) —used by the computer at the other end to determine if the block arrived intact.

Unlike the uncorrected ASCII file transfer, XMODEM can send every bit and byte in a file, not just the 128 ASCII characters. So it's useful for transmitting material like programs and spreadsheets.

XMODEM, however, like all protocols, slows down transmission time compared to transmitting straight ASCII. Also, it works only with files using 8 data bits, one reason why the 8, 1, and none combination is so popular. Another problem is that XMODEM needs rapid acknowledgments of those 128-byte packets, and many mainframes aren't brisk enough. CompuServe users must use a slower-than-normal version of XMODEM, known informally as "relaxed XMODEM." If you're having trouble talking to CompuServe reliably via XMODEM during the day, you might wait until the night, when traffic dies down.[8]

Different versions of XMODEM exist. Ideally your software will slide easily into either the checksum or CRC form of XMODEM and also use other popular protocols.

YMODEM is good for transmitting files faster than XMODEM can, as long as the lines are clean. Used by many university mainframes, Kermit allows excellent error checking, is fast, and permits wildcard transfers. That is, if you type *.LTR, Kermit will transmit all files on your floppy or in your hard disk subdirectory that end with .LTR—for example, IRS.LTR. You may also look for error-checking protocols such as X.PC (recognized on MCI Mail and Tymnet, among other networks). And if you're buying the Mirror communications program, investigate the possibility of adding an enhancement for MNP error checking (you won't need an MNP modem).

Yet another possible file protocol is ZMODEM, which, according to David Page, the Fidonet man, "is faster than nearly all other protocols and has better error recovery than all of the others. It's the one Fidonet uses to talk to Australia." ZMODEM is the favorite on David's BBS and a number of others. The faster people can transfer files, obviously, the more callers the BBS's can accommodate.

Amazingly, if you're disconnected from a BBS halfway through a file transfer using ZMODEM, you can call back later and resume the transfer where you left off. ZMODEM saves the half-sent file and graciously asks the sending computer to continue from where the line "broke."

---

[8]A handy protocol for CompuServe is CompuServe Quick B, which is faster on CompuServe than any other standard found there. YMODEM is another good protocol for CompuServe.

Question Three: What Are the Program's Other Traits and Features?

1. *Compactness*. If your laptop has a roomy hard disk, compactness may not matter. But suppose you're using a portable with either one floppy or none at all—just a memory chip with very limited capacity? Then you may evaluate communications programs in terms of their length. Try Mirror or another that, stripped down, without all the .HLP files, takes up several hundred K at the very most, ideally far less.

2. *Good error handling*—the human variety. Suppose you're in the "capture" mode and are about to "overwrite" an existing file by assigning the same name to an about-to-be-created file. Will the software program warn you? Some programs will not only warn you but give you the choice of whether to erase or add to the old file. Please note that while the ideal program will offer this feature, it's a feature you can live without—or at least I can, if pressed. You can capture material to a standard file name, then use MS-DOS's REN command to change the name to something more descriptive.

3. *Special features for the network you're on*. The Lotus Express communications program, for instance, can dial up MCI Mail regularly and "beep" you if it finds new messages. With it, you also can compose messages off-line, then dial up MCI Mail automatically. Moreover, Lotus Express can turn your spreadsheet or word processor file into ASCII characters acceptable to MCI Mail; then the other person's Lotus Express can restore the files to the usual binary format. Available through MCI Mail representatives or your Lotus dealer, Lotus Express lists for $150.

4. *Either a built-in word processor or the ability to call up your regular one in a hurry.*[9] Mirror includes a WordStar-like editor that you can summon up as an alternative to the clumsy on-line systems that many e-mail services inflict on their users. You can use the editor to create a quick ASCII file to respond to a message you've just seen; you needn't sign off the network first.

In the future, as modem speeds increase, e-mail services may be able to offer more nimble editors, but right now, most on-line editors are the pits. For instance, if you delete a number of words from a

---

[9] You might also consider a small, fast editor, such as VDE or QEdit, with an output that e-mail systems like.

paragraph, the remaining material in most cases won't reform automatically. Nor can you straighten out the margins with a quick command, such as Ctrl-B. Instead you may have to type out the word FORMAT or otherwise slow yourself down.

That's why the ability to edit easily off-line, on your own computer, is so valuable. If the communications software lacks its own editor, then ideally it will let you move back to your own in a hurry—a feature with which ProComm is blessed.

5. *Macros—the ability to consolidate keystrokes when giving commands*. Normally your software may require you to push the PgDn key, then select the ASCII file transfer method when you want to preserve material on your disk. With a macro, however, you can combine the two actions. Do not confuse macros with the ability to dial a phone number and arrive at many different settings just by loading in the proper command or script file.

6. *An easy-to-understand script language*. Earlier I alluded to script or command files that you almost could write automatically, just by having the communications program be able to re-create your keystrokes. Preferably, however, the communications program will let you edit the scripts easily and understand their contents. You also may want to be able to create scripts from scratch—perhaps using a word processor or other program that can produce ASCII.

7. *Background operation*. Can you boot up your modem program, start a file transfer, then resume your word processing or other activities while your modem and the other one exchange bytes? That's a lifesaver if you're on a deadline and are swapping long files. Bear in mind, however, that not all computers have enough memory for you to use this capability (which is available in Mirror, Relay Gold, and some other sophisticated communications programs). If you're word processing you may have to use a compact text-editing program, such as QEdit or VDE.

FAX MODEMS (AND ALTERNATIVES)

While editor of a magazine called *High Technology Import & Export*, I trained most of my writers to file by MCI Mail. But I couldn't help noticing what was happening on the business side.

Hardly ever did advertisers or subscribers "talk" to the magazine via our MCI Mail account, which I used daily, and from which I would

HOW YOUR CONVENTIONAL MODEM CAN USE MNP

You don't need a special modem to enjoy MNP 5's compression and sophisticated error control. A communications program called MTEZ lets ordinary modems—capable of 1,200 or 2,400 bps—do the job. There is a trade-off, naturally. Although you'll enjoy data compression, your modem's effective speed will be at least 17 percent slower than a true MNP modem. But that's still a big gain.

MTEZ is available from MagicSoft, P.O. Box 396, Lombard, Illinois 60148 (708-953-2374) for $79 with an MNP add-on. The product shares some of the look and feel of ProComm. It includes certain protocols such as XMODEM. And an optional module can add on Kermit, CompuServe B, and ZMODEM, among others.

MTEZ's MNP feature is also available as a module for Mirror III, the communications program from SoftKlone Distributing (327 Office Plaza Drive, Suite 100, Tallahassee, Florida 32301, telephone 904-878-8564).

SoftKlone and MagicSoft are reputable companies, but beware of unscrupulous modem-makers and dealers who bundle MTEZ with their wares, then pass them off as MNP modems. Make certain that an "MNP modem" is an MNP modem, regardless of the communications software in use.

Intriguingly, MagicSoft also sells a cellular module (for $49). The company says the cellular module and MTEZ will let your modem talk to an MNP 5 modem in a car, et cetera, and survive loss of carrier, which can occur when bridges, buildings, and hills interfere with radio signals. There is a big controversy about which kinds of protocols and modems are most effective on the road. For crucial applications, you might still want to rely on something proven like the SPCL protocol discussed in my appendix on cellular modems.

Considering the low prices, however, MTEZ and the cellular module might be worth trying, if you want to see if your regular modem will work in a cellular situation. According to MagicSoft, in fact, conventional modems can communicate—via cellular phones—if both ends use the company's special software.

have forwarded any messages. Instead the advertisers and subscribers favored fax. And they insisted on it despite the fact that the magazine carried the MCI Mail number as well as a telex number that linked up with MCI. That's not all. Later, after I became a telecommuter, editing *E&I* articles from my apartment, I found that the magazine preferred that I send in memos by fax rather than computer. The publisher and staff didn't want to run up a heavy MCI Mail bill or keep a six-thousand-dollar Macintosh turned on just for my messages. Moreover, even the resident technophobes could still pick up my faxes.

However plain may be the glories of computerized communications, much of the planet prefers fax or telex. More than three million fax machines exist.

A fax-laptop connection can double the number of machines to which you can speed your message. Fax is ubiquitous, not just in the United States but abroad, including places where the phone service is too bad for high-speed computer communications. Yasser Arafat, an example of faxmania, reportedly flies around the world accompanied by two facsimile machines. With a computer-fax connection, you can even use your laptop in some cities to order a pastrami on rye from a suitably equipped deli or wire in a prescription to a certain drugstore. More important, just as I have done, you can reach people or companies allergic to computers. Another benefit exists. You can send to a fax machine in your hotel, so you can obtain hard copy even if you're half a world away from your printer.

The above magic is all possible through either (a) facsimile modems or (b) network connections like CompuServe and MCI Mail, which can translate computer messages into fax format.

Mike Weiner, president of Microlytics, a software house famous for its spell-checkers and GOfer text-searcher, is sold on computer-sent faxes. At four in the morning in Hong Kong, Weiner miraculously awoke with answers to problems he'd hashed out at a late business dinner, details that were "better read than listened to." He wrote eight pages on his laptop, then fretted over how to print them. Then an idea dawned on him. Why not use CompuServe's fax connection? Within twenty minutes after he'd sent his file to CompuServe, the hotel delivered his fax. This message to himself had to travel thousands of miles—first to CompuServe's computers and their ASCII-to-fax converter, then back to Weiner in Asia. Presumably he racked up some hotel fax charges, which can be steep. Still, the expense must have been small, considering the value of the service.

Weiner didn't require a special fax modem in this case. His regular modem sufficed for CompuServe, which, like MCI Mail, can communicate with almost any fax machine in the world.[10]

Your needs may differ. For example, if you want to send faxes to people expecting them almost instantly, then a fax modem may be the real answer. Commonly, fax modems come as plug-in cards that slide into certain makes of portable computers, or as cigarette pack–size instruments that plug into the serial port of your computer. Many of the "pocket modems" combine fax-style functions with the conventional modem type.

This mix of modem and fax is no mystery. Both modems and fax use digitized information. And both rely on protocols. In the fax world, users have more or less standardized on the CCITT's Group 3 protocol and transmission speeds of 9,600 bps. Most Group 3 machines, however, are capable of slowing down to 4,800 bps, the speed of some of the cheaper fax boards. As of this writing, you can pick up portable fax modems—the fax-only kind that hook into the serial port—for around three hundred dollars. Here are the questions to ask:

Question One: Do You Really Need a Fax Modem or a Fax Machine?

You may find that you can get along splendidly without either a fax board or a fax machine.

Remember, via MCI Mail and CompuServe you can send your faxes almost anywhere. A short message within the United States costs maybe a dollar in 1990; a fax to Europe costs several times that much. Probably, however, your expenses will be a fraction of what they might be if you transmitted from a hotel. And of course, you'll be safe from a nosy fax operator, at least when sending.

Network-transmitted fax offers yet another blessing compared to most fax machines and fax modems. Thanks to the mail list powers of MCI Mail and cousins, you may be able to send messages to large numbers of people more easily than you can through other means. Many fax machines and fax modems can do this. But if you're talking about

[10]The Weiner example is from *CompuServe Magazine*, February 1990.

dozens or hundreds of machines and you're wrestling with hotel switch-boards, then it makes sense to send your faxes via a network like MCI or CompuServe.

The downside is that when you use a network to send faxes, you're not assured of instant transmission. On MCI Mail I've suffered delays of maybe forty-five minutes before a fax goes out. And of course, I have no control over the font that MCI uses. For the moment, anyway, my own fax board produces better-looking characters than does MCI Mail.

Also keep in mind that in some cases you may be able to get a fax out but not a computer message, since fax machines run at half duplex. If you can't transmit via computer, what good is a computer network that offers faxing?

There's also the cost factor. You'll want a fax modem if you regularly transmit computer-generated messages to certain locations, especially one that's just a local phone call away—without a toll. Sending a stream of memos to the magazine ten miles from me, I was better off with a fax modem.

Another negative has been that most e-mail networks can't *receive* faxes for you. This may change. Already, via a special service available through MCI Mail and other means, you can arrange for faxes to arrive as ASCII files. PANN Networks (P.O. Box 162, Skippack, Pennsylvania, 19474, (215) 584-0300), provides the service. Using optical character recognition (OCR), PANN achieves accuracy of 90 percent. That means one character in ten will be wrong, so you'd better be wary of the spelling of names and the correctness of numbers that reach you this way. Too, the messages should include just text since logos and other graphics might confuse the scanner. But the PANN service still could prove invaluable for travelers and others who don't want to mess with either fax machines or fax cards. The price is $15 monthly and $2 for every page turned into ASCII. (PANN also will allow you to *send* faxes.)

If you want to receive your faxes as graphics—so you're not at the mercy of the finicky OCRs—you might check out a service known as Xpedite, from Xpedite Systems, 446 Highway 35, Eatontown, New Jersey, (201) 389-3373. Faxes arrive via your normal computer modem. Through special software you can print out the faxes on a normal printer if you're patient; just one page may take five to ten minutes, depending on the speed of your printer and the complexity of the images received.

As of this writing you can send a page of text from the United States to Germany for $1.50 or less and to a U.S. destination for between $.55 and $1 (the charge varies with volume).

Xpedite isn't the world's best bargain for heavy users, who eventually may end up paying for a fax machine in fees to the service. But it's something to consider if you'd rather not buy any special hardware and you don't fax often. What's more, you can be on the road and just dial into Xpedite to pick up any possible fax messages. I'll be surprised if CompuServe, MCI Mail, or another big network doesn't follow Xpedite's lead.

Confronted with the need to receive faxes, you of course might also use commercial fax facilities—both on the road and at home. You could face the same privacy problems, however, that you do when entrusting your material to hotel fax machines run by humans other than yourself.

Question Two: Do You Want To Buy a Facsimile Modem Rather Than a Fax Machine?

The advantage of a fax modem—as opposed to a fax machine—are:

■ The ability to type your letter or report and have it go out directly over the wires as a fax file. You can work with your pet word processor, then convert the file to ASCII and feed the results to your fax modem. At no time need you ever mess with a printer or that primitive substance known as paper. Plus, you have a keyboard and the advantages of word processing. With an ordinary fax machine, however, you may have to revert to plain old handwriting on the road if a computer or typewriter isn't available.

■ Compactness and lightness. Fax cards can plug into the machine-specific slots of several major brands of laptops: Toshiba, NEC, Epson, and eventually Zenith and others, if products aren't available for them by the time you're reading this. And an external fax modem—plugging into your serial port—can be pocket-size and probably double as your normal modem. You might well be carrying a little modem anyway, right? At any rate, with a fax modem you won't have to lug around a portable fax machine.

■ Characters often look sharper at the other end than they do from normal fax machines. A fax modem has its own set of characters—of letters and numbers—built in. It doesn't have to scan paper. A friend liked the output of one of my fax boards so much that he suggested I could team it up with a fax machine and use the combination as a printer!

■ The ability to edit incoming or outgoing faxes electronically—with a graphics program. You can move paragraphs around, for instance, or erase them. Of course, the process isn't nearly as easy as it would be editing with a word processor.

■ The cheaper availability of sophisticated features, such as the ability to dial up preselected numbers at odd hours when the phone rates are low and transmit to many faxes. Regular fax machines can do this. But you might pay dearly for the features you want. Again, however, remember that e-mail networks may be the easiest way of handling mass faxings from the field, especially from hotels.

■ Greater security. You can store faxes on your computer disk rather than on paper.

■ No need to use that crinkly, flimsy paper. To preserve printouts from most fax machines, you must Xerox them.

The disadvantages of a fax modem are:

■ Complexity of operation. You have to master the software and install the fax modem properly in your computer. That's easier now than it was in the past. But problems still abound with some models, so try to buy your fax modem from a dealer who'll assist you if problems dog you. Needless to say, the concept of a regular fax machine is far easier to understand: just feed the paper in and punch a button while you transmit. And to receive? Just drop by the machine or await delivery of faxes from your secretary, mail room, or wire room.

■ The need for a printer to read material received. As of this writing, it is possible but still difficult to read faxed material on the screens of a typical laptop. The resolution of the commonly used LCDs just isn't great enough. What's more, you'll probably have to scroll through the electronic version of the fax. To avoid this you must carry a printer—maybe a tiny one, but still, it's one more box to cram into your carry-on bag.

■ Slower reception of faxes. A fax modem sends its output to your printer, which, even if laser, may take several minutes to print.

■ The fact that you normally can't transmit pictures, newspaper articles, charts, and so forth over a fax modem. It merely picks up electronic material, such as converted versions of ASCII files. To transmit any kind of graphics you must either (a) have to be happy with simply relaying fax files that you yourself received from another machine, or (b) use a scanner to create a graphics file based on a letter, report, or other material that you want to send. The latter process can take time. What's more, scanners aren't cheap and, certainly, will take up yet more space in your traveling kit.

■ Your not being able to receive anything—in the case of most fax modems—unless your computer is running. Some fax modems will require that you not use the computer for other purposes while awaiting a fax. This is more of a concern, obviously, if you're in a office than if you're on the road.

■ Just one faxed page can take up 50K or more of disk space. You can still use a floppy-only machine with most fax modems, but it may be a challenge.

Question Three: What Fax Modem Should You Buy if This Technology Is for You?

Answer these questions:

■ Do you want a fax card to plug inside your machine or an external fax modem that plugs into your RS-232 port? A fax card won't take up the space outside, which an external fax modem would. On the other hand, if you sell your machine, you probably won't be able to use the card again—especially if the new laptop is a different brand. Checkett's company, Holmes Microsystems (2620 South 900 West, Salt Lake City, Utah 84119, [801] 975-9929), makes cards. Stogel's firm, Touchbase Systems (160 Laurel Avenue, Northport, New York 11768, [516] 261-0423), produces external fax modems.

Another maker of external fax modems is Hayes Microcomputer Products; contact Hayes Customer Service, P.O. Box 105203, Atlanta, Georgia 30348, (404) 441-1617. As usual, I'm mentioning specific companies because their products are prominent in the laptop world or because their technology has stood out. Don't limit your choice to companies whose names I give. Shop around! Read articles and ads in *PC Magazine*, *InfoWorld*, and similar publications.

■ Will the modem be for both fax and normal computer communications? Touchbase's fax modems can do double duty. Another promising possibility is Vocal Technologies (323 Scott Boulevard, Santa Clara, California 95034, [408] 980-5181).

■ Can the fax modem communicate with major brands of fax machines? For the most part, there are fewer compatibility problems with fax devices than with computers talking directly. But not always. The first fax card I used, for instance, couldn't reliably receive messages from the machine at the offices of one of my clients. You should be able to buy a fax modem with the understanding that you can bring it back if it can't communicate with your major business contacts.

■ How fast can the fax modem go? At 4,800 bps, a page will take a minute or so to send—twice as much time as the same material will at 9,600 bps. Transmission speeds may vary according to kinds of material transmitted and according to line conditions. "I wouldn't buy anything less than a 4,800 bps modem, and I would prefer 9,600," says Glenn Checketts, the Holmes engineer, "but we sell both 48 and 96 because some people don't want to spend the money." He says a 9,600-bps modem's filtering and other attributes "make it that much better at 4,800 bps. So even if it has to fall back, it has fewer errors than a 4,800-bps modem."

■ Can the fax modem easily slow down when talking to slow machines or confronted with heavy noise?

■ Can it work with an acoustic coupler? The WorldPort fax/data modem, for example, can do this—an invaluable capability when a hotel telephone system might as well be a dreadnought in invincibility.

■ How much work, if any, must you do to make sure that the fax modem doesn't interfere with the overall operation of your computer? I won't discuss "interrupt requests" and IRQ settings other than to say that the settings for the fax modem should not interfere with those for the disk drive, the printer port, and so on.

■ Will the fax modem's software hog much RAM? What if the fax software is to remain constantly inside your RAM the whole time you're running your computer? Will you still be able to use SideKick and other TSR? A friend of mine sent back a fax card in disgust because it couldn't work with his TSRs.

■ In general, how easy is the fax software to install and learn? Is the installation automated, so you merely boot up the program disk and follow instructions from there? To what extent must you modify standard files in your computer, such as AUTOEXEC.BAT and CONFIG.SYS?

■ Is the software easy to use? Is it simple to enlarge parts of the documents you're viewing? Does it require much effort to move from one part to another? Can you rapidly toggle between part of a document and the whole document? Does the software keep automatic records of calls made and received, and can you easily view these files from the past?

■ Does the fax modem software include a simple word processor with which you can compose ASCII files on the fly without worrying about converting your normal word processing format? You don't need all the power of WordPerfect or XyWrite just to write a short memo.

■ Will the modem work with unconverted files in the format of your favorite word processor? This feature is far from universal. Some products, however, can accept WordPerfect or WordStar files, not just ASCII.

■ How easily does the factory-supplied software let you change the faxes you receive or transmit? Can you receive separate faxes and combine them into one monster fax?

■ Will the fax modem software gobble up much disk space, especially when using the "background reception"? (See the last item on this list for an explanation of the term.)

■ How much space do received fax files take up on your disk? Does the fax modem compress the files? Ideally a typical faxed page of text will consume just 50K or so of disk space, maybe less. Some fax boards, however, can use up to 2 megabytes to store just one page of information.

■ Can the board send and receive long faxes? Or will it fail at times when length exceeds five or ten pages?

■ Can you feed the fax modem a list of phone numbers and have it "broadcast" the material to a number of locations?

■ Can the fax modem run in the background so that you can receive fax messages while you're working on the computer? Please note that there are varying degrees of "background reception." The truest kind lets you keep on working without necessarily even knowing that a fax arrived. But that may not be the best solution for a laptop owner with limited battery power. One compromise may be the ability to be *notified* that a fax is about to arrive, so that you can save your report or spreadsheet, then shift to the fax mode. Ingeniously, Holmes reduces the battery problem by not really powering up its fax modem until the phone rings. Even then, the modem draws well under half a watt. As of this writing, typical portables can consume maybe eight watts total, meaning that the fax modem is hardly a formidable drain.

* * *

How's that merger going? Or that rumor about a merger? With luck you'll already possess a good laptop and modem and be close enough to the appropriate phone to speed the latest information back to corporate headquarters (or your newspaper). If the phone isn't right, however, there is help for next time. Ahead lie tips for laptop people confronted with *in*appropriate phones.

Chapter 7

HOW TO HOOK UP (AND HANDLE OTHER HASSLES) FROM ALMOST ANYWHERE

- A survival kit to deal with quirky telephone systems, electrical power problems, and strange printers and computers with which you might want to share bytes that you receive via modem. Page 201.
- A step-by-step plan for telephone victims. Page 214. Please note that this chapter will discuss the idiosyncrasies of cables, et cetera, that plague laptop users both in the United States and abroad. The next chapter will focus just on woes of *foreign* travel, with certain prominent exceptions, such as airport security, which nowadays is also a domestic issue.
- How to boss your modem via the terminal mode using Hayes-style commands. Page 221.
- Transferring data between your laptop and the office desktop(s), using floppy disks, memory cards, cables, modems, a conventional LAN, or a zero-slot LAN. Appendix 4, page 357.
- "A Fast Way of Using Floppies for Multi-file Transfers Between a Desktop and a Laptop. Appendix 5, page 361.

If a laptop users' hell exists, James Fallows has at least served time in purgatory. Fallows edits and reports for *The Atlantic*, and he traveled to Southeast Asia while not quite yielding the duties implied in his title—Washington editor. His electronic link was telex, followed by computer. He asked friends not to send him long e-mail messages, and the people back in the States soon learned why.

The acoustic cups of his modem could not slide atop the squared-off transmitter and receiver of the telephone in his house in Kuala Lumpur, Malaysia. Just as disturbing, he couldn't hook into MCI Mail. So Fallows ended up using pay phones downtown to dial a computer in Singapore that could reach MCI. When *The Atlantic*'s man in Malaysia wished to swap messages with the States, he would have to leave the house carrying a blue canvas sack with a Radio Shack notebook computer, acoustic cups, a cable for his modem, and "eighteen to twenty pounds of Malaysian coins," each worth eight American cents.

Arriving at a bank of phone booths, he would make a pile of the coins, anything left over would sag in his pants pockets, weighing enough to make him tilt. Fallows would bend his "right knee and brace it against the bottom of the phone," then "rest the computer on [my] now-horizontal right thigh, and connect the cable." Then he would dial a tortuous sign-on code full of gibberish, such as NQJFXOM-03106004759. In four or five minutes he would have to drop more money into the little metal maw.

Then, having filled up the coin box of the first telephone, he would "break contact, disassemble [my] equipment, and move to the next phone in line."

Fallows would gravitate to the same phone-blessed location again and again. Watching his forced buffoonery there, he says, the locals would "laugh openly at the sweaty, red-faced foreigner doing his *Modern Times* routine on the phones. The humiliation of the West is complete." Fallows grew nostalgic for the lower-tech medium of telex.[1]

He eventually learned to hook up more gracefully from Kuala Lumpur, after the Malaysian data network forged a link with MCI Mail, but thousands of laptop users are still suffering. Many must travel to countries whose phone systems are predictably hostile to Americans and their modems, while other users must battle balky telephones even in the States, especially hotel systems. The worst domestic monsters are old hotels with Eisenhower-era

---

[1] Fallows's account of his pay-phone tortures appeared in *The Atlantic*, February 1987, p. 24. Other Fallows quotes come from MCI Mail correspondence and an interview following his return to the States.

phone systems or else new, luxury hotels where everything is modern enough to be confusing. Often the safest bets are economy chains with telephones as plebeian as the furniture.

In the United States or abroad, the big issues are these:

1. Telephones are located away from either comfortable places to sit when working or the good lighting that you need to use LCDs that are not backlit. Or, if they're pay phones, you must go through contortions similar to those Fallows went through.

2. Many hotel phones cannot be unplugged from the wall to allow use of direct-connect modems.

3. Phone systems, especially foreign ones, don't always use the standard RJ-11–style jack that accepts the tiny plastic, modular plugs with which most Americans are familiar. Expect to find RJ-11–style jacks only in a few countries, such as the United States and Canada. Furthermore, even though some systems may use what looks like a standard RJ-11–style jack, the actual electronic connections may be quite different. Systems made by Rolm may offer the worst hazard of nonstandardization: they can even blow up the popular WorldPort "2400" modems, and perhaps other makes, for reasons of incompatibility. The two companies are now trying to resolve the problem. (WorldPort "2400" modems may also suffer damage from other makes of PBXes.)

4. You can't unscrew some transmitters to hook up wires to the modems. In other ways, too, phones may be impregnable.

5. More and more hotel phone systems are electronic, and you risk either burning out your equipment or at least blowing the fuse of a phone system if you don't know what you're doing. I'll tell you when you might want to cry uncle and perhaps use acoustic cups rather than the direct connections that computers and modems prefer.

6. You must face the complexities of dialing into packet-switching networks through hotel systems, corporate switchboards, and so on. I'll show mercy. After telling you step by step how to make the connection, I'll explain a key step in detail—the use of the Hayes command set for modems. Almost all modems for laptops employ Hayes-style commands.

In this chapter, I'll also tell what survival tools you should carry. For your convenience, the list won't deal just with communications-related issues. Rather, in one place I'll tick off what you need to overcome other problems, such as electrical connections. What's the point of having telephone connections if you can't power up your computer first? Moreover, what if you want to share the information with others via paper or disk? This survival kit should help.

After helping you outfit yourself with the necessary survival kit, I'll offer a step-by-step plan for hooking up from strange phones. Please note that shortcuts exist in some instances, such as renting a modem if you're not in a country observing U.S. technical standards; see page 247.

SURVIVAL TOOLS

A computer and modem are just a start; below are other items that electronic travelers often bring.

Batteries if Required

Are you using a notebook-style computer running off small batteries? Are you constantly on the move and don't want to tie yourself down to AC outlets? Or are you unsure whether the local power will work out? Then figure out how many hours a day you expect to use your computer on the average, then double it to be safe, and from there calculate your battery requirements—taking into consideration the normal life of the batteries.

Stock up on batteries in the United States if you can. Often batteries overseas may be two or three times more expensive than in the States. Their quality may be lower. Bear in mind, too, that to buy batteries overseas you may have to bring some samples along to the stores, since overseas people don't always refer to battery sizes in the same way that Americans do.

Other Power-related Items

Even if you're traveling just in the United States you may need an adaptor to turn a two-prong outlet into a three-prong outlet. After all, the whole country isn't wired up just for the convenience of laptop owners.

Here are some other possibilities:

■ An extension cord fifteen to twenty-five feet long. That's the obvious, common-sense solution to the problem of power receptacles that are far from telephone receptacles. Bill Howard, the executive editor of *PC Magazine*, came up with another solution. He uses power outlets in the bathrooms, in which, he says, some travelers have simultaneously accomplished more than one task. In any event, always count on the worst.

"You will seldom find an electrical outlet anywhere near where you will want to use your computer," says John Deakin, a pilot with Japan Airlines and an experienced laptop user. "In fact, in some hotels you will be lucky to find more than one outlet in the whole room, so it's worthwhile carrying a duplex or triplex electrical plug adaptor. That way you can have lights where you want them as well. I carry two triples, myself, so whatever was plugged into the wall socket can remain there, and then the end of my extension has three outlets for my computer, printer, and immersion-type hot water heater."

What about a possible socket for a modem adaptor if the voltage is right? "A lightweight extension cord," Deakin says, "is quite enough, as the average computer uses very little current. If you carry a Skil saw to handle rude bellpersons, you may want a heavier extension."

■ "A screw-in adaptor that allows you to turn a light socket into a 220-volt receptacle for your laptop power adaptor," an item recommended by Patrick Tyler, of the *Washington Post*. "This is essential in hotel rooms and bush country locations where a single light bulb hanging from a wire may be your only power. With your three-plug adaptor and halogen light, you will be able to set up an office in a grass shack in Angola, as I have done."

■ Adaptor plugs for wall outlets of foreign outlets. Some countries offer the U.S. standard outlet—the modern version—with a pair of flat holes and a single round one. Other places, such as Japan, may have outlets with just two slots for the plug. And some European outlets may have two or three round holes that are "somewhat farther apart than the U.S. style," Deakin laments, adding that "very few U.S. hardware stores" are familiar with these problems.

Harry Welsh, however, a resourceful systems staffer at the *Washington Post*, found a possible solution as close as the Radio Shack store next to his office building. For $7.95, Radio Shack sells an Archer 273-

1405B Travel Outlet adaptor that includes a "type A" plug for England, Hong Kong, Africa, and Israel; a "type B" for England, Europe, Asia, Africa, and the Middle East; a "type C" for Australia; and a "type D" for South America and the Caribbean.

Please remember, of course, that not all of the plugs will be the same in various countries; hence the overlap on the preceding list. Also, the plugs by themselves won't convert voltages. I mention the Radio Shack kit, by the way, simply because its stores are almost everywhere in the United States.

■ A universal AC adaptor, if your portable lacks one (you may find that the laptop maker is charging too much for its own adaptor). Consider Radio Shack's Archer 273-1650 universal AC adaptor, which sells for $12.95 and can run most battery-operated laptops off 120 volts AC. It includes six adaptor plugs for as many as sixty different kinds of power connectors. Rated at 300 milliamperes and drawing 8 watts off 120 volts (60Hz), it can produce voltages of 3, 4.5, 6, 7.5, and 9 volts. It also will work with 50Hz current. Hz is short for hertz. One hertz is one cycle per second.

Please note that most laptop power packs will be happy with fifty cycles, but not all computer equipment will. A friend of mine, for instance, lugged a printer to Leningrad—only to find that it wouldn't work, even with the proper voltage, because of the differences in cycles per second. Perhaps my friend would have enjoyed better luck if the printer worked off batteries, as most portable computer gear does. The batteries typically act as a buffer, making it easier for the equipment to cope with differences in cycles per second (and also, to an extent, with power surges). Even that, however, isn't a guarantee.

Just returned from England, Alan Garratt, a public relations executive with MCI Communications, told me: "Most U.S. portable computer equipment is powered by transformers and seems to work on recharge-able batteries. In theory, since charging the batteries does not involve cycles, a simple 220-volt-to-110-volt converter should suffice. In prac-tice, it did not work too well. My Diconix printer stopped trying to charge after about five minutes, and the lead-acid battery in the laptop did not fare too well." Moral? You may want to check with your computer or printer manufacturer if you're really determined to remove all uncertainty.

■ A fifty-watt travel voltage-conversion device to step down the 220–240 volts so often encountered abroad. Buy a device of the kind for cassette recorders, radios, and shavers; avoid the high-wattage models—for hair dryers and the like—that can burn out your laptop. Investigate Radio Shack's model 1405, which is designed to work with the 273-1405B plug adaptor set. Upscale department stores, appliance stores, and luggage shops may be other sources of voltage converters. I'm using the term *voltage-conversion device* rather than *power converter*, since the latter phrase can apply to primitive gadgets that lack transformers. Insist on a transformer! Power converters may offer average voltages of 110 but may let *peak* voltages in waveforms—which I won't bother to explain—leap up to 300.

Thankfully, many computers nowadays have switches to let you choose the voltage; just make certain that the switches are set right, especially when you're at the airport. Better still, an increasing number of machines can sense the foreign voltage and automatically adjust to it; I'm thinking of recent models from Toshiba, although even in those cases you'll want to read your instruction manual to confirm this. Abroad, of course, you'll still need a special AC plug to use your laptop.

A Small Halogen Light if Your Portable Lacks Backlighting

Does your portable computer lack backlighting? Tyler says that if you want to survive "in countries where the hotel rooms are devoid of all but twenty-five-watt lights," then you'd do well to take a small halogen light. I'll add a reminder to consider:

■ Voltage differences. Perhaps the solution will be to buy the light in your destination country.

■ The need for a proper extension cord or other means to use the light.

You might also consider a small, battery-operated reading lamp—with a clip—available in many stationery stores and bookstores.

A Portable Printer—or at Least a Cable That Will Go Between Your Computer and a Borrowed Printer

Amazingly, many foreign correspondents don't take along printers. I'm baffled. Wouldn't they want to print out modemed messages for easy reference?

My word processor, granted, allows me to split my screen into halves, quarters, and so on and simultaneously view different files—to see notes and book chapters at once, for example. But for me, nothing beats the convenience of simple paper. If you're a businessperson on a trip, you might consider buying a very small printer. If you don't want to lug around a printer, at least think about borrowing one from a regional or overseas office.

If you borrow, however, you'll need (1) a software driver for the appropriate printer and (2) a cable that will work between it and your computer. Try to check in advance to see whether the foreign printer will emulate one of the Epson series or Hewlett-Packard series of printers; those are as close as any to worldwide standards. Also, find out about printer connections ahead of time. Most computers use a parallel, or Centronics, port for their connections to a printer, and connections at both ends are more or less standard the world over. But don't gamble. Your host just may have an oddball computer that needs a bizarre hookup to reach a standard printer.

By the way, a few printers use serial ports instead of the parallel ones, and that can complicate matters. See an MS-DOS guide and your computer and printer manuals for how to use DOS's MODE command to get a serial printer to work with your serial port. Obviously, if you do own a serial printer, a serial port won't be available for your modem unless you have two serial ports.

Whether you use a serial or parallel printer, remember that many foreign printers employ different character sets. Even though you've successfully hooked up, you still may not be able to reproduce a cents sign—just an English pound sign or one for a French franc.

Finally, as a last resort, if you can't print the proper characters or for some reason can't make a printer hook up, you can use MCI Mail or another computer network to send an e-mail message to your hotel fax. Or you can use an e-mail net's ''hard copy'' option. Some hotels, however, may charge a dollar or more a page for received facsimiles.

A Modem Cable (if You're Taking a Modem!)

Don't grab a cable at the last minute and find that the connections at either end are wrong. A modem cable for a PC-style machine, for instance, won't get along with the serial port of an AT-style computer.

Telephone Extension Cords and Special Trimmings

Deakin recommends:

■ A twenty-five-foot phone extension cord with modular plugs at both ends.

■ A six-foot extension cord with alligator clips at one end and a modular plug at the other. "You can buy a standard telephone extension cord . . . that has 'spade lugs' on one end, and the modular plug on the other. Cut the little flat tines off the spade lug, leaving the part that is crimped/soldered to the wire, and insert that into the back end of the 'gator clips, soldering or fastening with screws as needed. Working directly with the very fine, fragile wires is fairly miserable." Don't, incidentally, worry about the yellow and black wires in the extension cord, just the red and green ones.

For alligator clips, Bill Howard suggests Radio Shack part number 270-378; the cost is $1.29 for ten. "They look like miniclothespins with steel teeth," says Howard. The completed cord with the clips can hook up either to telephones themselves or to the wiring leading to them.

Telephone Plugs and Converters for Different Countries' Phone Systems

The end of the cord with alligator clips could include a series of plugs for different countries' phone systems—wired in parallel. (See above.)

There is a variant on this. Whenever you go to a country, you might pick up some adaptor plugs at a telephone store. In England, France, and many other European countries, you can buy converters for RJ-11–style fixtures and the local equivalents.

RJ-11 is the standard in the United States for such fixtures. If you really want to be technical about it, as my consultant acquaintances insist, you should say RJ-11–style rather than just RJ-11, for reasons I won't bother to explain.

Surge Protectors and Lightning Protection

Power and phone lines abroad may give you strange voltages; what's more, some may lack the same protection against lightning that those in the States offer. Check with your computer and modem manufacturer about lightning protection. Computer surge protectors are ubiquitous, at stores everywhere, and for $23.95, Radio Shack sells a telephone surge protector. Traveling Software (18702 North Creek Parkway, Bothell, Washington 98011, 800-343-8080) offers for $49.95 a combination protector with RJ-11–style jacks for modem cables and outlets for computer and printer power cables.

The extra-prudent might check out the $79 TeleMax 2 surge protector or other models from Panamax (150 Mitchell Boulevard, San Rafael, California 94903-2057, 800-472-5555). The 1,200-watt Telemax 2 can guard your computer, modem, and printer. The protector includes just two sockets, though you can use a power strip to come up with more outlets. Unless you plug all equipment into your protector—a Panamax or any other make—the device won't be bulletproof.

What's interesting here is that Panamax doesn't just warrant its protectors for life. It also throws in a $2 million insurance policy.

"If a protector and the equipment connected to it are ever damaged by a power surge," says Ellen Rony, a Panamax public relations person, "Panamax will repair or replace them for free, forever." Panamax vice president Richard Cohen won't give statistics on the number of people taking the company up on the offer, but he says it's very low. Check with Panamax about the fine print. I warned Cohen of the menaces that Rolm switchboards pose for WorldPort modems, and as of press time, he was looking into the circumstances. I'm optimistic. Panamax prides itself on the broad wording of the warranty for its surge protectors.

What should you look for in a protector, especially one covering a laptop, modem, and printer? Consider:

■ The ability to limit voltage peaks on the AC side to less than 330 volts without overshoot. On AC lines, voltage peaks typically last 1 to 100 microseconds. Overshoot means to go above the rated level—above the 330 volts in this case—for even a fraction of a microsecond.

For phone lines, the voltage peaks should be no more than 220 volts without overshoot. Here, peaks typically linger 10 to 1,000 microseconds.

■ Whether the telephone side of the protector meets the standards of UL 497A from Underwriters Laboratories. The standard covers criteria ranging from safety to voltage peaks.

Please note that some excellent protectors haven't been tested. This is slowly changing as more makers of protectors discover the benefits of common standards (the U.L. test isn't prohibitively expensive to manufacturers—just several thousand dollars).

■ How narrow or broad the language is in the manufacturer's warranty. Does the language provide for replacement of the protected equipment, not just the protector?

Keep in mind, of course, that no protective equipment—or at least nothing portable—will make your gear 100 percent invincible. In particular that's true in tropical areas with primitive power and telephone systems and plenty of lightning. You'll still want to unplug the computer and modem when lightning flashes, especially if you're operating from a home. In Kuala Lumpur, a Zeus-like bolt left Fallows with a charred computer.

If you're staying in a hotel with small windows and a bad view of the sky, you might tune a little portable radio to an unused spot in the AM band and listen for the telltale crackle that suggests that all is not well on Mount Olympus. Lest your precautions still not work, of course, you might want to take along some spare modems. In his time, one foreign correspondent has burned out several.

An Eight-Dollar Telephone and a Neon Bulb Tester

Just before he boarded a jet for Europe, a laptop owner named Mel Snyder plugged his WorldPort 2,400-bps modem into a Rolm digital telephone system at the airport. "Within 30 seconds of connecting," he says, "the line-matching transformer within my WorldPort 2400 actually caught fire!"

You can prevent such disasters by carrying a little neon bulb tester from Radio Shack. "Mine is marked CG Electronics," Snyder says. "*Never* plug into a hotel or other RJ-11–looking line without it."

You might consider another tool as well to verify that the RJ-11–style jack is fit for your modem. Buy a small, cheap phone. When my old Chevy broke down a few years ago, I had a choice between paying two dollars less for repairs and acquiring an eight-dollar telephone for the two dollars. That's exactly the kind of phone you'll ideally be able to use as an amp tester. How much better that your eight-dollar phone die in the line of duty than your three-hundred-dollar pocket modem.

If nothing else, a throwaway phone will help you find the proper wires to which to hook your modem.

There's another reason for a throwaway phone. Some modem manufacturers suggest that in case of trouble, you plug in a telephone before blaming your problems on their miracle product. This is particularly true when wrestling with multiple line or electronic telephones.

If a toy-priced phone won't work, your modem probably won't either. There is one cause for hope: via an X1 or X3 modem command, you may be able to force a modem to dial even when there isn't a dial tone. Before you do that, however, use a neon tester or otherwise confirm that the phone line is safe for you to hook up to your modem.

A Telephone Modular In-line Coupler

An in-line coupler—a little connector with RJ-11–style jacks at both ends—can turn two short phone cords into one long cord. It's also handy to use, since many cheapie phones don't have jacks for plugs from cords, just wires that plug directly into the wall. And yet your modem probably uses jacks. Solution? Use an in-line coupler to turn a plug into a jack (Radio Shack part number 279-358, $2.49).

A Telephone Duplex Adapter

Available from Radio Shack, this Y-type connector will turn one jack into two. As Deakin says, this will "permit you to plug into a wall outlet, then plug your modem and the telephone into the same spot. Or you can plug into the wall and use the adaptor on the other end, plugging it into your modem, and this will allow you to use the phone right next to the computer" (Radio Shack part number 279-357, $4.95).

Two Screwdrivers—One Phillips Head and One With a Straight Blade

"A Swiss Army knife will do nicely, but keep it in your check-in baggage," Deakin says, "or security may take it from you."

A Knife or Razor Blade

"For educational purposes only," Bill Howard says that in a bind you might "take your Swiss Army knife and scrape the phone cord until you expose the wires inside, then attach the cable with the two alligator clips, and dial away.''[2]

Let me add some caveats:

■ I must suggest that you check with the hotel or a lawyer before engaging in procedures fraught with legal risks.

You're on your own here. I do not intend to sanction violations of any law, U.S. or foreign. Use care. You may not want to be too much of an electronic adventurer, for instance, in a totalitarian country with a low tolerance for deviations from the law. Instead you should stick to acoustic modems or authorized access.

Sooner or later an American or European is going to see the inside of a Third World prison in a land where the local telephone monopoly finds joy in stifling adventuresome businesspeople.

■ Furthermore, unless you're trained in electrical engineering or have experience working safely around electrical currents, it's not wise or proper to fool around with such equipment. You're perhaps best off consulting the hotel electrician or engineer, and perhaps working under his or her supervision. Second, do not count on an indestructible phone system in your hotel. "If you don't know what you're doing, you could fry a couple of thousand-dollar circuit cards," says Bill Degnan, a veteran telecommunications expert who has advised hotel chains. "The hotel management would probably frown on that."

Indeed, as I said in chapter 1, such woes reportedly befell a Radio Shack employee. Perhaps it was just an isolated set of circumstances, a horribly timed surge of voltage, but I'm ready to believe Degnan.

Even when using commercial products to make hookups easier, please be aware that no procedure is entirely free of risk. I'm not impugning the quality of commercial products here. Rather, I must emphasize that I cannot be responsible for unanticipated possibilities. (This book will self-destruct in thirty seconds.)

A Small Flashlight

Sooner or later you'll need to look under a bed for a telephone or power connector. You might, by the way, want to do this in your underwear

---

[2]The Howard quotes are from his *PC/Computing* article of October 1988.

or in the buff; this isn't the best of places for the Brooks Brothers suit in which you'll be meeting your client.

An Acoustic Coupler

If a direct connection turns out to be impossible and you can't rent a "native" modem or try another location, you might turn to an acoustic coupler. Howard notes the widespread availability of Radio Shack's acoustic coupler 2 (part number 26-3818, $59.95). Check also with Vocal Technologies.

The perfect coupler for the traveler will have separable cups for the transmitter and for the receiver—to accommodate the different types of headsets.

Ideally, too, the cups will be flexible so that you have a reasonable chance of overcoming problems with the exotically shaped headset. Perhaps you can use string, if need be, to position the couplers on the transmitter and receiver.

Use a pillow over the modem and headset if lines are weak or noisy or you are trying to send a fax or communicate at more than 300 bps. I won't make guarantees about 1,200-bps-plus speeds for acoustic couplers, just give it a try.

Please note that even acoustic cups aren't foolproof. Fallows tells me that when he used a Radio Shack coupler in Kuala Lumpur, he still found them ill-fitted to the local phones. Rarely, if ever, does he now bother to take around the cups.

Again, be aware that I can't approve of your "operating" on hotel telephone systems. You're on your own.

Commercial Products for Hooking Up With Telephones

I can see the uses of commercial kits, consisting of tools and wires and mysterious black boxes. They may lessen risks to your modem or the hotel's own equipment when, for instance, you're trying to hook up to a quirky, electronic phone system. If nothing else, they give you one more support number to call from Teheran or wherever if you're running into trouble. The commercial hookup products cost may be worth their price of fifty to one hundred fifty dollars in situations where your business depends on reliable communications at speeds higher than acoustic couplers can offer.

Do make sure, however, that *if* you're technically inclined, you're paying for more than tools or a connector that you could rig up on your own. Deakin says: "It is worth noting that there is a commercial device on the market that screws into the handset in place of the mouthpiece, with a modular socket in it. It sells for about $50. A six-foot cord with alligator clips is an exact functional equivalent, for a good deal less money, which weighs a lot less and takes up much less room in a suitcase."

On the other hand, the Deluxe Road Warrior, a hookup kit from Computer Plus (16321 Gothard Street, Huntington Beach, California 92647, 800-274-4277) could be a dandy investment. It may greatly simplify the installation of computers or facsimile machines in hotels or offices with private branch exchange (PBX) systems.

A small rectangular box from the kit hooks in between the coiled handset cord and the telephone. This box—called the CP+ Connection—even includes a voice/data switch so you can use the phone normally without removing the wires to your modem. What's more, the box apparently can adjust for the vagaries of various electronic phone systems. The instructions mention a setting for a Rolm system, as well as those for single-line phones and various systems from Toshiba, NEC, and Northern Telecom. But be careful. A Rolm system, after all, may damage a WorldPort "2400" modem, according to a WorldPort technical bulletin that was sent to me by someone at Touchbase Systems. Discussing the CP+ Connection, Jon Landre, a technical support staffer with Computer Plus, says: "We don't sell the CP+ Connection as a protective device of any kind." So check with whoever makes your surge protector or similar gadget.

The CP+ Connection is part of the aforementioned Deluxe Road Warrior kit, sold for $139.95. The basic kit omits the box but includes a waterproof pouch, a magnifying glass/flashlight, a telephone extension cord, and another cord with alligator clips—nice and convenient, but perhaps not worth the $49.95 that Computer Plus charges to shop for tools for you.

There is at least one other commercial product, the $99 MoFone from Traveling Software (18702 North Creek Parkway, Suite 116, Bothell, Washington 98011, 800-343-8080). Like the Deluxe Road Warrior kit, the MoFone works with both computers and fax machines and even includes a magic rectangular box that looks the same except for the paint job. The MoFone, too, is wired in between the handset cord and the telephone, and includes the same set of switches.

If you already own tools, the MoFone may be the better deal. Either product, however, could be a godsend when your boss is panting for an article or spreadsheet from a hotel or PBX-afflicted office. Just make certain you're comfortable with the direct approach—both legally and technically.

A Null Modem Cable

See appendix 4 for a discussion of null modem cables for transferring programs and data between computers—as well as a shopper's guide to commercial products for file transfers. Remember that at this point, most of the micro world uses 5.25-inch disks, whereas your portable most likely uses the 3.5-inch format.

A Gender Changer

A gender changer may come in handy for connecting your serial cable to one of the other gender—useful for assuring compatibility between computers and modem cables or null modems.

At the risk of sounding like the instructor in Sex Education 101, a plug normally would be a male connector and a socket normally would be a female connector. Some sockets, however, have pins sticking out and so would be described as male.

A DB-nn Adapter

Even in the United States, serial ports and the cables for them can vary. An XT-style serial port, known as a DB-25, will normally accept a 25 plug. An AT-style serial port is a DB-9 and has a male connector with nine pins sticking out—ready to accept a *female* plug. Most of the world's microcomputers use the DB-25, so consider wiring up a converter if you're traveling and need to hook into other people's equipment.

An Ample Supply of Floppy Disks

Abroad, floppies are almost always more expensive than in the States —sometimes more than several times the cost, especially if you need the high-density 1.44-megabyte disks.

What's more, some local brands of disks may not be as reliable as those from the United States. This will vary. Check with other computer users.

A File Transfer Program

Are you planning to exchange files and data directly with other, nearby computers—rather than "talk" to them through a modem? Then you'll want the appropriate software.

Chances are that your regular communications program will work. But if you're moving around enough files, you may want a special file transfer program.

Among the possibilities are:

■ A commercial file transfer program, such as the well-reviewed LapLink.

■ Shareware products, especially ZIP141, a good little program that allows transfers of data between computers at 115,200 bps.

You should keep one copy of the transfer program on a 5.25-inch disk and another in the 3.5-inch format.

For more information, see page 361.

A SURVIVAL PLAN

Here's an eight-step plan to reduce the possibility of nasty surprises from the time you leave home to when you hook up your modem and make your first connection. Common sense should be enough to tell you which of the steps apply to you and which you should skip. Don't worry if some of the information is sketchy about the steps relating to foreign travel—you'll see more about that in the next chapter.

Step One: Investigate the Customs Situation—Both the American and the Foreign—If You're Traveling Overseas

See the next chapter for details. If nothing else, protect yourself by carrying along copies of your receipts for your computer, modem, and other gear.

Step Two: Find Out About Phone Connections or About Packet-Switching Numbers

Almost everywhere in the United States, MCI Mail customers can dial 800-456-6245 to reach MCI Mail at 2,400 bps. Check with your MCI rep for the latest number and information for other speeds. Other large networks, such as CompuServe, have a slew of dial-up numbers in many cities or at least ways of hooking you in, via other systems. See pages 243–250 for details on connecting from abroad.

Step Three: Check With Your Area Office or Hotel in Advance

I know. Often you'll jet off into the sunset without the slightest inkling of what lies ahead. Still, you would do well to get the electronic lay of the land. Are you headed to a city where your company has offices? Then check with your people there; see if they can provide you with an alternative to a hotel—either as your regular plan or as an alternative. Can you borrow a modem, computer, or printer, or at least use one of the aforementioned? Between what hours of the day? Will you have the key to the office? If you're hoping to hook into the area office's modem or printer or exchange disks with a computer there, then you'll want to find out the technical specs, especially cabling.

Planning to work instead from a hotel? Then, directly or through the area office in the destination country if you have someone there you trust, you should investigate the phone system. Are RJ-11–style jacks available? Deakin reports that some chains, such as Hyatt, "are getting around to installing phones that have an extra 'data port' right on the side of the phone." Don't assume, however, that all hotels in a chain offer such amenities; you must check.

If this answer is no, then you're going to have to decide on your basic strategy. Should you install your laptop unofficially? If you do, you won't have to worry about the bureaucracy and possible expense if the hotel insists on calling its telecommunications expert to solve your problem. Chances are, no one will be the wiser. As I've said elsewhere, however, you just may face serious legal problems, especially in some foreign countries where, theoretically, users of unauthorized modems can undergo criminal prosecution. My advice here for such circumstances is to *stay legal*.

If you disregard my advice and expect your installation to be un-official, then you must shy away from asking risky questions about the kind of phone system the hotel has. Or you must, in a casual way, say that you hate electronic phone systems and wonder if the hotel has one with an old-fashioned bell and dial. If so, then you probably should be able to hook up physically without problems—although, as you'll learn later, an ancient switchboard system may wreak havoc when your mo-dem is dialing out.

Step Four: Check With the Airline—if Need Be

In 1988, terrorists hid a bomb in a cassette player aboard a jumbo jet that later exploded over Scotland. Even before the incident, many air-lines were leery of passengers carrying computers. If your schedule is going to be tight while you're traveling, it's a good idea to check in advance about (1) the security question and (2) whether you can operate the computer while in the air. (See the next chapter for more about this.)

Whatever you do, try to carry your portable yourself rather than entrusting it to the vagaries of the luggage handlers. If you must pack your portable, use twice as much padding as you otherwise would. Also, try to get an airline employee to sign off that the luggage contains your computer.

Step Five: Connect to a Pay Phone at the Airport or Elsewhere

Acoustic cups usually will spare you real trouble, both from the phone and from suspicious humans. At least that's true in the United States. When all else fails, you can always try a pay phone.

Needless to say, fresh batteries and enough small change will serve you well when you're using a pay phone; better, use a credit card if the phone will allow it and you think it's worth paying a little extra. See the hotel-related material (steps 7–8) for more information on direct connections through strange handsets.

Step Six: Arrive at the Hotel or Local Office and Prepare for the Installation

Why risk a bad back, tired eyes, or other problems just because you're on the road—especially if you're about to enter some important business negotiations?

In a hotel you probably won't be as comfortable as your office-bound colleagues blessed by ergonomic chairs, and as a visitor to an area office, you may not always lay claim to the best furniture. Still, you should make out the best you can with what's available. Consider the following:

■ Furniture. If hotel furniture is at an uncomfortable height for you to use with a laptop, you may be just as comfortable propped up on a pillow in bed, with the machine resting atop the part of your anatomy for which it was designed.

■ Lighting. If your screen isn't backlit, do you have a halogen or another appropriate light? Or you might try facing away from the window. Even with a backlit screen, you'll want to minimize problems like glare.

You'll also want to see how amenable to your activities the phone system is. Are you facing an electronic phone system that may self-destruct or ruin your modem under rare circumstances?

You're safe if the phone sports a dial and rings. Don't worry, in-cidentally, if the phone tingles when you dial; that's its friendly way of saying "I'm just a sweet, old-fashioned phone at your command." If, however, the phone has LED lights, touch-tone dialing, or a funky speaker, then you may not be so safe. Touch-tone dialing by itself usually is not a danger sign. Still, there are subtleties. In Europe, more so than in the United States, be careful of phones with LEDs. But don't worry about a garden-variety neon message light.

Please note that I am being cautious. Even with an electronic phone system, you still may be able to hook up. In those cases, however, you might confine your activities to the inside of the mouthpiece (described below). Or you might try to wire in your modem—or related equipment—between the main telephone and the handset. If you limit your action to those areas, you'll stand a good chance of getting the dial tone you need to proceed. Of course, any kind of electrical work can be hazardous, so don't try it unless you know what you're doing.

Before wiring yourself in, tell the hotel switchboard you don't want any rings to disturb you. Otherwise you may be in for a shock from the juice from the ringer voltage. Again, don't take chances with electricity.

Step Seven: Wire Yourself In

■ If there is an RJ-11–style outlet. Bingo! Very likely you can direct connect.

■ If you don't see a modular outlet and the phone wire vanishes Houdini-like into the wall. In the United States, anyway, you'll probably see an RJ-11–style outlet behind a cover plate. "Just unscrew the plate for access," Deakin says.

■ If you see a little square box attached to the baseboard. Unscrew the box. Then, even in hotels outside the United States, you may very well encounter some green and red wires—the colors to which you'll need to pay attention (rather than, say, yellow). The remaining leads are for carrying electricity to a call-alert lamp, a dial light, or some other purpose, such as grounding. Ignore those distractions; in fact, in foreign countries, you may see only two wires.

At any rate, if you find green and red wires in the box, connect the equivalent colors from your alligator-clipped cord. You can probably get away with scrambling the red and the green. But first try it the obvious way. Hook up your eight-dollar telephone via the alligator clips and the extension cord (mentioned on page 206) and see if you're in business. Or be brave and try your modem directly. Find out if it dials when instructed by your software or at least if you can hear a dial tone.

■ If the square box is behind a three-hundred-pound dresser or is otherwise inconvenient to reach, and you want to wire into the phone. Deakin suggests: "Look for a couple of screws on the bottom of the phone itself, which will allow the guts of the phone to fall out into your hand in one piece. With the cover off, you'll have to depress the phone hook with your fingers, a book, or a rubber band."

Put the alligator clips "where you see red [and] green wires inside the phoneset. You can usually 'dress' your wire so that it clears the insides of the phoneset, then run it right out" with the cord leading to the wall. After that, says Deakin, you should temporarily replace the phone cover.

What if, while wreaking mayhem on the phone, you get a "real phone call," as he describes it? "Have the microphone inside the mouth-piece, all ready to put back on. As soon as the phone rings, *don't* panic and pick it up, but smoothly pull the 'gator clips off, pop the mike and mouthpiece back into place, screw it down tight, and *then* pick up the phone and answer. With a little practice and mental preparation, you should be able to answer on the third or fourth ring. Without preparation, you'll instinctively pick up the phone and say 'hello?' and the party on the other end won't hear a thing, except for the click of the phone being picked up.''

■ **If you can't wire yourself into the phone.** "The next possibility," Deakin says, "is the mouthpiece. This is a little more clumsy, but still works very well. Pick up the handset, and unscrew the mouthpiece if you can, and a microphone will usually fall free. Inside the mouthpiece, under the mike, you'll see two spring clips. Clip right onto these with your 'gator clips (again, which is which doesn't matter), and you have the same connection as if you used any of the above techniques.'' The only extra requirement is that "you'll have to raise the hook to make a call.''

Assuming you have the hotel's permission, I'll add the following to Deakin's good advice: do not bend or otherwise damage the spring clips in the phone. That shouldn't be a problem if you're careful. Remember, too, as I've noted, that the mouthpiece solution may be a good place to start if the phone is electronic.

■ **If you're ready to use a knife** (on the phone, not yourself). The hotel people won't love you if they see your handiwork, and you already know my recommendation against this sort of thing. But if you're ready to use a knife, at least follow Deakin's advice and leave the phone system in good shape. Again, attempt the following *only* if you have the appropriate training or supervision.

Says Deakin, "With a razor blade or a very sharp knife, slit the phone wire lengthwise for about one inch to two inches (preferably in a discreet location). Bend it, and the wires inside should pop out into view. With the smallest straight pins you can find, puncture right through the center of the red and green (one pin each) wires about an inch apart, so that your clips will not short against each other.

"You may be able to drive these pins into the baseboard slightly, or into anything that will hold them firmly. Then just clip onto those pins with your 'gator clips, as usual.

"When done, remove the pins, pop the wires back inside, smooth out the slit, and wrap it with a couple of turns of tape (Scotch tape is nearly invisible). When you find this situation, first run your fingers along the wire, looking for a place where someone may have done this before you! That will save you some time and trouble, and will minimize further damage to the wiring.''

Step Eight: Make the Call

■ If the call is local. "Your modem and communications program should have no trouble at all," Deakin says. "You will need to set your dialing string to dial the 9 (usually) for an outside line, then a comma or two to give a small time delay, and then the number. If it's long distance and you can direct dial it, the same thing applies, although you may need to set a little extra 'time-out delay' in your comm program, as it often takes longer to complete the long-distance call."

■ If you need to use a credit card number or, to quote Deakin, "if you must go through the trauma of an operator-assisted call." In most cases you'll start out in the terminal mode (for important details about this mode, see page 221). Then, as Deakin advises, "dial manually whatever you have to, including the distant modem number, giving the operator whatever information you need to, or punching in your credit card number, et cetera." When you hear the other modem, type ATD and press your computer's Return key (in some cases it may be necessary instead to type ATX1D and press Return). The modems should exchange noises.

As soon as they do, says Deakin, "hang up the handset. You may see some 'garble' on the screen from that, but if you do it soon enough, it should not affect the log-on. A very few phone systems will rudely disconnect as soon as you hang up. The solution to this is not very elegant, but again, it works. Instead of hanging up, just put the handset down on the bed, and cover it with a pillow to cut room noise down. When done, don't forget to hang up the phone!"

Don't worry if you do not understand the reference to the ATD commands and other ways of telling your modem what to do. This is explained in the next part of this chapter.

■ If the phone's dial is the ancient rotary style. Deakin notes that many rotary phones "are actually hooked up to a line that supports tone dialing, and your modem may very well work using tones. If this is not the case, you may need to reset your dialing string to ATDP to use pulse dialing. If the exchange has only pulse dialing and you are using the mouthpiece method, you may have to manually dial the number and then have your modem do only the ATD to connect."

■ If the above fails. Fallows's experience notwithstanding, aren't you glad you took along an acoustic coupler? You'll probably be limited to 300 bps, but Deakin says that if the room is quiet and you use a pillow, you may get away with 1,200 bps. Harry Welsh of the *Washington Post* also swears by the pillow technique. A friend of mine claims to have heard of direct communication from Africa to the United States at 2,400 bps; I wouldn't count on the reliability of acoustic couplers under such circumstances, though.

■ If even an acoustic coupler isn't the solution—perhaps because the lines are so bad. Do the obvious and try another location. You may be able to isolate the problem to a specific building or area. If you're abroad and you can't communicate from your hotel, office, wherever, then you might try a phone at an airport or bank—in short, someplace where people in the host country have major business reasons for wanting acceptable phone service. Another, equally drastic solution would be to forget about normal computer communications and use a fax board to send out a facsimile. As I've said, there are occasions when faxes will work but computers won't.

Finally, be aware that in some rare situations, especially in Third World countries, telephone companies may use echo suppressors. Such devices make phones more pleasant for humans, but they may befuddle computers. With a defective suppressor in use, you may hear the other modem, but your machine may not respond. Try placing the call again to get a different long-distance trunk line with a working suppressor— one that will recognize a data signal. If you're still out of luck, ask the hotel or phone company if suppression is indeed in use, and if there aren't ways to suppress the suppressor.

HOW TO BOSS YOUR MODEM VIA THE TERMINAL MODE

Most modems obey the "Hayes command set, " named after the company that became the IBM of the modem makers for microcomputers. Even IBM itself got into trouble when a modem for one of its laptops wasn't Hayes compatible.

You can use the Hayes command set in two ways:

1. You can boss your modem with the Hayes set by way of the commands in your regular communications software. Let's say you're using CrossTalk. To dial a number, you may hit Esc and punch in **NU 555-1212**, press Return, then type **GO** and hit Return again. That's

HOW YOUR MODEM CAN COEXIST WITH CALL WAITING

People kept complaining that I might as well have been incommunicado. The busy signal again and again assailed their ears. I was always busy talking to some modem maven in California, a Canadian customs inspector, what have you. And yet for years I resisted call waiting. It was barbaric—in a class with answering machines (do you think I succumb to all technology just because I've perpetrated a few computer books?). My computer and modem felt the same way. Call waiting, after all, could make bytes go astray if someone phoned while I was transmitting.

Recently a friend told how she'd taken care of the computer problem by signing up for call forwarding as well as call waiting. That way, instead of ruining a data transmission, a call could go to a number where people didn't care if the phone rang. But it was still what computer folks would call a "kludge," a not-very-elegant, hastily improvised solution.

Now, however, my phone company has offered a better solution, something good enough to convert me to call waiting. Here's how it works. Merely by dialing ***70** before a phone number, I can turn call waiting off. That still doesn't solve the problem of having incoming calls interrupted, including those to the modem while it's in the "answer mode." But I'm willing to make the trade-off. See if your own phone company (or one in the city where you're visiting, and where your host may have call waiting) can offer an equivalent of ***70**. (The code **1170** often works for pulse-dial systems, too.)

In my area, anyway, the phone system needs time to handle a request to disable call waiting. But that's no problem; I just follow ***70** with two commas. Each comma creates a two-second pause before the modem dials the actual phone number.[3]

*   *   *

Oh, and about the answer machine . . . I finally succumbed in 1988.

---

[3]Many communications programs let you automatically insert prefixes—such as *70— in front of numbers you dial with the automatic dialer. Check your manual.

A HIGH-TECH ROLE MODEL FOR HOTELS (PLUS A LIST OF CHAINS WITH RJ-11–STYLE JACKS IN GUEST ROOMS)

Next time you're staying in a luxury hotel in a metropolis with a backwoods switchboard fit for Dog Patch, Arkansas, suggest that it follow the example of the Nob Hill Lambourne in San Francisco.

The hotel's phone jacks are modem compatible, and if your modem breaks down, you can use a 2,400-bps substitute at the hotel's business center, which features, incidentally, both PS/2 and Macintosh equipment, including an Apple Laserwriter.

Every guest room boasts a PS/2 model 30-286 with Lotus 1-2-3 and WordPerfect on a 20-meg hard disk, as well as a fax machine.

Progress, mind you, isn't cheap. Undiscounted, the room rates begin at $175, and suites are $250 (excluding taxes). The Nob Hill Lambourne is at 725 Pine Street, San Francisco, California, 94108, and the telephone number is 800-BRITINN, or (415) 433-2287.

Business centers with faxes, copiers, and other goodies are becoming increasingly common among luxury hotels. It's just that as of this writing, the Nob Hill seems to have outdone its competitors.

*   *   *

Laptop-friendly jacks would be a good start for hotels wanting to catch up with the Nob Hill Lambourne. *CompuServe Magazine* found that at least five chains could "claim rooms with either single jacks with switches, or double phone jacks for travelers who want to telecommute and still call out for a pizza":

- Hampton Inns: 800-426-7866
- Hilton Hotels: 800-445-8667
- Hyatt Hotels: 800-233-1234
- Ramada Inn Renaissance Hotels: 800-228-9899
- Westin Hotels: 800-241-3333

To this list I'd add the Motel 6 chain: 505-891-6161.

Don't let the above lull you into a false sense of security. If possible, before your visit, call up the hotel or motel to make certain you're in good shape at the location where you'll be staying. You just may be staying at one hotel in a chain that flouts the RJ-11 policy. Also, of course, phone ahead if you'll be at hotels not listed above. Find out what awaits you and your modem. In July 1988, Holiday Inns (800-HOLIDAY), the nation's largest chain in terms of number of rooms, mandated computer jacks in rooms in newly built hotels. But Holiday Inn cannot guarantee their availability in existing buildings. Nor can Marriott Hotels and Resorts (800-228-9290) promise a jack in every room. Marriott, though, will install a jack for free if you request one through the hotel's front office manager, preferably at least a day ahead of time.

RJ-11–style jacks, of course, are just one of the issues. You'll still want to find out if you must go through an operator—through a switchboard—before you can talk to the outside world from your hotel room. Luckily, major programs, such as ProComm, CrossTalk, and Mirror, at least when used with the appropriate Hayes commands, allow you to switch from voice to data after you've made the appropriate connection.

---

working within CrossTalk's own commands. The program will translate these commands into a language fit for a Hayes modem or equivalent.

2. If quirky phone systems confront you at home or abroad, you can manually tell the modem to carry out the Hayes commands directly—via the command set. That means you first get your communications program into a terminal mode, so your software will pass on commands from your computer to the modem just as you typed them. Then you type **ATDT 555-1212** and hit Return, and the modem dials. CrossTalk can enter the terminal mode if you press Esc, type **GO L**, and press Return. (*L* means "Local.") You can use this same mode for transferring files via your serial port and a null modem cable[4] hooked up to a serial port on the other computer. In my version of the ProComm program, the terminal mode is the one in which the software boots up. I can immediately start typing **ATDT** and so on without worrying about a command like **GO L**.

If you're going overseas and expect to be in some challenging situations, don't buy communications software that won't let you enter the terminal mode easily. You should be able to use the AT command set yourself and stay flexible amid adversity; some useful AT commands are listed below. For detailed AT information, check your modem's

---

[4]See appendixes 4 and 5 for more on null modem cables and on how to exchange information between laptops and desktops.

instruction manual. Please remember that unless I note otherwise, you should press the Return key after you give the commands below. Also, please note that if you're using a modem with a bank of switches, it may have a "dumb mode" that prevents it from using AT commands. See your instruction manual for ways to get out of the mode. Luckily, modems with the dumb mode are increasingly rare; the newest modems lack switches. Note, too, that to be on the safe side you should try the modem first while giving all AT commands in capital letters, especially if you're using an older modem. Above all, if your modem doesn't respond to the AT commands, allow for minor disasters, such as loose or defective cable.

Now for that list of handy AT commands.

AT This is really a prefix rather than a command. It goes before all commands other than + + + and **A/** (explained later). **AT** ("attention") can include mixes of different instructions; **ATDT 555-1212** and a Return, for instance, combines the dialing command with the **T** command for use with touch-tone telephone systems. **ATDP 555-1212** would be the same command for a pulse system. The AT command can be handy for seeing if your modem is working. If you type **AT** and Return, "OK" should appear on your screen (modems are less pretentious than some people and aren't afraid to use the colloquial if it gets the point across in a hurry).

A Make the modem try to answer, using the answer mode; the usual **AT** precedes the **A**, so that the full command is actually **ATA**. Remember, one modem must be in the answer mode, the other in originate. The **ATA** command is handy if you're talking the old-fashioned way to the other person and then decide to switch manually to computer communications. The first person should type **ATD** to the originating modem *first*; only then should the second person type **ATA** to the answering modem. Confusingly, in this situation, the answering modem always transmits first. So the originating modem must be ready. Like **AT,** the **ATA** command is useful for seeing if you've hooked your modem into the phone line properly. If the gods are on your side, **ATA** sends a dial tone through your modem's loudspeaker. (So would **ATD** or ATH1.)

ATH Disconnects (hangs up).

A/ Replicates the immediately preceding command. Do not precede with the normal AT, and don't follow **A/** with a carriage return (Enter). While I'm on the subject of repeat commands, let me suggest checking your modem manual for non-Hayes commands in the same family, such as > or **A>** (perhaps also used without the AT prefix and the carriage return). If available, they may let you automatically redial up to ten times or so.

B0 and **B1** An important command if you're using an American modem and are trying to answer a CCITT modem at 1,200 bps (CCITT V.22 mode). Then you would type **ATB0A.** The last **A** is for "answer." Use the usual Return after the **A.** Alas, the **B0** command won't work with the originating modem. But your colleague with the CCITT modem might be able to use a **B1** command to effect Bell compatibility when receiving.

B15 and The **B15** turns on CCITT compatibility for mo-
B16 dems at 300 bps, and the **B16** turns it off. These Hayes commands may not apply to other modems at 300 bps. They aren't part of the original AT command set.

+ + + Tells the modem "I want you to return to the state where you're awaiting commands." Don't follow with a carriage return. Please note that if you immediately type another character (including a fourth plus sign), this command won't work.

D A connect command for the *originating* modem, even if the **D** officially means "Dial" and can serve that purpose as well (as in **ATDT 555-1212**).

The normal AT comes before the **D**. So **ATD**— followed by the usual tap on the Return key— should connect you after you've dialed a number manually and you hear the other modem. But in some cases you may have to use other variations of this command. If you've already dialed manually, for example, no dial tone will be present, so you may have to use **ATX1D** to disable your modem's dial-tone detector. See the explanations of **X1**, **X2**, **X3**, and **X4** on pages 228 and 229.

E0 and **E1**	**E0** avoids an unwanted echo—the kind when you see two characters in a row. Normally your modem software should be able to control whether you're echoing or not. Most on-line services, such as MCI Mail, already echo. So you shouldn't. Use **E1**, the opposite of **E0**, if you're commanding your modem and want the characters you type to echo back.
H1	Picks up the phone line.
H0	Hangs up.
L1	Modem speaker set low. Some modems, of course, may lack speakers. Many modems lack the L command. Instead they have (gasp) a volume control. Crank it up if you own such a modem and have never heard anything!
L2	Medium-level speaker setting.
L3	High-level speaker setting.
M0	Quiets the speaker in all situations.
M1	Turns on the speaker only from when you pick up the phone to when your modem is talking to the other modem.
M2	The speaker is on always.
O	Use this command if you just typed + + + and you want to get back to talking to the other modem.
P	Allows you to dial with a pulse phone line—as in **ATDP** followed by the phone number and Return. On some modems this is the default setting,

the one from the factory. Chances are, however, that your communications software will include instructions for tone dialing.

S0   Sets the number of rings until the modem answers automatically. **ATS0 = 1** will make a modem answer on one ring, **ATS0 = 2** will answer on two rings, and so on. **ATS0 = 0** turns off the automatic answer and is the normal setting. Please note that failure to set the auto answer properly is one of the most common instigators of panic calls to "help" lines of modems makers.

S7   An extraordinarily important command for some travelers overseas and those at home beset by troublesome telephone systems! After dialing a number, most American-made modems allow themselves only thirty seconds to detect a carrier before they give up. In some cases, however, you may have to extend the wait time to sixty or more. You can increase the time to ninety via this dialing command: **ATS7 = 60DT 555-1212** (Return). The **AT**, of course, is the normal attention command, the **DT** specifies tone dialing, and the 555-1212 is the usual sample phone number.

T   Command for tone dialing. Please note that you can combine tone and pulse dialing. (See an example on page 230.)

X0   Default on some modems. It does none of the other special X functions. When you connect to another modem, it will not announce the speed, just the fact that you're connected.

X1   Use **ATX1D** when you must dial manually, or when you are already connected and are switching from voice to data. This command is for situations in which you can't expect a dial tone. It could cover those rare times when you're using a leased line without the tone. Also, the **X1** tells you what speed your modem fell back to, if it ended up talking to a slower modem. In fact **X1** always tells you the speed, at least if it's above 300 bps. Note

	that some older modems don't support **X1** or some other X commands. Still, **X1** is helpful in certain foreign countries where your modem may be unable to recognize the dial tone or busy signal and thus be unable to dial.
X2	Prevents the modem from dialing until it hears the first dial tone. This command might be invaluable at any time, but particularly if your hotel, nasty PBX, or foreign phone system takes forever to give you a dial tone. Note that **X4** also provides this capability, plus that of **X3**. You can embed the **X2** command in your dialing string via the following syntax: **ATX2DT 555-1212**, followed by Return. Of course, you can combine the X2 feature with the delayed time-out feature, via **ATS7 = 60X2DT 555-1212** and a tap on the Return key.
X3	Enables your modem to say "BUSY" on your screen and hang up the phone line when the line is busy. Normally you won't use this command, since it's part of X4. Almost always you'll use **X2** or **X4** when dialing.
X4	Combines **X2** and **X3**. This is the normal default of many modems. Normally you needn't mess with this command unless you're switching from an earlier mode. On most modems, at any rate, you may start out with an X4 setting.
Z	Reset modem settings. As in the command **ATZ**.

Below are commands that have special meaning when they follow the D command:

0 through 9	The numbers **0** through **9** represent the numbers you want to dial—as in **555-1212**.
# and *	The equivalents of the # and * buttons on your phone. Some phone systems use the # or * to turn off features, such as call forwarding or call waiting. Remember, call waiting can wreak havoc on modem communications.

,   A two-second pause prior to or during dialing; add
           more commas to lengthen the pause. This com-
           mand can be a must when you're dealing with
           switchboards or other sources of delay. In those
           cases, if your modem spits out the number in a
           hurry, the switches may be unable to keep up—
           especially the old-fashioned mechanical kind. What
           if you want to include a four-second pause when
           dialing from a switchboard that requires a delay
           after the "9" used to designate an outside call?
           Then you'd type **ATDT 9,,555-1212**. Inciden-
           tally, via your communications software, you can
           insert this comma in the program's own regular
           dialing sequence; you needn't be in the terminal
           mode. You simply include a comma as part of the
           regular phone number.

!   Disconnect for a half a second, but reconnect. This
           is for "flashing"—where you hang up, then in-
           stantly reconnect. It's equivalent to rocking the
           button on the phone cradle or to the button on
           some phones called "flash" or "tap." Please note
           that some older modems don't support the excla-
           mation point command.

W   Await another dial tone. A typical usage would
           be **ATD9W 555-1212**. That's when you're in a
           hotel and have to dial 9 to get an outside line and
           you want a wait after the 9 to get a second dial
           tone.

@   Waits for silence. Occasionally, your modem will
           reach a phone and not "hear" anything—no con-
           firmation. In fact, silence itself is the confirmation.
           The system isn't busy and it's not ringing; there-
           fore, the connection has been made.

Never forget that you can combine commands. Let's say you're at a
hotel where the phones require that you use pulse dialing to get outside,
and every outside call must start with a 9. And suppose your favorite
long-distance carrier uses tone dialing when you're giving an access

code and dialing the actual number. Then you would use the following: **ATDP 9 W 1 8009501022 ,,, T1 703 5551212, 1234567890** and a Return.

Here's what you're doing: The ADTP tells the modem to dial pulse. The 9 gets an outside line. The W says to await another dial tone. The 1 means you're dialing long distance. The 1-800-950-1022 is MCI's access number (or use that of another carrier). The three commas let you wait for MCI's dial tone. The T initiates tone dialing. The 1 means you're dialing long distance. The 703-555-1212 is the actual number you're dialing. The comma is a two-second wait. And the 1234567890 is a fictitious MCI security code. Please note that few modems can accept more than forty entries and that spaces don't count here. Considering that hotels typically slap a 20- to 40-percent surcharge on top of "normal" long-distance rates, the ability to dial the extra digits may save you a lot of money.

*   *   *

In this chapter I've dealt in general terms with the problem of making telephone connections, and other basic survival issues. In the next chapter, for the most part, I'll pass on some specifics aimed at overseas travelers. How do you use an American-based network from Europe? Just how do you protect your floppy disks against jungle rot? What about customs inspectors who, as one victim put it, "eat computers for breakfast"?

Heed—if you don't want Iraqi officials to use your laptop as a Frisbee or drop it eight feet to the floor, an actual occurrence. Or if you don't want your computer sitting on the docks for two months due to a customs snafu. Ideally, you won't just learn how to survive other people's imbecilities; you'll also reduce the likelihood of committing your own.

Chapter 8

THE ELECTRONIC TRAVELER ABROAD

McDonald's hamburgers recently opened up a big franchise in Moscow. This epitome of Western capitalism has given the Soviets a list of its proprietary ingredients, and it's even supplying seeds to grow potatoes for those famous French fries. I don't know exactly how McDonald's people are faring when they tote laptops into the Soviet Union, but I suspect that with the new emphasis on global trade, more and more electronic travelers from the United States and Canada will be at the mercy of officials in once-unlikely destinations.[1]

Even travelers to more familiar places—London, say—can encounter:

■ Airlines that think laptop cases may house bombs, a problem that could annoy travelers increasingly, even in this country.

■ Pilots who won't let you compute at thirty-five thousand feet,

[1]To be precise, the Russian deal involved McDonald's of Canada.

even if your boss wants you to modem in a polished spreadsheet within minutes after touching the tarmac.

■ The complexities of hooking up to MCI Mail, CompuServe, or similar services from abroad.

■ Equipment breakdowns. Venture beyond air-conditioned hotels in Southeast Asia, for instance, and you may soon learn about instant mold and similar joys of life in the tropics.

Don't let jungle rot and like tribulations discourage you; there are ways to survive and even thrive. Often you can turn the challenges to your advantage. Your rivals, in business, in journalism, in many other fields, may not show the same savvy that you do. For example, you may sail through customs and modem out your news story long before your rival who rubbed the inspectors the wrong way.

CUSTOMS

Horror stories fit for Stephen King have come out of even pedestrian destinations, including the ultimate one for American travelers—the United States.

"By far," says airline pilot John Deakin, "the greatest trouble will be caused by U.S. Customs to U.S. citizens. They do not know their own rules and make them up as they go along, often at the whim of the individual inspector that day." Deakin owns a Toshiba computer made in the USA in Irvine, California. By customs' rules, his laptop is a domestic machine; it isn't to be registered as an import. "Yet," Deakin says, "I've seen customs officials go nearly berserk when some-one tries to 'smuggle' a Toshiba back into the USA without such registration."

The incident is hardly one of a kind. In San Francisco, a customs agent confiscated four American-made printed circuit boards containing chips that said "made in Japan" and "made in Singapore." Deakin describes his tormentor as "an apoplectic, cursing, abusive inspector."

I believe Deakin. When I called customs to ask for tips for foreign travelers bringing laptops into the United States, the agency aggressively ignored me. I'm not surprised we're losing the drug war. Customs bureaucrats must be too busy bullying the computer-addicted. I suppose it's hard to hire good people nowadays; that's certainly true in Canada, where, although some customs officials were outstandingly intelligent and helpful with advice, the lower-level minions were nothing short of moronic. One man even used a false name to identify himself.

Meanwhile, to the south, Mexican customs can be equally ogre-like. Caryl Conner, one of the first women to become a White House speech-writer, went to Mexico to live and travel, and she died there of a heart attack in her late forties after a marathon-length row with officials who had seized her Toshiba T3100.

If the aforementioned can happen so close to home, then how about the rest of the world?

Granted, *most* travelers with laptops will breeze through customs in *most* countries. "In general," says the *Atlantic*'s James Fallows, "customs officials have become accustomed to seeing electronic equipment." But you cannot take bureaucrats for granted. A customs official seizing your hard disk laptop would be like a policeman invading your office and wheeling away your file cabinets and desk. So, given enough time, you may as well be ready for the disastrous exceptions, even if you're not on the way to Iraq.

Here are some precautions for the prudent:

Precaution One: Back Up Programs and Data

Keep copies of programs and data at your office or home; you'll feel much more relaxed around the customs inspector. If your nemesis is a Bedouin tribesman turned cop—as may happen in the Middle East—you won't have to worry about him destroying months and months of financial reports or spreadsheet work.

If you own a notebook-size computer without convenient storage facilities, consider modeming your data to your MCI or CompuServe account if you have one. If you own a floppy-only machine, copy to other floppies. If you own a hard disk machine, use floppies or a LapLink-style program to transfer the material for safe storage.

Needless to say, even stay-at-home businesspeople should back up their material often, In seven years of computing, I have suffered no fewer than four hard disk failures, amnesia that would have crippled me professionally had I not replicated my material beforehand on floppies. The forgetful machines ran on electricity from no more exotic a source than the Virginia Electric and Power Company.

Precaution Two: Contact the Appropriate Government(s) or Others Beforehand—At Least If There's Time

A copy of your sales slip—showing price, model, serial number, and the date of purchase of your equipment—may be helpful in placating customs bureaucrats of all nationalities.

William Claiborne of the *Washington Post* even suggests sticking a copy of the receipt in the laptop bag. That's what his colleague Jonathan Randal does. Randal also carries a "certificate of registration for personal effects taken abroad," U.S. customs form 4457 (06-02-80), issued by the U.S. Treasury Customs Service."[2] It:

■ "Duly notes, complete with official stamp from Office of Inspection & Control, the date [of issuance].

■ "Establishes that the Toshiba—including model and serial number—is my property [and establishes] its value at time of purchase. On [the] same certificate I also noted similar information about my Diconix 150 printer.

"Thus armed, I have never been challenged by any U.S. official."

David Bland of MCI offers similar advice. "No one's given me major problems," he generalizes about customs, "but there have been times when they've asked me to fill in a form which they kept a copy of and which I had to show when I was leaving."

Below are possible organizations to contact—besides customs—to forestall customs difficulties and other kinds of problems.

■ The U.S. Council for International Business (1212 Avenue of the Americas, New York, New York 10036-1689, (212) 354-4480, fax (212) 575-0327), which issues documents known as carnets to help you avoid paying customs duties on goods you'll be bringing back to the United States within a specified time.

Participating countries agree not to levy duties on "commercial samples" or "professional equipment." The council defines such samples as "any and all items which are temporarily imported solely for the purpose of being shown or demonstrated in the territory of importation for the soliciting of orders."

---

[2] Check with customs to see if you'll need a more recent form.

Professional equipment "includes, but is not limited to, equipment for the press or for television broadcasting, cinematographic equipment; equipment for testing or repair of machinery; tools; sporting goods; engineering, construction, surgical, electrical, archaeological, musical and entertainment equipment."

The council sends you a form listing the equipment that you'll be carrying and asks you to give the total value of the goods that the carnet will cover. On values between $500 and $4,999.99, you pay $100. Not everyone likes carnets; see page 276 for one traveler's generic complaint that they can cost too much and may not be helpful if you don't know all of the countries to which you're headed.

In case you're curious, the U.S. Council for International Business is a business group that presents "American business views" to international bodies and agencies, such as the World Bank or the General Agreement on Tariffs and Trade.

■ The U.S. State Department. Get an official American perspective on customs complications in such troublesome countries as Iraq and Iran, places where you *know* Americans are regarded with suspicion. The main State Department number is (202) 647-4000.

Ask the switchboard operator to refer you to a "country desk" that can brief you on current conditions. Perhaps someday Iraq will be a paradise for laptop users—after customs officials learn to distinguish between computers and Frisbees.

■ The Bureau of Export Administration, part of the U.S. Commerce Department, which may require you to register a powerful laptop with a processor, such as a 80386 or 80486, for reasons of national security. That's especially true if your machine packs more than 4 megs of RAM and 150 megs of hard disk space and is more rugged than the usual portable. You may be subject to registration even for some non-Communist countries. Vietnam, Cuba, Cambodia, North Korea, Libya, South Africa, and Namibia are among the nations to which the strictest regulations apply.

The U.S. government can be a tough customer, too. It once imposed a fine of hundreds of thousands of dollars on the Reuters news agency for sending high-tech terminals to East Europe.

Within the Bureau of Export Administration, call (202) 377-4188 to see if your computer is advanced enough to need a special permit. If you live in a large city, look in the phone directory for a local office of the bureau (under the Commerce Department listing).

■ The telecommunications authorities in the destination country. You might check with the consulate to see if this will be necessary beforehand to expedite your use of a modem. Alas, there may be a stiff fee. You may be better off just calling the United States directly and not bothering to register. Ideally the telecommunications people won't be that well coordinated with the bureaucrats in customs.

■ Not just the consulate of the destination country, but perhaps the office of the commercial attaché (if you're a businessperson) or the ministry of information (if you're a reporter). Alert the officials that you'll be using a laptop in your normal business and, if possible, ask for a letter explaining this.

Advice from an American journalist may as well be generic for the Third World: "Any time you are traveling to Iraq and want to take your laptop, just telex the ministry of information and ask for a protocol officer to meet you at the airport with a letter authorizing you to bring in your computer. It's a well-established routine. Be sure you exit Iraq in the same way, because that customs officer who eats computers for breakfast is bound to find you if you don't."

Contacting the ministry of information or other official agency beforehand, a visitor also may reduce the likelihood of being mistaken for a CIA agent because of his or her equipment. This particular correspondent can recall watching on television an anti-American speech in Teheran; the ministry of intelligence was exhibiting "spy" gear. "There in the middle of the screen were several personal computers, including a laptop, computer modems, and fax machines."

"In many parts of the Third World," says Claiborne, "computers are viewed as spy tools. When I went to Zambia to cover a South African Army bombing of African National Congress hideouts, I was arrested by the security thugs. As they were booking us and preparing to put us into the cells, they asked me what my Tandy 200 was. I told them it was for communicating and they got very interested and asked me to turn it on. When I did, the menu came up and showed a file that I had written the week before about an explosion at a post office in Johannesburg—slugged 'BOMB.' I had forgotten it was still in there. When they saw that they went crazy and immediately called for the chief inspector, certain they had a South African spy who was responsible for the bombing."

Still, laptops are becoming far more common than in the past in the

Third World, so you can expect much less trouble, at least for businesspeople who aren't in the middle of a war zone.

"Nobody arrests you on suspicion of being a CIA agent," James Fallows generalizes about Southeast Asia. "A computer aggravates this, but the suspicion is there anyway, so it doesn't really matter." Suspicions of spying are quite common and boring, indeed, in parts of the Philippines. Fallows jokes that spookhood is the only other possibility left for an American if he or she isn't a sailor or a car salesperson.

Precaution Three: Using Diplomacy When Dealing With Customs and Police (Even if You Wish You Could Strangle Them)

Once again an experienced traveling reporter gives some wise generic advice, even though he's speaking of Arab countries rather than the world at large: "When you get in a jam, never, never choose an angry course to try to bully your way through. It does not work; in fact it works against you. Many airport policemen are recruited from the Bedouin tribes that tend to be the fiercest fighters and most loyal subjects. In Bedouin tradition, a display of anger is a challenge to fight." It doesn't require much imagination to see the preceding observation as applying also to Latin countries, where the macho mindset tends to reign supreme.

"The best way out of airport jams," he says, "is a very respectful pleading of your case with frequent displays of sincerity and respect by putting your hand over your heart."

Body language at work! Who needs Esperanto?

"If things don't go your way, gather as much information calmly on the exact nature of the obstacle and solicit advice from any other authority you can consult before returning again to the person who is holding you up. The statement 'God Bless You,' to me, is one of the friendliest terms you can use in these situations."

Be diplomatic even in the face of political inanities, such as those that he suffered in Iraq. "The customs man said he had no authority to let me in the country with a computer," he recalls, "especially since it was the equivalent of a typewriter, and typewriters are forbidden in Iraq." It seems that "President Saddam Hussein, as a young revolutionary, used to write propaganda leaflets for the fledgling Arab Ba'ath party on his manual typewriter, and years later, when he got to power he decided he would not give anyone the opportunity that he had taken.''

Hence the brief confiscation of this journalist's computer. In indelible ink, a clerk wrote the number 205. ''This was the inventory number of my Toshiba when the clerk took it away to a room where most of the people handling it did not know what it was or whether it would break if you threw it across the room like a Frisbee.''

The reporter could have done an outraged American act. Instead, however, he turned to bureaucracy to fight bureaucracy. Within a day and a half, he was able to reclaim his computer, thanks to a letter from the information ministry saying that the government had authorized his visit.

If you're a businessperson, you might not be able to avail yourself of the same contacts that our friend did. But you can try different ones. Now do you see the arguments for working out the details of visits to difficult countries ahead of time? Get letters of introduction from clients, from branch offices, through banking connections, any way you can.

How to be diplomatic in the face of a demand for a bribe? This is one issue I won't address, other than to suggest that you consult with your company's lawyers ahead of time if you fear the issue may arise.

Precaution Four: Carry Your Equipment—Don't Ship it Ahead of Your Arrival

Try to avoid sending laptops ahead of time—at least not without doing plenty of homework—if you're visiting Asia and perhaps some Western countries as well.

''The general rule is that the customs officials are much easier on stuff that is accompanied by baggage that you bring in with you, rather than stuff that comes in as a separate shipment,'' Fallows says. ''What you bring in with you is done at the airport where they're more kind of in a rush; they want to get through things. Stuff that's sent in separately goes to the docks, where the customs inspectors have a lot of time, and they're looking for bribes. So, in all countries, that's the rule: bring it in with you directly.''

''Sending a computer in via DHL or whatever is a customs hassle,'' Claiborne says of delivery services. ''In South Africa it's 40 percent duty. So, best to just bring it in with you, or include it in your shipment that is cleared by a shipping agent.''

OF LAPTOPS AND BOMBS

Not long ago, a bomb hidden in the case of a cassette player blew up a Pan Am jet over Scotland. Two-hundred and seventy died. The bureaucratic response was inevitable: a proposal to banish electronics, such as laptops, from the air. That didn't happen. Increasingly, however, airport security staffers are making laptop users produce a cursor and an A> or C:\ prompt. As if terrorists couldn't miniaturize both a computer and a bomb!

"Security people are sometimes interested in stepdown transformers, wires, modems, alligator clip connecting wires, et cetera, because those things look like components of a bomb," says Claiborne. Still, he hasn't experienced any major hassles at airports, even in volatile areas of Africa and the Middle East.

Among the major issues for laptop owners are:

■ Giving yourself enough fudge time to allow for security-caused delays. MCI's David Bland jovially admits a little room for personal improvement: "I broke my record last week. I caught four flights showing up at the gate within a minute of the departure time. I'm not the best person in terms of checking in early."

Fallows, on the other hand, has tried mightily to reform. After moving to Japan he told me via MCI Mail: "I placidly arrive at the airport *at least* two hours before departure time—that way I don't have to get exasperated, and I can always just take along a book. Narita Airport is the worst major airport I've dealt with, among other reasons because it's so far out of town. I leave my house five hours and thirty minutes before the plane's departure time."

■ Preparing in other ways for the inspection. If you're toting a rechargeable battery laptop to the airport, make certain your machine has a full charge, and if the laptop is an AC-only model, just hope that there's a power outlet nearby. Be sure that your step-down transformer and plug adapter are handy, or that you've flipped the proper switch on your machine if it can handle different voltages but does not do so automatically. Tape a note to your machine if need be. Even experienced computer pros have fried their laptops this way at luggage inspection stations.

"It's a very easy thing to forget," says Bland, "when you're going through an airport security check in a hurry and plug your computer in to show that it works, and suddenly you've got 240 volts and there goes your power pack.''

■ Learning to live with airport X-ray machines. John Deakin, the Japan Airlines pilot, says, ''X rays are highly unlikely to do any damage whatsoever, and may be pretty safely ignored.

''The machinery driving those belts, and the magnetic detectors, may be somewhat more hazardous to your machine and to data, but to date no one in any of the IBMNET, CP/M, TAPCIS, AVSIG, or PCVEN (Section 10, Toshiba Tech Support) Forums on CompuServe has ever, to my knowledge, reported the slightest problem.

''I myself have put Kaypro 2s, 4s, 10s, 2000s, and two Toshiba 3100s through airport security hundreds of times, together with my archive and backup floppy disks, with no known problems.

''I don't think I'd care to put my floppy disks right up next to those magnetic arches, but that's about the only limitation I'd have, and I doubt even that would affect them. It actually takes a fairly intense, highly localized magnetic impulse to do anything to a floppy.

''Please, no lawsuits if I'm wrong; this is just my personal opinion.''

I'll add a caveat. It's been noted that while the X rays won't harm disks, the transformers of the machines may cause problems; that some units are better shielded than others; and that you may want to hand-carry your floppies. Perhaps the true solution is to go ahead and have your portable inspected, but insist on hand-inspection of backup floppies (which isn't to say that another set of backups shouldn't remain in your office).

LAPTOPS AND PILOTS (AND WORRIES OF RADIO INTERFERENCE)

You're thirty thousand feet over Nebraska; you punch a key to move to the next column of Lotus 1-2-3. Instantly the plane goes into a nose dive and crashes. You're not alive, of course, when the investigation winds down, but the conclusion is that radio waves from your computer jinxed the jet's electronics.

Luckily, the above scenario is as far-fetched as it seems, despite past talk of a federal ban on airborne computing. Some experts *theorize* that a laptop could cause harm in a plane with poorly installed wiring or another problem. John Deakin, however, while noting these fears, downplays the risks. He does say that the Federal Aviation Agency bans operation of most electronic gadgets—except when airlines have tested on their own and found them to be safe.

Japan Airlines, United Airlines, and surely many other carriers have satisfied themselves that laptops won't imperil planes. In fact, Deakin says the JAL operations manual "specifically states that 'Battery operated computers with LCD screens are permitted.' " (Ah! So Toshiba or Sony executives can blithely compute while flying back to their products' fatherland.)

MODEMS OVERSEAS: THE MORE, THE MERRIER

If you're going abroad—or at least to the Third World—one modem may not do.

■ In Third World countries with quirky electrical and phone systems, you may need some spares. A *Chicago Tribune* man carried three modems during a tour in Latin America. Many *Washington Post* reporters also believe in redundancy. You should, too, regardless of your business—at least if you're fighting deadlines and you know that a spare modem could take days to arrive.

■ Overseas, whether you're in the Third World or some developed country, you may have to buy a local modem to comply with local telephone regulations.

Be prepared, at any rate, for technochauvinism and other inanities. When James Fallows moved to Japan he had trouble registering his American modem. Then he said he was using a device made by Epson, the Japanese electronic company, and approval was instant. The Japanese are no longer so small-minded about the nationalities of modems; but don't be surprised if you encounter similar silliness elsewhere.

For information on international modem standards, please see Chapter 6.

At any rate, Deakin makes a good case for the safety of laptops aboard jumbo jets. "I have, on my own, done considerable testing inflight on 747s with a number of Kaypro and Toshiba AC-powered machines, in the cockpit, the cabin, and in the electronics compartment, with not the slightest effect on any aircraft system, radio, or navigation equipment. I have seen literally hundreds of passengers using laptops, often several dozen at once, with no known effect. I believe it to be safe on any modern jet transport. I would be much more concerned over such use in a small aircraft, where the antennae are located much closer to the cabin.''

HOOKUP TIPS FOR TRAVELERS ABROAD

You've got two main ways of connecting to a computer in the States:

1. A direct connection, dialed yourself like any other call. As you'll discover, this may be cheaper in the short run than the alternatives.
2. A hookup from your modem to an international packet-switching network, which you'll very likely use together with such services as MCI Mail or CompuServe. You can even employ your laptop to dig up information about using it overseas. In case you didn't know, a packet-switching network lets many computers at once use the same phone line—slashing long distance charges. Alas, some nations charge hundreds of dollars to start using their nets, hardly a good deal for short-term stays.

A Direct Connection to the United States

If you'll just briefly be in a destination country, then you and your wallet may be better off if you just phone directly to the States—to avoid the stratospheric fees that some of the foreign packet-switching networks charge. You might check with your regular telephone company for information on ways to reduce your communications bills from your travels.

Hotels love to gouge international callers. Why let them? In at least fifty-three countries, AT&T offers the USA DIRECT service, through which you dial a local number and hook up directly with an operator in the United States. Often, though not always, USA DIRECT is much cheaper (although it still may not beat direct dialing in cases where there are no hotel surcharges). To find out more about the service, call AT&T at 800-874-4000. You'll need an AT&T calling card if you aren't phoning collect. To obtain a card, call 800-225-5288. USA DIRECT is available even if you normally use another long-distance pany. Check with MCI, Sprint, Allnet, and other rivals about the availability of similar services from these carriers.

Also to reduce the cost of direct connections, you might try a file compression utility to shorten your material to perhaps two-fifths of its original length. Compression may or may not work with bad connections. But give it a shot. Check local BBS's for compression shareware, such as the popular ARC and ZIP programs.

Remember, of course, that with a direct connection, the transmission quality may suffer. You may have to be content with 1,200 or even 300 bps. What's more, you may have a problem with satellite echo, which can confuse some error-control schemes that encourage accurate transmission of data. Your transmission may stop because there are too many errors. If error control doesn't work, you might try a plain ASCII transmission, maybe in half duplex. You'll get errors, but at least the bulk of your file will transmit. The right modem can help. If you skipped the modem chapter, repent! Go back and read it.

If you're dialing to MCI Mail or a similar net from abroad, you might inquire about the half-duplex option. This option can eliminate the oft-confusing delay between when you hit the keys and when your screen flashes the characters back at you.

An International Packet-Switching Network

When I interviewed James Fallows for this book, I sent my questions to him via MCI Mail for just $1 per one thousand words or so. By contrast, I must have spent several dollars on gas and wear and tear on my car when he returned to the United States and I drove into Washington to meet him for lunch.

MCI Mail isn't a charity. What makes the cheapie e-mail possible is a technology called packet switching, which can drastically slash the costs of communicating via computer. Via packet switching, many computers at once can jabber away on the same phone lines.

Giant computer networks like MCI use many different lines, but still just a fraction of what they'd need if packet switching didn't exist. I won't bother with a technical explanation here. Just take my word for it. Packet switching, at least in theory, can be much cheaper than alternatives. In the case of MCI Mail, I dial an 800 number to reach MCI's packet-switching network directly. Overseas, however, you'll typically be calling a local number in either your host country or a country in that area of the world. Via satellite or cable, your modem signals can then go to the United States and, thence, to the main MCI network.

Unfortunately, although packet switching can lower transmission costs, foreign countries and companies often overcharge visitors trying to use the local nets that tie in with international ones. So Fallows's MCI costs per message from Asia averaged several times mine. On the plus side, packet-switching nets allow clear signals and a higher speed than does direct dialing to the States. Most of the time, packet switching is virtually essential if you're overseas and want to call home at 2,400 bps, at least without error control.

If only the electronic traveler could receive some on-line help about making an international connection as a client of MCI Mail, CompuServe, SprintMail, and other networks!

As a matter of fact, such assistance often exists. For example:

■ If you're on MCI Mail, you can type **VIEW INTERNATIONAL** from the main prompt and press the Return key to see MCI's International Access bulletin board.[3] Then type **SCAN** and hit Return again. Begin with the recommended "read this first" introduction; type the number for it, then press the Return. From there you can go on to other items, especially material for the country to which you're headed. You'll see, among other things, the names of telecommunications offices and rate information. The command **LEAVE** followed by Return will get you back to regular MCI Mail.

Before leaving the International Access board, however, take a look at the item about an MCI-licensed service called WorldMail. It supplies help in the local language and receives payments from local subscribers in their own currencies. WorldMail offers other services, too—services of interest to travelers. WorldMail licensees and MCI's international offices will provide telephone advice to visitors. There are different policies for on-site visits. WorldMail is available in twelve of the eighty countries to which MCI Mail has packet-switching connections: Bel-

---

[3]If you're using MCI Mail's Basic Service rather than the Advanced one, you might have to use somewhat different commands. Try typing **VIEW** from the main prompt, then press Return, and type **INTERNATIONAL** followed by another Return. Another way to find out about conditions would be to phone MCI's Customer Support office: 800-444-6245 in the United States; in Washington, D.C., or outside the United States, 202-833-8484.

gium, Chile, Colombia, Denmark, West Germany, Israel, Japan, South Korea, the Philippines, Spain, Switzerland, and the United Kingdom.

■ If you're on CompuServe, you can see some basic country-by-country information by typing **GO INTERNATIONAL**, pressing your return, and following the prompts. You'll find out (1) whom to contact in individual countries to arrange for connections with CompuServe and (2) telephone numbers and technical setting for some of the data networks there.

Going to Europe? Then type **GO EUROPE** and follow the menus, beginning with "Logon Instructions (Europe)." Even before you reach Europe, you can make contact with local people via CompuServe/ Forum, the European service. Ask CompuServe customer service (800-848-8990 or 614-457-8650) for the current names of European-oriented forums; or just plunge in and try typing **GO IBMEURO** from the main CompuServe prompt. (Maybe a Mac-oriented forum or others will exist by the time you're reading this book.) After you've logged on a forum, see if you can't learn who's in which country, and who might offer advice on telephones, supplies, repairs, and other useful information for your travels. You might even post a general request for help if the SYSOP—that's jargon for "system operator," or the person running the forum—can't point you to someone in your destination country. What a bargain for the traveler! You're not paying a penny extra to communicate across the Atlantic. By the way, try to oblige if you see a plaintive plea in a domestic forum from a European planning a visit to the United States.

What if you're in Europe and want to *hear* a *voice* offering you help? From anywhere in the United Kingdom, you can dial the CompuServe/ Forum Bristol office for free (800-289-458). The address is: CompuServe/Forum, P.O. Box 676, Bristol BS99 1YN, United Kingdom. On the Continent, dial 41-31-031-509-800 in Berne, Switzerland (not a free long-distance call). That address is: CompuServe/Forum, Laupenstrasse 18A, CH-3008, Berne, Switzerland. Depending on where you are, the extra charges for logging on from Europe can range from $9.50 an hour to $20.50.

See page 266 of the "Electronic Baedeker" chapter for information on hooking up from Japan.

■ If you use an electronic mail service on Tymnet, such as OnTyme, call a special number for international information. I won't publish a complete list but will pass along a number for northern Virginia that you can dial from afar: (703) 352-3136. After seeing garbage on your screen—perhaps a series of Xs—you should type A, then hit the Return. You'll see a request for you to log in. Type **INFORMATION** and follow the menu. Just as with MCI and CompuServe, you'll see detailed country-by-country information. This is a public service of Tymnet; you needn't even be a regular user to benefit from the country-specific facts.

Those services notwithstanding, you still may feel beset by the lack of telephone plugs in hotel rooms, different modem standards, and so on. What do you do if you'll be transmitting too often to get away with just direct connections to the States?

You might consider using the services of a company such as COMCO (short for "Compagnie de communication COMCO S.A."), which works closely with PTTs ("Post and Telegraph"), as overseas telephone companies are often known. In many countries the communications agencies are part of the post office.

Coincidentally or not, many of the PTTs can be as slow as postal systems. So COMCO, started originally to help roving journalists, can be invaluable in helping you deal with the bureaucracy. COMCO sup plies you with an RS-232–compatible modem tailored to the country you're in and makes certain that it coexists peacefully with the local telephone system and packet-switching network. You can employ your normal software, such as ProComm, CrossTalk, or Mirror.

To activate the modem, you use what Richard Dent, a COMCO officer, describes as a credit card–size smart card "whose computer chip contains the call charge units that pay for the call and other information that makes connection easier for the user. It is very similar to the European PTTs' different telephone cards with the significant difference that the same card works in every country where the service is available." When using the modem, Dent says, "you put your communications software in 'dumb terminal mode,' plug the COMCO-MODEM into the laptop," and then simply press the Return key.

"The COMCO-MODEM will automatically dial the COMCO gateway from which you will receive a welcome message in the language indicated automatically by your card. When asked what host computer you wish to call, pressing Enter automatically dials the NUA (network user address) that is stored in the card. Alternatively, any other NUA can be put in manually or typing the word COMCO will connect you to the COMCO information host." An NUA is a network identification number, an account number.

One way or another, COMCO connects to major services like MCI Mail, CompuServe, SprintMail, OnTyme, and EasyLink, Dialcom (now foreign owned), as well as equivalent services in Europe and elsewhere. Dent says: "For the user of MCI Mail with Lotus Express and COMCO in a Hilton hotel room in London, Geneva, or Tokyo, for example, it is simple to the point that you can plug your laptop into the COMCO-MODEM in your room, turn it on and go and have a drink while it automatically collects and sends your mail. This is possible because use of a COMCO-MODEM is the same everywhere, regardless of the country it is in."

You can use COMCO, as of this writing, in Australia, Austria, Belgium, Canada, Finland, France, West Germany, Holland, Hong Kong, Japan, Korea, Switzerland, the United Kingdom, and the United States. "COMCO," Dent says, "has central agreements with the Hilton and Swissotel chains. Individual hotels of other chains have also taken COMCO-MODEMs. We have an agreement with Swissair to equip their lounges around the world, but so far this is the only airline to have COMCO-MODEMs available.

"British Telecom, the Swiss, and Finnish PTTs are installing COMCO-MODEMs in selected locations. The list of locations of COMCO-MODEMs can be obtained on the COMCO bulletin board on MCI Mail," says Dent.

Use MCI's **VIEW INTERNATIONAL** command, followed by the **Scan** one, and you'll see COMCO information as one of the items in the international area. "COMCO also maintains a host information service that is free to users of COMCO-CARDs," Dent says. "The COMCO-MODEMs are provided free of charge in some hotels and in, for example, Swissair lounges. Other hotels may charge $10 to $15 per night."

In addition, COMCO charges according to how long you are on line. "The time allowed per call charge unit varies depending on the origin of the call and the speed of transmission," the company says in its electronically distributed literature. "As a guide, for a call from Switzerland to MCI Mail, one unit currently pays for 50 seconds at 300 bps, or 30 seconds at 1200 bps. The Card is debited one unit for the log-on."

There is no monthly subscription charge. Do check about equipment fees if you wish to buy rather than just rent COMCO gear; the portable card reader alone runs to $470, and the modem is extra, though COMCO says that WorldPort models work fine with the reader. Needless to say, before using COMCO or a similar service, you'll want to compare it very closely against the costs of dialing the States or other locations directly. For further information on COMCO, write:

COMCO S.A.
Route de Lausanne, 128
1052 Le Mont-Lausanne
Switzerland

You may also reach COMCO via telephone (41-21-36-51-05) or computer (41-21-37-01-10).

MCI Mail	COMCO
Dialcom	84:TXT047
Easylink	19037235 +

Mind you, COMCO isn't necessarily the only way to simplify billing and reduce technical problems and maybe costs. You might, for example, check with country contacts listed on MCI or CompuServe to find out about other ways of doing this. Some international data networks may make temporary arrangements for visitors to cut back hook-up charges, which normally may run as high as hundreds of dollars.

What's it like to log on from abroad? Let's say you're using a network run by the Computer Sciences Corporation to log onto CompuServe from a European country. Then, depending on local circumstances, you might do the following or something similar:

1. Dial the local access number. CompuServe/Forum will tell you the local number if you don't know it.
A "Connect" message will confirm the connection.
2. Press the carriage return—the Enter key—twice.
A pound sign (#) from CSC will appear on your screen.
3. Type the letter C and press the return key again.
4. Type CSF at the "CENTER" prompt. Hit the carriage return.
You'll eventually see a "USER ID" prompt—perhaps after some garbage characters.

5. Enter your CompuServe ID. Press the return key.
6. Type in your password, then hit Return.
7. Proceed as you normally would on CompuServe.

Mind you, there are many variants. Let's say you're reaching CompuServe through a network run by a local telephone company. Then you might:

1. Dial a local number—the "node," in network parlance.
2. Tell the network what kind of computer you're using. You might do this through a series of letters and numbers.
3. Wait for the network to confirm that you're logging on successfully. This might be just gibberish, in the vein of **LO3/231421323-123**.
4. Enter your user ID number, which the international network will give you.
5. Type out a number indicating the network address of CompuServe. You're just directing your connection to CompuServe rather than to another service. Before or after the number, you might type in extra characters. An **A** might tell a packet-switching network that you're about to give an address, and a **9** could say, "The address is outside the United States."
6. Having followed those steps, you might then see the same set of prompts that you normally would when logging on CompuServe from the States.

Obviously, the log-on process can be awkward if done manually. You can greatly speed it up through:

■ Automatic log-on scripts, which you can write in many programs, so that the modem software will automatically spit out the various routing codes and your identification. The scripts will be handiest for people remaining in a country a while. Even those lingering just briefly, however, might still go to the trouble of doing a script if they think they may return. Some communications programs, of course, can write the scripts automatically by memorizing the keystrokes you use while logging on.
■ Macros. You might be able to automate your communications software to spit out network IDs, et cetera, individually. This will be

most handy when you're hopping from country to country rather than tarrying.

EQUIPMENT BREAKDOWNS ABROAD

Via "The Murphy's Law Chapter," you already know that breakdowns happen. In fact, a problem confounded me earlier this week: my printer was working just part of the time. Ah! Nothing to worry about. I just tried a second printer cable to replace the cable that I'd mutilated to fit another machine.

But suppose I were in a more isolated, worse-equipped location; that's the big rub when you're computing in, say, the Andes. The ideal solution would do Noah proud: take along two of *everything*. If that's impractical, at least leave your haywire and your quirkier other gadgets behind when you're abroad. Here's other advice specifically for foreign travelers:

■ If you know you're likely to be going abroad in a hurry someday, check with the manufacturer *before* you buy, to see if the company boasts a far-flung network of repairpeople. It's obvious. IBM and Zenith are going to be much, much better off in this respect than an obscure company. Of course, you still might want to buy the offering of an obscure manufacturer, but be aware of the trade-off.

■ Follow my advice on surge protectors and the like; also, if you're buying a fleet of computers for a number of people to use overseas, you might look for those with automatically switchable power supplies, which can tell the difference between 115 and 230 volts before it's too late.

■ If you don't have a list of prospective repair locations, get it *now*.

■ Realize that in many cases, it just won't be worth having a micro repaired abroad, because of the cost, lack of experienced people, and/ or the time delays. When it comes to getting repair parts, not all cultures exist with an "absolutely, positively has to be there mentality." Even in the United Kingdom you may have to wait weeks for a part. Besides, who says the United States is perfect? Many manufacturers insist that local dealers send gear back to the factory for servicing. Also keep in mind that many micros are sold only in the United States, placing many manufacturers at a disadvantage.

■ If you're in a location well served by international air express, you might make plans with your home office or a regional one nearby to ship in a spare machine.

■ Don't count on buying a replacement overseas that will be worth taking home—because of differences in keyboards.

■ Even in the States, rental of equipment is expensive. If you're an MCI Mail subscriber, however, you might consider making temporary use of one of the computers in a local office of WorldMail—for a fee, of course.

■ Resign yourself to the fact that in the tropics or other special surroundings, computers just won't last as long as they would elsewhere, because of humidity, insects, and so on. See chapter 9 to learn how James Fallows coped in wet Kuala Lumpur. If you're using your micro on a beach, in a desert, or in some other area with sand or dust, you may do well to cover your keyboard with a plastic membrane of the kind I described in chapter 5.

*   *   *

So much for the general joys and frustrations of laptop use abroad. What's it like in London? New Delhi? Travel on! Ahead lies "An Electronic Baedeker."

Chapter 9

AN ELECTRONIC BAEDEKER

■ Tips on dealing with customs, telecommunications, and other plea-
sures in more than twenty countries. Page 254.
■ Power Plugs, Euro-style. Page 279.
■ The telephones of Europe. Page 281.

In Germany, if you use acoustic cups, you'll find that mouthpieces
on the telephones can be gigantic—perhaps too big for American
cups. If you're in certain tropical countries, especially if you
aren't staying at a hotel blessed by air-conditioning, you might
protect against jungle rot that can destroy your floppy disks. In
Iraq, customs people just might toss your laptop around if you
rub them the wrong way.

Via responses to BBS notes, CompuServe messages, memos
by *Washington Post* reporters, and other sources, I've informally
collected such odds and ends from Americans who have been
abroad. Among the other goodies here, you'll find a basic guide
to the power plugs and telephones of Europe.

This is not a scientific paper. I'll just try to give you a flavor
of what to expect. For better or worse, conditions are always
changing, and you'd do well to pick the brains of colleagues who
either have been to your destination or are there now.

Such changes are mostly good; consider Germany. In the late
'80s the Bundespost, the telecommunications organization, was
known as one of the world's most rigid phone companies. German
phones lacked plugs: they were just hardwired to the wall. Imag-

ine the joys for modem users. But word has just reached me that, gasp, even the Bundespost is loosening up. "All the world seems to be liberalizing their telecommunications policies, some more, some less," Alan Garratt of MCI says. "A few countries, Argentina, New Zealand and Chile and maybe others, have put their telecommunications organizations up for sale." Government regulators will still call many of the shots, as the Federal Communications Commission does in the United States. But the global trend is toward more competition, lower costs, higher-quality lines, and easier computer links.

Via high tech, you can avoid outrageous telex or fax charges or bypass antique telephones abroad.[1] When a Berlin correspondent for *Time Magazine* has trouble with a hotel telephone nowadays, he or she just might call New York by way of a cellular phone. And if American journalists and business people in Europe aren't already using cellular phones with laptops and modems, then many soon will be.

Portable computers and other high-tech gear are everywhere. Go to Ethiopia and you'll see Eritrean rebels using fax machines and a satellite dish. One American saw so many computers in the hands of famine-relief officials that he calls Ethiopia and Sudan "the land of the laptops."[2]

Africa (General)

"In South Africa," William Claiborne of the *Washington Post* says, "there are good repair shops for a number of computers, like Toshiba, Zenith, etc., mostly the ones they sell here. No repair available for Tandys. Elsewhere in Africa, limited repair facilities and for limited models."

There's still hope, however. "Every country has a local computer doctor," Claiborne says, "who deals with correspondents, usually a computer geek who is not affiliated with any company or service that normally does business with computers, but who knows hacks and deals with them. The one I have in South Africa is a genius."

[1] See page 341 for more on using cellular telephones with laptops.

[2] The examples involving *Time Magazine* and Africa are from "The Compleat Reporter," Gib Johnson's article in the May 1990 issue of *The Washington Journalism Review*, page 17.

Claiborne says that the telephone lines are "excellent" in South Africa. "Elsewhere on the continent, the lines aren't so great, but the hotel connections often are possible through the usual alligator clips. . . . When calling from a hotel or through an international operator, I suggest that you tell the operator you are making a 'telefax call.' They seem to understand the term and will get you on the line before the access number starts ringing. You must remind the operator to stay the hell off the line and not break in to ask if you want to continue with the call or that the three minutes are up, or whatever. I've left finger marks on the necks of several hotel operators in Africa."

Algeria and Tunisia

The *Post*'s Jonathan Randal has experienced no difficulties with U.S. customs, thanks to the bureaucratic precautions mentioned earlier. But he says that at various times, customs agents in Tunisia and Algeria "have tried to make me pay duty," until he "wasted a considerable amount of time negotiating with their superiors and explaining that the Toshiba T1000 was a glorified typewriter. Some Middle Eastern airport security people confiscate batteries, thus endangering battery packs."

In the eyes of some officials in Third World countries, all batteries are bomb detonators until proven innocent.

Arab/North African Countries (General)

"Increasingly," Randal says, "I choose hotels in function of their telephone plugs, rather than their other services, with those equipped with American RJ-11 plugs at the top of the list. Unfortunately, hotels throughout the world are increasingly equipped with metering devices which cause transmission problems." Off the top of his head, Randal recommends "the Africa in Tunis, the Nile Hilton in Cairo, the Hilton in Bahrain, the Sheraton and Hilton in Kuwait, the Intercontinental in Amman."

Asia (General)

James Fallows says that "in most cases you won't have customs problems if the machine looks like it's not brand new—if it's obviously part of your own belongings. Worst problems are in the most primitive and corrupt economies—Burma, Vietnam, sometimes China. But in general people are getting used to these things. The main problem is with airport security detectors. Every time you have to take the machine out of the bag, turn it on, show it's not a bomb.

"In my experience, in most Asian countries *except* China, Indonesia, Vietnam, and sometimes the Philippines, the phone lines are good enough for direct calls back to the U.S."

Australia and New Zealand

"Australia and New Zealand use a funny outlet with canted slots," says Richard Talley, a Toshiba owner I ran across on CompuServe. Take along a converter from 220 volts. "The weight of the transformer made it hard to keep the adapter in place unless it was propped up with something," he says. "The salvation was the shaver adapter in the bathroom. Only one of four hotels failed to have a 110-volt, U.S.-type outlet in the bathroom. So my T1000 got charged up in the bathroom."

Brazil

Surprise! "It is rare for Brazilians on private lines to ever use anything less than 9,600-bit modems," according to Don Kimberlin, the telecommunications consultant mentioned earlier in this book.

"You'd have a hard time selling a Brazilian anything less than 9,600 bits because their inter-city communications network is all brand new, spanking and sparkling. However, in the city centers of the old major cities, in Rio de Janeiro, São Paulo, etc., the local telephone exchange cable network has been fabulously rotten. And so you're talking through a funnel to get out to that great inter-city network." Just the same, as Kimberlin observes, "sometimes the most remote locations in the least developed countries can do some amazing things for you."

Oddly, when Mary Williams Walsh was in Brazil for the *Los Angeles Times*, she had less trouble getting telephone connections through to the United Kingdom than to the United States. Mysteriously, Brazilian telephones would rather talk to the English ones. Do the phones have accents? Just what's going on here?

There is at least one other issue in Brazil: customs. The Brazilians are fiercely protective of their high-tech industries. Walsh says one American reporter there was so concerned that he never left Brazil while carrying an expensive laptop, just a cheap little Radio Shack model. That way he wouldn't have to worry so much if Brazilian officials seized his machine on the way back in.

Canada

Some American laptop users can breeze through Canadian customs and avoid paying any taxes or duties on high-tech gear. A midwestern business executive, however, passed on some vague but ugly rumors about harassment of laptop owners by Canadian customs officials.

The rumors probably are true. Some Canadians might spend a little more time puzzling out the laws that they're supposed to enforce. I wasted a healthy amount of money in long-distance tolls while trying to answer two simple questions: "What are the relevant laws here? And how can business travelers ease their way through customs if they're carrying laptops?"

Customs Inspector X, who wouldn't give his name, told me that Americans no longer had to worry about paying duties on laptops. Not necessarily so. More knowledgeable officials said that if your computer was made outside the United States, you might indeed have to pay a 3.9 percent duty.

Even if your equipment is of American manufacture—Toshiba and some other Japanese companies have U.S. factories—you still may get stuck with a 13.5 percent national sales tax or security deposit of the same amount. Mercifully, on January 21, 1991, the tax is expected to drop to 7 percent under the new Goods and Services Tax, which will replace the sales tax. The deposit too, presumably, will be lower.

You may or may not recover the deposit. If you stay longer in Canada than you expected, you may have to forfeit the money. Luckily, I'm told, this does not happen often.

Here are some tips to increase your chances of breezing through customs without payments of any kind:

■ Realize that the main question is (1) Are you bringing in the laptop for temporary personal use without modification, or (2) are you in Canada to have the machine sold, repaired, or upgraded? My sympathy if the official insists you're in the second category. Inspector X said that inexperienced colleagues could be inconsistent when asking the foregoing question.

■ Bring a letter from your employer explaining why you are in Canada, where you will go during your visit, how long your visit will last, and just how you will use your laptop. A letter from a client may help, too, if your stay will be long.

■ Ideally, come with a round-trip ticket or additional evidence that your stay is temporary. Or drive rather than fly. The scuttlebutt is that the customs agents at the airports are tougher than those inspecting automobiles.

■ Also bring an invoice or other document establishing the cost of your computer. Otherwise, in calculating a possible tax or security deposit, the Canadian authorities will arrive at a figure of their own. By the way, a good way to arouse suspicion is to drastically underestimate the value of your laptop.

■ Cooperate with the official asking you to fill out form E29B, a "temporary admissions permit" for goods.

■ Think about a carnet, especially if your laptop is sample merchandise. (See page 235.)

■ Check with Canadian officials in advance if you're really worried. For questions about whether your laptop would be subject to duties—because of its place of origin—you should contact Paul Colpitts, acting manager of the Machinery Policy Unit of the Tariff Programs Division of Customs Programs, Sixth Floor, 64 Connaught Building, Mackenzie Avenue, Ottawa, Ontario K1A OL5. His number is (613) 954-7006. I found Colpitts to be outstandingly helpful when I called, and I'm letting him have the last word here in my interpretation of Canadian customs laws.

■ If you have questions about whether you can be exempted from customs duties even in connection with non-American-made laptops, you should call David Hotchkiss or Rick Teal with the Duties Release Program of Tariff Programs, (613) 954-6887. Their address is the same as Colpitts's. Hotchkiss also can answer questions about security depositions and E29B and similar forms.

■ For questions about sales taxes interpretation, call Veronica McGuire, Excise Tax Interpretation Section, Excise Operations, Sir Richard Scott Building, 191 Laurier Avenue, Ottawa, Ontario K1A OL5. Her telephone number is (613) 954-2288.

Please, I can't guarantee that you'll pass the border without anyone nicking your wallet. But there's hope. Mary Williams Walsh, now reporting in Canada, paid no deposit on the GriD laptop she brought in from the United States for a long-term assignment.[3] She astutely observes that laptops may present less problems than desktops. A laptop seems natural enough for a traveler to bring in and out of Canada; a fifty-pound IBM clone does not.

As you may expect, Canada isn't exactly a paradise for laptop shoppers. A Toshiba laptop, discounted to as little as $550 in New York, cost the Canadian Press $1,245 in Canadian dollars. Even with the Canadian dollar worth about 80 cents at the time, that's still steep. Batteries, disks, and other supplies, too, are more expensive. So are repair parts, which must be flown in from the States. What's more, Canadian dealers may not honor American warranties on the same brands.

Canada, however, is a wonderful country for modem users. Storer H. ("Bob") Rowley, Toronto correspondent with the *Chicago Tribune*, even ran across a special telephone jack for modems at the old Hotel Vancouver. Telephone service itself is first rate. In fact, your own telephone company in the States may be using Canadian gear.

How about AC power? Within a few months, Walsh suffered several electrical outages in her Toronto neighborhood, but Andrew Glenny, a staffer with the communications department of the Canadian Press, believes that "our power is more reliable than in the States," perhaps because of Canada's many hydroelectric dams. In the main, at least when you're not talking about confused customs inspectors, Canada comes across as a country that *works*. That's no small criterion in deciding if a place is fit for happy computing.

China

Computers can be just as much at risk as political dissenters. Fallows tells of "an extremely unreliable national power network in China which permits very large voltage spikes to get through. All you can do is take your chances." Spikes zapped his computers twice—once in Beijing and again in Shanghai. In the second case, says Fallows, "just when I was plugged into the hotel's power source, some enormous voltage

---

[3]Walsh says her good luck might have resulted from her being a journalist. Maybe. Obviously, however, as shown by the horror stories of other reporters who have tangled with customs officials in other countries, that isn't universally true.

spike came through and just blew up the computer, blew out the power supply and burned some chips.''

Please note that Fallows lacked a spike protector. Still, even with protection, you'd better tote a spare computer to this nation that claimed two of Fallows's MultiSpeed laptops. And bring the right power supply, too. *Sans* spikes, power is normally 240 volts.

Egypt

Whew! *PC/Computing* says that "phone lines throughout Egypt and the gulf countries are clear and reliable. Egypt's packet-switching service is based here, and you can dial international calls directly. U.S.-type Bell-compatible modems, not CCITT modems, are the standard. Phone lines are not heavily monitored; you can reach Israel and the Arab states directly. Cairo's many computer stores sell software and hardware, but getting support is difficult. Generally no customs problems.''[4]

France

As in most of Europe, French power will be exotic to American machines—220 volts in this case. But users of individual brands may enjoy some nice surprises. People with Toshiba 3100e's, for instance, already know that their power supplies are most cosmopolitan. And in a pinch you may make some useful discoveries. Jim Millard, a Zenith 183 owner, traveled to Paris and "found that the old power supply for the 183 (large brick with long cables) worked just fine on 200 volts, 50 Hz. I have heard that the new power supply is not as forgiving of such use. My power supply that worked is marked as: Model 150-308, Input: AC 120 60Hz. Output: DC 16.5V, 2A. I tested it in the United States before leaving, and it runs hot but suffered no damage. This can make life a little easier on the traveler not having to cart a lot of power supplies around.'' Beware! Confirm Millard's findings at your own risk!

On the modem front, Millard found that when he visited France, the quality of the phone lines didn't quite match those in the United States.

---

[4]The *PC/Computing* material in this chapter is from "Letters from the Road: Around the World with a Laptop," July 1989, page 106. *PC/Computing* uses the phrase "laptop Baedeker."

"You must use pulse dialing," he adds. "They do not have tone dialing. The phones have buttons on them that dial with pulses, quite a bother to wait for."

Check, however. France has made considerable strides in telecommunications, and his observations soon may be out of date. *PC/Computing* has described the French phone system as "excellent"; perhaps the magazine's writer and Millard simply happened to be in different parts of the country.

According to the magazine, "the Mac is the current favorite, but DOS hardware and software are widely available. Software stores thrive even in bucolic villages, and you can reach the packet-switching service in Paris through the ubiquitous Minitel system. Repair services are available for Compaq and Zenith laptops. Generally no customs problems."

In some parts of France, however, you may have a battery problem. "The price for triple A cells for a small town in France," says Barry Berkov, a CompuServe executive, "was about 100 percent more than I pay at a discount store in the States."

Germany

Bring your biggest, most flexible acoustic cup. "Some of the country's telephone mouthpieces are rather large," says the telecommunications consultant Don Kimberlin. "What's the old sociologist's and anthropologist's joke about the long jaws of Northern Europe?"

Germany and neighbors in Western Europe boast better phone lines than do the southern European countries; Kimberlin notes German technical triumphs. But all is not joyous. While England and France have deregulated their phone systems, Germany is the home of what Kimberlin once described as "one of the world's most bombastic telephone companies. [The Deutsche Bundespost] absolutely forbids plugging foreign attachments into their telephone lines! They monopolize terminal equipment totally. They have begun in the Bundespost to permit user-owned apparatus of a few types, but my last recall was that it would allow only dedicated private-line data modems. It wasn't dial-up modems that could be plugged into the line at random, anyplace.

"What really happens in countries like this," Kimberlin said in late 1989, "is that practical travelers do a fair amount of skullduggery. I went ahead and blasted away and did something. That means I went over there on the wall and took the cover off the terminal block that the telephone was wired up to. I used a screwdriver, a small pair of pliers, and an American-style connector that would fit the plugs from my devices, and wired them in.

"To be brutally honest, there is no such thing as people who sit around listening to telephone lines or automatically monitoring to see if you're sending data on the line. If anybody does discover you, it's because somebody happened to be on the line and heard something strange and they also knew at the same time exactly what the line was for. So your chances of getting caught are very low.

"The telephone man is the telephone man most any place in the world. He's usually very busy drinking coffee and installing telephones rather than going around looking for people playing tricks on his network."

Bill E. Badger, a resourceful army captain and a veteran user of Radio Shack's Model 100, reports that German phones were a problem to hotwire. Sagaciously he says you should practice on phones at home before hitting the road. Just the same, your hometown phone is no challenge compared to some of the more impregnable German ones; you may as well be trying single-handedly to sink the ghost of the *Bismarck*.

Luckily, like the *Bismarck*, the German telephone system is yielding to its adversaries. I've just learned that the Bundespost is becoming more liberal about the use of equipment from other sources—modems, say. No longer will virtually everything be hard wired; you might even be able to pick up RJ-11 adapters; who knows, maybe the Germans will soon be buying the equivalent of our ten-dollar phones, if they aren't already. The changes, though, won't happen completely overnight. Hard wiring will linger in many a hotel. So even if the legal situation is wonderful by the time you're traveling in Germany, you might still want to take along your burglar's kit.

Greece

Greece isn't the friendliest territory for modem users, at least not the rustic parts. One hapless traveler, according to Badger, "blew up his modem and took a whole village's phone system with it."

Hong Kong

Avoid the illegal software and bargain-priced clones, unless you're willing to gamble on tech support back in the States. Needless to say, telecommunications in Hong Kong is far superior to that of most of Asia. To avoid excessive hook-up charges, consider COMCO if you're going to be in Hong Kong just briefly.

David Ensor of ABC News reports fine telephone connections, just as I'd expect from a world trade center.

Hungary

This is Silicon Valley East, the most advanced country—in micro terms—in the whole Soviet bloc. Aided by the Taiwanese and other Asians, the Hungarians are churning out IBM clones and, for all I know, may even make some decent laptops. Their PS/2 LAN boards are so advanced that when Hungarians went to an American trade show, people joked about their having problems on the way home—getting their own products past U.S. inspectors worried about American national security

This technological savvy could bode well if your laptop breaks. No promises, but there are probably enough garage-style entrepreneurs lurking around, waiting to take a stab at it and brainy enough to succeed even if they've never before beheld your brand of computer. You just may need time to scare them up.

Telecommunications isn't so promising. "It takes two to three years to obtain a private phone," notes *PC/Computing*, "but most hotels and post offices have public phones. Telecommunications lines are in abysmal shape, though you can dial directly to the West. Salzburg is the best gateway for data transmission. To use the experimental packet-switching service available through the Post Central Telegraph Office's Development Department, you must rent the government's strange and clumsy 300 bps asynchronous modems. Some Western software and hardware are available on the black market. You can buy batteries for cash, but avoid the locally produced ones; they leak acid." The same caveat may apply in some Third World countries.

"Customs," the magazine says, "wants to see you leave with what you brought in"—hardly a desire unique to Hungarian bureaucrats.

India

India's phone lines "are generally terrible," in the opinion of William Claiborne. "Often you have to try several times to get a good enough line."

This could improve, however, at least if you're trying to make international connections from major cities. Indian programmers can now offer their services to American companies and have their work beamed back to the United States via satellite. Ideally travelers one day will be able to avail themselves of such hookups, if it isn't possible now.

"The communications picture is changing rapidly in south Asia," says Steve Coll, the *Washington Post*'s present correspondent in India. "Packet switching is available now in Bombay, New Delhi, and some other major cities. One difficulty in using regular lines while calling the U.S. is that the Indian phone system has some beeping meter signal to keep track of the time of the call that comes in behind your modem signals and disrupts the data transmission.

"A solution now offered here short of packet switching is access to regular trunk lines where the timing signal is turned off, which makes it easier to connect and dump data. Only CCITT will work in any case. Connecting to phone lines is generally no problem in first-class hotels in capital cities."

In hotels without direct dialing, however, "you may have to jigger with the software in order to wait for the operator to ring back with the completed call." See page 225 for a summary of Hayes-style modem commands, which just may be the answer here.

Computers with automatic power switching between 110 and 220 volts are essential in India, according to Coll. "Without that flexibility," he says, "it would be very difficult to deal with hotel power systems. If you stayed in one place, then it would be easy enough to build in surge protection and transformers." As for computers and supplies, he says: "You won't want to buy any of that stuff in these parts." Like Third World batteries, presumably, the quality of the computers themselves does not always match that in the United States. Western software is "widely available" in Bombay, *PC/Computing* says "though most of it is pirated."

Iraq

Journalists are a vanguard of sorts for businesspeople, and some Fourth Estate workers must feel like martyrs on behalf of high tech. Consider the outrages visited on correspondents at Saddam International Airport in Baghdad.

"Iraqi customs officials are surly, abusive, and life threatening to computers," an American reporter says. He tells of a respected journalist, an Egyptian to whose nationality a bigoted customs official did not cotton; the Iraqi held up his victim's Tandy 200, then dropped it eight feet to the airport floor. "How," asks the reporter, "would you like to see that happen to your $4,000 NEC MultiSpeed with a 20-meg hard disk and backlit screen?" His modest little Toshiba T1000 still bears scars from the black marker pen of an Iraqi customs official who briefly confiscated it.

"A word on batteries in Iraq," he says. "Take them out of everything in your hand luggage or the police will seize them and throw them in the trash. Same thing with audio tapes. Put them in your checked luggage or you will lose them, and, believe me, there is no appeal."

Italy

Remember the gossip writer scurrying from scandal to scandal in the movie *La Dolce Vita*? I wonder: just what would life hold for him today in this era of cellular phones, laptops, and modems? I doubt he'd want them. His editors might get rid of him because he kept the phone and laptop switched off too often while he was plying the orgy beat. Whatever the case, like most of the rest of Europe, Italy is in the throes of a communications revolution. "More digital lines are being added," says Bruno Corrada, an Italian who frequents CompuServe.

Just the same, life in Italy isn't yet entirely *Dolce* for people with laptops and other high tech. "Telephone lines are sometimes bad," Corrada says. "The best are in Milan and in the big cities." For transoceanic calls, he recommends a modem with MNP 5 correction, or else software that can help a conventional modem emulate MNP. David Ensor, who worked as a correspondent in Rome for ABC News, says direct connections to the States seemed to be iffy. If you try one, think about using a service like USA DIRECT to avoid the steep charges that the Italian telephone companies make on calls to the United States—

see page 243. You may prefer to use a packet-switching network. Before you leave, make arrangements through MCI Mail, CompuServe, or whatever other net that you or your company relies on.

The hotel telephone wires may also hold surprises of their own. Badger, the army captain mentioned earlier, says he couldn't fathom a pattern in the colors of the wires inside telephone cables. "The real problem is to use modems in hotels," confirms Corrada, who nonetheless has performed successful surgery on the innards of a hotel phone in Tuscany, near Florence.

Electrical power isn't always what you'd expect. "Occasionally in Rome," Ensor says, "the power dies in a whole section of the city." He says blackouts can last several hours. Corrada is more sanguine about the country as a whole. "Power may fail occasionally, due to interruptions, but it's very rare."

What about Italian customs? "We at ABC News have had trouble getting high-tech gear in and out of Italy," Ensor says "but never with laptops. They seem to be accustomed to laptops."

Japan

The fatherland of many of America's laptops is, in many ways—though hardly all!—a hospitable place for portable computers. To give one example, subways in Tokyo may be crowded, but your chances of having your machine snatched are low compared to, say, New York. There are other bright spots, too. Batteries may sell for a third more than in the United States, but that's a bargain in a country where a business meal can cost $200 (American).

Also, wall voltages in Japan are kinder, gentler, than in many parts of Asia. The power is quirky but not lethal.

Fallows says 100 volts is the usual for the bulk of the country, "from Osaka and Tokyo and on to the east. Most American equipment works okay on either system, including the bricklike converters for portable computers. If the machinery is hypersensitive to 100 volts, you can buy a 100-to-110 transformer in the big electronics district of Tokyo.

"Phone lines are, predictably, good in Japan," Fallows says. To avoid bureaucracy, "the casual traveler should just bring his portable modem and call the number in the U.S.—which you can direct-dial from almost any hotel in Japan and from most good hotels in other countries." Less encouragingly, "the phone cable problem is worse than in the U.S. Very few phones, except in new homes, have RJ-11 jacks. The handsets don't fit acoustic modems, which are unreliable and a pain anyway.'' So Fallows travels with his ''little burglar's tool kit,'' in the vein of the one Deakin and the others described in chapter 7. ''Sometimes I've been in hotels where the switchboard setup defeats these attempts,'' Fallows says. ''Then I give up.

''The network hookup situation is extremely complicated and would take too long to explain. Contact Mr. Kenji Tanaka at Japan Tympas (a Tymnet affiliate), Tokyo phone number 262-8711. He can explain how the system works here. If you want, you could call him ahead of time from the United States but it really doesn't speed things up at all.'' In my opinion—and this is Rothman speaking, not Fallows—advanced planning is normally worth the effort if there's time. ''Tanaka's system,'' Fallows goes on, ''is the first government-approved competitor to the previous monopoly, Kokusai Denshin Denwa (International Telephone and Telegram).''

As in the case of other countries, MCI Mail users should use **VIEW INTERNATIONAL** to see what awaits them in Japan. Short-term visitors may find it easiest to do a direct connect to the States. Before leaving town, call MCI customer support at 800-444-6245 for information about the least expensive modem numbers to dial.

What about CompuServe? Here are the two main possibilities that the company recommends:

■ The FENICS network. FENICS means the Fujitsu Enhanced Information and Communications Service, and it's available through NIF Corporation, CompuServe's distributor in Japan. NIF stands for Network Information Forum. Telephone NIF in Tokyo at 81-03-221-7363 (the 81 is the country code and the 03 is the city code—not necessary in Tokyo itself). NIF's address is Kojimachi Koyo Building, 1-10 Kojimachi, Chiyoda-ku, Tokyo 102 Japan. If you're dialing Tokyo from the United States, precede the numbers with the usual 011 for international calls.

This FENICS service costs 70 yen a minute. At currency conversion rates in effect in April 1990, that meant between $26 and $27 an hour beyond CompuServe's normal $12.50 charge for either 1,200 or 2,400 bps.

''The lines are *superb*, as clean and snappy as any node in the U.S.A.,'' pilot John Deakin says, ''with only a couple of minor extra

steps to log on, no joining formalities, no joining fees, et cetera.'' The
FENICS service is available in forty-five locations all over Japan.

■ Another NIF-related service, costing less: 40 yen a minute, or
$14 to $17 an hour using exchange rates of April 1990. You can reach
this economy service from the same forty-five locations. The catch is
that you can't use it to send or receive e-mail or hook into services
other than the CompuServe Information Service. Investigate the forty
yen service by calling the number mentioned earlier. In Tokyo you can
dial up the forty-yen-per-minute service directly without going through
FENICS, but the cost is the same and the above restrictions apply.

Ironically, and unhappily, Japan's domestic computer prices are
higher than in the United States, perhaps lending some credence to those
who charge dumping. Fallows flatly states, ''There is no piece of electronic equipment that is cheaper in Japan than in the U.S. None.''
Computer supplies such as floppy disks cost more in Japan, he says—
just as they almost always do in Asia, with certain exceptions such as
Singapore and Hong Kong.

Fallows says, too, that ''laptop repair is a big problem. The root of
the problem is that the famous Toshiba and NEC models we know from
the U.S. are *not sold in Japan*. This is only partly conspiracy: it's
mainly also because of the different language and different marketing
patterns—very few Japanese can type. So unfortunately the short-term
visitor should assume that his computer can *not* be repaired while he
is here, even though he may be able to see the Toshiba or NEC headquarters from his hotel room. It can be done on longer term, but for
instance, it took me two weeks to get a ni-cad battery replaced on an
NEC.''

Patience might also serve you well when you're dealing with customs
in Japan. ''Japanese customs officials,'' Fallows says, ''are fairly lenient
on things you bring in by yourself but extremely strict on things you
have shipped or sent to you in Japan. Once I left an overcoat at a hotel
in the U.S., asked them to mail it to me, and had to pay $20 import
tax on my own coat. Hesitate before asking to have anything shipped
to you—mail order from the U.S. is no good here.''

Oh well, at least the airport security in Tokyo might not be as bad
as some travelers fear in other countries. The security people at Narita
Airport have never asked Nobuyuki Makita to turn on a laptop to see

the cursor to verify that it isn't a bomb. In the States—even though he's a copilot for Japan Airlines—such security checks are usual.

Jordan

"Phone lines vary enormously," Randal says, "and not just in the quality of line. Jordan, for example, is notorious for burning out modems, as is Israel." I hear that Israel's telecommunications situation may be improving; still, play it safe.

Kenya (Nairobi)

"The phone lines are fair in this Westernized city," *PC/Computing* says, "but, oddly enough, Kenya lacks a packet-switching service." Ask about packet switching. For a while Kenya did have a demonstration packet-switching project, and it may be back. Meanwhile, laptop users may want to check with the ministry of communications; find out about using a special line that lacks a suppressor to squelch sound echoes. Echo suppression can wreak havoc on computer transmissions.

"Hardware and software are available on the open market," *PC/Computing* says. "Compaq maintains a dealership here." Even as far back as 1985, Kenya had an Apple users group with five hundred members.

As a rule, you shouldn't have problems with customs people in Kenya.

Korea (South)

"Look," Fallows's Korean friends once warned him, in effect, "you should assume that the things you're sending out over the state data network can be overheard." He never confirmed that this was going on. Besides, mercifully, the Korean regime has changed in recent years; what's more, the increasing volume of traffic may have overwhelmed Big Brother's modem squad. "They wouldn't be able to make cars or anything," Fallows quips, "if they spent all their time trying to oversee all the computer traffic." Beware in all Third World countries, however, if your business is politically sensitive; it doesn't require that much savvy to monitor computerized communications, especially if there are only a few links to the world at large.

Latin America (General)

"Problems filing stories are horrendous in Latin America," Storer says, recalling his days there with the *Chicago Tribune*. "Practically all the signals get weakened by hotel switchboards or local phone lines, which often can take up to several hours to get your international call out anyway.

"The acoustical couplers are notoriously bad in these situations and they get progressively worse the farther you get from the home office.

"We found that the direct connect modems were nearly impossible to use in Latin America." (Most of the phones in hotels lacked modular plugs.) "I usually had to use the couplers. Then when really desperate I would fashion a direct connect modem into a clip on the job, cutting off the plug and putting alligator clips on the end which I would then attach directly to the two metal clips inside the phone mouthpiece. Just like radio reporters do. This would often work as a last resort.

"Another emergency measure was to go to the hotel office and use the fax line, which was often direct and clearer and didn't go through any switchboard."

"Central America's phone lines," says Harry Welsh, the laptop guru at the *Washington Post*, "are so poor it might take eight to ten tries to get into packet switching. Usually when you connect to a packet-switching network in a Central American country there'll be a big click, click on the telephone lines." In some places your call may go through both manual and electronic switches; try following the ATDP and ATDT instructions in chapter 7, as appropriate, to adjust to this situation.

Local phone companies can be intractable. "Calling out in Nicaragua could take hours because you had to go through an operator," Storer Rowley says of his days as the *Chicago Tribune*'s Latin American correspondent. "El Salvador was difficult, the phone lines breaking off occasionally half the time when I tried to file via Honduras packet switching from the Camino Real Hotel in San Salvador. Sometimes, though thankfully not too often, you simply can't help blowing a deadline."

Rowley is no fan of Central American electricity. "Local power problems are worst in Nicaragua, El Salvador and Panama. . . . War and natural disasters, or simple bad management of the economy, are forever cutting off power. I wrote a lot of stories by candlelight or flashlight in those places but still managed to send them out by phone or dictate.''

In Central America, you may be searched and asked to turn on your computer at airport security posts. Rowley says that in Honduras authorities may actually try to ''impound your computer when you visit. Then you protest loudly and they take the serial number down at customs. You can keep it, but then you are required to pass through the customs checkpoint again on your way out of the country and show them you're taking it with you.''

Malaysia

Computer-menacing thunderstorms are chronic in Malaysia. But they're obliging enough to be relatively predictable, so you can reduce the risks. ''Almost every day in Malaysia,'' Fallows says, ''there are huge violent thunderstorms between four o'clock and seven o'clock in the evening, three hundred days a year.'' Powerful surges can rip ''sometimes through the power system but often through the telephone wires, and they can be so powerful that the telephone sets will explode or burst into flame, and anything connected to a phone line, such as a computer through a modem, can be destroyed. The solution to that, whenever you're in a tropical country, is to disconnect everything when you're not actually using it.''

Oh, but what about that jungle rot? Fallows didn't fight it by storing his computer in a special bag or taking similar precautions, because of the awkwardness of wrestling with the cables. Rather, he resigned himself to the fact that his Compaq portable in Kuala Lumpur wouldn't survive to a ripe old age. The Compaq, the bulky twin-floppy version, eventually did fall victim to the humidity.

''There would be random errors, or it wouldn't boot, or certain controller chips would fail,'' says Fallows. ''The humidity must have been causing minor shorts in the system. Finally it just rotted out the mother board. So if you can arrange it, it's better to have air conditioning because it keeps the computer from getting wrecked. And if you can't arrange it, then you just know that the computer will age rapidly, part of the hardship of the foreign life.''

Does this mean that people should avoid hard disk computers amid the rigors of the tropics because the humidity might destroy the delicate memory devices? An amazing study suggests the opposite. Teaming up with an IBM man on sabbatical, researchers at Northwestern University and the University of California showed that a hard disk should fare *better* if the relative humidity is above 50 percent. Why? Because a hard disk builds up "wear debris" as it spins. The researchers learned that the debris is "much finer" in humid air and thus will harm the disk less. Working in the tropics, Fallows himself would rather use a hard disk laptop than one with just floppies—if only because the tropics can be as deadly to floppies as to motherboards. He lost a whole pile of disks to the moisture of Kuala Lumpur.

If, like Fallows, you end up in the tropics and venture beyond the world of air-conditioned hotels and high-rise offices, then you might pick up some special storage boxes at a camera store. They're the size of beer coolers and somewhat resemble fish aquariums.

Mexico

My unfortunate acquaintance Caryl Conner, the woman who died of a customs-precipitated heart attack, isn't the only victim of Mexican officialdom. After power surges destroyed two modems of a *Washington Post* reporter, the newspaper repaired them and mailed them back. The modems were in customs at least two months. "When we send stuff by DHL, even with a cover letter," Harry Welsh says, "they still tie it up in customs and require duty to be paid."

Still, savvy travelers can reduce the likelihood of problems with Mexican officialdom. Mary Williams Walsh of the *Los Angeles Times* says she "got off easy. I explained my computer was like a typewriter and I needed it for my job. You try to avoid trouble in the beginning because otherwise it could only get worse. A sweet, agreeable disposition can go a long way. People in Mexico don't have a kindly disposition toward us. They owe American banks all this money, and they've been invaded by the Marines." Sensitivity, please!

In the telephone department, Mexico also can be a challenge. My friend Barbara Sturken, a travel writer, had to wait several hours to get a line out of Zihuatanejo, in the western part of the country. Moreover, don't expect to escape such problems by remaining in Mexico City. If anything, because of the city's growth, problems could be worse. The telephone company can't keep up with the demand. You may end up living decades in Mexico City before a telephone installer materializes.

Free-lance installers roam the streets; you flag one down to get your line put in. Further taxing the system, some Mexicans run pirate wires from the main lines to their homes. The preceding is of interest to the traveler for the simple reason that the phones so often fail. "Sometimes," Walsh recalls, "there wasn't even a dial tone. You'd wait and wait for one. Or you'd hear the tone going up and down."

Similarly, Mexican power (it should be 115 volts, 60 Hz, but check to be on the safe side) isn't world class. "There are a lot of power failures and spikes," Walsh says. For a desktop computer, Walsh used a surge protector the size of a microwave oven. It isn't clear whether the size reflected backwardness in surge protector technology or the size of the surge problem.

Finally, beware of Mexican repair shops if your computer breaks down. Many technicians in the United States exaggerate their prowess, and south of the Rio Grande, you're not exactly immune to such a phenomenon.

Pakistan

Pakistan is a mixed bag. It isn't Peoria—the phone lines are disasters and international direct dialing is far from universal—but batteries are more plentiful than you'd imagine. Jon Anderson, owner of a Toshiba T1100+ and a Radio Shack Model 100, did fieldwork in the Hindu Kush mountains. "The Model 100 was easier," he says, "because batteries are available everywhere. For the Toshiba, I had to carry around a 20-pound voltage regulator-transformer for recharging the battery, which was a hassle; but with its six-hour working time, I could usually get to someplace that had mains current (220 volts, 50 Hz). This would not be a problem now since Toshiba now has a universal connector." What's more, presumably, he could use solar cells.

"Supplies and repairs are obtainable in Karachi and Islamabad, and increasingly in provincial cities, although most reliably in Karachi and Islamabad from firms which range from big trading houses to small entrepreneurs. There is high-tech talent in the country. Several shops in Islamabad and Karachi can supply peripherals like printers. I had my Toshiba screen repaired twice at EGS in Islamabad, although it was the first they had seen in the country." (Alas, Anderson no longer has EGS's phone number, which, perhaps, is traceable through another computer shop if you make it to Islamabad.)

"There was no hassle getting these machines into or out of the country in 1985 and 1987," Anderson says. "Although I did get a license from the Pakistan embassy in D.C., customs never asked for it. Some people, however, had told of being held up, having to post bonds, etc."

A second American laptop user says the Pakistani customs people seem fuzzy about their own rules. Among other things, he suggests that you try the old trick of passing your computer off as a typewriter. "I've never heard of a customs agent challenging this, and there are no controls of duties at all on old typewriters." Some may be dubious of such an approach, given the growing numbers of business travelers toting laptops; you just may turn yourself into jail bait if you don't notice that the person behind you is carrying an identical laptop and describes it as such. Still, do what makes you feel comfortable.

"Another problem," says the user, "is security. Pakistan International Airways and other airlines in this area prohibit any battery cells to be carried in hand luggage. The security people relish catching you with batteries, so much so that I wonder whether they're looking for knives or guns at all. You can check your PC battery pack with baggage, but you can't use the computer on board. The trick I have used without fail so far is when they ask whether the computer runs on batteries, I say, 'No,' take out the AC adapter pack, and say, 'Power pack,' and this has ended the discussion every time."

Somalia

Jerome Glenn, a foreign aid consultant, futurist, and author of the book *Future Mind*, contradicts Fallows and swears by acoustic cups.[5] He recommends them especially in dictator-ridden countries that regard unauthorized modem hookups as gross intrusions on national sovereignty. Hmm. I suppose that with acoustic cups you can always jaw up a good excuse—for instance: "Please, Your Omnipotence, it isn't a direct connection. It's just air pressure. Just a little sound from the modem. Do you think a little air can bring down your perfect country's phone system?"

---

[5]Remember, of course, that in some cases the shape of the phones may just plain rule out the use of acoustic couplers, with the possible exception of the new models mentioned on page 170.

In not-so-democratic Somalia at the time I talked to Glenn, the lines were working fine at 300 bps but unfortunately were shut down from time to time due to a little distraction, a two-front civil war.

Soviet Union

Why can't the English and the Mexicans be as easy to get along with as the Soviets—or at least the customs people who let *Washington Post* people breeze through? "We had two reporters carry two IBMs on either arm through the airport for Moscow," Harry Welsh says, "without any problem."

Moscow voltage is 220; take the usual precautions; use a transformer-style device to bring the voltage down to a digestible level for the more provincial of the American laptops.

Consult with Soviet telecommunications officials about modem requirements if your company will be there for awhile; Welsh says that the Soviets recommended that the *Post* use MNP modems because of their error control. Like many international travelers, Welsh is gung ho on WorldPort modems for telecommunications-backward countries such as the U.S.S.R. He says many built-in modems in laptops "aren't powerful enough to get on packet-switching networks" from afar. If you own a Radio Shack Model 200 notebook computer, for example, you may have to have a technician tweak it before the modem signal will be loud enough for international use. You'll have to perform the surgery back in the States.

Describing the situation in Leningrad but perhaps also the circumstances in the U.S.S.R. as a whole, *PC/Computing* says: "All things PC-related are prized commodities here. Software and hardware are officially available, but impossible to find—except on the black market, where you can expect to pay $75 for a blank diskette. Batteries are a rarity, too." In Leningrad, at least, you may find that "long-distance circuits may be better than local lines. You can hook into a direct satellite link to the United States through the San Francisco/Moscow Teleport (415/931-8500), which also offers an e-mail service and gateways to others. The national packet-switching service in Moscow operates only occasionally. Customs notes what you bring in and expects you to leave with it." Still, if the *Post*'s experiences with the IBMs are representative, Moscow customs officials may be recognizing Glasnost.

On the other hand, you might heed the warning of a businessman who visited the Soviet Union recently and reports via CompuServe: "Laptops fetch up to 100,000 rubles on the black market and are prime targets for theft. Indeed, it is reported that gangs have staked out Moscow Airport and have hijacked foreigners on the road to town for their equipment. Carry the smallest machine you can, and try to camouflage it—no Cordura cases!"

Switzerland

Jonathan Randal boasts of knowing a free lancer with "the only RJ-11 in captivity in the U.N. press room at the Palais des Nations." Alas, ethics compel me to keep the lucky man's name a secret.

A hacker friend of mine says the Swiss are wonderfully whimsical toward modems. The authorities growl if you buy an unapproved external modem, but they wink at internal versions of the same products.

United Kingdom

U.K. customs agencies presumably don't employ Bedouins as customs inspectors, but I wonder if tribesmen haven't at least coached the British in the art of creative harassment. "I have been interrogated for hours upon entry into the U.K. by Customs and Excise officials," says Kevin R. Grantham, director of product sales, switching products, for the International Division of DCS Communications in Plano, Texas. "I have never had to put up a bond, nor had the laptop seized—normally for return upon leaving the country—although that has happened to people."

In fairness to the British, let it be conceded that, as Grantham says, "the European countries as a whole and the United Kingdom in particular are becoming more and more upset about people bringing laptop computers into the country without paying duty on them." So the British have "instituted a system of 'carnets' which basically are a promissory note from an insurancy agency that covers payment of duty and fines should the person bringing the laptop leave it in the country."

Grantham is talking, of course, about services of the kind that the U.S. Council for International Trade arranges. Such services—and I'll speak generically, since Grantham didn't use the U.S. Council's service—are not without disadvantages. As he himself notes, they are not free; and they may inflict on you "the hassle and inconvenience of knowing which countries one will visit, which make a carnet's use very limited." Somehow it seems not so cricket for the United Kingdom and other countries to make innocent travelers suffer for the sins of the unscrupulous. Am I hoping for too much? Perhaps.

Security, as you may expect, is tough in England. "Trying to board American Flag carriers," Grantham says, "I have been requested to switch on the laptop so the inspector could type a few keys, in order to see if it really worked or was just a shell hiding something else such as drugs or explosives." Technically speaking, the security X rays at airports in the United Kingdom and on the Continent have presented "nary a problem" for Grantham's laptop. But he warns laptop owners to beware of the powerful magnets that focus the X rays: "These alternating field magnets can introduce data errors if the diskette happens to be close to the magnet and the operator decides to inspect the item at full power with the belt stopped. I have never experienced data loss in the computer although I have experienced data loss on floppy diskettes."

As for metal detectors, says Grantham, "I have heard that some of the metal detectors use active magnetic fields rather than the passive ones; I have never had a diskette scrambled from a metal detector. On the other hand, I usually hand the box of diskettes around to the inspector, good reason to keep diskette boxes."

Don't count on good pickings at the United Kingdom's computer stores, according to MCI executive Alan Garratt. But the stores may be handy at times. "Tottenham Court Road," he says, "is sort of the 'radio row' of London. Several stores there sell an adaptor which translates the Bell RJ-11 jack into the standard British Telecommunications receptacle. It costs about six dollars." Just as others have found, Garratt concludes that modems of the Bell 1200 variety seem to be compatible with the CCITT 1200.

According to Garratt, "Ireland has the same electricity, plugs, and telephone connections as England."

United States

I'll insert here a few words for non-Americans taking a laptop to the United States.

The ugliest Americans are not the ones who go abroad. They're the vermin who, if you visit a large city here, steal your laptop computer and camera. You've already read on page 136 of the computer theft that my business acquaintance suffered. If anything, I expect such incidents to increase as laptops become almost everyday appliances, like toasters and TV sets. Plan accordingly. The United States may enjoy some of the world's best telephone connections and high-tech repair shops galore; but when it comes to the safety of personal effects in big cities, it's still a developing country. Above all, watch where you travel. Try not to tote your laptop around bad neighborhoods, and if you must ride big-city subways, stay away from the end cars, the most dangerous. Don't be compelled to choose between Laptop and Life.

"Take out insurance," advises Nobuyuki Makita, a Japan Airlines copilot; he says "safety is a big problem," especially in New York and Los Angeles.

More encouraging, if you're here for an extended stay, you may make friends quickly with members of user groups—computer clubs; some even have special interest groups for laptop owners. To locate a club, check with computer dealers. You may even want to make friends beforehand through one of the laptop conferences on CompuServe. See chapter 8 for tips on arranging phone connections. Just as services such as COMCO can help Americans adjust abroad, they may help you feel more comfortable in the United States—or at least tell you where to go for assistance. Also on the bright side, you'll find the laws laxer on the use of modems than in many places, despite the oft-ignored requirements of phone companies that modems be registered.

Check out the customs situation—with your own governments and the American officials issuing your visa—if you're going to shop for computer equipment here. Are you buying a 386- or 486-style machine? Then at some point you might consult with the U.S. export control authorities, even if you're from a non-Communist country; see page 236. If your stay will be long—and if you're a stickler for observing the law—you might explore the question of whether your laptop will comply with regulations of the Federal Communications Commission. The FCC prohibits the use of computers that it hasn't tested for radio and television interference.

Hong Kong prices are lower, but just the same, the United States well deserves its reputation as a shopper's nirvana. Japanese laptops often sell for less than equivalent models in Tokyo. So laptops in American stores may be bargains if you can put up with the quirks of keyboards and screen displays.[6] Read *The New York Times*, at least on Sundays and Tuesdays, when the paper is full of computer ads from discount stores in the Forty-seventh Street area.

If possible, consider a subscription to an American computer magazine *before* business takes you to the United States. *Some* possibilities (in no particular order) are:

■ *The Computer Shopper*. P.O. Box 51020, Boulder, Colorado 80321-1020. This magazine consists mostly of mail-order ads, prices from which you may on occasion use to bargain down computer stores. Speaking of prices, check with *Computer Shopper* and the other magazines for the latest on the cost of a subscription from overseas.

■ *InfoWorld*, P.O. Box 5994, Pasadena, California 91117.

■ *PC/Computing*. P.O. Box 40078, Philadelphia, Pennsylvania 19106-9868.

■ *PC Laptop*. P.O. Box 16927, North Hollywood, California 91615-9966.

■ *PC Magazine*. P.O. Box 51524, Boulder, Colorado 80321-1524.

■ *PC World*. P.O. Box 51833, Boulder, Colorado 80321-1833.

■ *Portable Computing*. Attn. Reader Service Dept., P.O. Box 5252, Pittsfield, Massachusetts 01203-9850.

■ *Mobile Office*, P.O. Box 8937, Boulder, Colorado 80328-8937.

Finally, keep in mind that I hope to do another edition of this book and will welcome your own impressions for this "Electronic Baedeker" section—whether about laptop conditions in your own country or those in the United States as seen through your eyes.

A FEW MORE WORDS ON POWER PLUGS, EURO-STYLE

Courtesy of Kevin R. Grantham—a well-traveled executive with a Texas high-tech company—here's a guide to the wall outlets of Europe; keep in mind that exceptions may abound within individual countries. Remember as well that a trip to your local Radio Shack store could

---

[6]Make certain, of course, that the computers and printers can handle characters in your language.

provide an immediate solution to your problem. The chain sells multicountry adapters, and so far the *Washington Post* seems to be getting along fine with them. Just the same, to give you a preview of what you're in for, let me share Grantham's tips, some of which go beyond the question of plugs per se:

■ Most Western European countries. "They use a two-prong plug with round prongs. Some countries have the socket flush with the wall, some have it recessed. The little Franzus plug adapter works very well to reach the recessed ones." The Franzus, please remember, is just a *plug* adapter, not a way to reduce voltage; it's available from drugstore chains such as Eckerd's and Boots and appears to be a variant of the Radio Shack adapter. Grantham goes on: "Try to avoid getting a machine that requires a ground (earth). The Toshiba I've used required it, but the Franzus adapter doesn't support it, and therefore one occasionally got zapped, which in retrospect was foolishly dangerous. There are grounded plug adapters available, but they generally do not work in the recessed socket."

Laptop makers, or at least their legal departments, would tend to side with Grantham and insist that grounding is necessary. Out of caution I'll say "Amen." But not everyone would. Many knowledgeable users of computers with three-pronged plugs report full success operating them in locations such as Japan, where only two prongs are commonly found. As one put it to me, "there's no chance of danger to the machine and very little danger to users, unless they make it a habit to work while standing in a water puddle." That's someone else speaking, not me. Regardless of some hackers' protests to the contrary, I would still worry about static buildups and threats to the well-being of the chips—not to mention your own safety.

■ France. The ground lug protrudes from the recessed socket, which can make it difficult to plug in a plug adapter.

■ Germany. "In most of the Germanic countries, the plugs have a third prong for a ground."

■ Italy and some parts of Spain. "There is what looks like a Eurostandard socket, but in fact the holes are closer together and smaller. The Franzus plug adapter will fit these quite nicely, although in some of the more modern hotels and such there will be scattered around the room a few Eurostandard plugs."

■ Scandinavia. "The earth point often consists of two metal strips on both sides of the recessed socket, so that a grounded plug will ground out before the prongs make contact with anything. Swedish and other such plugs are generally not polarity sensitive, but some United States equipment with three-prong plugs is, so one can damage the equipment plugging into a socket backwards."

■ United Kingdom. "They use a behemoth three-prong plug. Usually, there must be a ground prong, because that operates a sliding door to expose the other holes. This is to prevent children from inserting objects into a live mains point, and is a great idea. U.K. sockets are always polarized, in the same way as U.S.A. three-prong plugs, so compatibility is easier. U.K. sockets also have a switch on the socket, so that the power can be switched on or off at the wall. In the U.K., as in the rest of Europe generally, 'up' is 'off,' and 'down' is 'on.' This is backwards from the U.S. The U.K. mains wiring often uses a different scheme than that in the U.S.A., where each group of wall outlets is on a separate circuit breaker. In the U.K., they can run a 'ring' from appliance to appliance and outlet to outlet, all over the building. Thus, there is a huge circuit breaker somewhere. Plugs in the U.K. have a fuse built into the plug. It is illegal to use an adapter like the Franzus, since it does not have an internal fuse. It is also dangerous, although I did it for a long time. Getting nervous, however, I purchased a Eurostandard-to-U.K. adapter that has a fuse in it, and used the Franzus Eurostandard adapter to connect the Toshiba to that."

THE TELEPHONES OF EUROPE: HOW ONE TRAVELER HANDLED THEM

"Telephone lines in Europe vary wildly," says Grantham, who has traveled widely with a Toshiba laptop.

"Fortunately for most laptop users, there is no need to set up the laptop for automatic answer. There are technical problems because the ringing setups are so different. For example, in the U.S.A. there is a ringing capacitor in each phone. In the U.K., there is a ringing capacitor for the whole house!

"In most countries, the center two wires of whatever kind of plug they use are the two to be connected to the red and green (center two) wires of the laptop's modem.

"I always carried a small screwdriver with a flat and Phillips on each end. I also carried a double-ended RJ-11 cable, a duplex adapter (the kind that lets two phones use the same line) and a short RJ-11 cable with spade lugs on one end (Radio Shack special) to which I attached a couple of insulated alligator clips. When in the States, either connecting directly to a hotel phone jack (and plugging the hotel phone into the modem) or using the duplex adapter worked. In Europe, I would plug the cable into the modem and into the duplex adapter, plug the alligator cable into the other side of the duplex adapter, and then disassemble the telephone or the wall plate to find some wires to attach. In worst cases, I clipped onto the contacts in the mouthpiece, but this often reduced me to 300 bps with errors, whereas going straight to the wires got me to 1,200 and often to 2,400 bps.

"The biggest problem I found was that European PABX systems, such as those used in hotels, often use delta modulation or other compressed voice digitalization schemes that are totally incompatible with data transmission. Sometimes it was so bad that no data transmission was possible at all. Time to change hotels!" You might try a MoFone or Road Warrior–style device—between the receiver and the telephone itself—and see what happens, although Grantham is skeptical about whether they'll do much good. Even using such a device, you'll probably still have to dial by hand.

Different voltages are yet another challenge and indeed, at least theoretically, a danger. "In the U.S.A.," says Grantham, "we use a 'constant-voltage' loop. That is, the voltage across the loop is 48 volts nominally, and speech is added by varying the current. In the U.K., they use a 'constant-current' loop, which carries speech by varying the voltage. Most transformer-coupled phones will work on either system. However, because the U.K. is constant current, when you hang up the line, the phone system tries for a brief moment to drive the same current through the now-open pair. This means that peak voltages of nearly 200 volts can be experienced, with a good deal of power behind it. As a result, BABT (the organization that certifies phones and things for connection to the phone lines, much as the FCC grants permission in the U.S.A.) will not certify many U.S. instruments, including modems. For good reason. They can be destroyed by this 'normal' operation of the phone system in the U.K. Not only that, but in the destruction, harmful voltages found inside the device might leak through to the phone network.

"There is not much one can do about this, except [to] look for a modem that is BABT approved, or (illegally) go ahead and connect it, and hope for the best. I never had any modems destroyed, but it is a real possibility."

*   *   *

Okay, so you've hooked up from "abroad," wherever that may be. But how do you keep up with the latest news and other essential information from afar? The connection is just the start. *Something* has to come across it to justify the trouble. The next chapter, 10, "A Quick Tour of Some On-line Services," will offer an overview of electronic newspapers and libraries and briefly discusses electronic mail. Chapter 11, "Some Basics of Electronic Mail (Including How To Send E-Mail, Faxes, Telex, and Paper Letters Via CompuServe and MCI Mail," will explain e-mail in greater depth. But first let's go on the general tour, with a brief detour to visit Dr. Sysop.

Chapter 10

A QUICK TOUR OF SOME ON-LINE SERVICES[1]

- Brief descriptions of on-line services offering everything from electronic mail to searches through massive databases. Page 285.
- A mini-explanation of databases. Page 289.
- CD-ROMs: One Way to Augment On-line Information Services. Appendix 6.

I once compared local bulletin board systems to bars. Each comes with its own crowd. I myself hate bars and cholesterol. Maybe that's why I hang around a health-oriented BBS where people call the system operator "Dr. Sysop"; David Page, in fact, *is* a doctor.[2] The board's regulars don't just delve into computer matters and the usual political and social issues. They also debate such cosmic questions as the best ingredients for low-fat yogurt and whose cat is the homeliest or meanest. Every once in a while, the owner of a mirror-breaking cat leaves town; but via the phone lines the human can still visit our electronic bar. We're stuffy, of course. Maybe someday I'll go on a wild long-distance spree and again log on "The Lee County Jail" down South.

If BBS's are bars, then on-line services are whole cities, com-

---

[1] Material for this chapter comes from my book *IZE Examined* (Homewood, Ill.: Dow Jones–Irwin, 1989), as well as additional personal experiences. I've also relied on the books of Dvorak and Glossbrenner.

[2] David Page's BBS is busy enough as it is. So, selfishly, I won't reveal either its name or the phone number.

plete with the electronic versions of ticket counters for airports, reservation desks for hotels, stockbrokers, shopping malls, newspapers, and of course libraries—with text and programs. Dr. Sysop's hard disk contains a rich trove of software. But in this respect even his BBS pales next to national services, such as CompuServe and GEnie. Nor can it offer the striking color graphics of Prodigy.

Below are quick descriptions of some major on-line services. For more information call the numbers below. You may also see *Dvorak's Guide to PC Telecommunications* (Berkeley, Calif.: Osborne/McGraw-Hill, 1990), $49.95, by John C. Dvorak and Nick Anis. The book comes with a disk providing a mock tutorial that shows how to use major services. Other excellent resources are Alfred Glossbrenner's *How to Look It Up On-Line* (available for $18.95 plus $1.95 for postage and handling from Cash Sales Department, St. Martin's Press, 175 Fifth Avenue, New York, New York 10010) and his *Complete Handbook of Personal Computer Communications* ($18.95 plus $1.95 for postage and handling, also from St. Martin's Press).

BRS and BRS After Dark (800-345-4277)

You're a part-time consultant, and you can't spend hours and hours at the library during the day, looking up the arcane technical facts you need to serve your clients. Some information reaches you in your regular job. But your clients' hours aren't always the same as your employer's.

What to do? BRS or BRS After Dark may be the answer. They're a collection of databases in such fields as medicine, biochemistry, law, mathematics, education, and the arts and humanities. Prospective clients for the regular BRS service would include schools and large companies. But the After Dark service just may be cheap enough for professors and students whose schools haven't favored them already with access to on-line knowledge. And of course it could be a natural for consultants and small-business people.

Both the regular service and the reduced-rate one are especially strong on health matters. In fact, BRS's founders worked for the Biomedical Communications Network of the State University of New York.

I gave BRS a test spin, searching the mysteriously initialed ABI/INFORM database for articles on telecommuting. ABI/INFORM isn't part of BRS, just a database that BRS resells. Still, I wondered what might be there for me. Lots, it seems. I found 138 "telecommuting" citations.

From California—via an article in *Industry Week*—came details of the state's laudable telecommuting experiment. "Increases in productivity of 30%-100% have been reported by firms that have implemented telecommuting, such as Rank Xerox and Barclays Bank," said an article in a British journal called *Accountancy*. I may have run across *Industry Week* at my local library. But *Accountancy*? Or *Management Services*, another publication in the United Kingdom? Or *British Telcom World*?

For years I've been pushing the idea of an Electronic Peace Corps to transfer knowledge from the United States to the Third World, but, as my BRS confirmed, we hardly hold a monopoly on knowledge. Someday, let's hope, the databases will be full of telecommuting insights not just from London but also from New Delhi.

And someday, too, ideally, all these wonders will be cheaper. BRS After Dark, the lower-cost version of BRS, has a sign-up charge of just $75. But you must spend at least $12 a month, whether or not you use the search time. Expect to pay anywhere from $8 to $80 an hour and to be charged a bit more for, say, looking at a document rather than just seeing a citation. By database standards, mind you, BRS After Dark is a bargain.

There are at least two other important differences between the deluxe and economy offerings:

1. As you'd expect from the name, BRS After Dark isn't available during regular business hours.
2. You can only tap into some 100 of the 150 BRS databases. Luckily, the National Newspaper Index, a collection of material from major newspapers like *The Los Angeles Times*, is among the 100.

Even in the regular BRS service, the number of databases is still a fraction of those on the rival DIALOG, which offers at least 355.

Just the same, like a small college, BRS seems friendly enough. The support people were patient—very. BRS has even set up a User Advisory Board, which, according to Alfred Glossbrenner, the database maven, is taken "very seriously." Yes. Logging on the deluxe service, I saw a bulletin for a two-day "BRS User Meeting" in the Washington, D.C., area.

CompuServe ([614] 457-8650 or 800-848-8990)

CompuServe is to on-line services what New York and Tokyo are to cities. You can find almost *anything*. And often it's the biggest and best. CompuServe lets you dial up the giant DIALOG Information Service. You also can find scads of other databases as well as electronic forums where you can read and post messages, BBS fashion.

On CompuServe you can log on forums for owners of Toshiba, Zenith, and Tandy laptops, and many other popular machines—plus special areas for small business people and for professions ranging from journalism to law.

Among other subjects, various forums cover:

- WordPerfect, WordStar, Tapcis, Lotus, and countless other programs. One forum even devotes itself to the microcomputer operating system from which MS-DOS is descended: the CP/M Forum (John Deakin, the airline captain and laptop maven, is the CP/M SYSOP).
- IBM-related topics ranging from programming to communications and hardware.
- Computer consulting
- Working from home
- Travel
- Foreign language
- Science fiction
- Sailing (attention, William Buckley: check this out)

CompuServe is especially valuable for international travelers (try the **GO TRAVEL** command from the main prompt). You can tap into a wealth of schedule and reservation services, such as those operated by the Official Airlines Guide and EAASY SABRE. CompuServe, moreover, contains a forum for small businesses with somewhat of an international slant.

Numerous other attractions are on-line. You even can order goods from an electronic mall, for instance, and you can converse with other people instantaneously via a "CB Simulator" (not recommended to the socially inclined with tight budgets!).

Not surprisingly, CompuServe is the largest of the on-line services in the United States, with more than 550,000 subscribers. Glossbrenner has observed that the IBM-related areas alone "have more than 20,000 members.'' So ''your chances of encountering someone who can answer your questions or help you find the hardware or software you're looking for are much greater than on smaller systems.'' The newest, hottest shareware and free programs show up on CompuServe, home of more than twenty-seven thousand programs in these categories.[3] Not only can you download the programs for laptops and other machines, you can also communicate with the shareware authors and pass on suggestions.

Through CompuServe, too, you can dial up more than 1,400 databases, including an electronic encyclopedia, the on-line database of the National Institutes of Health, and of course articles from magazines ranging from *Consumer Reports* to *Byte, PC Magazine, PC Week, Computer Shopper, Mac User*, and *A +* .

As you'd expect, CompuServe is a news junkie's paradise. Glossbrenner says CompuServe's financially related offerings are ''extensive'' enough to ''rival'' those of the Dow Jones News/Retrieval Service. ''Not only that,'' he says, ''you may find that CompuServe gives you the identical information at a far lower price.''

You can even set up CompuServe's Executive News Service (ENS) to automatically file away items mentioning certain key words—you have, yes, an electronic clipping service. What a boon to travelers who worry about missing out on news during their trips! You can read stories from the Associated Press, Reuters Financial Report, and the *Washington Post*, among others. To reach ENS, type **GO ENS** from CompuServe's main prompt.

Does CompuServe have a catch? Sort of. The usual one: cost. It's tolerable to many companies (especially when compared to the Dow Jones News/Retrieval service), but not so palatable to small fry. On local BBS's, from time to time you read of ''Compu$erve.''

At 1,200 bps and above, the basic rate is at least $12.50 an hour, excluding connection charges. Some of the databases peddle their wares at around $100 an hour on top of that. Not all, of course. The Executive News Service, for example, is a mere $15 an hour above the basic rate!

Luckily, you can somewhat lower your expenses by using special software such as the Tapcis program (shareware—$79 if you like it) to shorten your on-line sessions. You also can compose your e-mail mes-

---

[3] Shareware isn't free; public domain software is. The authors normally aren't expecting a payment.

sages off-line. For sending extremely long files, CompuServe is a better deal than MCI Mail is. Certainly it and MCI Mail are both bargains compared to long-distance telephone (imagine the condition of my bank account if I'd regularly used voice to reach John Deakin, who flies between Tokyo and New York as others would commute between Manhattan and Greenwich).

See chapter 11 for information on sending e-mail and fax through CompuServe.

DataTimes ([405] 751-6400 or 800-642-2525)

DataTimes describes itself as "a network of full text newspaper and newswire archive information covering four continents and over 140 cities." Perhaps DataTimes can help track down information about foreign clients.

Among the offerings are the New York *Newsday*, the *San Francisco Chronicle*, the *Chicago Sun-Times*, the *Louisville Courier-Journal*, the *Washington Post*, *USA Today*, *Congressional Quarterly*, *American Banker*, and (via gateways) many Canadian, British, Australian, and European publications.

DIALOG Information Service and the Knowledge Index (800-334-2564)

The American space program didn't just give the world Tang and that pseudo–ice cream on sale at the Smithsonian Air and Space Museum. It also gave us DIALOG. Lockheed Missiles and Space Company set up the system under a different name for its own use during those heady days when we were aiming at the moon.

A MINI-EXPLANATION OF DATABASES

A database can be as simple as a pile of recipe cards. It's nothing more than an assortment of related information. Normally the term *database* means information stored in electronic form—either in your own computer or someone else's. If you want to call your recipe cards a database, that's fine with me. Just don't expect to sell it to Mead Data.

The related information can include full texts of writings within the database's category (for instance, health, business, agriculture, or something more specific). But it can also be limited to citations of books or articles. So you *still* may need to troop over to the library in the snow. Sorry.

In many databases on-line, you'll often locate information by typing a word and seeing what references pop up. If the database is a full-text one, you'll be able to see the actual articles after you type the proper word.

Word is a little misleading. You may need to specify a whole series of words to narrow your search. How? Let's say you're looking for articles about John Smith. Then, using your database, you might employ Boolean logic, named after George Boole (1815–1864), an English mathematician whose theories proved surprisingly useful when computers at last came along. Boolean logic depends heavily on three magic words: *AND*, *NOT*, and *OR*.

■ **SMITH AND CAPTAIN** would call up only articles with the words *Smith* and *Captain*—one way to help narrow the search to "Captain John Smith" in a database on Virginia history.

■ **SMITH NOT CAPTAIN** would give you all the articles about "John Smith" except those that used both of the search words. Try this combination if you're looking for information about a Smith other than the fabled captain (the one saved from execution by the Indian maiden Pocahontas).

■ **SMITH OR CAPTAIN** would call up a list of all articles containing either the word *Smith* or the word *Captain*.

Boolean logic can be much, much more complex than the aforementioned, but this should give you a general idea.

Mind you, the Boolean approach isn't the only one. Some of the smartest databases can help novices find the right material quickly— even if they think that the word *Boolean* means space aliens rather than a dead mathematician. See the listing earlier in this chapter for Dow Jones News/Retrieval to find out about the marvels of DowQuest.

Now, however, the Knight-Ridder newspaper chain owns DIALOG. Lucky thing, too. K-R is one of the country's better mass media companies. "No one," Glossbrenner says, "could figure out what a missile manufacturer was doing in the information business in the first place."

Still, it isn't as if Lockheed bungled the job. Not until 1988 did the company sell DIALOG, and by then the service had become like the space program itself: a veritable showcase for the American brain. Worldwide DIALOG has attracted more than one hundred thousand users. It isn't just DIALOG's powerful computers that are a triumph, but also what's inside them.

"DIALOG represents itself as the 'World's Largest On-line Knowledgebank,' " John Dvorak and Nick Anis say in their authoritative telecommunications guide. "This is no idle boast. DIALOG has over 325 databases, ranging in subject from aerospace to zoology. There's information on art, music, and the humanities, business articles, company news, and industry assessments. Research resources include the hard sciences: biology, chemistry, and physics." In fact, as Dvorak and Anis observe, DIALOG is beyond a database. It's a data*bank*, a whole collection of databases.

You'll find, among other things, material from or about:

- Academic papers
- Patents
- Trademarks
- Statistics
- Local newspapers
- Medical matters
- The Associated Press, United Press International, and Knight-Ridder Financial News
- Other financial sources, including Standard & Poor's, Moody's, and Dun & Bradstreet

Imagine the possibilities for the traveler away from the United States and needing to access arcane medical or technical information.

Unfortunately, like the space program, DIALOG is pricey. Retrieve a full SEC record about a company from the DISCLOSURE database and you're out twenty dollars or so—at least several times what Dow Jones would charge you. And Dow isn't exactly for the economy set!

But wait. There is a little hope. It's in the form of the Knowledge Index, an offshoot of DIALOG available outside the normal business day. The Knowledge Index's offerings aren't as extensive. But you can access many basics, such as the *Marquis Who's Who, Books in Print*,

Magazine Index, and, yes, ABI/INFORM. The charge is $24 an hour or 40 cents a minute.

That's still a far cry from the cost of a trip to the library, and I'd hope that such costs will come down in the future. Still, the price has declined to the point where even students will want to consider the Knowledge Index as an alternative to a session in the proverbial Dusty Stacks.

Dow Jones News/Retrieval ([609] 452-1511 or 800-522-3567)

A year or so ago a friend of mine was scrambling to find a British writer who, last she knew, was somewhere in rural Asia. A movie studio held out hopes of a big deal if she could buy his life story. She got a tip that an article had appeared about him in the past several years, but she had no idea of the date.

"No problem," I said, and within five minutes had dug up 2,500 words about the man in the *Washington Post*.

I did so just by keying in the man's name and waiting for Dow Jones News/Retrieval //TEXT service to do its job. Among other material, it gave me access to the *Post*, selected Dow Jones News Service articles, *Business Week*, *Baron's*, the PR newswire, and many articles from *Forbes*, *Fortune*, the invaluable *American Demographics*, *Consumer Markets Abroad*, *Financial World*, *Money, Inc.*, and the *Wall Street Journal* (no other database carries the full text of the *Journal*'s stories).

All it took in my friend's case was one article from the *Post*, and she was off to England, having found that the man was writing for a British newspaper. The Hollywood deal, alas, hasn't yet materialized, but if it does, Dow Jones News/Retrieval certainly will have helped make it possible.

At that time I was using the command //TEXT, but that doesn't provide the menus that you'll see if instead you key in //TEXTM. You can also invoke DowQuest, which is even simpler to use. Type in keywords and DowQuest will spew out a list of stories. You can then examine the stories in depth and end your search there; or you can go a step beyond and identify material that shows more precisely the kind of topic you're after. You can, for instance, choose a paragraph that uses *star* in the astronomical sense rather than the TV one. And so on. DowQuest will get the hint and narrow your search.

Needless to say, Dow Jones News/Retrieval is a premium-priced service—an extended search can cost hundreds of dollars if you don't plan ahead and know the system. But many will find the service to be worth the cost. Want to know about business conditions in Baton Rouge, Louisiana; Orange County, California; or Alberta Province in Canada? The service can call up regional publications from those and other areas.

Besides the ability to retrieve news stories, you can benefit from access to such goodies as:

- 10K filings with the Securities and Exchange Commission
- Credit information
- Standard & Poor's on-line
- Information from major stockbrokers and investment banks
- *Wall Street Week*
- The Mutual Funds Performance Report from Media General
- Comp-u-Store
- Peterson's College Guides

By the way, instead of subscribing to Dow Jones directly, you may use the service through an electronic connect with MCI Mail. You may find this route a little cheaper and more convenient, especially if you're sending and receiving computer messages more often than you're searching for information.

GEnie (800-638-9636)

In the 1970s, when CompuServe started, William H. Louden was subscriber number two. He went to work for CompuServe shortly thereafter, and played a notable role in shaping the consumer information service. Some four years later, after Louden had left CompuServe, General Electric hired him to start a similar service for GE. So if you log on GEnie and see more than a few traces of CompuServe, you aren't hallucinating.

Among other things, both services offer:

- E-mail. At one point GEnie's e-mail wasn't as sophisticated as CompuServe's, but that may well have changed.
- News-clipping services. For $25 a month—the fee may have changed—you can specify as many as ten search terms or other identifiers.

■ Electronic malls. On GEnie you can even respond with an order after seeing a list of the wares from Tiffany.

■ Other news-related products. On GEnie you can read stories from the Associated Press, United Press International, even Xinhua (the Chinese News Agency). Moreover, through GEnie you can log onto the Dow Jones News/Retrieval Service. Those inclined can even download RockNet Entertainment News, which the Dvorak guide describes as "the latest, most accurate information in the world of rock and roll."

■ Services for the traveler. On GEnie you can dial up the Official Airline Guides as well as the EAASY SABRE reservation service.

■ Special interest groups in a number of areas. "Round tables" include everything from "Writers' Ink" and "Legacy Law" to laptop and WordPerfect forums. Certain professional groups, moreover, are on-line. GEnie is the electronic home of the Computer Press Association. It's also where you'll find PhotoSource International, which matches photographers with magazine assignments.

■ Vast libraries of shareware.

■ Databases. Want to do a genealogical search? GEnie's Genealogy KnowledgeBase can point you in the right direction. Want to know about Microsoft products? Check out the KnowledgeBase inside the Microsoft Round Table.

■ Instant-time discussion areas à la CompuServe's CB simulator. You can even create files showing electronic faces to use during conferences.

Not surprisingly, by last year GEnie had enrolled some two hundred thousand subscribers. Surely by now the number is much higher. In membership GEnie is far behind CompuServe, but it's been among the faster growing of the on-line services.

Rates are constantly changing. GEnie's offerings do not encompass the range of CompuServe's, however, so you'll probably find that the cost of the newer service is lower. Either is a good bet. As Glossbrenner observed, the price competition "bodes well for the consumer."

MCI Mail (800-323-0945)

MCI Mail is one of my favorites because the clock is never ticking when I'm sending electronic mail. Basic subscriptions cost just $25 a year, a wonderful source of amazement to friends new to computers.

They always wonder if a catch exists. No! You can send about one thousand words for just a dollar. Reception is free.

Besides, MCI Mail is easy once you get the hang of it. To get a letter on its way, you just type **CR** (or **CREATE**) from the main "command:" prompt and press the Return key. MCI guides you from there.

Unlike Prodigy, which includes an e-mail net, MCI Mail is a serious business network. I suspect that most of the Fortune 500 subscribe. Some impressive-sounding corporate listings, of course, may involve nothing more than branch offices or low-level management people. Don't count on reaching the chairman of General Motors this way! "People may have accounts on different systems," Glossbrenner correctly says, "but *everybody* is on MCI."

MCI Mail is also a true business network in the powers it can offer. Unlike Prodigy, MCI lets you prepare your files in advance with your favorite word processor, and you can store messages from other people on your disk.

What's more, you can simultaneously send the copies of the same letter via e-mail, fax, telex, and paper mail to the different recipients.

■ E-mail copies can go to as many other MCI subscribers as you want. They can also reach people on other networks such as CompuServe and AT&T Mail and even some corporate networks. Of course, to reach people not on MCI, you must know the appropriate routing codes and identification numbers or letters.

■ Fax copies can reach machines anywhere in the world. You can arrange for MCI's facsimile to make X number of tries. MCI itself, by the way, operates a fax network.

■ Telex copies can go to old-fashioned companies without either computers or fax machines. Much of the Third World still uses Telex because transmissions can go over primitive, crackly phone lines.

■ Paper copies. MCI Mail can print them out as regular letters and have them mailed in cities close to the recipients. Or through an arrangement with an express service, MCI can offer overnight delivery. You can enjoy overnight service to many if not most of the world's capital cities.

This isn't to say MCI Mail is perfect and all powerful. When, oh when, for instance, is MCI going to have an easy-to-figure-out way of zapping messages that you decide to kill? Once I deleted a message from my "out" basket. I thought it was dead. But it went on to the recipient anyway.

Just the same, MCI Mail is terrific for a wide range of users. Consider sales departments. As I show in chapter 4, traveling reps can log on MCI Mail from anywhere, then follow "scripts" to enter orders, expense account information, and other routine data.

Bulletin boards are another, not-so-well-known wrinkle of MCI Mail. The number isn't as great as on CompuServe, and many are private, but there are some offbeat, publicly viewable ones that come and go. Alfred Glossbrenner, for example, writes that he ran across "Medmal Lawyers (30 cents per minute), offering medical malpractice expert witnesses for malpracticing attorneys—'Court appearances welcome!' " The thirty cents, by the way, isn't the lawyers' fee, that's the viewing charge on MCI Mail. Some boards cost nothing, including MCI Mail News. To reach a board by name, type from MCI's command prompt: **VIEW MCI NEWS** or an equivalent command, then hit the Enter key.

Through MCI Mail, you also can dial up Dow Jones News/Retrieval. If you're interested in Dow it may make more sense to use it through MCI Mail rather than subscribe directly. Please note that as of this writing, Dow Jones isn't available to overseas MCI. This could change.

Regardless, MCI Mail is well-suited for employees visiting or living in foreign countries. MCI ties into major packet-switching networks, so it's truly a worldwide service, reaching some eighty countries. Via WorldMail, an MCI-licensed service in twelve countries, you can receive technical help if you're abroad and are having problems hooking up your modem.

See chapter 8 for some international access information and chapter 11 for information on MCI.

NEXIS Mead Data Central (800-227-4908)

Every now and then a reporter writes, "No stories about Topic X have appeared in any major American newspaper in the last X years." How can the journalist make such a sweeping statement? It may be that he or she is tapping into NEXIS, which offers full texts—not just summaries—from at least 650 sources of news. You can even find *Playboy* articles on-line. If I were NEXIS, I'd launch a sales campaign among the librarians in the Bible Belt whom the more obnoxious evangelists were harassing. "Look, Mrs. Jones," the NEXIS reps could say, "buy our service and we'll even throw in *Playboy* without the pictures."

NEXIS, to borrow a phrase from a computer-crazed writer, is an infomaniac's dream. When I asked a newspaper to do a NEXIS search for an article I was writing on Star Wars, NEXIS coughed up citations from everywhere; it even listed a transcript from the British Broadcasting Corporation.

"Perhaps its greatest prize," Glossbrenner has said of NEXIS, "is the full text of *The New York Times*. The final city edition is on-line in its entirety within 24 hours of publication, and the file dates back to June 1, 1980. That means the Sunday magazine, the book review, the Sunday regional supplements—everything. Nobody else has it."

NEXIS, moreover, offers full texts of Securities and Exchange Commission *on-line* in some cases.

Such marvels aren't cheap. NEXIS costs a minimum of fifty dollars a month. You might do well to buy communications software from Mead so you can most efficiently use the service and keep your costs down.

What if you want searches from time to time, but would rather not incur the fifty dollars a month? Your salvation may be the DialSearch service from Mead Data Central. Call DialSearch (at 800-843-6476 outside Ohio or 800-227-8379, extension 5505, in state) and explain your precise needs. DialSearch will then gather the information for you. Reportedly, $140 is the average charge for a search.

You might ask other information providers, by the way, if they can offer similar one-time services or refer you to independent information brokers who can do the work.[4] Ideally the searchers can make the material available not only on paper but also in the appropriate disk format so you can better digest large chunks of information. Who knows, maybe the searcher can even modem you the results. Do, however, check to make certain that reproduction on a disk (for personal use) wouldn't violate any copyright laws.

---

[4] Another way to find an information broker—someone to track down material on-line for you—is a book called *Directory of Free-Based Information Services*, which Alfred Glossbrenner highly recommends. The price is $37 for 250 pages. Write: Helen Burwell, Burwell Enterprises, 3724 F.M. 1960 W., Suite 214, Houston, Texas 77068 (713) 537-9051.

Speaking of laws, attorneys almost surely know already of a sister service from Mead, LEXIS, through which they can obtain legal citations. So I won't mention it further here.

Prodigy (800-PRODIGY, Extension 205; Also Available Through Many Chain Stores, Including Radio Shack and Sears)

Prodigy is a videotex service. It doesn't just fill your screen line-by-line with the usual letters and numbers. Instead, whole pictures pop up. If your monitor is color—yes, monochromes are the rule among laptops, but this will change someday—you'll think at first glance that you're beholding a video sales presentation. It's no accident. Prodigy was created not just to serve subscribers, but also to sell, sell, sell. Garish ads keep turning up at the bottom of the screen. The hope is that you'll use the "look" command a lot, find out more about the ballyhooed products, and buy, buy, buy.

Despite all the dazzle, Prodigy is s-l-o-w. It's like a bus. I'm not talking about the computer kind, with cables going every which way; no, I mean the one that rumbles down the street and belches diesel fumes. You hand over your money, you let Prodigy move you at its own pace.

The e-mail commands aren't as direct as, say, MCI Mail's. Prodigy designed them for newcomers to computers—nice, except that you may happen to be a faster learner than the man in the aisle seat.

Also, you pay for the flashy video display in terms of the time it takes for new views to show up on your computer. With a 12-megahertz computer and a 2,400 bps modem, Prodigy often needed half a minute or so to move on to the next screen.

Screen is indeed the word. To draw another parallel, Prodigy is like, well, network TV. With some justification, snobs could say that Prodigy has been dumbed down. You won't find all of the information choices that you enjoy on CompuServe. "Choices" could also include such exotic indulgences as being able to transmit already-typed files or to save messages on your hard disk. You can't even print out the terse news bulletins. Prodigy is a copyright lawyer's dream.

I wonder, too, about this "family-oriented" service's commitment to freedom of speech and thought. Supposedly for lack of customer interest, Prodigy dropped a health forum where people were discussing

AIDS. I'm baffled. Since Prodigy can tailor itself to different members of a family signing on, why couldn't it just limit access by children? Or do the same for adults who might be offended? Some years ago, a famous Apple commercial—shown during the Super Bowl—depicted IBM as Big Brother–like. IBM and Sears own Prodigy Services Company jointly, and although the management there is independent, the alleged censorship seemed to validate the Orwellian stereotypes. One minute the health forum existed. The next, it didn't. It was like *1984* where Big Brother's minions were rewriting back issues of the *London Times* to suit their whims.

The above notwithstanding, I'm a Prodigy booster. I can see myself enjoying the service in the same way I can appreciate public transportation during rush hour, bad TV movies, and sales at Sears.

Like good old Bus #13, Prodigy is cheap. You pay just $49.95 for a start-up kit (including a month's free service) and then $9.95 a month. That's it. You needn't worry about unknowingly racking up huge bills. Another delight is Prodigy's lively and fresh computer news section, where you can learn about the latest products. The day I first logged on, for instance, I could read the major technical specifications of new laptops from Toshiba. I was pleased, too, to see an offbeat feature called Computer Quirks.

On top of everything else, Prodigy offers weather maps for the traveler, as well as the ability to make airline reservations without paying for the costs by the minute. Prodigy is superb for domestic travelers curious about the weather at their destinations (subscribers also can call up local news bulletins three thousand miles away). The service also may be handy when you're too tired to shop after that five-week vacation in the Himalayas. You can order virtually anything on-line—from a book to a cellular telephone. If you live in certain ZIP codes of some cities, such as Washington, D.C., you can even type in an order for groceries.

Yes, Prodigy is a brazen creature of our consumer society. But so what? The garish ads are one reason, maybe *the* reason, for the bargain rates of $9.95 a month. You can ignore the ads the same way you tune out laxative spiels on television. (Of course, if you see a pitch on Prodigy for a laptop book from St. Martin's Press, it will be an aesthetic and literary triumph.)

Let's hope that Prodigy can survive and increase the range, depth, and seriousness of its free offerings—perhaps using volume to bargain down the charges of expensive information services. Prodigy is a massive money loser right now, even with the ads.

IBM and Sears, however, are looking ahead. New technology should cure the major problems. Over the next decades, for example, many local phone systems will convert to ISDN (Integrated Services Digital Network). ISDN or other advanced techniques such as voice-data multiplexing could turn the Prodigy bus into a Concorde. Tweaking of Prodigy's existing software will help. So should 9,600 bps modems, the prices of which are plummeting. Sirajul Islam, Prodigy's manager of telecommunications technology, says Prodigy already is receiving requests for 9,600 bps modems and will add them in markets with sufficient demand.

Too, Prodigy in the next few years might be able to send binary files. Then you could whiz half a megabyte of WordPerfect or XyWrite material across the country for free or at least for a fraction of what the e-mail services now charge. You'd no longer have to wrestle with the Prodigy clumsy on-line editor. Sooner or later, perhaps, Prodigy could even be able to transmit home video tapes.

Meanwhile, if it's all just a plot for Big Blue and Sears to sell ISDN adapters or ultra-fast modems someday for $69.95—well, I won't mind.

USA Today Update (800-828-4414; [703] 276-6940 in Virginia)

USA Today Update isn't as good as Dow Jones for detailed financial information but could be helpful to marketers and other students of trends. The service's USA Today Decisionline offers news summaries for executives in categories ranging from real estate to international news.

VU/TEXT (800-323-2940; [215] 574-4400 in Pennsylvania)

VU/TEXT may be the service to use if you're scouting for new geographical markets or a new plant site and you want to know *everything* about an area. VU/TEXT offers stories from dozens of local newspapers, especially those of Knight-Ridder, the newspaper chain that owns the service. You can dial up stories that appeared in Knight-Ridder and non-Knight-Ridder papers in Detroit, Miami, Los Angeles, the New York area, and many other locations.

*   *   *

Notice? The computer world is a long way from one master service that will take care of all your needs. Some services will shine as inexpensive learning tools to acquaint you with life on-line (Prodigy); others, in the area of business news (Dow Jones, for example); and still others, as ways to meet mavens who might solve technical problems (CompuServe, to name one such service). For many people, however, e-mail will be the primary use—if not now, then later as more of their friends and business contacts join the networks.

Ahead lies a discussion of e-mail in general, followed by some detailed tips for users of:

■ CompuServe, distinguished by its number of "mailboxes"—at least 550,000—as well as by its ability to send long files cheaply.

■ MCI Mail, which some computer experts rate as the best-run e-mail service, is certainly one of the more interesting possibilities for small businesses and private individuals wishing to communicate with large companies.

If you have any doubts about the utility of e-mail for many people, then John Deakin's story in the next chapter should help dispel them.

SOME BASICS OF ELECTRONIC MAIL (INCLUDING HOW TO SEND E-MAIL, FAXES, TELEX, AND PAPER LETTERS VIA COMPUSERVE AND MCI MAIL)

- How to type messages on-line, then send them to other CompuServe users. Page 305.
- Sending already typed messages to other CompuServe users. Page 308.
- Transmitting to a mailbox on MCI Mail. Page 310.
- Sending to fax machines. Page 311.
- Communicating with a telex machine. Page 312.
- Creating an old-fashioned, paper-style letter on paper that CompuServe will print out for you and mail. Page 314.
- Receiving e-mail on CompuServe. Page 315.
- Logging off CompuServe. Page 316.
- Similar advice for MCI Mail. Page 316.

A few years ago the non-Japanese pilots of Japan Airlines were at odds with the American company that "leased" them back to the airline. It was an ugly, bitter fight over retirement benefits.

John Deakin joined twenty-seven other pilots in a lawsuit against the U.S. company. The suit was a logistical nightmare. "We were flying full, heavy schedules all over the world," he says, "and often went for months without seeing each other. Plus, the company headquarters were located in San Francisco, while we were based in Tokyo and Anchorage."

One day, however, a open-minded vice president of the leasing company saw Deakin's name in an IBM-related section of

CompuServe. The two began swapping electronic mail. Both owned Toshiba 3100s, and they enjoyed a surprising rapport.

"As a direct result of that relationship," Deakin says, "we were able to agree that it might indeed be better to negotiate a settlement rather than continue the litigation, much to the disgust of the lawyers involved." The two men drifted into the positions of chief negotiators for their respective sides. In full privacy, they could exchange hundreds of pages of arguments, honing them along the way. Time zones and distances no longer wreaked havoc on negotiations.

The upshot was that the leasing firm and the pilots saved many months of hearings and slashed their legal costs by thousands of dollars. They hammered out a settlement that Deakin says was "satisfactory to all."

Electronic mail, to be sure, isn't for everyone. Instead of painstakingly trying to lay out arguments, some people may insult the person at the other end. Settling a lawsuit via computer can demand just as much etiquette as doing so in person or over the phone. Just the same, e-mail's rewards can be big. If Deakin and the corporation could settle their bitter labor-management suit this way, imagine the less trying situations.

Consider this book. Deakin has hacked for 13 years and owned seven portables; he's a font of wisdom about laptops; he can tell you, for instance, how to cope with Tokyo electricity, or which packet-switching networks are best for CompuServe members visiting Japan. So I expressed to his San Francisco hotel a 3.5-inch disk containing my electronic manuscript. Deakin's review of my first chapters came from Tokyo. He sent other suggestions and corrections from across the planet in New York, all within a few days, then flew back to Japan and continued from there.

A central computer bank was key. Via the global communications networks, Deakin and I both hooked in. He left messages in the computers for me. I left messages for him. The computers could have been anywhere between Alexandria, Virginia, and Tokyo, Japan; the location didn't matter, just so the two of us could send e-mail to our respective mailboxes inside the memories of the central machines.

He and I also can communicate with many, many other mailboxes on CompuServe: at least 550,000, or more than on any other e-mail service in the United States. More than 8 million Americans are on e-mail nets, according to Eric Arnum, editor of *Electronic Mail & Micro Systems*, but many can't dial into CompuServe or other commercial networks.[1] They may be on internal corporate networks that lack connections with the outside world. This will change as more and more networks include electronic bridges over which people can send messages to other systems.

CompuServe, of course, isn't the only e-mail possibility for small businesses and private individuals. Many users, at least those who hate the clock to tick away, will find MCI Mail a better deal for shorter messages. MCI charges by the number of characters transmitted, not by how long it takes to send the material (see page 316 of this chapter for more on MCI).

On the other hand, CompuServe is an amazing bargain for swapping long files, perhaps even the world's best buy. Eric Arnum says 100,000 characters would cost just $1.50 to send and $1.50 to receive on CompuServe, compared to $14 to transmit on MCI Mail.[2]

What's more, you can use programs such as TAPCIS, Navigator, Information Manager, and other CompuServe-specific software. Each can lower the cost of shorter messages. With them you can more easily compose and read messages off-line when the meter is off. "If you're not doing on-line work this way," Deakin says, "you aren't using on-line services properly."

How can you benefit from CompuServe's electronic mail capabilities? Below are instructions for sending messages to:

■ Other CompuServe members—in this case, when you're composing messages while hooked up to the service's main computers.

■ Other CompuServe users, when you are sending them already typed messages.

---

[1] The address of *Electronic Mail and Micro Systems* is P.O. Box 1716, New Caanan, Connecticut 06840. The telephone number is (203) 966-2525.

[2] MCI Mail subscribers do not pay to receive messages.

■ People on MCI Mail. CompuServe uses a routing symbol—a >—to show that a message is going to another system.

■ Those with fax machines. "No doubt," Arnum says, "ten to fifteen million Americans have access to fax machines."

■ Telex users. They're a dwindling breed in the United States, but Europe and the Third World still have plenty.

■ People without computers. A printing site will print your message for mailing as a normal letter—to either an American or overseas destination.

In addition, I'll tell how you can "read" from your mailbox—fetch messages from it—and disconnect from CompuServe when you're done.

The CompuServe people are constantly refining their service's commands and the menus that list various possibilities. So I'll try simply to give you a quick overview. This material isn't a replacement for the *CompuServe Users Guide* ($12.95 if not included with the introductory kits available through many computer stores, or by calling 800-848-8199) or the useful book *How to Get the Most Out of CompuServe*, by Charles Bowen and David Peyton (New York: Bantam Books, 1989, $26.95). From these other sources you can learn how to hook up to CompuServe, which is a simple, semiautomated process. And via "help" commands (type **HELP** and hit the Return key) you often find explanations on-line. So don't count on everything being here. I'll explain just a few of CompuServe's many e-mail capabilities.

CompuServe Information Service, by the way, is much, much more than simply the part called CompuServe Mail. For example, as you'll recall from the previous chapter, you can tap into hundreds of databases and call up the latest news bulletins. Also, you can read and leave notices on bulletin boards covering computer-related topics and scads of other subjects ranging from aviation to law.

HOW TO TYPE MESSAGES ON-LINE, THEN SEND THEM TO OTHER COMPUSERVE USERS

At speeds of 1,200 bps and higher—the normal standard for business modems—CompuServe costs can add up for heavy users. The rates are at least $12.50 an hour if your modem is going faster than 300 bps. So try not to compose messages on-line unless they're very short. Here's what you do to send your first message, once you're a CompuServe member:

1. Log on to CompuServe. In cities with local CompuServe numbers, you'll see a message asking you to enter the name of a host computer. Just type **CIS** and hit the Return key. You'll see a request for a CompuServe number

2. Type in your CompuServe number. The format will be something along the lines of: **12345,6789**. Keep the commas in the right place or CompuServe won't understand your entry. Hit the Return key. You'll next see a request for a password.

3. Enter your password, then hit Return. CompuServe in this respect is merciful toward users. In my case, anyway, it came up with two easy-to-remember words joined together by a space or @ or other symbol (nope, I won't give anything away).

4. Type **GO MAIL** and press Return.[3] (Now that you're in the habit, I'll delete references to the Return key.) You'll see a menu offering options.

5. Select the option to "Compose a new message." Please note that by the time you're reading this, CompuServe might have different but similar wording. Also, don't forget: You're not using CompuServe the most economical way. Later I'll show you how to compose off-line so the clock isn't ticking away while you polish your message.

Having selected the option to compose a message, you'll see the words "Enter message (/EXIT when done)" and the start of line numbers.[4]

6. To the right of the "1," you should start typing away as if at your old manual typewriter. You'll even press the Return key at the end of every line. If you want, you can skip lines between paragraphs. You can even use the Backspace key. You can type up to 80 characters per line.

---

[3] Actually, on CompuServe, you can type **G** instead of the word **GO**.

[4] The example given in paragraph 6 assumes that CompuServe is in the LINEDIT mode, where you see the line numbers when you're composing on-line. Consult your CompuServe manual for a discussion of LINEDIT and EDIT. The latter mode is for more experienced users.

Your message will look something like this:
Enter message (/EXIT when done)
1:Jim,[Press the Return key]
2:[Return—not visible on CompuServe]
3:It's official now. We've got word that Slim Pickens[Return]
4:has been quietly buying up stock.[Return]
5:[Return]
6:I say, Let's break out the poison pill![Return]
7:[Return]
8:Yours,[Return]
9:Fogarty[Return]
10:/EXIT[Return]
The **/EXIT** doesn't refer to the departure that Fogarty will make from the company if Pickens or another corporate raider wins. It simply marks the end of the message. The **/** is there just because it normally doesn't occur that often in letters (well, the nontechnical kind, anyway). It's a good way to show that you're really done.

After you type **/EXIT**, you'll see a menu with such possibilities as "Send," "Edit," and "Type." Read your CompuServe manual for further explanations, especially if you want to edit.[5]

7. Right now, just press the number for "Send." You'll see a screen with this or a similar message:

Send to (Name or User ID):

8. Type in the other person's CompuServe number. You can't enter a name (unless it's in a CompuServe "address book," a shortcut that I won't explain here). Once you've entered the ID, CompuServe will then request a subject.

9. For a subject, you can type up to 40 letters, numbers, or symbols.

---

[5]When novices send a letter the first time, they might type out the text on paper beforehand so they don't have to mess with the on-line editor. Later they can experiment with the "Edit" option. That will take them to another menu. On that menu, "CHANGE characters in line" will allow replacement of characters, words, and so on within the line. "REPLACE line" will let you type in a whole new line. "DELETE line" will let you erase a line. "INSERT new line(s)" similarly will do what it says. "TYPE all lines" will cause them to display on your screen with line numbers. "TYPE/POSTAL all lines" will show how the material will look when printed out. And "SEND message" will move you out of the editing mode and into the one where you'll add such information as the CompuServe ID number of the person receiving the message. See your CompuServe manual for more details.

You'll then see a request for your own name (unless it's already in the address book).

10. Enter your name. CompuServe Mail will then display what you've entered and ask:

Is this correct? (Y or N)

11. Type **Y** if the information is correct, and your message will be on the way. Is the information wrong? Press **N** and pick out the appropriate choice, probably #1, and supply the proper information.

SENDING ALREADY TYPED MESSAGES TO OTHER COMPUSERVE USERS

Okay, so you know in a pinch how to compose a CompuServe message on-line and send it.

You and your bank account, however, will be far, far better off if you learn to send messages that you've already typed out. Already typed messages without protocols can be up to 50,000 characters, or close to 9,000 words long. If they're longer, you can split them. "Binary" messages, using protocols such as CompuServe B, can push slightly past half a million characters.

If you compose a message off-line, you can do any of the following:

■ Use a word processor such as QEdit or VDE that creates files in ASCII (text files) with carriage returns at the ends of all your lines. CompuServe and most other e-mail systems favor this kind of output. By the way, the ASCII files mustn't contain lines more than 80 characters long.

■ Convert the output of WordPerfect, WordStar, whatever, to ASCII. See the instruction manual of your word processor for proper guidance.

■ Uploading via a binary technique, using CompuServe B, XMODEM, or another protocol. That way you'll transfer every bit and byte of a file so the person at the other end can download the file and read it in ASCII, WordPerfect, WordStar, XyWrite, or whatever you used in the first place. Of course, the other person ideally will use the same word processor. Otherwise he or she will have to translate, just as if the material had arrived on a disk rather than over CompuServe.

For simplicity's sake, I won't discuss protocols here. See your

CompuServe manual (and the one for your communications software). Or type **HELP UPLOAD** at the main prompt of CompuServe's mail menu. Please note that CompuServe's own protocol transfers files more quickly on CompuServe than XMODEM does.

Now, here is the procedure for sending already typed material:

1. Follow steps one through four in the preceding section. In step five, instead of "Compose a new message," choose to "Upload a message." You'll see a list of protocols available.

2. Select "No protocol." Please note that this isn't a mandatory choice, it's what I'm using in this example for simplicity's sake. "No protocol" works only when files are in ASCII. You can use a protocol to transfer an ASCII or binary file, however.

Once you understand your communications software, you may experiment with various protocols. But not now. In this case, transfer the file (to CompuServe's computer) without using a protocol.

Transfers of this kind are more susceptible to transmission errors than those with a protocol such as XMODEM. Also, you won't be able to transmit the format of your favorite word processor (unless it's plain ASCII with carriage returns at the end of each line) Those are negatives. The positives are that ASCII transfers take less time, since the computers aren't bothering to see if the information got through accurately.

After selecting "No protocol" or the equivalent, you may see a message with wording such as:

> **No error detection/correction**
> **Do you want to be prompted for each line (Y or N)?**

3. Type **N**.

CompuServe will now say something like:

> **Begin sending your data.**
> **Use /EX to indicate the end of your data.**

4. Tell your communications software to start sending the ASCII file.

5. Type **/EX** (or **/EXIT**) when the transmission ends. In the future, by the way, you might experiment with including /EX in your files when you prepare them.

You'll now see a message such as:

> ***** File Transfer Completed! *****

6. Press the Return key, if CompuServe instructs you, and you'll see "Send Menu" or the equivalent.

7. Select "Send."

8. Follow the remainder of steps eight through eleven in the preceding section.

SENDING TO AN MCI MAILBOX VIA COMPUSERVE

There's no mystery here at all. Just do what you do to send to people on CompuServe, with one big exception—the obvious one: address your message differently.

You won't type in a CompuServe identification number. Instead you'll enter the recipient's MCI Mail ID. Two important points here:

■ Do not confuse his or her MCI Mail identification with the "user name" with which the person logs on MCI. It's a different animal. The MCI Mail identification number is just that—a number, a unique one. Your recipient can find out his or her number by using MCI Mail's "Create" command, typing in the name, and finding out what number comes up beside it.

■ You also can use the recipient's registered name on MCI Mail, but ideally you won't, since it may not be unique. That isn't just a problem with "John Smith" or "James Jones."

What's the exact format for an MCI Mail address? After the usual "Send to (Name or User ID)," you must enter an MCI Mail ID this way:

>MCIMAIL:MCI ID

In other words, you type:

>MCIMAIL:123-4567

Or else if you're certain the name is unique:

>MCIMAIL:Attila T. Hun

Remember:

■ You must include the >**MCIMAIL:**.

That's how CompuServe knows to route the message to MCI Mail.

■ Your message can't exceed 50,000 characters.

■ It must be a text message, not binary.

■ Each line can be no more than 80 characters long.

CompuServe charges extra for MCI Mail messages according to the following formula:

> "Up to 500 characters $.45
> 501–7500 characters   1.00
> Each addtl. 7500 characters 1.00"

MCI Mail, incidentally, isn't the only other e-mail service you can reach through CompuServe. You also can reach Internet, an electronic mail system linking governmental institutions, military branches, educational institutions, and commercial companies. And through Internet you can reach Bitnet and Arpanet.

To learn how to use Internet, type from within the mail menu: **HELP INTERNET**. You'll learn all you need to know. (By the way, if you'll be communicating with a Local Area Network via CompuServe, the service should be similarly informative on-line. Just type **HELP LANS**. The LAN feature will be available by 1991.)

USING COMPUSERVE TO SEND TO FAX MACHINES

CompuServe lets you reach facsimile machines anywhere in the world. After the prompt to "Send to (Name or User ID)," enter the fax telephone number the following way:

>**>FAX:7035551212**

The 703 is the area code; the rest is a seven-digit telephone number. Do not insert a 1 before the area code. Treat Canadian and Caribbean numbers like domestic ones. The area-code format is the same.

What if your target is a fax machine elsewhere on the planet? Then you'll need an 011 to show that the call is an international one, followed by the country code, the city code if there is one, and the number of the destination fax machine. Hence:

>**>FAX:01144112345**

Suppose you want to send to more than one fax machine? Use this format:[6]

---

[6]The same idea will work with regular CompuServe numbers. Hence: **12345,1234; 23456,2345**. Notice the semicolon between the different numbers? By the way, you can simultaneously mix media (including regular CompuServe addresses) with those for faxes, MCI Mail, telex, Internet, or the Postal Service. For example: **12345,1234; >FAX:0114411234;>MCIMAIL:123-4567;>TLX: 1234567 ABCDEF;>POSTAL**.

>FAX:6145551234;>FAX:2125554321

After you enter the number(s) of the receiving machine(s), CompuServe will ask you for the name(s) of the person(s) and the subject, request that you confirm the location(s) and phone number(s), and tell you how much the message will cost. You'll see something like:

To: >FAX:7035551212
Attn: Attila T. Hun, third floor
FAX message to Virginia

From: Cyrus MacBride
Subj: Henchmen's Escape from Lorton Reformatory

Mail to Fax $.75
Is this correct? (Y or N)?

Type **Y** and you'll be on your way. CompuServe will automatically give you a format of 55 lines per page unless you press Ctrl-L to create other page breaks. Please note that facsimile delivery is not instant. When the message arrives—probably well within an hour if the fax at the other end isn't busy—CompuServe will send you a message that the facsimile got through.

Domestic faxes cost $.75 for the first 1,000 characters; $.25 per 1,000 beyond that. Type **HELP FAX INTERNATIONAL** for rates overseas.

HOW TO REACH TELEX MACHINES VIA COMPUSERVE

Telex is a bit of a fossil nowadays in this country. Eric Arnum estimates that while some 600,000 telex machines are pounding away in Europe, only 50,000 are operating in the United States. "I've heard there are one and one-half million telex in the world," he says, "but where's the rest of them?" In Latin America, Asia, and elsewhere in the Third World! Tisha Gray, a marketing manager for CompuServe Mail, says that's where most telexes go nowadays. Whatever the case, a telex is still a must for international business. And, as with fax, you can use CompuServe to make the link—to any Telex I or Telex II (formerly TWX) machine.

Send a telex by entering the following after the prompt "Send to (Name or User ID):":

>**TLX: (machine no.) (answerback)**

Thus:

>**TLX: 1234567 ABCDEF**

Notice? The "1234567" is the telex machine's number; the "ABCDEF" is an answerback—a way to confirm that the message arrived. Don't use answerbacks if you're not certain. It's tricky. Certain machines require that the answerback contain all or some of the machine number; others don't. With a machine number included in the answerback, you might enter:

>**TLX: 123456 123456 AB CDE**

CompuServe says it won't accept the blame for telexes not arriving because of incorrect answerbacks. Fair enough.

You can send telexes in the continental United States for $1.15 per 300 characters. Type **HELP TELEX INTERNATIONAL** to learn prices and procedures for sending telexes elsewhere, and to look up country codes.

Helpfully—considering the high cost of telexes compared to alternatives—CompuServe informs you of the exact charges when it asks you to verify the address that you've entered. Telexes, by the way, can't exceed 50,000 characters; also, do not use lines wider than 72 characters. That's the standard for domestic telexes. If you're sending internationally, limit the number to 69 characters.

To receive a telex in your CompuServe mailbox, tell the sender to:

1. Address the message to the following telex number: **3762848**. The answerback is: **COMPUSERVE**.

2. Type a **TO:**, a space, and your CompuServe ID number on the first nonblank line of the message. RE: and a space precede the subject of the message. Hence:

    TO: 12345,1234 (This is required.)

    RE: TEST MESSAGE (This is optional message subject.)

    See, our telex-to-CompuServe connection worked fine!

In some countries, the senders of telexes must insert a prefix before the CompuServe machine number. Type **HELP TELEX PREFIXES** for a list of prefixes.

What if the sender wants to reach more than one CompuServe box? Then use this format:

TO: 70001,1234;71110,1111
RE: INFORMATION YOU REQUESTED

SENDING OUT PAPER MAIL THROUGH COMPUSERVE

In a surprising number of offices—even in the United States—IBM Selectrics still reign supreme and even fax machines are missing. How to reach those people? Easy: Use CompuServe to mail ordinary letters, the paper kind. CompuServe operates seven print sites around the United States and directs the letters to the sites closest to the recipients. International letters go out of Washington, D.C. For more information type **HELP POSTAL**.

To create a paper letter, do the following:

1. When you create your file, make certain that your letter isn't more than 60 characters wide or 279 lines long. (If you're typing on-line use the ''Compose/Postal'' option; see your CompuServe manual.)

2. Enter the ''Send'' menu. After the usual prompt to ''Send to (Name or User ID):'', type: >**Postal**

3. Then answer the prompts that appear. Here's the format in which you'll work:

Recipient's name: Hank Lawson
Title/Company (optional):
Address Line 1: 134 Donnelly Place
Address Line 2 (optional)
City: Lorain
State or Province: Ohio
Zip: 44052
Would you like to edit this address? (Y or N): n

Enter your return address.
Enter ''CANCEL'' to exit the address prompt.

Name: David H. Rothman
Title/Company (optional): c/o Editorial Department
Address Line 1: St. Martin's Press
Address Line 2 (optional): 175 Fifth Avenue
City: New York
State or Province: New York
Zip: 10010

Would you like to edit this address? (Y or N)? n

Would you like to save this name and address so you do not have to type it in the future? (Y or N)? y

Subject: World's Largest Concrete Easter Egg

To: Hank Lawson
    134 Donnelly Place
    Lorain, Ohio 44052
From: David H. Rothman

    c/o Editorial Department
    St. Martin's Press
    175 Fifth Avenue
    New York, N.Y. 10010
    Subj: World's Largest Concrete Easter Egg

CompuServe Mail to Postal $1.50
Are your message and address correct? (Y or N)? y
Message sent to Hank Lawson
Did you see the reference to saving "this name and address"? And the "yes" when CompuServe asked if I wanted Hank Lawson saved? From now on, instead of typing >**Postal** and going through the whole routine, I can just type in "Hank Lawson" and CompuServe will be smart enough to give me his address.

Address books can also simplify the entry of other addresses—those on CompuServe itself, those on MCI Mail, telex, and so on.

RECEIVING E-MAIL ON COMPUSERVE

It's easy to receive e-mail. (Novices should remember, of course, to put their communications software in "capture" if they want to save the messages to their disks.)

After you've typed **GO MAIL**, you should see something similar to the following:

             1 READ mail, 2 messages pending

Now:

1. Type 1 or any other number designating the "Read" option. You'll see a "Read menu"—for example:
1 Raid!
2 Poison Pills
2. Pick your choice. (See your CompuServe guide or use on-line help to learn what to do about files designated "binary." You can't read them the normal way; you'll have to download them with CompuServe "B," XMODEM, or another protocol.)
3. Respond to the next menu:
1 DELETE this message
2 FILE in PER area
3 FORWARD
4 REREAD message
5 REPLY
6 SAVE in mailbox
7 DOWNLOAD message
See your CompuServe manual on on-line "help" for a full explanation of the above.

Want to read the message again? No problem. Just choose CompuServe's "REREAD message" option. Use "REPLY" if you want to respond on-line and have the other person's address already inserted. Remember, however: CompuServe is much, much less expensive if you compose off-line.

LOGGING OFF COMPUSERVE

Careful. CompuServe may charge you a little for extra time if you don't disconnect properly. Don't simply snap off your modem.

Instead, type **OFF** or **BYE** after exclamation point on the usual command line. You'll see how much time you've used during your session. Then CompuServe will disconnect.

AN INTRODUCTION TO MCI MAIL

"God" has left MCI Mail. Half a dozen years ago I found him when, out of curiosity, I typed "God" after MCI's TO: prompt. "God" was a West Virginian.

I never did learn whether he was a preacher or a businessman associated with a very distinctively named company. No matter. MCI Mail is still a splendid network for both business and personal use even if you can't reach the Almighty. Via MCI I found three "CIA"'s (not *the* CIA, just initial-sakes), one "Department of Defense," scores of famous corporate names, ranging from "NBC Radio News" to "Euro Disneyland," and seven "Rothman"'s (no apparent relatives, though I could see the potential here for genealogy buffs).

MCI Mail is far from the largest commercial network in the United States—that honor belongs to CompuServe, with more than five times the number of mailboxes—but you still feel in touch with the whole universe. There are bridges to:

■ CompuServe
■ AT&T Mail
■ Dialcom. In spring 1990 this link was experimental. Check with MCI for the latest.
■ Western Union's EasyLink (probably in effect by now)
■ General Electric/GEnie (probable)
■ SprintMail (the old Telemail)
■ Internet
■ The PT Postel service in Italy
■ The MISSIVE service in France
■ INFONET (probable)
■ TRANSPAC France (probable)
■ Telecom Australia (probable)
■ OTC Australia (probable)
■ DACOM Korea (probable)
■ The usual fax and telex connections. You could not use a computer to *receive* faxes via MCI as of spring 1990. But that might have changed by the time you're reading this book.
■ Many links to corporate computer networks.

I'm also an MCI fan because of the organization of the commands. Like any e-mail net—including Prodigy, designed largely for computer novices—MCI Mail isn't 100 percent understandable to new users. But it's as easy as any other. Plus, MCI Mail is fast and powerful, offering the ability to consolidate commands in many cases. It's what Prodigy *should* be.

Above all, I like the fact that MCI Mail doesn't punish me if I upload a file, see the wrong information flash by during the transmission, and decide to delete the message and start up again. MCI won't bill you a cent for unsent messages.

MCI Mail's fees, incidentally, are terrific for small users—just 45 cents to transmit a message of up to 500 characters or less, 75 cents for 501 to 2,500 characters, and $1 for 2,501 to 7,500 characters. The character counts include not only the messages but also the letters and numbers in the electronic address. Seventy-five hundred characters is around 1,000 words. Savings are possible through MCI's Preferred Pricing option. To be sure, even with discounts, MCI Mail isn't always the cheapest; long files are less expensive on CompuServe, and AT&T Mail bills just 80 cents for every 7,500 characters that you upload. Still, MCI Mail is a great deal. It's a wonderful tension preventer when you know you can take your time without paying extra except in special situations, such as when you're abroad.[7]

Below are brief instructions for using MCI Mail to send messages to:

■ Other MCI mailboxes. MCI boxes are not just in the U.S. but overseas. You pay no more to transmit to Australia than to send to an office across town.

■ CompuServe mailboxes. Reaching CompuServe subscribers is a cinch—hardly any more effort than communicating with those on the MCI net itself.

■ Fax numbers. If you only need to *send* faxes and you're not doing so constantly, then MCI Mail may be the perfect affordable solution. There is a downside. You can send just text, no images other than laser-scanned graphic letterheads and signatures. But that's fine in most cases. Why bother to print out what's already on your disk?

■ Telex addresses.

■ Postal addresses. This section also includes information on using MCI to send letters for overnight delivery.

---

[7]Obviously MCI Mail won't pay for the cost of dialing it directly from overseas. Nor will it pay for long-distance calls in the United States to numbers other than the 800 dial-up numbers. And of course it won't pay the minute-by-minute costs of other networks that you may use to reach MCI Mail.

I'll also tell how to receive messages via MCI Mail—whether they're computer messages or from telex machines.

Please note that MCI's commands may vary somewhat according to whether you have "Basic" or "Advanced" service. ("Advanced" is the service MCI normally comes with, at no extra charge.) Too, the instructions below won't replace the MCI users manual or on-line help features. If you're serious about MCI Mail, you might also read *The Complete MCI Mail Handbook* (Bantam Books, New York: 1988), $27.95, a fine guide by Stephen Manes.

SENDING TO ANOTHER MCI MAIL SUBSCRIBER

1. Dial MCI Mail. As of this writing, an 800 number works for 2,400 bps transmissions without MNP error correction: 800-456-6245 (preceded by the usual 1). Call MCI Mail's toll-free voice number, 800-444-6245, for more information.

If your communications program doesn't log you on automatically, press the Return key and follow the next two steps.

2. Type your user name (for example, **DROTHMAN**) after MCI says:

Please enter your user name:

3. Hit the Return key. You'll see:

Password:

4. Type your password, then press the return again. You'll see a message in the vein of, "Connection initiated...Opened," followed by "Welcome to MCI Mail," a promotional message; the day's headlines from the Dow Jones News/Retrieval service; a message telling you what version of MCI Mail you're using; notification of how many messages are in your "inbox," and finally an all-important word:

Command:

5. After the word **Command**, type **CR**, which in this case means "Create." Press the Return key. You'll see:

TO:

6. Type the name of the person you're trying to reach. MCI Mail will display different possibilities if more than one exists. Here's what you may see if you type "Wilford Brumley" and reply MCI's prompts:

TO: Wilford Brumley
There is more than one:

No. MCI ID Name Organization Location
0 NOT LISTED BELOW. DELETE.
1 NOT LISTED BELOW. ENTER AN ADDRESS.
2 123-4567 Wilford H. Brumley   WHB, Inc. Alexandria, VA
3 876-5432 Wilford X. Brumley   New York, NY
Please type the number: 2 [The 2 is what you enter.]
123-4567 Wilford H. Brumley   Alexandria, VA
After you've entered Brumley's name, you'll see another:
TO:
That's MCI's way of giving you a chance to route the message to
yet another person.

7. Since you're only sending to one person, just press the carriage
return and MCI Mail will ask whether you want an electronic ''carbon''
copy of the message sent to someone else. If you do, enter another
address. If not? Just press the return key. You'll now see:

Subject:

8. Enter the subject and press the carriage return. Now the screen
will display:

Text: (Enter text or transmit file. Type / on a line by itself to end.)

9. Either type your message out or use your communications software to send a file. You can take your time composing on-line. Unlike
CompuServe, MCI Mail won't charge. Its billing machinery cares only
about length of messages, not the time you spend writing them.

Messages must be no wider than 80 characters. But they can be any
length you want. MCI does have an editor to edit material typed on-
line, just as CompuServe does, but I won't explain it here, since this
is just a quick introduction. Below, however, are several handy commands that you *generally* can use while composing.

—**Ctrl-H** backspaces and rubs out, just like the Backspace key.

—**Ctrl-W** wipes out the word to the left of the cursor.

—**Ctrl-X** deletes *everything* from the cursor to the start of the line
that you're on.

SENDING ALREADY TYPED MESSAGES VIA MCI MAIL

What if you're uploading—sending files composed before you logged
on MCI?

Keep your material no more than 80 characters wide, and make
certain it's in pure ASCII. The only exception would be if you're using

special software. That would include such programs as Desktop Express (for the Macintosh) or Lotus Express, which can transmit files from WordPerfect, Lotus 1-2-3, and so on, while preserving the original formats. As with CompuServe, the ASCII should have carriage returns at the ends of all lines.

Unlike CompuServe, MCI Mail normally cannot accept binary files, sent with protocols such as XMODEM. You can't transmit spreadsheets or word processors in their native formats with boldface, underlining, and so on, at least not without products such as Lotus Express. But this could change. Check with MCI Mail for the latest. Meanwhile, if you use certain dial-up numbers, MCI Mail will recognize error-control procedures of MNP modems. That could be no small help if you're dialing up an MCI node in the States from, say, India.

10. After you've finished typing out the message or sending the file, type / at the beginning of a line and press Return. That tells MCI Mail, "Hey, I'm done!"

You'll see:

Handling:

11. Just press Return. Once you're more familiar with MCI, however, you can use "Handling:" to give the message special treatment. For example, by typing **RECEIPT**, you can ask MCI Mail to tell you when the recipient reads the letter.

(By the way, you can also type **RECEIPT** or enter other special handling features when you're addressing the letter. The format would be similar to this: **WILFORD BRUMLEY (RECEIPT)**. That's right. Skip a space and put the name of the feature in parentheses.)

12. After you see **Send?**, type **Y** and press Return. Your message is on the way!

HOW TO SEND TO COMPUSERVE

Without any extra charge, MCI Mail lets you send messages to CompuServe subscribers. And the procedure couldn't be simpler.

1. From MCI Mail's main command line, type **CR**.
2. After the **TO:** prompt, type the name of the person you want to reach, but add **(EMS)** after it.

Hence:

TO: WILFORD BRUMLEY (EMS)

You'll see:

Enter name of mail system.

EMS:

3. Type: **COMPUSERVE**

MCI Mail will respond:

   EMS 281-6320 COMPUSERVE

Columbus, OH

Enter recipient's mailbox information.

MBX:

4. Type the CompuServe number:

12345,6789

You'll see:

If additional mailbox lines are not needed press RETURN.

MBX:

5. Press the return, since you don't need another mailbox line. MCI will say:

TO: WILFORD BRUMLEY

   EMS: COMPUSERVE / MCI ID: 281-6320

   MBX: 12345,6789

Is this address correct (Yes or No)?

6. Type **Y**, hit Return, then proceed with the message as if communicating with another MCI subscriber.

Similar procedures will allow you to reach subscribers on other electronic services. For on-line guidance, type **HELP** followed by the name designating the service you want to reach:

For AT&T Mail use: **HELP ATTMAIL**.

For Dialcom use: **HELP DIALCOM**.

For Internet use: **HELP INTERNET**.

For SprintMail use: **HELP TELEMAIL**. By now, MCI may have changed the command to **HELP SPRINT** or **HELP SPRINTMAIL** to reflect the service's latest name.

For information on other networks, contact MCI Mail customer support at 800-444-6245 if the combinations of HELP and their names do not work.

SENDING TO FAX MACHINES VIA MCI MAIL

MCI Mail lets you call almost any fax machine in the world.[8] To learn fax prices, type **HELP**, skip a space, then enter the name of the country. You'll get information not only about fax prices and other odds and ends, but about information about telex, postal, and courier service to the country involved. Sorry, I must say "almost any" rather than "any" fax machine. As of this writing, alas, MCI Mail can't send faxes to Tibet.

Here's the fax procedure for most of the rest of the planet:

1. Once again, you'll use the old parentheses to tell MCI Mail you're going off the system. In other words, after the **TO:** prompt, you'll type:
WILFORD BRUMLEY (FAX)
MCI Mail will ask you to:
Enter country of recipient. Press RETURN if USA.
2. Follow the instructions from MCI. Press the Return after entering the name of the foreign country, if that's what you're doing. You'll now see a request for the recipient's fax number:
Recipient Fax No:
3. Type in the person's fax number and hit the Return key. There's no need to enter a **1** as you would for normal domestic faxes via long distance, or the country codes for foreign faxes. MCI Mail will provide them.
Now MCI will ask:
Options?
4. Type **N** for "No" when you answer the "options" question; then hit the return key. (Let's not clutter up this example with too many complexities. Not that these features are a waste—just try them later. They include the ability to change the number of times MCI tries to dial up the fax machine. Also, you can include your phone number and fax number on the cover page. There's no charge for that page.)
You'll now see:
Alternate Delivery?
5. Again, type **N** and press the return.

---

[8]You can even include pre-registered graphics, such as letterheads and signatures, in faxes sent via MCI. What better way to distribute press releases internationally when the material is time sensitive?

Then MCI will flash back at you something like this:
   TO: WILFORD BRUMLEY
   FAXno: 703-555-1212
   Is this address correct (Yes or No)? y
   6. Type **Y**, hit the return, and from here on treat the fax as you
would an ordinary MCI Mail message.

Delivery won't be instant; at times I've had to wait an hour or more.
Obviously you'll suffer a delay if the other person's fax machine is
busy. Then again, MCI's fax feature is so versatile that, in case one
machine is tied up, it can direct your message to another fax. Or the
message can go to a telex, electronic, or postal address. See your MCI
Mail manual for explanations.

TELEX ADDRESSES

You can send up to 100,000 words per telex—clearly a waste of money
at that length considering the economies of computerized mail. Lines
can be no more than 69 characters; answerbacks, no more than 15.
Again, remember that you can find out prices by typing **HELP** and the
name of the destination country.

Here's how to send telexes:

   1. After the **TO:** prompt, type the name of the recipient followed
by **(TELEX)**. Hence:
   TO: WILFORD BRUMLEY (TELEX)
MCI will ask the country of destination.
   2. Just press Return if you're sending a telex within the continental
United States. You'll see a list of carriers; choose the appropriate one.
   If the telex is going elsewhere—such as Alaska—enter the name of
the country or the telex country code. Have you typed in a code? Then
MCI Mail may give you a list of countries. Select the item number for
the destination.
   3. When asked for the recipient's telex number, type it in. You'll
see the country code. Do *not* type it in yourself. It's already there! Just
enter the telex number, avoiding letters, spaces, or punctuation. Avoid
mentioning the answerback. Hence:
   Recipient Telex No: 391-
   Recipient Telex No: 391-1128237

MCI Mail will now ask you for the recipient's answerback—telex's way of confirming that the message reached the right machine.

4. Type in the answerback if you *definitely* know it. If not, just hit the Return key. You'll see:

TO: WILFORD BRUMLEY
TLX: 3911128237 1128237 ABC BR
Is this address correct: (Yes or No)?

Type **Y** if the address is accurate, **N** if it isn't.

If you type **Y**, you now can go on to the rest of the message. If you type **N**, you'll re-enter the address.

MCI Mail will confirm the arrival of the telex, which may be delayed if the destination machine is busy. If the telex doesn't arrive, MCI Mail will say so.

USING MCI MAIL TO SEND PAPER LETTERS (INCLUDING EXPRESS DELIVERY)

For $2, you can send paper letters of up to three pages ($1 for every three additional pages) within the United States. Obviously you'll get more for your money if you single-space!

MCI Mail has printing offices in all regions of the U.S. and in several locations overseas. For details, use the trusty **HELP** command with the name of your destination country. You'll find out how long you can expect it will take letters to arrive—well, sort of. I notice that the listing for the U.S. says, "subject to local postal schedules." In Europe, that typically can mean several days.

The appropriate HELP section also will give you the details about express services. Domestically, overnight courier service costs $9.00 for up to six pages and $1.00 more for every three pages beyond that.

If you're sending a paper letter, do the following:

1. After the **TO:** prompt, type the person's name followed by a space and **(Paper)**.

In other words:

TO: WILFORD BRUMLEY (PAPER)

But if you're using the overnight service, do not type the above. Instead type:

TO: WILFORD BRUMLEY (ONITE)

You'll see:

Enter country of recipient. Press RETURN if USA.

2. If the letter is domestic, press the return and you'll see:

Destination is USA.

Fill out the address lines, confirm the information when MCI Mail asks you to do so, then go about your business if you're sending a normal MCI message.

3. If the letter is headed overseas, the procedure is the same, except that MCI will request the name of the country.

RECEIVING MESSAGES ON MCI MAIL

What if "God" returns to MCI Mail and wants to reach you that way rather than via a thunderbolt? How will you pick up a message from him? Or from a business associate? Almost as soon as you log on MCI, you'll see notification—in the form of:

Your INBOX has 1 message

Here's what to do next if you have "Advanced" service, the most common kind on MCI Mail.

1. After the word "Command:", you'll type **RE IN**, then press the Return key. You're telling MCI, "Let me read the contents of my 'inbox.' "

(Please note that, rather than just presenting you with the command line, MCI accounts with "Basic Service" are set up to display a menu of options. From the list, you can select "INBOX" or something similar. Press the return after you've made your choice.)

As soon as you press the Return key, you'll see the message scroll across your screen. MCI Mail will stop after displaying a just short of screenfull of text. It will say:

Press RETURN for more; type NO to stop

2. Hit Return to cause the message to continue, assuming there's any left.

Type **NO** and hit Return to bring you directly to a list of other options.

What are the other options? You'll be given chances, for example, to **ANS**—answer the message—without having to key in the sender's address. And if your inbox contains more than one message, an **NE** (short for "next") will help you retrieve the next one. Hit the Return key after typing **ANS** or **NE**.

3. From MCI's "Command:" line, "Advanced" subscribers can use the Read command for perusals of other material besides the contents of their inboxes:

RE DE retrieves messages that you've read before. The **DE** means "desk." After a week or so, MCI will delete automatically old, already read messages to make room on the system for more. Note the "already read." A message will sit months and months in your MCI mailbox if you don't read it.

RE OU fetches messages that you've already sent in the past week or so. The "OU" of course is short for "OUTBOX."

RE AL brings up "All": the contents of the Inbox, the Desk, and the Outbox.

What if you just want to see a list of messages—with the subjects and the names of senders and recipients? Need you read every one? No. Just use MCI Mail's **SC** option. For example **SC IN** will give you a list of all the messages that you haven't read, while **SC AL** will supply a list of everything sent and received in the past week.

You can target Read and Scan commands to bring up precisely the material you need. For instance, **RE INBOX SUBJECT "LAPTOPS" ON APRIL 2ND** brings up a message on the specified subject on the specified day. You can omit the day if you want to read *everything* about "laptops." **SC INBOX "LAPTOPS"** will give you a list of all messages on that subject without your having to read each (you could pick a number to select the message to peruse).

Please note that the fancy abilities to combine commands aren't available to people who use MCI Mail's "Basic Service." But normally MCI sets up accounts with "Advanced Service" at no extra charge. Ask for advanced. Otherwise you'll see cumbersome menus scrolling across your screen. The menus—the list of commands—will be easier to use at first, but they'll slow you down in the long run.

Whether you have "Basic" or "Advanced" service, be aware of some helpful commands for reading messages:

- **Ctrl-S** freezes a message as it's scrolling across your screen.
- **Ctrl-Q** resumes it.
- **Ctrl-O** followed by a Return will freeze the display, then take

you back to the command line. (These commands won't work with all
keyboards and all communications programs.)

There's another trick, too. If you're downloading a file, you can use
the "Print" option—**PR**—rather than the **RE** one that you normally
use to read messages. The **PR** will cause the message to scroll steadily
across your screen; meanwhile, your software can be saving the material.
PR, in fact, is handy even if you're just reading messages. You can
use it with **Ctrl-S** and **Ctrl-Q** to stop and resume the display whenever
you want, rather than halting in the places MCI Mail wants you to.

Here's one final tip—for people who favor the **RE** command over
the **PR** one, but who hate it when MCI Mail keeps asking them to press
the Return to move on to the next screen.

Type **ACCOUNT** at the "Command:" prompt. Then increase the
number of lines specified for your screen.

The default setting is 24 or 25—it's fewer for smaller screens. I
increased it to 80, my personal choice. Now I can watch maybe 800
words of text scroll past me before I must tell MCI I want to see more
of the message. Except when viewing the longest messages, I don't
have to press the carriage return to fetch new screens.

Via **Ctrl-O** and a tap on the Return key, I can stop the scrolling
whenever I want.

LOGGING OFF MCI MAIL

No problem here! Just type **EX**—short for "exit"—while you're on
the command line; then press Return.

THE TOP COMMERCIAL E-MAIL NETWORKS SERVING THE
UNITED STATES (AND A FEW ODDS AND ENDS ABOUT THEM)

CompuServe, with 550,000 mailboxes, is Network #1 in popularity in the
United States. It will be a good buy for many readers.

When shopping for an e-mail net, however, remember that what really
counts isn't the number of people on a network. The big question is
something else: How many of the subscribers do you really want to contact
or hear from? Consider the needs of your profession. Writers, for instance,

seem to favor CompuServe, MCI Mail, and GEnie because of the lower fees. At any rate—no pun meant—e-mail nets soon will be like telephone companies. Most should be hooking up to the others. Price, then, may become paramount.

By way of *Electronic Mail & Micro Systems*, here's a list of major commercial services and the present links between them. The list includes the number of mailboxes that you can reach on each e-mail service. The numbers come from statistics that the services or EM&MS editor Eric Arnum gave me. Be forewarned that some individual boxes can be entrances to major corporate systems, with hundreds or thousands of boxes of their own. Also, the mailbox statistics are rapidly changing.

■ CompuServe (800-848-8199 or 617-457-8600) has 550,000 mailboxes. It connects with MCI Mail and Internet (a net for academics and researchers). Via Internet, subscribers can reach BITNET and ARPANET. Also, as of 1991, CompuServe can exchange messages with many LANs; it can function as a hub, in fact, for messages from one LAN to another—a bargain for small users transmitting large files. See chapter 10 for more on CompuServe, GEnie, Prodigy, and MCI Mail.

■ Prodigy (800-PRODIGY, extension 205) has 340,000 mailboxes. Prodigy is a special case. This consumer-oriented service has enrolled 200,000 households, and each household can have more than one box. Unfortunately, Prodigy lacks links to other services. Prodigy wasn't designed with serious e-mail at the top of the list. Its special software—you can't use your normal communications program—won't even let you save your messages to your disk. On the other hand, you can send all the e-mail you want for free, as long as Prodigy's phone number is in your toll area.

To start up, you pay $49.95, giving you (as of this writing) a month's free service. The monthly charge is $9.95.

■ Dialcom, a service of BT Tymnet (800-872-7654), has 318,000 mailboxes; it connects with AT&T Mail and MCI Mail. Dialcom is internationally oriented and has databases galore—it's more focused toward business and government than toward individuals. Network charges are $5 an hour to reach Dialcom via Tymnet, plus connect time of $14 an hour for light users, and $.05 a kilobyte transmitted. $25 a month minimum. Part of British Telecom.

■ Western Union EasyLink (800-779-1111) has 250,000 mailboxes. It connects with AT&T Mail and General Electric Information Services.

EasyLink's market is primarily corporate. Twenty-five-hundred character messages cost $.68 when sent at 1,200 or 2,400 bps during business hours (20 percent during off-peak hours). There's no registration fee, and the minimum usage fee is $25 a month, starting with the second month of service. Among EasyLink's specialties are telex connections and links with corporation office automation systems. With EasyLink, you can converse instantaneously with other telex users.

■ GEnie (800-638-9636) has more than 200,000 mailboxes. Presently it has no links with the other networks, though this may well change. Forums, software, games, and shopping are the main attractions here, not e-mail. Registration is $29.95. The basic after-hours rates for 2,400 bps should be $10 or less in areas with local dial-up numbers for GEnie.

■ SprintMail, once known as TeleMail (800-835-3638), has 200,000 mailboxes and hooks into AT&T Mail, Dialcom, and MCI Mail and a number of foreign systems, including those licensed for the same technology. SprintMail is very good for communications with LANs. SprintMail has local access points abroad, meaning easier and cheaper connections. Recently Sprint International, the provider of US SprintMail, announced plans for a major data communications service in Russia. Annual registration is $25. The monthly minimum, not to be confused with a flat rate, is $20. SprintMail charges between $.94 and $1.25 for 7,500-character messages, depending on the time of day. For longer messages, the rates would be cheaper. Users of BBS's might check out a sister service, PC Pursuit, which for $30 a month gives your 30 hours of connections outside business hours to thousands of local BBS's. Call the same number, 800-835-3638.

■ MCI Mail (800-444-6245) has 110,000 mailboxes. It connects with CompuServe, Dialcom, SprintMail (the old Telemail), AT&T Mail, Internet, the PT Postel service in Italy, and the MISSIVE service in France, among others. "They price their services," Eric Arnum says, "to be attractive to individuals." What's more, many Fortune 500 companies are on MCI Mail, including IBM. Typical cost: $1 for 7,500 characters. MCI Mail, needless to say, is a hit with many consultants and other individuals doing business with corporate America.

■ AT&T Mail (800-624-5672) has 80,000 mailboxes and connects with Dialcom, MCI Mail, SprintMail, and Western Union EasyLink. There are also some interesting international connections here: Telecom-Canada-Envoy 100, Transpac-Atlas-400 (a French network), KDD Nessavia (Japan), TeleDelta TEDE 400 (Sweden), OTC MPS400 (Australia),

DACOM DACOM MHS (Korea), P&T Telephone MailNet 400 (Finland), and the Helsinki Telephone Company (also Finland).

AT&T Mail seems keen on going after the economy-minded MCI Mail market. In many ways it's still more expensive. But in at least one shocking way, as you'll discover in a moment, AT&T may be undercutting MCI.

Messages on AT&T cost $.40 for 400 characters or less (plus $.20 for the message-creation time if you're composing on-line—an expense not incurred on MCI Mail). Charges are $.80 for between 401 and 7500 characters; they're $.80 for additional blocks of 7,500 characters. You pay $.45 extra per 7,500 characters for composing on-line, but not if you're uploading with communications software.

And now for the shock: an AT&T customer support representative tells me that there's no charge for communicating with MCI Mail boxes. Apparently, then, if you compose off-line, you spend just $.80 for 7,500 characters to reach a colleague on MCI Mail—less than the usual MCI-to-MCI cost of $1. What's this? *AT&T* underpricing MCI? Is the cheapest way to use MCI to use AT&T?

Registration and annual renewals are $30 a year for basic AT&T Mail service. That excludes mass storage of files, among other things, available through an enhanced service at another $10 a month.

Like many of the other networks, AT&T Mail offers fax, telex, and postal links.

There is one little wrinkle that AT&T provides without charging extra —something still rare in commercial e-mail: the ability to retrieve a message from a *telephone* rather than a computer. Just dial up an 800 number from an ordinary touch-tone phone and AT&T will read your mail in an electronically synthesized voice. Not bad for $30 a year! Theoretically some people without computers could sign up for AT&T Mail—just to use this feature to retrieve messages intended for them.

AFTERWORD

Years ago, in my book *The Silicon Jungle*, I alluded to a friend of my parents, an old woman who bragged about a song she had written: "Marconi, Marconi, the World Is at Your Feet." That was her mindset. Perry Como was visiting America's living rooms in living color, even then the videorecorder may have been around, but she was still stuck on Marconi.

Are we not, many of us, just like the woman? Is anything more ephemeral than the latest technology? I wrote my *Jungle* on a Kaypro II portable computer twenty-five times the weight of the more powerful Poqet.

Today's technomarvels—the Poqets, the Psions, the fax cards for laptops—will pale beside the surprises of the future. Even the Dynabook may one day seem passé. The Dynabook? Yes. Alan Kay, the computer expert, predicted a laptop through which users could call up billions of bytes of knowledge from everywhere. Already several computer manufacturers have named their laptops after his "Dynabook." Maybe they can get away with it. It was Kay, after all, whose imagination helped pave the way for the laptop industry.

Eventually, perhaps, a true Dynabook will be born. But I can also see a much different kind of portable computer: one built into a pair of spectacles. Don't confuse CompuSpecs with the Private Eye discussed on page 45. CompuSpecs would look like true eyeglasses, and their frames would house the whole computer—hardly a pipe dream if you bear in mind:

■ The unceasing miniaturization of circuits.

■ The fact that in the next few decades computers may be able to understand our every word, through advanced voice recognition.

■ The possibility that the screens and trimmings can be refined. In the future a quick voice command could shrink or expand the computer-generated images. So, wearing the CompuSpecs, the user won't feel overly detached from the world at large.

Move ahead a few more decades. Even the glasses might go. So, too, might the need for voice recognition. Instead, CompuBands would replace CompuSpecs. These bands, worn around the head, would pick up brainwaves through which we would give commands and enter data. The process would work in reverse as well—through the same human-machine ESP. (I use the term *ESP* loosely. Here, it means an electronic equivalent of what a few brave researchers at Duke and Princeton have been investigating. I don't know if ESP exists naturally.)

No skin would be pierced, no electrodes implanted. Just by removing the band, the human could divorce from the machine. CompuBands, in short, might save us from the grotesque human-machine unions that Strangelovian futurists have on our agenda.

However far off the CompuBands might seem (for now I'll leave it to crazies outside the White House to pick up brainwaves), please bear in mind a statement by Arthur C. Clarke. He said that experts are more often wrong in claiming that something can't be done than they are in saying that it can. Anyone who thinks otherwise—anyone who can't see far enough past the laptops of today, whether in forecasting the next century or the next gaggle of new product introductions—may as well be singing the Marconi song.

APPENDIX 1
SCREENWRIGHT:
A DELIGHTFUL $49.95 PROGRAM
FOR SCREENWRITERS
AND PLAYWRIGHTS

Screenwriters are naturals for laptops. They're a peripatetic crowd, even if some of the travel is only back and forth from the den to the swimming pool. Whether screenwriters use laptops or desktops, old problems dog them. Hollywood script formats have long bedeviled even the brightest of computerized writers. You must use one set of margins for dialogue, another for stage directions, and so on; and you can't split up characters' speeches between pages, at least not without a "continued." Even theatrical scripts can be hair pullers for technophobic playwrights. To hell with computers. Anyone for Mont Blanc pens? In the 1980s a program called Scriptor took care of the main formatting problems, but another woe remained for many writers—coughing up several hundred dollars for the software. Even Scriptor left some things to be desired.

Luckily, Paul D. Nadler, a playwright hacker in Brooklyn, has been tinkering over the years with a low-cost rival to Scriptor. ScreenWright Professional 5.0 is a good bet for laptops and desktops alike.

ScreenWrite Professional is more than just a formatter to turn ASCII files into scripts. It's a word processor that responds to WordStar-style commands or whatever others you assign to the customizable keyboard. Of course, you can still compose on your own word processor, just so it can produce ASCII for the formatter.

Even Nadler admits that ScreenWright lacks some of Scriptor's wrinkles; for example, his software can't arrange for a sentence not to spill over to the next page. However, he says he's addressing that problem and others. After six years of tinkering, ScreenWright has reached the point where the National Film Board of Canada considers it its official software. A typist for *Back to the Future II* and *Back to the Future III* used Paul Nadler's brainchild, reportedly, and Nadler has heard that a number of ScreenWright-created scripts are on the verge of production. Nadler himself is the author of four plays, including a one-act work that Common Ground, a New York theater, was to produce in 1990. Not having seen *Cabin Fever*, I don't know if it's good. Nadler, however, just may have written the world's first software documentation bound for Broadway. In SWTRY.ME, the program's sample script, a mythical user named Sam holds a ScreenWright diskette in one hand and a peanut butter sandwich in the other while his partner Hilda scolds him.

```
                                      MEDIUM SHOT
                    HILDA
               (Grabbing the
               diskette away from
               him)
Hey, you want to get P.B.J. all over it?
Let me make the backup now; then you can
drool on it all you want.


                                      MEDIUM SHOT
                    SAM
Oh, yeah?  And what "safe place" are you
going to put it in?


                                      MEDIUM SHOT
                    HILDA
               (Inserting the
               diskette in the
               computer)
Someplace where you'll never touch it --
the laundry room.
```

Nadler has designed ScreenWright with movie scripts and teleplays in mind, although the formatting powers also will be useful to some playwrights.[1] His software, alas, can't do the double-column format

---

[1]Many playwrights, maybe even most, will find that their usual software suffices, since the formatting demands are less rigorous than those of screenplays.

used by documentary producers, especially the TV variety. A fix is coming. Meanwhile, regular word processors, such as XyWrite and Microsoft Word, can offer the double columns.

ScreenWright won't please everyone. A Washington-area writer complained that the commands were too difficult. Even in its more recent, polished version, the program does demand time to learn. Then again, other people—especially old WordStar hands—may pick it up easily.

Limitations notwithstanding, ScreenWright is fast and adequately powerful and flexible; it offers, for example, the ability to copy and move blocks, WordStar fashion, or to set margins. Thrifty scriptwriters or playwrights could probably get along with ScreenWright as their only word processor (it will suffice for letter writing and other light work). Almost any printer will run ScreenWright if you give the program the proper commands; Nadler says he'll aid owners of oddball machines. What's more, you can adjust the color settings if the program does not display properly on your LCD screen.

At more than 300K—including a 73K help file with which you may dispense—ScreenWright is hardly as compact as a QEdit-style program. But it's still a dwarf compared to WordPerfect, Word, or some of the other programs used to create scripts. Remember, ScreenWright includes a complete word processor for scriptwriters, not just a formatter.

For a copy of ScreenWright, send $49.95 to Paul D. Nadler, 338 Prospect Place, Apartment 4C, Brooklyn, New York 11238, telephone (718) 638-0103.

APPENDIX 2
SOFTWARE TIPS FOR OWNERS
OF THE MAC PORTABLE

Jerry Oppenheimer, the author of *Barbara Walters: an Unauthorized Biography*[1] and coauthor of a biography of Rock Hudson, swears by his Mac portable. If I owned a Mac, I'd swear at it. As I said earlier, I hate mice, and I'm not fond of trackballs, either. Even at the Macintosh Portable's recently lowered price ($5,499 for a model with a 40 megabyte hard drive) this is not the best computer for me. It won't ever be, in fact, not unless the Mac can run my favorite word processor, sell for still less, and be more luggable by non-Olympians.

Think I'm full of it? My friend Jerry Oppenheimer certainly does. In an ecumenical spirit, however, I'm passing on a list of programs that he finds useful for the portable Mac. He hastens to point out that because the portable Mac's screen is so sharp, the laptop can run just about any Macintosh software. There are exceptions, such as older graphics programs that won't work with the latest operating system that the portable requires. "But," Jerry says, "you can use newer, better programs to do the same things."

Here are some of Jerry's favorite programs:

■ The Mac version of Microsoft Works. "I like version 1.1 better because 2.0 has a built-in macro facility that I don't like. It isn't as flexible and easy as the add-on macro program that I do use. The other reason is that Works' macro facility takes up space on the menu bar

[1](St. Martin's Press, New York, 1990, $19.95)

where I'd rather have a clock and calendar." Microsoft is at 1 Microsoft Way, Redmond, Washington 98052 (telephone 206-882-8080). Version 2.0 costs $295 (ask about 1.1 if you prefer that instead).

■ The Tempo 2.0 macro program. "It's simple to operate. Just a couple of steps and you've automated your keyboard for whatever commands you want. When you make a macro, you can make it a universal one. You can use it in other programs on your hard disk. Within the Tempo menu, you just select 'Record.' And then you type what the macro is to be. And then you save it. It's easy to choose whether you want the macro to apply to all programs or just the one that you're in." Tempo 2.0 costs $149.95 from Affinity Microsystems, 1050 Walnut St., Suite 425, Boulder, Colorado 80302 (303-442-4840 or 800-367-6771).

■ WriteNow 2.2, from T/Maker Company. This is "a backup word processor" for Jerry that he uses from time to time when he wants a change of pace from Works, which in version 1.1 lacks a word counter. "WriteNow is packed with a lot of power and it takes up a very small amount of disk space compared to other word processors. If you're traveling, especially with a portable without a hard disk, WriteNow leaves plenty of space for the operating system and your data. You can see the page numbers, headers, and footers on the screen with your copy. It's true what-you-see-is-what-you-get. I don't use WriteNow all the time simply because I'm more used to Works. I've had Works macroed so long that I can work with it blindly. But WriteNow is easy to learn. If Works disappeared from my hard drive and I didn't have a backup, WriteNow would be my immediate next choice. It's the word processor that Steve Jobs bundled with the NeXT computer." WriteNow 2.2 sells for $195 from T/Maker Company, 1390 Villa Street, Mountain View, California 94041 (415-962-0195).

■ Microphone 1.1. The software house, Software Ventures Corporation, is at least up to version 3.0, but Jerry Oppenheimer's philosophy here is, "If it ain't broke, don't fix it." He likes Microphone 1.1 because "like many other Mac programs, it's easy to use. My basic use of a modem is to get on a BBS or send copy to publishers. It does it easily. It also easily downloads software from bulletin boards." Ask about the price and availability of Microphone 1.1. The program can be bought in at least two forms—Microphone 1.5 ($149) and Microphone II, Version 3.0 ($295). Software Ventures Corporation is at 2907

Claremont Ave., Suite 220, Berkeley, California 94705 (800-336-6477 or 800-336-6478).

BigThesaurus, informally known as BigThes. "It's incredibly powerful and gives you synonyms, antonyms, complete definitions on-line. It's also a desk accessory [RAM resident]. You can write a macro to call it up with one keystroke. Say you're writing the word *bizarre*. You can hit the menu to 'Look up selected' word, and it does it. Then you can replace it. It's amazing. I couldn't live without it. You can set up the program so you have only the features you need and don't take up memory space with others. Any writer with a Mac should have BigThes." The program costs $99.95 from Deneba Software, 3305 Northwest Ave., Miami, Florida (305-594-6965 or 800-622-6827)

■ The Mac version of GOfer. "Your whole hard drive becomes a database. GOfer lets you find any one word. If you wrote the date January 15, 1942, in a small file that's one of hundreds on your disk, GOfer could find it in seconds. And you could call it up and insert it in the file you were working with. Your disk literally becomes a complete database for you without having to put in keywords. GOfer is a desk accessory, and if you're working on a major project like a book, it's invaluable." Contact Microlytics, One Tobey Village Office Park, Pittsford, New York 14534 (716-248-9620 or 800-828-6293). Price is $79.95.

■ DiskTools Plus. "It's a really good calendar and scheduling program. You can have it on your 'desktop' always. You can write a macro to call it up. You can schedule way into the future. I use the calendar on a daily basis. I used to write my things to do on a desk calendar.[2] Now I do it on the Mac since it's portable and always with me. If I need a calculator, I can use the DiskTools Plus calculator." DiskTools Plus costs $49.95 from Electronic Arts, 1820 Gateway Dr., San Mateo, California 94404 (415-571-7171 or 800-245-4525).

---

[2]Oppenheimer uses paper to back up references to his most important appointments.

APPENDIX 3
CELLULAR MODEMS FOR LAPTOPS

Donald Trump, the man who must have been born with a car phone in his hand, may be together with Ivana once more. I don't know. News of the breakup has just filtered out. Whatever happens, I can imagine the teeth grinding of the Trumps' respective public relations people as charges ricochet back and forth. What do you do if you're Donald or Ivana's PR man, you're stuck in a traffic jam on the way back from the Hamptons, and the car radio has just passed on dirt from the other side? Let's say you want to retaliate instantly with a detailed written statement typed on your laptop. Your favorite gossip columnist is approaching her deadline, and her fax is broken. If only you could modem the whole truth directly from your car to her e-mail box! Besides, in preparing statements, you may want to dial up a database to make sure your forthcoming statement won't conflict with a past one.

The answer could be a cellular modem, a way to send computer messages from your car.

Yes, the above example is exotic and outrageously hypothetical. But others aren't. Miles from the nearest telephone, a real estate agent may want to fetch data from her multiple-listing file immediately, while the client is in the right frame of mind. A conscientious executive can more easily keep atop corporate business while camping in the Rockies. And a savvy newspaper reporter, sending stories from a hotel with a horrid switchboard, may favor a cellular hookup over the "land-line" variety. So may a field service technician working in a client's office.

Cellular phones and cellular modems aren't just for the road—or for the rich.

But why *cellular* modems? Cellular systems don't recognize the dial tones that a normal modem sends. One solution would be to use the cellular phone to dial the connection, then tell a conventional modem to start "talking." Another would be to buy a tone-conversion device. Just the same, that still leaves open other questions. Normal modems might be perfect for many people, but they aren't the best if you want the fastest, most reliable transmission of data. With a conventional modem you may even have to slow down to a poky 300 bps.

Consider the basic cellular concept. In a car, you're moving from cell to cell—areas covered by the radio telephone equipment that is your link to the regular phone network. As soon as you pass from one cell to another, you disrupt computer transmissions and reception. The vagaries of cellular radio can even jumble communications with cellular equipment that stays put. That's largely because of the dynamics of cellular radio networks. Suppose an army of commuters is "parked" on a crowded freeway near you. Then, even if you haven't left your hotel room, you may be passed on to another cell because you're closer to it than some of the commuters are.

This "hand-off" problem won't defeat MNP Class 5 and some other popular protocols, even if they weren't designed for cellular use. Many engineers say mobile businesspeople don't need cellular modems. (See page 188 to learn about an add-on to MagicSoft's MTEZ communications program, which is supposed to let even non-MNP 5 modems work over cellular phones.)

Still, hand-off is just one of many possible glitches. The results haven't always been happy when users of regular modems tried them on cellular systems under harsh conditions. Radio waves fade in fringe areas, and different versions of the same signals bounce off hills and buildings and clash with each other. The cellular networks add their own noises. Under the worst circumstances—and you just know that Murphy's Law will prevail when you have a crucial draft of a contract to transmit—a modem in the car can't even begin to talk to the one in the office. None other than Microcom, the same company that created the MNP protocols, is aware of MNP's 5's limits. It now offers MNP 10, a new protocol for cellular modems. Spectrum Cellular Corporation, meanwhile, the first maker of cellular modems, has long had a standard of its own. With SPCL Adverse Environment Protocol, the company claims 100 percent error-correction. ("SPCL" is short for "Spectrum Cellular.")

Outside the United States, similar protocol wars rage, and it could be years before the Consultative Committee on International Telephony and Telegraphy (CCITT), the organization responsible for global communications, straightens out the mess.

I won't enter the cellular protocol debate, then, and say you must buy your cellular modems from company X or Y. Spectrum claims to have the largest user base of cellular modems, more than ten thousand, but there are a number of companies either making cellular modems or on the verge of doing so.[1] Look around! Compare a whole range of traits and features. The following questions should help.

Question One: Is the Modem Internal or External?

Spectrum now makes cellular modems on cards for major brands of laptops. Other manufacturers surely will follow. And if you don't want too many boxes to clutter up your car, an internal modem certainly holds promise.

The advantage of an external modem for cellular is the same as with one for normal purposes. You can plug it into the RS-232 ports of a number of machines.

You may find that an external modem won't be that large. Spectrum by now may be marketing a pocket-size cellular modem. Touchbase Systems and Vocal Technologies very likely will have similar products out. Vocal's modem may sell for as little as several hundred dollars and be able to transmit fax as well as data.

[1.] Spectrum is at 2710 Stemmons Freeway, 800 North Tower, Dallas, Texas 75207 (214-630-9825). Some of the other players include Microcom, 500 River Ridge Drive, Norwood, Massachusetts 02062 (617-551-1000); Telebit, 1315 Chesapeake Terrace, Sunnyvale, California 94089 (480-734-4433); Touchbase Systems, 160 Laurel Avenue, Northport, New York 11768 (516-261-0423); Vocal Technology, 332 Scott Boulevard, Santa Clara, California 95034 (408-980-5181); and Compuquest, 801 Morse Avenue, Schaumburg, Illinois, 60193 (708-529-2552). As of this writing, Hayes isn't marketing cellular modems. Presumably, however, it too will be a very major player. Contact Hayes Customer Service, P.O. Box 105203, Atlanta, Georgia, 30348 (404-441-1617).

LAPTOP-CELLULAR COMBOS: A SHORTCUT FOR THE ELECTRONIC TRAVELER

Laptops are enough of a mystery to many computer novices. How can you make certain that your portable PC will work with a cellular phone and modem? The best bet may be to buy everything in one swoop. Here are some companies to contact:

■ GRiD Systems (415-656-4700). It's selling two laptop-cellular combinations. Priced at $7,290, the eighteen-pound deluxe model uses an 80386 processor that can coast more than four hours on a single battery charge—not bad at all for a zippy 386. An economy version with a slower 8086 processor goes for $4,545. You can remove the cellular equipment from either of the computers. GRiD claims that its error correction will preserve modem links when you're driving into the next cell.

■ Intelligent Technology Corporation (800-356-3493). It makes several laptop-phone-modem combos listing for between $2,400 and $8,695, including an 80386 machine that boasts a VGA display and runs at 16 megahertz. The company as of this writing uses the MNP class 5 protocol rather than the SPCL protocol. But it seems headed in the direction of MNP class 10, another protocol designed with cellular in mind.

■ Spectrum Cellular (214-630-9825), which works closely with computer manufacturers.

In addition, you might see if the industry has come up with yet another possibility—a cellular modem built into a cellular phone. "We've been in contact with many different kinds of manufacturers— those of telephones, hand-held computers, laptop computers, and special systems integrators," John Rule, now Spectrum's president, told me as he sped along a Florida freeway. "They're all thinking about cellular communications as part of the solution." That day Rule had been in Boca Raton, one of the spawning grounds of the original IBM PC (although, as you'd expect, he wasn't about to answer the obvious questions).

Question Two: What About the Connection With the Cellular Phone?

Here are some possibilities:

■ A cellular phone with a cellular modem built into it.

■ One with provisions for letting cellular modems go between the transceiver (the main part of the cellular phone) and the handset.

■ A cellular phone with an RJ-11 jack. General Electric and Radio Shack sell such products.

■ A device like the $480 "CelJack," from Telular of Wilmette, Illinois—intended for both cellular and conventional modems. The CelJack goes between the transceiver and the handset and includes an RJ-11 for the modem. The CelJack can even provide a dial tone that a noncellular modem understands; you can dial out the normal way with your regular communications program, such as ProComm or CrossTalk.

"The CelJack will physically and electrically support all modems," says Bill DeNicolo, president of Telular. "We support both the auto-dial and auto-answer functions of a modem." So people can leave you computer messages while you're on the go. You can bypass the ignition key and have power reaching your computer and modems at all times.

CelJack-like products, needless to say, work with fax. For all practical purposes, a CelJack is a pseudo–telephone line.

Telular is at 1215 Washington Avenue, Wilmette, Illinois 60091; the telephone number is (708) 256-8000.

■ What Spectrum calls an IntelliJack. It's expected to list for $295 and offer an RJ-11 connection for cellular modems. Yes, as you might guess, you can use the same modem back at the office, plugging it into the wall.

As the general rule in computerdom, never, never buy any equipment without confirming that it will get along with the other boxes. If you really want to play it safe, you might consider a laptop that comes with a cellular phone and modem (see "Laptop-Cellular Combos: Shortcuts for Electronic Travelers" earlier in this appendix). Contact the maker of your laptop if you already own a portable. You may find that the company has teamed up with a manufacturer of cellular-related equipment to market a full system. Then you'll know where to go for the cellular modem and the rest.

Question Three: How Does the Cellular Modem Handle the Issue of Talking to Ordinary Modems at the Other End?

Remember, a cellular modem may very likely not be compatible with a normal model—unable to communicate directly. Spectrum has offered several choices:

■ Dialing a special number at a cellular telephone company equipped with a device to relay the call to a normal modem in a format that the second modem will appreciate. There in the car—or wherever you are—you may punch an asterisk or pound sign and dial the appropriate number at the phone company. Then, after a delay, you'll dial the number of the ordinary modem that you're trying to reach. You probably can include all of the numbers in the dialing string that you enter through your communications program. Remember, you can usually use a comma to indicate a two-second delay, or however long you need. Not all of the local cellular service providers may offer this special number option, but Spectrum says it's available in more than one hundred major markets throughout the United States plus all those in Canada. The company hopes to add European, Pacific Rim, and Latin markets next.

■ Calling a modem in your own office that uses the cellular modem's error-correction protocol. For maybe $500 or $600 list—prices may be lower now—Spectrum sells a cellular modem that plugs into an RJ-11–style jack.

■ Phoning (from the field) a special device in your own office that will act like the gadgetry at the phone company. That is, it will redirect the call to the conventional modem you're trying to reach. The destination modem—let's say it's a customer's—then receives the call in a form it can handle. For several thousand dollars Spectrum will sell SpanNet, a conversion device that can serve two people dialing into it at the same time.

■ Dialing up a network, such as CompuServe, that has numbers that accept calls from cellular modems. The person you're trying to reach can then handle information like anything else received over CompuServe. Needless to say, you can use a cellular to tap into databases on CompuServe and other compatible networks, such as Telenet (which your cellular modem can dial up on an 800 number).

Of course, some cellular modems can double as conventional modems—sending and receiving the normal signals—so you don't have to buy both varieties. Remember, if mobile cellular modems are extremely versatile, they may work with RJ-11–style jacks back at the office.

Question Four: Does the Modem Respond to AT Commands and Handle Normal Communications Software and Protocols?

Ideally this won't be an issue. At least in Spectrum's case, the emphasis seems to be on the use of regular AT commands.

So conventional communications software probably should work fine. *Should.* I have no idea how file-transfer protocols, such as XMODEM, will respond under cellular conditions, even with error correction. Check with the modem maker.

Typically, file-transfer protocols like XMODEM and Kermit should work within the cellular modem protocols. Rule says his company will make some modems with the V.42 and V.42bis protocols as well as the proprietary SPCL protocol.

Question Five: How Fast Does the Modem Go?

Among cellular modems, the claimed speed champ as of this writing seems to be the Telebit CellBlazer, which lists for $1,495 and works with an RJ-11 adapter. Give the CellBlazer a good connection, and it supposedly may race as fast as 16,800 bps. Skeptics say 16,800 is a "clear-day" speed and a more typical speed is 6,000 to 8,000 bps. And it's true; you can't judge by peak bps alone. Size, weight, power type (AC or DC?), power consumption, and ease of interface with cellular telephones also matter. Still, my hacker friends love Telebit's "land-line" modems, the ones for normal phone lines. The modems cleverly adjust the speeds in small increments to give you the maximum bps possible under conditions of the moment. Telebit's PEP modem protocol is renowned for being the telecommunications version of the Land Rover: a vehicle, so to speak, for all terrain. That's one reason why I'm not going to say, "Buy MNP 10" or "Get SPCL!" You decide.

Do, however, insist on at least 2,400 bps. That is the standard now.

And it's rising. For example, a new modem from Spectrum, for both office and car, uses V.42bis with SPCL protocol to whiz up to what the companies say is an effective speed of 9,600 bps under ideal conditions. V.42bis can more than triple the speed of data transmission if everything is right. And that's not such a bad idea, considering the great expense of cellular communications compared to the land-line variety. Typical costs are $.35 to $.65 a minute during the business day. So modems going at 2,400 bps and even higher speeds may justify your investment faster than you'd expect.

Please note that modems are only part of the speed equation. The quality of the signal matters a lot and may even be the difference between using a regular modem and having to buy a cellular one. If you haven't selected your cellular phone company, see which one offers the most cells in the area where you'll be. And try to buy a cellular phone with an output of three watts, the highest available.

Also consider buying an external antenna if you'll be in a fixed (nonmobile) location in a rural area. Ideally the antenna will be directional, which will boost your effective power and allow faster transmission of data; it also will lessen the chances of your being handed off to another cell site. Such antennas commonly are about two feet long or less.

Finally, if you want the powerful signal, see if you can't power your cellular modem from a car battery or other external source, rather than from the ones inside the cellular radio itself.[2]

Question Six: Can the Modem Handle Fax as Well as Data?

Fax capabilities should become quite common in cellular modems. Vocal already is designing a fax-data combination, and Spectrum expects to be selling one for $695. You can see the present trend. It's toward multipurpose devices that can fit into the existing world of data communications.[3]

[2]Most of the suggestions related to signal strength come from John C. Dvorak and Nick Anis, *Dvorak's Guide to PC Telecommunications* (Berkeley, Calif.: Osborne/McGraw-Hill, 1990).

[3]IBM and Motorola have teamed up to market a new nationwide mobile data network (not cellular based). Let's hope that the network allows all brands of modems to be used. If not, that would be a blow against the compatibility and competition that could lower the costs of sending data from portable equipment.

John Rule, Spectrum Cellular president, told me that his company will woo the same customers who would buy the usual, premium modems (with high speeds, fancy error-control schemes, and the rest). Let's hope that this strategy works for Spectrum and similar companies. If the price gap isn't that big between a cellular modem and the normal one you need, then you may as well buy the former. That's the direction in which cellular modems ideally will go.

The alternative would be for cellular modems to be exotic gadgets affordable only to Donald Trump's retinue and the rest of the limousine set.

CELLULAR GOES INTERNATIONAL[4]

Some 3.2 million cellular phones are in use in the United States, and almost 5 million worldwide. By the year 2000, however, if the optimists are right, there'll be between 100 and 150 million subscribers. You'll be able to drive from Nome to Santiago, Chile, and be in constant touch. As soon as 1992, cellular radio coverage will blanket almost the entire United States.

Luckily, the United States shares—or is expected to share—a common cellular standard with Canada and a number of other countries:

■ Australia
■ New Zealand
■ Mexico
■ Most of the Caribbean
■ Most of South and Central America

If you go to any of the above countries, check with your local cellular provider about the possibility of your transmitting calls from those areas. It will depend on whether your cellular company has an agreement with sister companies abroad.

If so? Then you may be able to start making cellular voice and data calls as soon as you step off the plane. What a contrast to having to struggle with strange and balky switchboards at your hotel. You may even be able to receive incoming calls if you leave the necessary numbers with the people who'll be calling.

[4]Thanks to Bill DeNicolo for information for this sidebar.

Mind you, your host country will have to use the U.S. standard for cellular radio: Advanced Mobile Phone Systems (AMPS). Two other standards are:

1. Total Access Communication System (TACS), in use in the United Kingdom and Kuwait.
2. Nordic Mobile Telephone System (NMT)—favored in Iceland, all of Scandinavia, part of West Germany, Turkey, Saudi Arabia, Spain, Malaysia, and Indonesia.

Unless you use different cellular equipment, you'll probably be out of luck in those countries if you're hoping to benefit from cellular radio.

APPENDIX 4
FROM LAPTOP TO DESKTOP (OR VICE VERSA)—AND A FEW WORDS ABOUT LOCAL AREA NETWORKS

How can you get your laptop to share files more easily with your desktop or with other computers at your office hooked up to a local area network? Among the possible techniques are:

1. Using the same formats for floppy disks.
2. Taking advantage of memory cards.
3. Piping your material by cable from computer to computer.
4. Modeming it over the phone lines.
5. Using a LAN card or other LAN adapter.
6. Hooking into a zero-slot LAN, a term for a network that doesn't require a special card or other adapter.

Floppy Disks

This is one of the easiest ways of sharing files, and the method I normally use. When I bought my present desktop, an AT clone, I insisted that I have drives for both 3.5- and 5.25-inch disks. I was working on a WordStar book then, and I wished to be able to try out WordStar customization procedures on my desktop and write up the results on a borrowed laptop. I wanted to *write* as I tinkered with the program, not just take notes and compose later. So I had to be able to (1) take a partly completed chapter on a disk from the desktop, (2) add new material to the floppy while I was writing with the portable, and (3) copy the expanded file back to the desktop's hard disk.[1]

There are other occasions when I relish disk interchangeability. If I feel trapped up inside my apartment and want a change of scenery, I may want to relocate to the banks of the Potomac River. When I return, I don't want to have to mess with cables or modems.

Granted, complications do exist. Some desktop computers don't have enough bays in their cabinets to allow for an extra drive, or their disk controllers work only with 5.25-inch drives, or their Basic Input Operating System (BIOS) is incompatible, or they use early versions of the MS-DOS operating system that aren't designed for 3.5-inch drives.

How can you cope with the different formats, then? Consider the MegaMate drives made by Micro Solutions (132 West Lincoln Highway, De Kalb, Illinois 60115, 815-756-3421). It comes with a card that even novices can install. The card fits in the half-size card slot of a PC-, XT-, or AT-class machine. There are cheaper products—the MegaMate listed for $349 in late 1989—but this one includes special software, hooks up much more easily than many of the others, and has garnered wonderful reviews. MegaMate will even work with the ancient DOS 2.0. What's more, it can format and otherwise use both 720K and 1.44-meg disks. Even if your portable can work only with 720K disks, the 1.44-meg capacity may come in handy for backing up small databases, long reports, book manuscripts, and other lengthy documents.

You can also go in the opposite direction and buy an external 5.25-inch drive for your laptop. Ideally you can use a drive from the manufacturer; consider buying by mail to keep the price down. There are also third-party drives available, though before buying you should check with other owners of your make of machine to be certain those drives are absolutely compatible with the computer. Also, be careful about another kind of incompatibility. In the 3.5-inch world, almost all 1.44-

---

[1]Thanks to my BBS friends David Labell, Paul Lazar, and Bill Parke for helping me sort out the oft-confusing facts on floppy formats.

meg drives can successfully format 720K disks to be read later on 720K drives; but in the 5.25-inch world, not all 1.2-meg drives on AT-class machines can successfully deal with 360K floppies. If your desktop can't reliably write 360K disks but your colleague's machine reads in that format only, you may have to buy an external 360K drive for one of your machines. A laptop external drive could cost anywhere from $150 to $300.

If you order the appropriate external drive—truly compatible with your laptop—you should be able to hook it up almost instantly. Probably it will just plug into your parallel port or into a special drive port. If you do use the parallel port, you won't be able to use the printer at the same time. But how many people want to print and transfer files at the same time?

Memory Cards

Some notebook computers—the Portfolio, Psion, and Poqet, for instance—accept memory devices the size of credit cards. (See chapter two.) Such machines can be a quick way of swapping information between your laptop and desktop, if you can buy add-ons to let the latter read the cards. As of spring 1990, the cards were costly, but this should change, perhaps very quickly. Meanwhile, if your budget is tight, you might instead use a cable to zip files back and forth. A third approach would be to plug an external disk drive into your portable computer, write to a floppy, then have your desktop computer read it. Not all laptops, of course, allow use of external drives with a format that desktop machines can read. Check with the maker of your laptop.

Using a Cable Between Your Desktop and Laptop

Since your desktop and laptop speak the same language—bits and bytes—you won't need a modem. There's no tone or hissy sound to translate. You will, however, need to rig a null modem cable (the computer-to-computer kind) or buy the commercial equivalent.

You have three choices:

1. Do everything yourself, including the wiring. In most cases this really isn't worth the trouble.

2. Have someone rig up the cable for you; then you can try to use

your existing communications program to effect the transfer. You might also be able to buy a cable through regular commercial channels.

3. Buy a cable and file-transfer software intended to work with each other (and also function with a variety of machines). Among the better-known products are LapLink, the Flying Dutchman, Fastwire, or the Brooklyn Bridge.

A null modem cable links the serial ports of the respective computers. Not all wires in the null modem cables will go to the same pin numbers in the source and destination computers. Typically, for example, pins two and three are reversed to allow for pin two to transmit data and pin three to receive it. Pin seven might serve as a ground. Check with manufacturers or supply stores about the proper null modem cable.

Once you've bought the null modem cable, you'll still need software to do the transfer. Often you can use your communications software and go into the appropriate mode (such as the one you reach in CrossTalk by hitting your Esc key, typing **GO LOCAL**, and pressing your Return key). Then you may use XMODEM, Kermit, or other transfer protocols, the same ones as you would when communicating over the phone wires. Set up one program in the ''originate'' mode and the other in ''answer''; also, as when communicating by phone, be certain to use the common settings for data bits, stop bits, and parity.

If you buy a LapLink-style product instead of the alternatives above, look for the following features, all of which aren't necessarily present in one product:

■ High rates of transfer from one computer to another. The best products, for instance, can whiz data through serial ports at up to 200K baud. And they have provisions for using parallel ports, which offer even faster rates. All of the models available should offer transfer rates many times faster, perhaps hundreds of times faster, than those you achieve using your trusty 2,400-bps modem.

■ The automatic setting of port, bps rate, and ways of error checking.

■ Cables that can easily connect different kinds of computers. A serial port for an AT-style computer, normally, will use a different shape of connector from that on an XT-class machine.

■ The proper hardware to transfer from an IBM to a Macintosh, if the latter can't read IBM disks (some of the newer, more expensive Macs can).

■ A good, easy-to-understand manual that clearly outlines the risks. Even the manual of the highly regarded LapLink warns: "You may seriously damage your equipment if you (1) connect your computers through the serial port on one and the parallel port on the other or (2) attach one of the serial connectors to a monitor (RGB) port. If you are uncertain, you are strongly advised to seek help from your computer dealer, the manufacturer of your computer, or a computer users' group." Don't let this frighten you from buying LapLink or otherwise transferring data. Just try to minimize the risks. An ideal transfer product would contain the electronics to prevent equipment damage of any kind.

■ The opportunity to know when you're about to write over existing files—that is, replace them with new material under the same file name. Ideally the software will warn you.

■ The ability to easily identify the files you want copied, erased, and so on. When you boot up LapLink you'll see a long list of files, over which you can slide a cursor bar, a bar of light that you move with cursor arrows. Via the bar and a tap on the key representing "tag," you can pick out the files or groups of files you want to work with. Or, alternatively, you can use "wild cards" to identify groups of files to work with. For instance, you can type **D*.*** to pick up files with such names as DOUG and DON.NEW, or you can type ***.NEW** to look up anything with a NEW extension. And so on.

■ Provisions for writing "batch files"—files that, step-by-step, tell the transfer program what to do; a batch file can mention specific names for copying, deleting, and so forth. With batch files you can automate procedures that you often follow.

■ Being able to stop the execution of commands quickly, in case you make a mistake or change your mind.

■ The ability to view individual files on the screen so that you can make certain you are erasing, copying, or taking other actions on the right ones.

■ Quick sorting of file names—for instance, listings by alphabetical order or by order of date of creation.

■ Easy production of lists of files—either full lists or lists of files beginning with certain letters or created after certain dates.

If you don't want to pay for commercial transfer software, you might try ZIP143 (or successors), a shareware program by Eric Meyer, the same hacker who wrote the speedy little VDE editor. ZIP143 can send data and programs from one computer's serial port to another at 115,200 bps. It's available in a compressed form known as ZIP143.ARC and can be found on some local BBS's or in the IBM Communications Forum of CompuServe, known as IBMCOM.

ZIP143 and the usual form of LapLink are for MS-DOS machines. What if you own a Mac or a Radio Shack machine that uses a different operating system? A product called LapLink Mac III (from the seller of LapLink, Traveling Software (18702 North Creek Parkway, Bothell, Washington 98011, 800-343-8080) should be of interest to owners of MS-DOS portables who want to hook into the Macintosh. Owners of Tandy Models 100, 102, and 200 machines and similar laptops from NEC might check out a product from Traveling Software called LAPDOS II if they want to swap files with their MS-DOS machine.

Modeming Over the Phone Lines

When I went to work at *High Technology Export & Import*, I infiltrated a Mac shop—a magazine with several Macintoshes and not one of the IBM-style machines to which I was accustomed. I, a XyWrite user obsessed with speed, hated the Macs' mouse and poky word processor. So I brought my MS-DOS machine to work. That still, however, didn't solve the problem of incompatible disk formats at a magazine that at the time could ill afford to pay for expensive converters or hookups between machines in different offices. But I survived anyway, just by dialing up the other modem in the office. That took care of the disk issue. And since XyWrite is essentially just plain ASCII, the Macs easily could work with my material once it reached them. Our office, moreover, had several telephone numbers and maybe half a dozen phones. How did we do the communications? We engaged in some friendly chit-chat via the computers to verify the connection, then began an ASCII file transfer of the contents of the issue that I'd just finished editing. There at *E&I*, we didn't have to overcome the problem of having just one phone line and not wanting to move any equipment. The answer, however, would have been simple. We could have sub-

scribed to an inexpensive e-mail service, taken out two accounts, and
sent from one to another.

Modeming over the phone lines isn't a good solution, though, if you
want to transfer files often and the files are very long; at 1,200 bps, the
contents of our magazine didn't transmit instantly; this method would
have been intolerable had we been working frequently with book-length
manuscripts. The transfer speed was a fraction of what it would have
been with a cable directly between the computers.

Local Area Networks

More and more companies want networks between computers to share
data files, programs, and peripherals such as high-speed printers or
modems for transmitting faxes or data. Local area networks, or LANs,
can function as an electronic mail system for a lone office or for a whole
complex. They also are handy for leaving messages—one way to reduce
the accumulation of memos and pink slips on employees' desk.

With LANs becoming so common, then, it's helpful to be able to
hook up your laptop to these networks of machines, not just to one
isolated computer.

Fortunately, solutions exist:

1. Dialing into modems hooked up on the network to read e-mail
or send small files. This method is slow. Remember, most modems
today work at 2,400 bps or less.

2. Phoning not the network directly but a desktop computer hooked
in. You can use Carbon Copy or other remote-access software that gives
the "remote" computer control of the keyboard of the one machine on
the LAN.

3. Using a full-fledged LAN adapter. Some models plug into a slot
inside your laptop; some can connect with your computer's serial port.

4. Transferring files—from your laptop to a machine hooked up to
the network—via a product like LapLink Plus or the Brooklyn Bridge.
You won't enjoy all of the powers that a network adapter would give
you, of course, and you'll be keeping the networked machine busy. But
you'll enjoy transfer capabilities at a fraction of the cost of a LAN
adapter.

This book is a guide to laptops, not local area networks. Still, here are a few questions to ask when buying adapters:

■ What kind of LAN will the adapter work with? Networks come in many forms nowadays. LANs can consist of anything from coaxial cable or twisted pair to fiber-optic cabling; what's more, there can be major differences in the ways machines communicate on the network. To give one example, Xerox is famous for its Ethernet system but it isn't enough just to know that the LAN is an Ethernet—not when the exact configuration could take one of a number of forms.

■ Will the adapter be a card plugging into a slot in your computer, or will it be an external model connecting to one of the machine's ports? Xircom (22231 Mulholland Highway, Suite 114, Woodland Hills, California 91364, [818] 884-8755) makes a compact adapter (for Ethernet, among others) that weighs less than a pound and hooks up to a laptop's parallel port. As for plug-in cards, Megahertz (4505 South Wasatch Boulevard, Salt Lake City, Utah 84124, 800-LAP-TOPS or [801] 272-6000) sells Ethernet versions for various Toshiba laptops. Pure Data (1740 South I-35, Suite 140, Carrollton, Texas 75006, [214] 242-2040) offers ARCnet and Ethernet adapter cards for many Toshiba models and ARCnet cards for the NEC MultiSpeed series. Connect Computer (9855 West Seventy-eighth Street, Suite 270, Eden Prairie, Minnesota 55344, [612] 944-0181) makes accessories into which owners of some Toshiba, Zenith, and Epson models can plug LAN adapter cards. Connect uses the brand name WonUnder. In addition, major laptop manufacturers offer expansion accessories for LAN adapters and many other kinds of cards. And the Mac Portable and its clones (machines using the Apple ROM) all have AppleTalk Ports.[2]

■ Will the LAN administrator, your corporate micromanager, or another person approve (1) the concept of your buying a card and (2) your choice? Make sure you and that person have the exact specs for your company's network before ordering. If you're about to buy the Xircom attachment, for instance, know whether you're ordering a version for coaxial or twisted cable.

---

[2]The list of makers of network adapters comes from Craig Zarley, "Laptops to LANs," *PC/Computing*, September 1989, p. 165. Thanks to Paul Chernoff, an Apple-oriented hacker, for the Mac information.

Zero-Slot LANs

Zero-slot LANs are poor but worthy cousins of the normal networks. Regular LANs require fancy hardware, such as plug-in cards; the zero-slot networks need only software and cables. You needn't plug a special LAN adapter card into one of the slots in your portable—assuming that your laptop has the appropriate slot in the first place, which many don't.

These cheapie networks can allow your laptop to exchange files with two or more PCs and to share printers; typically data can whiz over the networks at speeds exceeding 100 kilobits per second. That's still slow compared to traditional kinds of LANs, which require expensive hardware but can hook up many more machines. But zero-slot LANs may be perfect for small businesses.

Check out offerings from Traveling Software and Grapevine LAN Products (15323 Ninetieth Street N.E., Redmond, Washington 98052, [206] 869-2707), among others.

Especially, however, you might consider a product with the price in its name, "The $25 Network," from Information Modes (P.O. Drawer F, Denton, Texas 76202, [817] 387-3339). When I logged on a techie-oriented BBS in the Washington area and asked for wisdom about laptops and LANs, a $25 Network customer named Mike Lambert responded with a paean to "the best software for the buck I've ever spent." The $25 Network's transfer rate can exceed 100 kilobits per second; in real life, if you consider equipment limitations, you can probably transfer a file several thousand words long in just a few seconds or a 500K file in a minute. Longer files transfer more efficiently.

The net can link as many as three different computers. It takes up just 14K of RAM, one-tenth the amount of memory that some other products need. Plus, the $25 Network works with simple cabling—just the usual null modem cables, the kind described on page 353. A fifty-foot cable from Information Modes costs just $25.

In action, The $25 Network lets you treat a hard drive on your desktop machine as if it were on your laptop. Call it drive C: if your laptop has just A: and B: drives. Then you use simple MS-DOS commands for copying. The command **COPY B:MIKE C:** (Return), for instance, can transfer the MIKE file from your laptop to the hard drive on your desktop. More important, people in most cases can use the same programs simultaneously and share peripherals, such as printers. Be careful, of course, to avoid having more than one person edit files from word processors, accounting programs, and the like; also be aware of the legal implications of using software simultaneously.

If you're using three machines, one will need two serial ports to act as a hub. The cost of an extra port, however, at least on the typical desktop, will be a fraction of the expense of an adapter card.

Now imagine the possibilities for a law office. A secretary could operate a desktop with a hard disk and hook up to the portables of the lawyers there, the machines they tote on trips or to court. "I've sold to a lot of lawyers, doctors, and accountants with simple needs," Don Jindra, the developer, says, "and at least one-tenth of them use portables. My niche market is people who aren't even sure they need a LAN in the first place. But they see they would enjoy sharing information and, occasionally, programs." A hefty program can take several minutes to load to another machine. If, however, you'll be using the software for two hours, and if there's no other alternative, then you won't mind.

Unfortunately, like some other zero-slot LANs, The $25 Network probably won't let you copy files from a machine with a higher version of DOS to a lower version when the higher version is 3.0 or above. But normally a simple DOS upgrade can solve that problem.

APPENDIX 5
A FAST WAY OF USING FLOPPIES FOR MULTI-FILE TRANSFERS BETWEEN A DESKTOP AND A LAPTOP

- The FROM.BAT file (for transferring material from the first computer). Page 363.
- The TO.BAT file (for transferring material to the second computer). Page 364.
- After you've been working on the second computer. Page 365.
- How to do a mass transfer without naming individual files. Page 365.

For MS-DOS machines, you can write batch files. With quick, simple commands, they can automate such operations as the copying or deletion of named files. So why not use batch files to speed the mass transfer of material—for example, book chapters—from your hard disk desktop to your hard disk laptop?

For floppy-only machines, of course, you generally can just remove data files from one computer and stick them in another if the formats are identical. But what about speeding up the transfer of files if two hard disk machines are involved? Or what if the desktop is a hard disk and the laptop uses floppies? The ability to transfer many files at once will be especially valuable to users of XyWrite and other people whose software lets them scoot quickly from one file to the next. The plans for IBM's new 2.8-meg floppy standard should also whet the interest of people who'd like to automate transfers via disks.

Here I'll explain how to write a batch file, then give you an example of how I used two of them to streamline my transfer procedures—so I could simultaneously dump a number of files to my laptop, then later return the expanded files to my desktop.

1. Realize that you'll write batch files in ASCII. Just about all word processors nowadays have ways to convert files into ASCII, and some, such as XyWrite, are already ASCII or close to it. Check your software manual. You also can write an ASCII file by working within your original word processor and converting to ASCII through a program provided with your software. In addition you can use MS-DOS's COPY CON command.

2. Type the words **COPY CON** followed by a file name, which to work for a batch file must end with the extension .BAT (as in TEST.BAT).

3. Press the Return key.

4. Type the first line of the batch file, then press Return again.

5. After you reach the last line, hold down the Ctrl key and press Z (Ctrl-Z), then Return. You needn't mess with Ctrl-Z if you're composing a batch file in your regular word processor for conversion to ASCII.

Put your batch file in the main directory of your hard disk, if you're using one; that's the root directory, normally identified as C:\. Subdirectories, the rough equivalents of drawers in a filing cabinet, have designations such as **C:\XyWrite\Book**. The "Book" is actually a sub-subdirectory within the C:\XyWrite subdirectory.

"But," you say, "I don't know how to move within my hard disk. How did you get to C:\XyWrite\Book in the first place?" Easy. I read my DOS manual. If you want to cheat, however, here's a quick lesson on moving around on a hard disk to log over to the appropriate subdirectory:

■ **CD ** followed by a tap on the Return key brings me to the C:\ directory, the main one.

■ **CD XyWrite** takes me to a subdirectory called XyWrite (also known as C:\XyWrite).

■ Once I'm in XyWrite, **CD Book** and the usual tap on the Return key log me over to a subdirectory called Book.

■ If I want, I can go directly to **C:\XyWrite\Book** from C:\

or anywhere else on the disk—for example, **C:\Procomm**. The command? Just **C:\XyWrite\Book** followed by Return.

■ **CD . .** and Return bring me one level closer to the root directory. In other words, if I'm in **C:\XyWrite\Book**, such a command will take me to C:\XyWrite.

The above example, of course, shows the directory structure of my own hard disk. Do not panic if your disk uses other subdirectory names, as it almost surely will. Are you a devotee of WordPerfect? Then in place of C:\XyWrite and C:\XyWrite\Book, you may have C:\WP5 and C:\WP\Book.

Consult your DOS manual if you have difficulties. I cannot promise that the above procedures for moving from place to place on a hard disk will work with all versions of DOS. Most likely, however, they will.

THE FROM.BAT FILE (FOR TRANSFERRING MATERIAL FROM THE FIRST COMPUTER)

Here is the batch file that I now have in the root directory of my hard disk to send three book chapters and other files to a floppy for use on a hard disk laptop. I've called the file **FROM.BAT** to remind me that I'm sending material *from* the hard disk.

> **Copy c:\xywrite\book\modems a:** [The same file name will appear on drive A.]
> **Copy c:\xywrite\book\hook a:**
> **Copy c:\xywrite\book\abroad a:**
> **Copy c:\xywrite\book\appendix a:**
> **Copy c:\xywrite\book\dir2 a:**
> **Copy c:\xywrite\pers.spl a:**
> **Copy c:\remind.dta a:**

The first line copies the MODEMS file to drive A. The files with which I'm working at the moment normally go in the sub-subdirectory called C:\XyWrite\Book—within the C:\XyWrite subdirectory. The A drive is my AT clone's designation for the 3.5-inch floppy. By the way, I haven't bothered to say ''(Return),'' since it's clear that you must press Return to reach the next line.

Lines two, three, and four, of course, respectively copy the HOOK, ABROAD, and APPENDIX files to the floppy. HOOK is short for HOOKUP.

Line five copies my phone directory, the DIR2 file, stored in the same sub-subdirectory.

Line six copies PERS.SPL, through which I can tell the XyWrite spelling checker not to beep at the oddball names and other bizarre spellings that I use—for instance, "Kuala Lumpur." Notice that PERS.SPL is in the main \XyWrite subdirectory rather than the one for the book-related material? I need to take PERS.SPL to the laptop, of course, because I'm constantly making new entries.

Line seven in FROM.BAT copies REMIND.DTA from the root directory, the C:\ directory. REMIND.DTA lists my appointments and, like PERS.SPL, is another file whose contents I want 100-percent current.

With me so far? Via the batch file, I'm telling the desktop computer which files to copy to a floppy. Just by typing FROM (don't type the .BAT) and pressing the Return, I can trigger the mass copying of MODEMS, HOOK, ABROAD, DIR2, and PERS.SPL, as well as REMIND.DTA. I do this while I'm in DOS (seeing the C:\XyWrite\Book prompt) rather than in my word processor.

THE TO.BAT FILE (FOR TRANSFERRING MATERIAL TO THE SECOND COMPUTER)

By reversing the FROM procedure, I can bring the material to the laptop. It has a hard disk. And the directory structure matches that of the desktop. So you'll see some familiar names in the aptly named batch file known as TO.BAT, which, by the way, is on the root directory of the laptop's hard disk:

```
Copy a:modems c:\xywrite\book
Copy a:hook c:\xywrite\book
Copy a:abroad c:\xywrite\book
Copy a:appendix c:\xywrite\book
Copy a:dir2 c:\xywrite\book
Copy a:pers.spl c:\xywrite
Copy a:remind.dta c:\
```

As soon as I stick the floppy in my hard disk machine and type TO, the floppy of the laptop whirs, copying all of the files to the appropriate locations on the portable's hard drive. As you'd suspect, drive A is the laptop's designation for the floppy drive, just as it is for the larger machine's floppy. Wait. What if you're using a floppy-only laptop? Simple. You'll just treat the data disk—the floppy you copied from the hard drive—like any other.

AFTER YOU'VE BEEN WORKING ON THE SECOND COMPUTER

Needless to say, once I'm through writing on the hard disk laptop, I can effortlessly transfer the material to a floppy that I'll later insert in the desktop. After all, the root directory of the laptop, too, has a FROM.BAT file. I just type FROM and hit the Return key to start transferring files from the portable to the floppy.

Some novices may object, "What if I accidentally type TO while I'm in MS-DOS and accidentally copy the material from the floppy to the more current files on the hard drive?" My response? Remember that the TO won't have an effect unless you hit the Return. Also keep in mind that if you're working with several files at once, you may want to use the FROM command regularly to back up the files from your hard drive. Use several backup disks and give one a "vacation" each day. Then an accident won't destroy that much work. Many word processing and other programs, incidentally, let you duck back instantly to DOS, then return to the applications software. So using FROM won't be a big deal.

Finally, keep in mind that if you're worried about confusing FROM and TO, you may substitute names with which you feel more comfortable.

ANOTHER METHOD OF MAKING CERTAIN YOU TRANSFER ONLY THE FILES YOU WANT

My hard disk doesn't just contain the electronic manuscript I'm working on at the time. The C:\XyWrite\Book area of my hard disk also includes *notes* for the book. So you can see why I wrote a TO.BAT file that would pick up just the specified chapters and other files I was super paranoid about. If the TO.BAT file had copied up the whole works, I never would have had room, even on a 1.44-meg disk.

Many writers and businesspeople, however, are stricter about what goes into the individual subdirectories of their hard disks. They may, for example, reserve space just for a manuscript.

If you're so lucky, then you can transfer files from your hard disk to the floppy with one easy command in MS-DOS:

COPY *.* A: (Return)

Press the Return key once you've typed those letters. As soon as you do, the floppy in drive A (or C, or whatever you designated) will pick up everything from the subdirectory to which you are logged. Just make certain that the contents of the subdirectory won't overwhelm the 720K or 1.44-meg disk or whatever else you're using.

You can also use the *.* routine to copy in the other direction—from the floppy to the appropriate subdirectory of the hard disk. While logged onto the right subdirectory, just type:

COPY A:*.* (Return)

APPENDIX 6
CD-ROMS: ONE WAY TO AUGMENT ON-LINE INFORMATION SERVICES

At $75, $150, even $200 an hour, many information services are too pricey to use *constantly*—even if you're an executive at a major corporation. On the other hand, you're not about to hit the road with a complete set of professional or trade journals in your field. Nor do you want to have to search for an English-language library open at 1:30 A.M. in Karachi. Besides, some extra-arcane information just might not be available on-line, period.

One solution might be CD-ROMs—compact disks similar to those that can play Billy Joel or Beethoven.

If you already own a laptop, investigate the possibility of using it with a portable CD-ROM reader. CD Technology (780 Montague Expressway, Suite 407, San Jose, California 95131, 408-432-8698) offers a battery-powered reader that you can use off and on for an hour without recharging the batteries. By *portable*, incidentally, I mean a reader the size of your laptop or even tinier. Even normal CD-ROM readers should work fine with your machine—just so it includes the proper port or slot.

Already, portable computers are appearing with CD-ROM readers built in. Among the first is a lunchbox machine, a gas plasma model from CD Technology. At $4,795, the basic model with 640K RAM includes a 1.44 megabyte floppy and a 20 megabyte hard disk in addition to the CD-ROM reader. The processor is an 80286, which unfortunately runs at a snailish 10 megahertz, a big disappointment for a lunchbox-style machine. Still, a faster model might be out by now. And whatever the case, this computer could be a natural for sales reps—especially those hawking CD-ROM databases.

Yet another choice may reach American stores in the next year or two. Sony has developed what some call "an electronic 'book' player," which could hold 100,000 pages on one CD-ROM. The machine uses 3 inch disks, weighs just 1.2 pounds, offers a little LCD screen, and already should be selling in Japan for just under $400. See if this "Data Discman" can send data to another laptop or desktop. Also, find out whether the disk format will serve your needs.

Don't buy CD-ROM data equipment for *any* format without seeing if your colleagues and your computer dealer know of disks useful in your occupation. You'd be surprised at the range of disks. Optical Publishing in Fort Collins, Colorado, for example, puts out a full list of the federal procurement regulations. This disk's sales won't rival Billy Joel's, but the product just might make the Top 40 among companies that sell to the U.S. government. What better reference to consult in your Washington hotel room?

Suppose you're in the computer department of a large accounting or consulting firm. Then you might check with your company and with organizations such as the Internal Revenue Service to see if libraries of helpful data exist. If so, your field people could carry CD-ROM readers with them to fetch citations instantly—right there in the client's offices. As a matter of fact, Price Waterhouse has purchased two thousand readers.

If you're visiting an obscure Third World country, you might check out *The CIA World Factbook*, from Quanta Press of St. Paul, Minnesota; this almanac contains unclassified information on two hundred forty-eight countries. Businesspeople may want to catch up, too, with a CD-ROM from Dow Jones offering back issues of the *Wall Street Journal*.

Moreover, as you'd expect, a list of CD-ROMs is available on one of the silvery disks themselves. The publisher is Diversified Data Resources, at 6609 Rosecroft Place, Falls Church, Virginia 22043-1828, (703) 237-0682.

Researching this book, I relied on a desktop CD-ROM reader borrowed from Amdek, the Laserdek 2000, which worked flawlessly and saved me uncounted hours of tedious page flipping through back issues of computer magazines. If I wanted to learn about keyboards on Zenith laptop computers, for example, I merely typed in **ZENITH AND KEYBOARD AND LAPTOP** and the Laserdek whirred and summoned forth a list of citations. Then, one by one, I browsed through the articles. I was using the Computer Library, a CD-ROM version of *PC Week*, *PC Magazine*, and other major publications owned by Ziff-Davis (although the same disk summarized material from other sources and even included full texts in some cases). Monthly updates of the Computer Library cost $765 a year.[1] That's beyond the range of many independent professionals with limited research needs. On-line searching makes more sense there. Indeed, the Computer Library is available via CompuServe.

Still, the CD-ROM version could be the real answer for procurement officers with large corporations, especially those who travel and who want to be constantly armed with a complete rundown in a product category when they bargain with vendors.

Similarly, well-equipped sales reps, especially those in high tech, may travel with CD-ROM readers to bone up in a hurry on technological options and on prospective customers. Lawyers might want to seek out laws on CD-ROMs for instant retrieval during trials. Doctors can take advantage of disks based on the computerized files from the National Library of Medicine.

On the negative side beyond the price the access speed of the typical CD-ROM drive is slower than that of a hard disk. However, I found that the longest of my searches took all of a minute or two after I'd booted up the CD-ROM software. It was a fraction of the time that a manual search would have needed.

Another problem with CD-ROMs, compared to on-line services, is that the information isn't as current. The solution? Use on-line information services, but, if possible, tell them to search for articles only back to a certain date. What's more, you may augment the CD-ROM information the old-fashioned way—by keeping clippings of the articles that have not yet been stashed away on the little disks.

---

[1] Contact Ziff Communications Company, One Park Avenue, New York, NY 10016 (212-503-4400).

APPENDIX 7
SHOULD YOU BUY A MAC PORTABLE?
(AN APPLE OWNER'S SIDE)
BY PAUL J. CHERNOFF

(Paul J. Chernoff works as a computer consultant and attends to the care and feeding of laptops, local area networks, and other computers for Partners of the Americas, an international volunteer group in Washington, D.C.)

A careless Apple dealer drove over his Mac Portable: the case cracked but the Mac still worked. Clearly this is the Timex of laptops. As they said in the old Timex commercials, "it takes a licking and keeps on ticking." True! And in other ways, too. The Mac Portable is a dependable, high-powered machine that can go as as long as twelve hours between battery charges. A model with a 40 meg hard drive lists for $5,499 and the floppy-only version for $4,799, and, yes, that's pricey. But this laptop should make the MS-DOS crowd drool with envy.

Designing the portable Mac was no easy trick; we Mac people expect more of our machines than the IBM people do. We all want a graphics interface. Most of us hate to type out the mumbo-jumbo commands with *.* or those weird \-style slashes. We don't want to say DEL OLDFILE when we're erasing a junk file; we'd rather just click on the file with a mouse and drag it to a picture of a trash can.

So the central processing unit, the main brains of the Macintosh Portable, had to be more powerful than the CPU of the typical IBM laptop. And the screen had to be able to change images fast, so it could keep up with the trackball, the Mac Portable's equivalent of the famous mouse. That's why it will be a long time until you see a Mac laptop as small and cheap as an MS-DOS machine such as the Toshiba T1000. In the end, you have three options:

1. Buy the floppy or hard disk version of the Mac Portable. My wife loves their high prices because they prevent me from taking one along on vacation. I hate the price tags for the same reason. (I already own a Mac Plus and use a Mac II at work.)

2. Get a Mac work-alike that uses the read-only memory (ROM) chip and perhaps other parts from a legal Mac.

3. Purchase a non-Mac laptop as a second machine.

In chapter 2, David Rothman told you about the Mac's sharp, high-contrast screen, and long battery life; a Mac can charge overnight and be ready to use during most of the following business day. But that's just the beginning of the Mac's features. Even the basic portable comes with one megabyte of random-access memory and a drive that can read or write to IBM-style 3.5 inch disks, not just its own 800K and 1.2 meg formats. You can expand the memory up to two megabytes, which suffices for virtually all Mac programs. This is a true do-all computer, not a mere laptop. The Mac Portable weighs just a little less than the Mac SE and runs faster. In my opinion, Apple is stretching the definition of the word ''laptop.''

If you don't like the Macintosh Portable, you can buy a work-alike machine—an Apple-made Mac with a new case and other niceties. Some choices are:

■ The Colby SE-30 with a base price of $6,699 from Colby Systems (2991 Alexis Drive, Palo Alto, California 94304, 415-941-9090). It's a repackaged Macintosh SE-30 and garnered some impressive reviews. Colby also sells the Colby SE ($5,499). With batteries, both models weigh fifteen pounds.

■ The 10-pound Stealth—an about-to-be-released laptop that Colby will sell under a different name. Colby bases the $2,995 economy model on the motherboard (the main printed circuit board) of the Mac Plus. The Stealth's Plus version uses a Motorola 68000 chip running at 8 megahertz. This basic model includes an 800K, 3.5 inch floppy drive. Based on the SE/30 board, the high-end model uses the Motorola 68030 chip, which races at 33 megahertz. It's expected to sell for $4,999 with a 1.4 megabytes floppy drive (check about the availability of a 20 or 40 megabyte hard drive).

Colby claims that the Stealth will be the most technically advanced 10 pound laptop on the market, IBM world included. Even the low-end Stealths will offer optional voice recognition for $799.

For $999 you can also buy the Private Eye, a screen that you wear somewhat like a pair of eyeglasses when you want privacy (see page 45 for more on the Private Eye). With the Private Eye and voice recognition, you could even use the Stealth while it's inside your briefcase.

By the time you're reading this, the Stealth should have reached the stores.

■ The Dynamic SE/30, designed for the person who must have everything. It's a repackaged SE/30. And it comes with a 16 megahertz Motorola 68030 processor; two, five, or eight megabytes of RAM; a hard drive of between 40 and 200 megabytes; compatibility with all Apple monitors, including color models; the usual SE/30 expansion slot; and a built-in modem that can send data at 2,400 bps and faxes at 4,800 bps. The price is a mere $8,995 and up from Dynamac Computer Products (14001 East Iliff Avenue, Aurora, Colorado 80014, 800-234-2349). Dynamac also has less expensive models based on the Mac Plus and Mac SE.

■ The Outbound, from Outbound Systems, once known as Wallaby Systems (4840 Pearl East Circle, Boulder, Colorado 80301, 800-444-4607).

Selling for less than $3,000, the Outbound stands apart. How? Instead of buying Macs and repackaging them, Outbound makes a Mac portable without the Macintosh ROM.

You must already own a Mac Plus or SE to use the Outbound. The dealer performs a little surgery and transplants the ROM from the Mac to the Outbound. You connect the Mac and Outbound together to create a single large computer with two functional screens. You can disconnect the Outbound from the Mac and take it on the road, leaving behind a non-functional Macintosh at home.

The Outbound comes with *either* a floppy disk drive or a 20 megabyte hard drive. If you choose the latter, you can transfer files by using the drive of the Mac in your office or home. Best of all, the Outbound weighs only nine pounds with battery included.

Rather than a portable Mac or clone, however, you might instead buy a DOS machine or other non-Mac, especially for light writing or spreadsheet use. Many Mac fans have purchased the MS-DOS Toshiba T1000 and the non-DOS Cambridge Z88 ($699 and up, from Cambridge North America, 424 Cumberland Ave., Portland, Maine 04101, 800-888-3723 or 800-366-0088). The Z88 even comes with special transfer utilities and cable to make it easier to swap files between it and your Mac.

If using a MS-DOS portable, a Mac person might want programs that work somewhat like Macintosh software even if they're for IBM-style machines. Here are examples:

■ Microsoft Works, an integrated program with word processing, spreadsheet, database, and basic communications features. Microsoft is at 1 Microsoft Way, Redmond, Washington 98052 (telephone 206-882-8080). The IBM price is $149.

■ The Excel spreadsheet from Microsoft, which recommends it only for machines with 80286 chips or more powerful ones. Price: $395.

■ Word, the best-known word processor from Microsoft. Price: $395. Word runs best on computers with chips at least in the 80286 class. A VGA screen helps, too.

Using a MS-DOS computer means learning a machine that most Mac users dislike. But you can transfer files from computer to computer to reduce the amount of time spent away from the Mac. All newer Macs, except for the Plus and older SEs, can read and write to MS-DOS 3.5-inch disks using the Apple File Exchange.

The Apple File Exchange program is free with every Mac. See your dealer if you don't have it.

Other file transfer programs are available, too. For instance, DOS Mounter from Dayna Communications ($89.95, 50 South Main Street, Fifth Floor, Salt Lake City, Utah 84144, 801-531-0203) allows easier use of MS-DOS disks in Macintosh 1.4 meg drives. And a more complete solution comes from LapLink Mac III ($189.95 Traveling Software, 18702 North Creek Parkway, Bothell, WA 98011, 206-483-8088 or 800-343-8080). LapLink includes cables and software. MacLinkPlus/PC Version 4 ($199 from DataViz, 35 Corporate Drive, Trumbull, Connecticut, 06611, 203-268-0030) is a similar product.

Compared to a real Mac Portable, most of the other approaches may involve tradeoffs in power and battery life. But sooner or later Apple could wake up to meet the needs of the people ads describe as "the rest of us," so we can all enjoy the real thing. Rumors persist that the company is working on a smaller, cheaper version of its laptop. Something is bound to happen. Apple has long wooed the education market, and what could be more natural for students to take to the library than a cheaper, notebook-sized version of the powerful Mac Portable?

TRADEMARKS, REGISTERED TRADEMARKS, AND SERVICE MARKS

This book mentions the following trademarks, registered trademarks, and service marks, among others:

XyWrite—XyQuest; WordStar—WordStar International; Techno-klutz—Stephen Banker; Windows, Microsoft Works, and MS-DOS —Microsoft Corp.; Word/Perfect—WordPerfect Corp.; Apple and Macintosh—Apple Computer; Compaq—Compaq Corp; CrossTalk —Microstuf, Inc.; Xword—Ronald Gans; Mirror—SoftKlone Distributing Corporation; PFS:Write, PFS:First Choice, First Graphics, and Harvard Graphics—Software Publishing Corporation; Home Office Computing—Scholastic Publishing; Freelance Plus, Lotus 1-2-3, Magellan, Agenda, Lotus Express, and Symphony—Lotus Corporation; SideKick—Borland; Eye Relief and No-Squint—SkiSoft Publishing Corporation; Double Disk—Vertisoft; Squish Plus—Sundog Software; CompuServe—CompuServe; GEnie—GE Information Services; MCI Mail and WorldMail—MCI; Sharp Wizard—Sharp; GRiDPAd and GRiD—GRiD Systems; ViewLink, LapLink, and Battery Watch—Traveling Software; Ethernet—Xerox; $25 Network— Information Modes; DataShow and Diconix—Kodak; Atari Portfolio—Atari; Poqet—Poqet Computer; ACT!—Contact Software; Psion—Psion; Selectric, PC, PC XT, PC AT, and IBM—International Business Machines; Agilis—Agilis Corporation; PC/5000, MicroPalm Computers; Private Eye—Reflection Technology; PC/ Computing, PC Magazine, PC Week, The Computer Shopper, and

the Computer Library—Ziff Communications; PCLapTop—L.F.P.;
Portable Computing and Infoworld—IDG Communications; Mobile
Office—CurtCo Publishing.

PC World—PCW Communications; Personal Computing—Personal
Computing Magazine; Kaypro II—Kaypro; Ultra-Lite and Multi-
Speed—NEC; Aerobic Power—Dreisbach ElectroMotive; B.O.S.S.
—Casio; PWP 7000LT—Smith-Corona; Won Under—Connect Com-
puter; Translate—FinalSoft; dBASE—Ashton-Tate; FileExpress—Ex-
pressware; PC-Write and PC-Brows—Quicksoft; QEdit—SemWare;
ZEdit—Telcom Library; Radio Shack—Tandy; IZE—Persoft; Prime-
time Personal—Primetime Software; Palette Plus—Polaroid; Present
—SML Services; Graph-in-the-Box—New England Software; Quick-
Graphs—Sumak Industries; DeskJet and PaintJet—Hewlett-Packard;
Calendar Creator Plus—Power Up Software; TimeSlips—North Edge
Software; DAC Easy-Light—DAC Software; Quicken-Intuit; Turbo
Tax—ChipSoft; Sideways—Funk Software; 3-2-1 Blastoff—Front-
line Systems; ABC Audit and ABC Quick Statement—Hemming
Moore; Accelerate!—Spreadsheet Solutions; Accounts Payable, Gen-
eral Ledger, Report Maker Plus, Inventory, Payroll, Payroll Admin-
istration, and Purchase Order—Great Plains Software; APS Fixed
Assets—Professional Services Microsystems; Check Writing Manager
—RD Software; CPA Tickler—Front Row Systems; Cruise Con-
trol—Revolution Software; Ready-to-Run Accounting-Manusoft; Fast!
—Prentice-Hall Professional Software; EZ Flow—Haven Tree; Sil-
verado—Computer Associates; Secret Disk II—Lattice; SpinRite II—
Gibson Research; ViziFlex—ViziFlex Seels.

Wristrest—Hypermedia Group; KB Pillow—Computer Giftware;
WorldPort—Touchbase Systems; Stowaway—Vocal Technologies;
TrailBlazer and CellBlazer—Telebit; TeleMax—Panamax; ProComm
—DataStorm Technologies; USA DIRECT—AT&T; Prodigy—Prod-
igy Services; ScriptWrite—Paul Nadler; Tempo—Affinity Microsys-
tems; WriteNow—T/Maker; Microphone—Software Ventures
Corporation; BigThesaurus—Deneba Software; GOfer—MicroLytics;
DiskTools Plus—Electronic Arts; SPCL Adverse Environment Proto-
col, The Bridge, and IntelliJack—Spectrum; CelJack, The Bridge, and
IntelliJack; CelJack—Telular; and MegaMate—Micro Solutions.

I'm publishing this list simply as a courtesy to the aforementioned
companies. Because of time constraints, it is not complete. If your

company is in *The Complete Laptop Computer Guide* but not on the list, and if you want it to be included, then please write St. Martin's Press, 175 Fifth Avenue, New York, New York 10010, and we'll correct the omission in the next edition.

INDEX